Euripides

and the Poetics

of Sorrow

Euripides and the Poetics

of Sorrow

ART, GENDER, AND

COMMEMORATION IN

ALCESTIS, HIPPOLYTUS,

AND *HECUBA*

Charles Segal

Duke University Press   Durham and London   1993

The excerpt from "On Not
Knowing Greek" from *The Common
Reader* by Virginia Woolf, copyright 1925
by Harcourt Brace & Company and
renewed 1953 by Leonard Woolf, is
reprinted by permission of
the publisher.

Frontispiece: Votive relief,
ca. 460 B.C., of mourning Athena.
Athens, Acropolis Museum.
Foto Marburg / Art Resource, N.Y.

FOR

JEAN-PIERRE VERNANT

ὃ δ' ὄλβιος ὅντινα Μοῦσαι φίλωνται

Contents

Preface   ix

1. Introduction   3
2. Euripides' Muse of Sorrows and the Artifice
    of Tragic Pleasure   13

Alcestis

3. Cold Delight: Art, Death, and Transgression
    of Genre   37
4. Female Death and Male Tears   51
5. Admetus' Divided House: Spatial Dichotomies
    and Gender Roles   73

Hippolytus

6. Language, Signs, and Gender   89
7. Theater, Ritual, and Commemoration   110
8. Confusion and Concealment: Vision, Hope, and
    Tragic Knowledge   136

Hecuba

9. Golden Armor and Servile Robes: Heroism and
    Metamorphosis   157
10. Violence and the Other: Greek, Female, and
    Barbarian   170

11.   Law and Universals   191

12.   The Problem of the Gods   214

13.   Conclusion: Euripides' Songs of Sorrow   227

Notes   237
Bibliography   283
Index   303

Greek tragedy gives us a sense of a remote world and across a vast gap of time reminds us of what we may share with men and women in very different historical and cultural circumstances. To audiences and interpreters in our century, Euripides has seemed both contemporary and remote; this volume attempts to explore some aspects of his fascinating combination of the archaic and the modern. The view of Euripides as an extreme radical that descends ultimately from Aristophanes' *Frogs* is an exaggeration; but it is true that he continually and self-consciously exploits the tensions between tradition and innovation, between the communal voice and the voice of criticism and iconoclasm.

This book has many continuities with my previous writing on Greek tragedy, particularly my concern with Euripides' self-consciousness about his art and about language, signification, writing, and poetics in general. It places more emphasis, however, on the ways these issues are connected with the representation of the difference between male and female experience and with the ritualized forms of mourning and commemoration, the female lament, and male heroic monumentalization. Consequently I am especially concerned with tragedy's affective dimension, the emotional response that it asks of its audience. The first two chapters introduce this approach. They are not limited to Euripides, although chapter 2 includes an extended discussion of Hecuba's lament over Astyanax in the *Trojan Women*. The chapters on *Alcestis* move from the play's implicit poetics to the themes of lament, domestic life, and the contrasts of male and female responses to death. Those on *Hippolytus* emphasize tragedy's social context, particularly its role as a voice of social memory and its use of ritual commemoration; and the chapters on *Hecuba* examine how Euripides explores the darker side of human behavior by combining traditional myths with contemporary intellectual discussions.

I draw on some of the insights and methods of poststructuralist and deconstructionist criticism, especially in chapters 3, 6, 7, and 10, but I obviously reject the limitations of self-referentiality that such approaches often contain. My concern with issues of representation and signification tries always to keep in view how the highly conventional and coded art form of Greek tragedy interprets those areas of experience that, thanks to the Greeks, we refer to as "tragic"—that is, innocent suffering, meaningless death, destructive and self-destructive passions, war, violence, and cruelty.

Anyone who interprets a historically remote literature has a twofold responsibility: to understand the past in its own unique, culturally specific terms and to refamiliarize the past in terms that are meaningful to the present. In practice the two activities are inseparably entangled, for the interpreter has to measure the otherness of the past by his or her own present. If literary study today differs from that of previous generations, it is in our pervasive awareness that the very activity of interpretation, including publishing a book or an essay on Greek tragedy, is defined by and is part of the special historical circumstances of the present. It is the Heisenberg principle of literary study today that we know that we change the phenomena by the very act of looking at them; indeed, by the very fact that we want to and have the means to look at them and can disseminate the results of our observations through a complex, technological, economically and politically created network of institutional and commercial media. In other words, we can look critically at past literatures only by bringing them into our own interpretive focus, using methodologies that define, exclude, describe, combine, and organize these texts or parts of texts. It is the beginning of critical wisdom to acknowledge

that there is no way of looking at texts without methodology, even if
that be only to collect and record isolated facts (assuming that such
could exist).

Earlier versions of chapters 3–5 and 7–12 and parts of chapters 2
and 6 have been published elsewhere and are here brought together,
with substantial revisions and additions, in the hope that looking
closely at three plays from different but complementary perspectives
will illuminate the meaningful intricacy and variety of Euripides'
dramatic and poetic art. I thank the editors, journals, and publishers
of the following publications for permission to reuse this material
here.

Chapter 2. "Song, Ritual, and Commemoration in Early Greek Poetry and
Tragedy," *Oral Tradition* 4 (1989): 330–59. Pages 341–56 are used here.

Chapter 3. "Cold Delight: Art, Death, and Transgression of Genre: Euripides' *Alcestis*," in *The Scope of Words: In Honor of Albert S. Cook*, ed.
P. Baker, S. W. Goodwin, and G. Handwerk (New York: Peter Lang, 1991),
211–28.

Chapter 4. "Female Death and Male Tears in Euripides' *Alcestis*," *Classical
Antiquity* 11 (1992): 139–54. Copyright by the Regents of the University of
California.

Chapter 5. "Admetus' Divided House: Spatial Dichotomies and Gender Roles
in Euripides' *Alcestis*," *Materiali e Discussioni per l'Analisi dei Testi Classici*
28 (1992): 9–26.

Chapter 6. "Signs, Magic, and Letters in Euripides' *Hippolytus*," in *Innovations
of Antiquity*, ed. Ralph Hexter and Daniel Selden (New York and London:
Routledge, 1992), 420–55. Pages 427–38 and 441–44 are used here.

Chapter 7. "Theater, Ritual, and Commemoration in Euripides' *Hippolytus*,"
Ramus 17 (1988): 52–74. Reprinted and revised with the permission of the
editors of *Ramus* and Aureal Publications.

Chapter 8. "Confusion and Concealment in Euripides' *Hippolytus*: Vision,
Hope, and Tragic Knowledge," *Metis: Revue d'anthropologie du monde grec
ancien* 3 (1988): 263–82.

Chapter 9. "Violence and the Other: Greek, Female, and Barbarian in Euripides' *Hecuba*," *Transactions of the American Philological Association* 120
(1990): 109–31.

Chapter 10. "Golden Armor and Servile Robes: Heroism and Metamorphosis in the *Hecuba* of Euripides," *American Journal of Philology* 111 (1990):
304–17.

Chapter 11. "Law and Universals in Euripides' *Hecuba*," in *Sprachaspekte als
Experiment: Beiträge zur Literaturkritik in der Antike und Neuzeit*, ed. T. Vil-

jamaa, S. Jäkel, and K. Nyholm. *Annales Universitatis Turkuensis*, series B, vol. 187 (Turku, Finland, 1989), 63–82.

Chapter 12. "The Problem of the Gods in Euripides' *Hecuba*," *Materiali e Discussioni per l'Analisi dei Testi Classici* 22 (1989): 9–21.

The introductory chapter, which sets forth some of my critical assumptions and concerns, is new, but I have transposed here, with changes, some methodological remarks in the originally published version of chapter 7 (*Ramus* 17 [1988]: 52–53). Chapter 2 develops pages 341–56 of the article originally published in *Oral Tradition* but contains much new material. To chapter 4 I have added a few pages from the introductory portion of my essay "Euripides' *Alcestis*: How to Die a Normal Death in Greek Tragedy" (in *Death and Representation*, ed. Sarah Webster Goodwin and Elisabeth Bronfen [Johns Hopkins University Press, forthcoming], used with the permission of the editors and the Johns Hopkins University Press). Chapter 6 is based on the indicated portions of my essay on *Hippolytus* in the Routledge volume, recast to focus more sharply on the issues of the present volume. In Chapter 8 I have incorporated, with permission, a few sentences from page 155 of my essay "Solar Imagery and Tragic Heroism in Euripides' *Hippolytus*" (in *Arktouros: Hellenic Studies Presented to B. M. W. Knox*, ed. G. Bowersock, W. Burkert, and M. Putnam [Berlin and New York: Walter de Gruyter, 1979], 151–61). In chapters 11 and 12 I have incorporated a few paragraphs, also recast, from my essay "Violence and Dramatic Structure in Euripides' *Hecuba*" (in *Themes in Drama*, vol. 13, *Violence in Drama*, ed. James Redmond [Cambridge: Cambridge University Press, 1991], 35–46), with the permission of the editor and the Cambridge University Press.

In addition to stylistic revisions and additions of interpretive detail throughout, I have made some excisions and also some transpositions between essays in order to bring these studies into closer relation with one another and to avoid overlaps. I have also abbreviated or deleted some of the notes. To make the book accessible to the nonspecialist, I have translated all of the Greek, aiming at reasonable closeness to the original rather than literary elegance. I have also reduced the number of quotations in Greek and transliterated individual Greek words and short phrases wherever confusion would not result. I have taken account of a number of scholarly publications that appeared subsequent to the original publications when these seemed especially relevant, but I have not attempted a systematic updating of the notes or bibliography.

Most of the essays in this volume were written or conceived during fellowships from the National Endowment for the Humanities in 1985–86 and from the Center for Advanced Study in Behavioral Sciences, Stanford, California, in 1989–90. Financial support at the latter was provided by the National Endowment for the Humanities (#RA-20037-88) and the Andrew W. Mellon Foundation. I am grateful for sabbatical leaves during these periods from Brown University and Princeton University, respectively. In 1985–86 I also benefited from the generous hospitality of the Institute for Advanced Study in Princeton, New Jersey, and from a term as Resident in Classics at the American Academy in Rome. Research for chapters 2 and 4 was greatly facilitated by a sojourn at the American School of Classical Studies at Athens in August and September 1985. The Department of the Classics at Harvard University has supported this work in many ways. To all these institutions I am deeply indebted for their material aid and for their support.

I thank again the lecture audiences and the many friends and colleagues who commented on portions of this book in earlier versions, especially Albert Henrichs and Gregory Nagy of Harvard University. The encouragement and advice of Rachel Toor of Duke University Press and of several anonymous readers improved the final form of this volume. I am grateful to Mindy Conner for copyediting that was both meticulous and sensitive, and to Pam Morrison for efficient and courteous handling of details at the Press. For help in the preparation of the manuscript I am indebted to the professional expertise and patience of Lenore Parker, Elli Mylonas, Gregory Shomo, and P. Lowell Bowditch. Whatever deficiencies or errors remain are, of course, solely my responsibility.

I cannot sufficiently thank my wife, Nancy Jones, for a unique combination of loving support and sound literary advice. For more than two decades the brilliant writings and lectures and the personal generosity and friendship of Jean-Pierre Vernant have been a constant source of inspiration, and to him I dedicate this book in gratitude and affection.

Cambridge, Massachusetts
October 1992

With the sound of the sea in their ears, vines, meadows, rivulets about them, they [the ancient Greeks] are even more aware than we are of a ruthless fate. There is a sadness at the back of life which they do not attempt to mitigate. Entirely aware of their own standing in the shadow, and yet alive to every tremor and gleam of existence, there they endure.

—VIRGINIA WOOLF

"On Not Knowing Greek," in *The Common Reader,*
First Series (New York: Harcourt Brace
Jovanovich, 1925), 38.

Ἂ δὲ φουσκώση ἡ θάλασσα, ὁ βράχος δὲν ἀφρίζει,
κι ἂν δὲ σὲ κλάψη ἡ μάνα σου, ὁ κόσμος δὲ δακρύζει.

If the sea does not swell, the rock does not foam; and if your mother does not weep for you, the world sheds no tears.

—Modern Greek ritual lament
(Margaret Alexiou, *The Ritual Lament in Greek
Tradition,* 127).

1

Introduction

This book explores how Euripides' poetic imagination shaped his vision of tragedy in three plays: *Alcestis, Hippolytus,* and *Hecuba.* The first two have long been recognized as masterpieces of Greek drama and remain among the most discussed works of Greek literature. *Hecuba,* neglected in this century, has recently begun to regain the high esteem it enjoyed from antiquity through the sixteenth century.[1] All three plays belong to the early phase of Euripides' maturity. The *Alcestis* was presented in 438 B.C., the *Hippolytus* in 428, and the *Hecuba* probably in the mid-420s. All three examine the divisions and conflicts of male and female experience. All three also experiment with the limits of the tragic form. *Alcestis* combines tragedy and the satyr play and, in what is still the most economical explanation for its peculiarities, was probably presented in place of the satyr play that usually followed the three tragedies at the dramatic festivals.[2] *Hippolytus* not only introduces a new kind of tragic protagonist—a male virginal devotee of Artemis with mystical tendencies[3]—but, like *Alcestis,* resumes Aeschylus' bold device in the *Eumenides,* presented thirty years earlier, framing the action by the conflict of two divine powers who appear onstage. *Hecuba* is the only extant tragedy to begin with a ghost; yet, after this striking opening, divinity completely disappears from the action. The play depicts the extremes of human suffering in war with a power rivaled only by Euripides' other great war play of a decade later, the *Trojan Women*.

In all three plays, Euripides works with an extreme self-consciousness of his dramatic art, transmuting suffering and sorrow into the paradoxical beauty of tragedy. He thereby draws on the ancient traditions of poetic and ritual commemoration, particularly epic song, but he is also conscious of refashioning these traditions through his new art, an art inspired no longer by the muse of epic martial glory but by a Muse of Sorrows.

It is not only the sad aftermath of death that this Muse of Sorrows sings. Like his predecessors in tragedy, Homer and Sophocles, Euripides knows that death more than any other event shows what a human being is. Each of the three plays brings us to or near these revealing final moments. We experience Alcestis' clarity of self-sacrifice; Phaedra's ambiguous mixture of hatred and heroism, guile and honor; Hippolytus' overwhelmed innocence and bitterness, into which a manly endurance and generosity surprisingly enter at the last; and Polyxena's change from helpless despair to a cold recognition of the lifetime of slavery that awaits her and the consequent courage of her choice. Euripides uses these deaths, especially the deaths of women, to question traditional values and the familiar definitions of male heroism.

Greek drama, unlike its modern counterpart, is a form of public discourse in a holistic society; that is, a society all of whose parts are visibly and inescapably related to one another. The chapters on the individual plays examine how tragedy explores the dynamic relations of analogy and contrast between different areas of personal and social life. To take a central nucleus of meaning in the *Hippolytus*, for example, the cleavage between appearance and reality is replicated in the dramatic movement between interior and exterior, the contrast between house and city, the conflict between female and male, and the clash of lying and truthful speech. Dichotomies between male and female in obviously gender-related categories like sexuality extend to less obviously gender-related categories like space and language. Phaedra's self-defense takes the form of leaving behind, inside the house, silent, closed-up tablets that have to be unfolded to the open air in order to communicate their message. Hippolytus, on the other hand, defends himself in set speeches to his father, the king of the city, in declarations that mirror the civic proceedings of the law courts and assemblies.

Euripides also exploits paradoxical mixtures and inversions of these relations. *Alcestis* combines the male, outward-facing obligations of guest-friendship with private mourning. *Hecuba* brings together primitive ritual and politics, intense maternal feeling, and questions of ethical universals. Its ending moves a mother's personal and characteristically female vengeance for her child into a public setting that reflects both a court of law and a debate on state policy.

As a form of civic discourse, Greek tragedy reflects on the ways in which its society represents itself through such collective expressions as myth, ritual, festivals, and political institutions, and through their explicit statements of civic ideals (and ideologies) in epideictic oratory or funeral eulogy. Tragedy includes and utilizes such forms of civic self-presentation. These surround the tragic performance in direct, concrete ways. Before the audience in the theater at the Greater Dionysia the tribute of the empire was displayed, talent by talent; and the young men who had been reared at public expense as recompense for the deaths of their fathers in battle were paraded forth.[4] But tragedy has a dialectical structure lacking in civic ritual or in such monologic forms of civic discourse as the epitaphios, or funeral speech.[5] It combines the distancing effect of myth and fiction with the agonistic model of debate and conflict. It speaks to the assembled citizens of the polis in the here and now of a time full of crises, dangers, and conflicts; but it uses a frame of remote, legendary events that enables the poet to look far beyond the passions and anxieties of the present moment. The tragedies therefore view the attitudes, practices, expectations, and latent assumptions of the assembled community not just as ideals but also as problems and sources of contradiction, not for empty praise (much as the Athenians enjoyed it)[6] but for critical reflection. All the plays studied in this volume, I believe, were intended to stimulate this kind of serious thought.

Tragedy not only reflects on the discourse of the city and the self. It also reflects on its own discourse. Like all Greek literature, from Homer on, it is concerned with fashioning monuments of itself. Like epic poetry, it is also its own monument, for in immortalizing the stories that it records, tragedy immortalizes its own power to create works of lasting beauty for the city, and indeed for all humankind. Although the plays were intended for a single performance, the tragedians became increasingly conscious of their survival in an immortality of fame. The growing literacy of the late fifth century and the proliferation of written texts of the plays doubtless contributed to this self-conscious monumentalizing. Euripides is particularly interested in making various types of monument—temples, rituals, statues—serve as figures for the peculiar kind of commemoration that tragedy creates. By calling attention to the survival of his tale in the city's collective memory and to the community of the theater that the play itself creates, he places his work in the commemorative tradition alongside oral epic, choral lyric, civic statuary and architecture, and other public symbolic forms. But he also intimates the unsatisfactoriness or even the emptiness of those communal forms of consolation in the face of the suffering that the audience has just experienced, as he does in *Hippolytus, Trojan Women,* and *Bacchae.*[7]

It may be, as Roland Barthes suggests, that the ultimate subject of the modern novel is love, a subject that corresponds to the novel's mode of reception if, as Barthes also suggests, reading, privacy, and desire are closely intertwined:

> Of this eroticism of reading, there is perhaps no purer apologue than that episode in Proust's novel where the young Narrator shuts himself up in the Combray bathroom in order to read . . . : "I went up sobbing to the very top of the house, to the room next to the schoolroom, under the roof, a little room smelling of iris, and also perfumed by a wild currant bush sprouting between the stones of the wall outside and which thrust a flowering branch through the open window. Intended for a more particular and vulgar use, this room, from which one had a view, during the day, all the way to the donjon of Roussainville-le-Pin, long served me as a refuge, doubtless because it was the only place I was allowed to lock myself in, for all those occupations of mine which required an inviolable solitude: reading, reverie, tears, and pleasure."[8]

If privacy and desire underlie the novel's mode of reception, its special form of pleasure, and its implicit relation to its audience, then death, absence, and commemoration underlie Greek tragedy's reception, special pleasure, and relation with its audience.

One source of tragedy's paradoxical pleasure is its always precarious equilibrium between the sadness of loss and the recuperative power of art. Alongside the destructive and self-destructive forces that tragedy reveals in man and his world, works such as *Bacchae*, *King Lear*, and *Hedda Gabler* also imply a creative energy inherent in the act of representation. The very form and social context of tragic drama surround potentially meaningless suffering with some sense of stability and continuity. In Greek tragedy the closing public acts of mourning and ritual commemoration often imply future survivors and spectators who will hear, remember, and learn. The end of *Hamlet* is perhaps modern drama's most familiar example (5.2.330ff.):

> *Hamlet.* Horatio, I am dead:
> Thou livest; report me and my cause aright
> To the unsatisfied.
>
> *Horatio.* Never believe it.
> I am more an antique Roman than a Dane;
> Here's yet some liquor left.
>
> *Hamlet.* Give me the cup. Let go. By heaven, I'll ha't.
> O God! Horatio, what a wounded name,
> Things standing thus unknown, shall live behind me!
> If thou didst ever hold me in thy heart,
> Absent thee from felicity awhile,
> And in this harsh world draw thy breath in pain,
> To tell my story.

The gestures here are not only those of ritual commemoration; they are also intertextual and metatheatrical in the way they imply the classical literary tradition ("antique Roman") and the living continuation of that tradition in the performance itself. The play reaches out through its literary and ritual traditions to embrace the present audience, who thus sees both the conclusion of Hamlet's "story" and its future perpetuation in Horatio's (and Shakespeare's) telling. It thereby also incorporates those who have participated in similar rituals in the past and those who will hear this "story" (via Shakespeare's play) in the future.

In Euripides such commemorative closures often contain a self-conscious reminder of the artifice and artistry within the play itself. This aesthetic self-reflexivity has often been noted, but the connections with the ritual lament and epic commemoration have not always been fully appreciated. Because it is embedded in these traditional forms of expressing sorrow, this aesthetic self-consciousness can coexist with the most powerful tragic effect and need not imply a breaking of the illusion or the dramatic frame.[9]

In addition to ritual commemoration and aesthetic self-consciousness, I am concerned with a third feature of these plays: Euripides' awareness that the communities he depicts are divided by the sharp dichotomy between male and female experience. In all three plays gender questions and disturbs the unity of the civic institutions. Men enjoy power, privilege, and access to public life and public space, while women must find ways of compensating for their relative powerlessness, which they do with results that usually undermine the male-dominated political order with which the plays begin.

We should not assume that these plays faithfully represent the actual condition of Athenian women; they are symbolic constructions, not true-to-life depictions of real behavior or even of the range of possible behavior for women in that society.[10] The separation of women from political life, for example, was not so absolute as the tragedies might suggest. Motherhood had its political function, particularly in the parallelism between marriage for women and war for men, in the rearing and bearing of children as future citizens of the polis, and in women's concern in time of war to help their men, knowing the fate that awaited them if their husbands, fathers, and brothers should fail to keep the enemy outside the walls.[11] Nevertheless, tragedy's almost obsessive embodiment of danger and destruction in female characters shows that these situations of male-female conflict did preoccupy the Athenian audience.[12] All three tragedians repeatedly project into the mythical situations of the plays and the choral odes the fears, tensions, and potential violence in marriage and in family life in general.[13]

With its very one-sided view of male and female relations, tragedy presents anxieties that perhaps could not easily be verbalized or otherwise represented. Tragedies concerned with love and marriage, one might argue, indirectly validate the (desiderated) norm of female submission to father and husband by showing the disastrous result of "deviant" behavior. Nevertheless, in a society that limits the woman's economic and emotional autonomy by placing her disposition in marriage largely in the hands of her father or his surrogate, the tragedies also bring out the dangers of the social system; permit the repressed fears, resentments, desires, and fantasies on both sides to find expression; and then illustrate how ruinous it is to allow full rein to these passions, especially the erotic passions, which women are supposedly less able to resist.

As we shall see in more detail in the following chapters, tragedy frequently expresses these destructive sexual conflicts in spatial terms. All three of the plays studied in this volume project the unity of the city upon tangible, specific spaces in the lives of its citizens, spaces that can easily symbolize the most important institutions of the society. In *Alcestis*, grief for the dying queen reaches out from her domestic realm to include Admetus' entire kingdom. In *Hippolytus* the destructiveness of passion and its denial is played out in a three-way contrast of house, wild nature, and the political entities under Theseus' rule. The city of Athens and its Acropolis (lines 29ff.) are the background to the play's events at Troezen and to the contrast between Hippolytus' hunting grounds and the secluded women's chambers. In *Hecuba* the assembly and law court of the victorious Greek army contrast with the secrecy and private spaces of the crafty Trojan women.

The boundary between male space and female space is a zone whose dangers all the tragedians elaborate in subtle variations. As appears from the richest such elaboration, the tapestry scene in Aeschylus' *Agamemnon*, this is the area where male power yields to female persuasion and seduction. In Sophocles' *Trachiniae* the wife overcomes the great hero of exploits in remote lands by means of the robe, emanation of female guile and erotic power, sent to him from within the deep "enclosures" (*muchoi*) of the house. Although Deianeira is attempting to preserve her marriage, she follows the Clytaemnestra-like pattern in which the woman inside the house collaborates with a seducer who finds his way to her heart.[14] In this case the stranger from outside is the dead Centaur Nessus, who persuaded her to accept the treacherous gift of his poisoned blood as a love charm and to store it in her chambers. In this indirect way he works within her interior realm as a co-conspirator who kills the returning husband.

In Euripides' *Medea*, which may have been influenced by the *Trachiniae*, the protagonist's skillful persuasion of Creon gains her a day's grace so that she can deploy her sinister magic. Although this magic works primarily in female domestic space, it moves from the women's chambers outward to affect the future of kingdoms.[15] Medea not only destroys her own children—her husband's successors—but also ends a dynasty and obliterates her husband's political ambitions. In the *Bacchae*, which plays with inversions of wild and domestic space and male and female roles, seduction takes the form of persuading the king himself to become a woman and leave his palace for the wooded mountain. There he is stripped of his power and seductively led to helplessness and death before a demonized version of maternal rage.[16]

Euripides' *Helen* produces a happy-ending version of the seduction pattern by reversing the roles of husband and seducer. Helen's husband, Menelaus, arrives in Egypt as the stranger and outsider, gradually wins over Helen's affections, enlists the women of the household as silent co-conspirators, plots against the man who possesses her in his palace (the Egyptian king Theoclymenus), and, in a replay of Paris' original seduction, sails away with her on board. In a happy twist of the ironies, however, he is carrying her off as her legitimate husband, her *kurios* (lord and master), and so has a more rightful claim to ownership than had the household where he found her. But even here Euripides is careful to tone down the Aeschylean overtones by keeping the plotter/usurper outside the house so that he does not quite fill the pattern of an Aegisthus.

The *Iphigeneia in Tauris* uses a displaced version of this pattern. The brother, Orestes, takes the role of the husband in *Helen*, and Iphigeneia's ritual service as priestess of Artemis under the barbarian king Thoas replaces the quasi-marital possession by an Egyptian king. Orestes wins his sister away from a male guardian through a female-aided conspiracy that culminates in the intruder's carrying off both woman and treasure from the land, another replay of Paris' seduction and abduction of Helen.[17] As in *Helen* too, the female betrayal is neutralized by the fact that the seducer/conspirator is the woman's more appropriate *kurios*.

Both the Euripidean and the Sophoclean *Electras* self-consciously reverse the crime of Aegisthus and Clytaemnestra by having an outsider (Orestes) plot with the woman inside the house (Electra) to kill its master; but again this plotter is, in fact, the rightful *kurios*, and he undoes the previous betrayal of male space in the symmetry of poetic justice. Even so, the horror and risk of female betrayal from within is kept within bounds by the fact that Orestes, like Menelaus in *Helen*, remains somewhat outside the house itself for most of his plotting. In Euripides' play, the killing of Aegisthus is kept entirely outside the house, whereas Sophocles' Orestes forcibly marches Aegisthus back into the house, there to reclaim his patrimony and reestablish the woman's proper *kurios* in a house where the rights of the father have been vindicated.

In *Andromache* the young wife, Hermione, acknowledges the authority of a woman's two *kurioi*, her father and her husband (cf. 987–92). Paradoxically, however, by abandoning her home with a stranger from outside (Orestes), she is here reenacting the story of her mother, Helen, the most notorious defiance of marital authority in Greek myth. And she simultaneously recalls the story of her aunt, Clytaemnestra, by associating with the man who has just plotted her husband's murder.

The *Hippolytus* offers another version of the betrayal story: Phaedra is a potential Clytaemnestra, plotting with a young lover and kinsman of her husband while the latter is away. An audience of Greek men might be inclined to regard Theseus' violent response less as oedipal jealousy toward a sexually mature son than as a husband's justifiable self-defense against sexual betrayal in his own house. Theseus might well assume that the next stage in the would-be seducer's plan would be to imitate Aegisthus and eliminate the husband entirely, taking over the kingdom along with the wife and the bed. The speech writer Lysias' *Defense for the Killing of Eratosthenes* shows in real life how much anxiety is felt about a lover in the house and how much sympathy and justification is aroused for a husband who kills him.

In the *Hecuba*, a woman's guile in a quasi-domestic interior seems justified by the atrocities it avenges. But this plotting also demonstrates the horrors that women can perpetrate, and so it is brought back under male control in male-dominated, quasi-public space in the courtroom scene at the end, with Agamemnon presiding. Yet even this apparent stability is open to further risk, for the ending indicates that the cycle of female violence, guile, treachery, and victory in the interior of the house will continue in the sequel, eliminating the arch-*kurios*, Agamemnon, in a betrayal far more threatening than Hecuba's justified deception and violence against a barbarian king and his sons.

In addition to depicting the human space of social institutions, the three plays with which we are concerned are typical of Greek tragedy in that they also represent the wider space of the world order: the supernatural and the gods. All three plays show or imply the opposite poles of what lies beyond human vision—Hades and Olympus, the mysterious and terrifying realm of the afterlife and the remote heavens from which the gods enter the human world for brief but labor-intensive visits. They also include the geographical limits that set the local action into a frame of universal significance: the eastern and western borders of Admetus' kingdom in *Alcestis*, Ocean and the remote western rivers in *Hippolytus*, and the border territory that divides Greeks and barbarians in *Hecuba*.

All three plays, like most of Greek tragedy, create a privileged mythical space that can make visible forces both within and beyond us that are usually hidden or denied. *Alcestis* and *Hecuba*, for example, open with exchanges between representatives of the lower and upper worlds. Above and below the magical circle of this theatrical space, and wondrously in contact with it through the evocative poetry of the choral odes, the remote celestial regions of the Olympians and the gloomy land of the dead become present, in varying degrees of clarity or obscurity. The stars and paths of the sun, the vast reaches of the night sky, the eastern and western horizons appear not just as rhetorical figures or elevating hyperboles but as the markers, at once literal and symbolical, of a mythical space where human passions, fears, and energies intersect those unyielding ultimate realities that the Greeks call gods.

2

Euripides' Muse of Sorrows

and the Artifice of Tragic

Pleasure

TRAGEDY, SONG, AND RITUAL

We are accustomed to look at tragedy retrospectively, as a fully developed literary form, and indeed as the jewel among the literary achievements that crown the culture of classical Greece. Our familiarity with centuries of tragic drama and our use of the terms *tragedy* and *the tragic* as categories that extend beyond the literary to the realm of moral philosophy make us forget how unique is the Greeks' blending of the song elements of their poetic tradition with the gripping staged narrative of suffering and questioning to which we give the name "tragic." If we view tragedy in prospect rather than retrospect—that is, as a creation that still lay ahead of the largely oral culture of archaic Greece—we become more aware of its indebtedness to the earlier poetry's forms for commemorating noble deeds and lamenting suffering. At the same time, we need to bear firmly in mind that tragedy is radically new as well as traditional and that whatever it uses it also transforms.

In this chapter I shall consider Greek tragedy, and especially Euripidean tragedy, from three different but interrelated perspectives.

First, I explore some continuities with the traditional forms of a largely preliterate culture, especially the ritual lament. My second topic is a less familiar and rather less obvious feature of these works, and one that is especially marked in Euripides, namely, tragedy's indirect comment on its desired emotional response. We shall see how in Euripides' *Hippolytus* and Sophocles' *Oedipus Tyrannus*, for example, the effect of emotional release is mirrored back to the audience through the play's stage action of weeping, either by the chorus or by a major protagonist. The response of tears and pity is marked as a specifically theatrical response: it implies the response expected of the audience watching the play.

My third area of exploration, which applies particularly to Euripides, though not exclusively so, is the tragedian's self-awareness and self-interrogation of his own poetics. This awareness includes his relation to epic commemoration, his self-conscious use of ritual, and his sensitivity to how the play's formal, aesthetic framing of its painful events brings together and holds in balance (sometimes a dissonant balance) both the pleasure and the pain. These concerns also inform the detailed studies of the three Euripidean plays in the following chapters.

Both drama and ritual consist of mimetic actions. Ritual is itself a symbolic-mimetic performance. From our secular perspective, it too creates a make-believe world, but it is a world that has a special claim and exerts a special influence over those who participate in it.[1] Ritual, however, is transitive in a way that drama is not: it is meant to have an effect, however indirect, on the "real" world; drama meditates on or reflects that "reality" but does not aim to change it. In the terminology of J. L. Austin and John Searle, ritual is "perlocutionary," whereas drama is "illocutionary."[2]

Because tragedy acts out its rituals with live performers before an audience of onlookers, who are therefore also vicarious participants, the boundaries between its fictive actions and ritual are more problematical than in epic or other nondramatic forms. Greek tragedy is often self-conscious about the fact that it is an imitation of a ritual within a ritualized communal context.[3] In the celebrated second stasimon of the *Oedipus Tyrannus*, for example, the chorus frames the question of justice in terms of their own choral performance in the city: if there is no reward for justice and if the unjust man can flaunt his crimes before the gods, they sing, then "why should I dance?" (884–96). In other words, why should they participate in choral songs that honor the gods and their harmonious world if the laws of that world do not work?[4]

In archaic Greece, song was directly tied to performance, often to a specific, ad hoc performance. A threnos (dirge), paean, marriage song, or encomium was sung at its specific cultic occasion.[5] The tragedian, however, cuts the song loose from the specific occasion. His chorus, performing its songs and rituals for situations largely invented by the poet, can range over many possible choral forms, or combine several different forms, or play one lyric genre off against another, mingling contrasting or contradictory ritual forms.[6] To re-cast the famous lines of the *Oedipus Tyrannus* cited above, what song should he sing? In a well-known chorus from the *Heracles*, for exam-ple, Euripides uses the hymnic phrase "I will not cease singing," alludes to symposiac song and epinician ode, and then turns the victory ode into a dirge, or threnos, for the "victor's" slain children.[7] The tragic Muse's shift from victory hymn to dirge is the choral counterpart to the reversals enacted onstage.

In using different kinds or genres of choral song, tragedy not only synthesizes elements from the preexisting song traditions but also represents different activities in the city and different areas of the civic religion. It thereby compares and explores the various voices of authority in the city and asserts its own right to speak about the values of the community and about the meaning and values of human life in general. The mythical aetiologies that end many Euripidean plays (*Hippolytus*, for instance) also give a histori-cal dimension to the rituals that tragedy represents, thus adding to its authority the claim to speak about the origins of communal forms.[8]

Tragedy's assimilation of different choral forms also fosters its artistic self-consciousness. The dirge that we hear and watch is sung over an actor or even a dummy, not an actually dead body. We are thus involved in the paradox of voluntarily submitting to what we would normally consider unfortunate, if not calamitous. Euripides sometimes calls attention to these paradoxes by direct thematic discussion, as we shall later see in the parode of the *Medea*.

All of the three extant tragedians incorporate within their plays the rites of lamentation that we know from archaic poetry and from other premodern societies.[9] All draw heavily on the function of song in an oral culture to give ritualized expression to intense emotion and to provide comfort, solace, and security amid anxiety, confusion, and loss. By absorbing the cries of grief into the lyricism of choral lament, the tragic poet is able to identify the emotional experience of suffering with the musical and rhythmic impulse of choral dance and song. Indeed, what Friedrich Nietzsche sees as the influence of Dionysiac energy in the "spirit of music" at the origins of tragedy may belong in part to the more somber ritual energy of lament.[10] Tragedy's transformation of cries of woe into song constitutes at least part of the creative power of the *poiêtês* (poet-as-maker) and of his divinity, the Muse. Pindar is perhaps aware of this process when he relates how the wail for the dying Medusa is transformed by Athena into the flute song performed at musical competitions (*Pythian* 12). Euripides specializes in this technique of tearful lament, doubtless expertly performed by virtuoso singers able to milk the audience's emotions with the quavers that Aristophanes parodies in the *Frogs*.[11]

As a part of civic and religious festivity, tragic poetry has aesthetic aims similar to those of epic recitation and choral song, namely *terpsis*, or pleasure; but it extends the Homeric paradox of "joy in lamentation" to new areas and gives it a new intensity, especially in its choral lyrics. Tragedy's linking of pleasure and pain is even more paradoxical than the epic's "delight in weeping." The Muse of Tragedy has little of the radiance and sheer delight that attend the Muses' presence in epic. When the tragic Muse is present, it is often in the form of negated music.

All three tragedians use the rhetorical figure of negated song ("unmusic singing," "lyreless Muse," "unchorused dance," or the like) to express these paradoxical relations between art, beauty, ritual, and tragic suffering. These oxymora call attention to the fact that the joyful songs and dances being performed have as their goal the representation of joylessness. They thus point to the fruitful tension between the mythical threats of disorder in self, city, and world enacted on the stage and the order-enhancing celebration of community inherent in the civic performance itself. Song itself thus becomes a part of the tragic action. As the release of grief, it offers momentary relief from the tragic events, but it too suffers the destructive forces that dominate the tragic world. In the *Hecuba*, for example, the lyric exchanges between mother and daughter are songs of mourning, like the nightingale's lament (154–215); but these can only reflect the desperation and sorrow back to the captives themselves and depict their ineffectuality in moving their captors to pity (334–41, cf. 296f.).

In a number of tragedies the crisis itself takes the form of imperiled speech. The worst effect of misery or terror is the paralyzing numbness of the tongue and the silencing of the voice that could give shape to the fears or communicate them to others to gain help or solace. Familiar examples are the mood of anxiety that hangs over the muffled past in the first scene of the *Agamemnon* or the agony of noncommunication in the Cassandra scene later. Aeschylus' *Niobe* and Sophocles' *Ajax* convey the protagonist's suffering through an initial stage silence that only reluctantly (and unexpectedly) breaks into the sharp, painful lyric of lament.[12] Aristophanes brilliantly parodies the effect in the *Frogs* (919f.).

The figure of the joyless song of lament has an intermediate status between metaphor, enacted gesture, and the ritualized expression of intense grief as we see it in the funeral laments of Homer. By transforming the celebratory lyric of choral or symposiac music into the oxymoronic form of the "lyreless tune" or "unmusical Muse," the tragic poet connects his work with the traditional, communal role of the poet in archaic society, but simultaneously also stakes out his unique, problematical place within that tradition. The figure of the "unmusical song" is all the more paradoxical because that song is actually being performed before us and because the emotional expressiveness of tragedy, as a *Gesamtkunstwerk* (total work of art), is enormously enhanced by its use of music, voice, dance, and rhythmical, choreographed gesture in combination with narrative and dialogue.[13]

Euripides is particularly fond of the figure of negated song. In the parode of the *Trojan Women*, for example, Hecuba's grief at Troy's calamity appears under the figure of an inverted Muse. Hecuba utters "elegies of tears," and the Muse "sings her disasters, unchorused, to the unfortunate" (119–21). This is a Muse of Sorrows whose only song is lament. In the next ode, when Hecuba collapses in despair over her own and her daughters' suffering, the chorus of Trojan women sings an ode that mingles song and tears as they recall the night of Troy's fall. The Muse they invoke is truly a Muse of Sorrows, of whom they ask, "Sing to me with tears a funeral ode of new hymns" (511–14). The Muse's dirge is all the more bitter because it contrasts with the songs of joy and the all-night dances when the Trojans, deceived by the Greek stratagem, brought the wooden horse within their walls (529–55).[14] "How sweet for those in misfortune are tears and the groanings of dirges and the Muse who holds pain," the chorus says in iambic trimeters, just after the ode (608f.). These lines bring together the Homeric "joy in lamentation"; the motifs of tears, song, or music (the Muse); and the ritualized lamentation of the dirge, itself a form of song.[15]

In Euripides' *Suppliants* the shared grief takes the form of "smitings that sing in harmony" and "a dancing that Hades reveres" (ξυνῳδοὶ κτύποι . . . χορὸν τὸν Ἅιδας σέβει, 73–75) or "an insatiable joy in lamentations" that "leads one forth," as in the dirge or the dance (ἄπληστος ἅδε μ' ἐξάγει χάρις γόων, 79). Iphigeneia, lamenting her loneliness in the Taurian play, sings to her attendants how she holds to "ill-dirged lamentations, unlyred elegies of a song unfavored by the Muses, in pitiful cries over the dead" (*Iphigeneia in Tauris* 143–47). The chorus replies with "antiphonal songs" that consist of "a woeful Muse amid dirges for corpses that Hades hymns in his singing, far removed from paeans" (179–85). Helen calls out to the Sirens of the Underworld to accompany her grief, "songs joined with her tears" and "deathly music in harmony with her lamentations." She would offer Persephone a grim "paean for the perished corpses in her dusky halls below" (*Helen* 167–78). When the chorus responds sympathetically, she sings "a lyreless lament" (*aluron elegon*, 185).

In Sophocles this figure of the unmusical song, and indeed the metaphorizing of song in general, is relatively sparse (at least as far as the limited remains of his work allow one to generalize). Electra's lament in her opening lyrical exchange with the chorus comes closest, but even here, as in Homer, the lamentation remains distinct as lamentation. Thus, when Electra compares her constant weeping to the plaint of the nightingale (the metamorphosed Procne) that cries, "Itys, Itys" for her son, she speaks directly of "lamenting" (ὀλοφύρεται, 147) and does not use a metaphor for singing. A little later she uses a bolder metaphor, "wings of sharp-toned laments" (πτέρυγας ὀξυτόνων γόων, 242f.), but here too the "laments," though qualified by an adjective that can also apply to singing, have their proper, nonfigurative word, *goos*. So too Antigone, crying over Polyneices' body like a mother bird bereft of her young, "laments in the sharp *voice*" of sorrow, but not actually in song (ἀνακωκύει πικρῶς ὄρνιθος ὀξὺν φθόγγον, *Antigone* 423–25).

In *Oedipus at Colonus* Sophocles does use a full-fledged metaphor drawn from song, but he is describing not the personal emotions of the speaker or chorus but the sadness of the human condition in general. In the third stasimon the chorus commiserates with the aged protagonist and describes death as "the portion of Hades without the marriage hymn, without the lyre, without the dance": Ἀΐδος . . . μοῖρα ἀνυμέναιος ἄλυρος ἄχορος (1221f.). The three epithets make death the negation of the joys of social life, and therefore of festive music, and so appropriate to Oedipus' misery and isolation. The passage reveals the tacit assumption that the communal rituals, accompanied by their music, are an indispensable part of what makes life worth living for men and women.

Sophocles seems more restrained than Euripides in relating the emotional quality of lamentation to the emotional expressiveness of music. Despite the emotionality of his characters, then, Sophocles may be reacting against the Aeschylean lyricizing of grief that we have seen in the passages discussed above. Euripides, with his taste for archaic ritualizing effects, seems to be deliberately recalling the practice of Aeschylus, who is still closer to the pre-Sophistic song culture. Euripides, however, combines this lyrical expressiveness with contemporary theorizing about the power of language to evoke and manipulate feelings that we see in Gorgias' *Helen*.

Tragedy's figure of negated music is appropriate not only to the sadness of the context but also to its double paradox: it evokes and adapts the rituals of communal festivity for situations that divide or threaten civic life, and it incorporates the art forms of lyric celebration for enactments of pain and suffering. In one of our earliest examples, Aeschylus' *Suppliants*, the chorus of Egyptian maidens calls down blessings on the Argive land that has received them, praying that no disaster should "arm Ares, the one of no choruses, of no lyre, begetter of tears, nor arm violence within the city" (*Suppliants* 679–83, especially 681, ἄχορον ἀκίθαριν δακρυογόνον Ἄρη). Such statements indirectly remind the audience that in seeing and hearing this choral song they are at that very moment enjoying the blessings of peace. War is the enemy of song. The sounds of the dance and the lyre fill the city blessed with peace. The sounds of the city at war are of tears and lamentation.[16] Stesichorus begins his *Oresteia* with an invocation asking his Muse to join him in "expelling wars" (πολέμους ἀπωσαμένα πεδ' ἐμεῦ) as she sings of the "marriages of the gods and the banquets of men and festivities of the blessed ones" (fragment 210 Davies). In the case of tragedy, the citizens are attending to the festive music and dance of the performance; they are not hearing the dissonant sounds of war, such as those evoked by Aeschylus at the beginning of his *Seven Against Thebes* (cf. 83–108, 150–73), nor the cries of lament such as those that fill the *Persians*, the woeful sounds that attend a city's defeat.

The wails of mourning for fallen warriors in Aeschylus' *Persians*, Sophocles' *Antigone*, and Euripides' *Suppliants* are more than just atmospheric effect. The members of the audience, as parents, children, and kinsmen, regularly attended state funerals for those fallen in battle. But what is repressed in the austere official ceremony of the funeral oration, as we see it in Pericles' funeral speech or in the *epitaphios* ascribed to Lysias, can appear in the unrestrained, though formalized and mythicized, laments in the tragedies.[17]

EURIPIDES AND THE TRAGIC PARADOX

Euripides reflects explicitly on the paradoxes of the pleasure of tragic song in the parode of his *Medea* (191–203):

> You would not be mistaken in calling foolish and in no way clever those men of previous time who invented songs as pleasurable hearing at celebrations and feasts and banquets. But no one has invented a way, by music and many-stringed songs, to put an end to the hateful sufferings of mortals, from which deaths and terrible misfortunes overturn houses. To heal these things by song would be a gain for mortals. Yet for banquets to produce their happy feasting, why do men strain [exert] their voices in vain? The present fullness of the feast, from its own self, holds pleasure for mortals.[18]

Euripides certainly knows the tradition, going back to Hesiod and indirectly also to Homer, wherein song "heals," or at least distracts from sufferings of this kind.[19] Indeed, the lines in the *Medea* seem to echo Odysseus' praise of the delights of hearing a bard's song amid full tables and abundant wine in Alcinous' palace (*Odyssey* 9.1–11). But for Euripides' banquet, the aim of song is not just physical or sensual, it is also moral and even psychological, alleviating the distress and pain inherent in the condition of mortality. Whereas symposiac or hymnic song suspends the sorrows of life in joyful oblivion and beautiful diversion (Hesiod, *Theogony* 98–103), the music of tragedy produces almost the opposite effect in its performative setting, dwelling on the sudden reversals and misfortunes that life may hold. Indeed, on one view, this effect of tragedy constitutes a kind of inoculation against unexpected suffering, a reminder that a life cannot be called happy until its last day is past.[20]

In a famous ode from the *Heracles*, the chorus expresses its devotion to the Muses (673–86): "I shall never cease mingling the Graces with the Muses, a yoking most sweet. May I not live without musicality, but may I always be in the company of garlands. The old singer still celebrates Mnemosyne. I still sing the victory song of Heracles, in accompaniment to wine-giving Bromios and the song of the seven-stringed lyre and the Libyan flute. Never shall we cease from the Muses who have set me in the choral dance." Interpreters have read this passage as Euripides' personal cri de coeur, the poet's affirmation of his calling and the steadiness of his aims. That may be so, but the expression "Never shall we cease from the Muses" is an allusion to the hymnic formula, "I shall never cease singing such-and-such a god," common as a closing motif of the Homeric Hymns. It thus recalls the traditional, generic character of this song as a hymn to poetry and the Muses. As a formal hymn, it also participates in the transformations that the ritual functions of song undergo in the play.[21] In this case, the joy of celebrating Heracles in the victory song (τὰν Ἡρακλέους καλλίνικον ἀείδω, 680f.; cf. 570, 582) becomes part of the massive change from cries of joy to sounds of horror and lamentation (cf. 891–99, 914, 1025ff.).

In such cases the Muse of Tragedy is not only the divinity behind the technical skill of the bard as singer and composer, as she is in Homer and Hesiod. She is also available to the poet as the figure who registers the horror in his world. She is the index by which he can measure the distance of this tragic world from the happiness of men, both communally and individually—the festive happiness that is associated with song in archaic culture. In Euripides' *Trojan Women*, for example, as Cassandra generalizes about silence as the appropriate response to her overwhelming suffering, she at once names the divinity of song itself, the Muse (384f.): "Better to be silent about shameful things; may I have no Muse as singer to hymn my woes" (μηδὲ μοῦσά μοι / γένοιτ' ἀοιδὸς ἥτις ὑμνήσει κακά). A little later in the same play, Hecuba, to arouse pity for her misfortunes, would "sing out" her sufferings (472f., ἐξᾷσαι).

TRAGEDY AND RITUAL CLOSURE

The tragic poet is both heir to the ritual and commemorative functions of poetry in early Greek society and at the same time one who questions, probes, and inverts those traditions. As a narrator of inherited cultural property, he is, as John Herington has emphasized, the successor of the epic singer and rhapsode.[22] On the other hand, he "narrates" those myths in a unique way, for unlike the rhapsode or choral lyricist, he is himself absent from the performance. Absence is itself a dominant figure for tragedy, from the elusive, wraithlike image of Helen in Aeschylus' *Agamemnon* and Euripides' *Helen* to the statue surrogates of lost spouses in Euripides' *Alcestis* and *Protesilaus*. The very fact of staging the myths as dramatic performances leaves the action with no single, unambiguous authorial voice that can claim absolute right or justice.[23]

Euripides, who is so fond of ending his plays with the foundation of a cult, goes furthest in this probing or ironizing of ritual.[24] But in Aeschylus and Sophocles too one can see this special property of tragedy: namely, achieving full ritual closure, on the one hand (signaled obviously by the closing choral pronouncement and exit), and, on the other hand, opening the myths to the maximum questioning of the social and ritual forms. Aeschylus' *Oresteia* is perhaps Greek tragedy's most problematic example of an ending that brings a ritual resolution through purification and communal celebration. Yet Athena's persuasion of the Erinyes at the end of the *Eumenides*, by its very abruptness, cannot answer the trilogy's deep conflicts between male and female, Olympian and chthonic, the claims of the Erinyes and the claims of Apollo.[25]

To take a less difficult and more positive example, Sophocles' *Ajax*, the hero's lonely walk to the washing places of the sea for an ambiguous "purification" by the blood of self-slaughter (654–56) is made good at the end by a shared, communal purification with fire and the "holy ablutions" of water (ὑψίβατον τρίποδ' ἀμφίπυρον λουτρῶν ὁσίων, 1404f.).²⁶ Solidarity is reestablished among the community of the Salaminians, whom Ajax's half-brother, Teucer, urges to draw together, "all" of them, in their special bond of closeness (*philia*) to their leader (ἀλλ᾽ ἄγε πᾶς, φίλος ὅστις ἀνὴρ / φησὶ παρεῖναι, σούσθω, βάτω; "But come, let all who claims to be present here as a friend proceed in haste"). Teucer's call brings us from the intimate, familial *philotês* of the son touching the body of his father (φιλότητι θιγών, 1410) to the broader *philotês* of "all" who would honor Ajax. The outcast and polluted criminal can now receive both heroic monumentalization and the rite of burial (1415–17):

τῷδ' ἀνδρὶ πονῶν τῷ πάντ' ἀγαθῷ
κοὐδενί πω λῴονι θνητῶν
[Αἴαντος, ὅτ' ἦν, τότε φωνῶ].

[Make haste] toiling for this man, noble in every way—no one of mortals grander [than Ajax when he was, I utter this].²⁷

The quasi epitaph that constitutes the near-final lines reinforces the unifying effect of the ritual, for it evokes the value system in which the hero can now find a place and simultaneously suggests the extension of his existence into the future through the social memory, including his cultic status in Athens and elsewhere.²⁸

This public ritual of shared grieving brings an emotional resolution of Ajax's private shame. It is also the visual, performative enactment of the emotions stirred among the audience in the theater, with all the feelings of pity, sorrow, loss, triumph, and vindication that the ritual lamentation evokes. The audience's identification with the lonely hero thus moves from the agony of hopeless, isolating pollution to identification with the forces of solidarity and reintegration available to the community, which in this case comprise the funeral ceremony, implications of cult worship, and the theater itself.

The ceremonial action effects closure; but the exclusion of Odysseus, the mournful nature of the rite itself, and the reminder of the great body still "blowing out its black force" (1412f.) continue the mood of conflict, waste, and suffering. These funerary rites for Ajax at the end also say nothing of Tecmessa or female lamentation in general, even though this has been prominent elsewhere in the play

(*Ajax* 579f., 624–34, 937–45). The exclusion shifts the emphasis from the ritual mourning per se, which might suggest the hero's defeat, to the restoration of his place in his society. What Ajax had valued most was his honor among his male peers; and the kind of funerary ritual that he receives at the end, so different from that of Hector in *Iliad* 24 or of Achilles in *Odyssey* 24, confirms his reintegration into that warrior society. He receives a warrior's burial with an entirely masculine focus: his armor, his son, his comrades, his wound. This narrowing of vision in the closing ceremony is both his triumph and his tragedy.

The ending of the *Hippolytus* is characteristic of the intellectual and emotional complexity of ritual closure in Euripides (1462–66): "This woe came without expectation as a common grief to all the citizens. There will be an oar-beat of many tears; for the tales of the great that are worthy of grieving do more prevail." This passage, to which I shall return in a later chapter, is like the final speech of Hamlet in connecting the mourning ritual with the survival of Hippolytus' story in the memory of the community. The chorus's beating of breasts, hands, and feet in communal mourning gives physical expression to the emotions that the spectators may feel but cannot act out so openly in the public theater. Yet this closing lament over the dying youth, as a "common grief for all the citizens" (κοινὸν τόδ' ἄχος πᾶσι πολίταις), points to the emotional participation that binds "all" the members of the theater together in the collective experience of the dramatic performance. The "tales of the great" in the last lines, which endure as the memory of a past suffering, also refer to the task of the tragic poet, here viewing himself as the voice of the communal memory, just as the epic singer was.[29]

The commemorative role of the tragic poet, however, is far more complex, partly because the drama contains many competing voices and because the values to be transmitted are more controversial, in fact are defined by the tragedy as controversial because they emerge only from conflict with other, competing sets of values. The tales of the great at the end of *Hippolytus*, for example, include a cult song, promised by Artemis, to be performed by Troezenian girls as part of the marriage ritual. But when Artemis presents this song as a metaphor (a "Muse-fashioned concern" and a grieving that Hippolytus will "pluck," 1427–29), she pulls it away from its social function as ritual and toward the aesthetic self-awareness of the poet's art. The grief to be expressed by these future (and anonymous) performers of cultic song is made tangible as a "fruit" of tears that Hippolytus will "pluck"—in place of the sexual ripeness of the maidens he has renounced.

The distancing effect of metaphor is analogous to the geographical remoteness of the grief of Phaethon's sisters, "dripping amber-bright beams of tears into the purple wave" of their western river in the second stasimon, the so-called Escape Ode (737–41). In this ode the aesthetic framing of grief by metaphor is reinforced by the combination of embedded myth and geographical distance. The effect of transposing grieving into metaphor is very different from the effect of epic, where gods and mortals can be literally joined in the funeral ritual for Achilles. Here the mortals share the lament with the Muses' dirge and Thetis' keening. It is a magical, radiant moment of community and glory in the midst of suffering (*Odyssey* 24.58–65):

> Around you [Achilles] the daughters of the old man of the sea took their places, lamenting pitiably, and they were clothed in raiment immortal. And all the nine Muses lamented over you, responding in lovely voice. Then you would not have seen any one of the Argives without tears: so stirring a song rose from the clear-singing Muse. For seventeen nights and days we lamented over you, immortal gods and mortal men together; and on the eighteenth day we gave you over to the fire.

The tragic mood is much more subdued. Whereas epic keeps the immortal fame in the foreground, tragedy, even when it promises cultic immortality, keeps this at the margins and places mortality in the foreground.[30] Artemis' words at the end of *Hippolytus* do not even convey much emotional involvement by the maidens, who, in any case, are reluctant celebrants of Hippolytus' death. She herself cannot be defiled by the sight or sound of dying (1437). Her emphasis is therefore on the contrivance of song, the artifice of the "Muse-fashioned concern." It is left for the human sufferers to blend singing and grieving, to strike their breasts with the "oar-beat of many tears," and to feel the "common grief" for loss.

LAMENT AND CATHARSIS

The closures of ritual lamentation that end so many tragedies may help us understand Aristotle's meaning in his enormously controversial description of tragedy as "accomplishing through pity and fear the catharsis of such emotions" (*Poetics* 6.1449b24–28). Without entering into the labyrinth of catharsis scholarship, I accept the traditional view that catharsis refers primarily to tragedy's emotional effect on the audience in performance and not just to intellectual "clarification" of the events of the drama. As proponents of the intellectualist view point out, even the purgation or purification of emotions involves an intellectual component, for learning combines emotional experience and intellectual perception; and so we should not entirely exclude the intellectual meaning.[31] Yet the parallels with chapter 14 of *Poetics* and with the discussion of catharsis and music in the *Politics*, taken together with Aristotle's attempt to answer Plato's attacks on tragedy, make it extremely likely that his emphasis in the catharsis theory is on tragedy's emotional effects on its audience.[32] He may even have chosen the term *catharsis* precisely because it includes ritual, affective, and intellectual responses.[33]

On this view of catharsis, the release of tears in the communal laments embodied in the chorus, especially in scenes of closure, effect a "cleansing" of the strong emotions stirred by the tragic performance. Such scenes help to direct the audience toward the kind of pleasure appropriate to tragedy, what Aristotle calls its *oikeia hêdonê* (*Poetics* chap. 14). This special "tragic pleasure," then, includes a sense of community in the shared arousal and resolution of the tragic emotions of pity and fear. Aristotle here, as often, is firmly within Greek cultural practice, in this case the free expression of emotion in weeping. Although he does not speak of tears explicitly in connection with pity, the two are closely associated in Greek views of emotional response.[34] When Gorgias combines pity and fear in his *Encomium for Helen*, he uses the expression ἔλεος πολύδακρυς καὶ φόβος περίφρικος (most tearful pity and most shuddering fear, chap. 9). Aristotle himself describes fear in terms of the physical effect of the accompanying "shudder" (14.1453b5).

Such emotional participation enlarges our sympathies and so our humanity. Aristotle's closest approximation to "humanity" in this sense is his term *to philanthrôpon*, and he associates it with pity and fear in one passage (1452b38) and with the tragic in general in another (1456a21).[35] This expansion of our sensibilities in compassion for others is also part of the tragic catharsis. We can be moved to such compassion because we accept the fears as our own and acknowledge that the pity and grief for the tragic protagonist's suffering imply pity and grief for the suffering of all men and women and do, in fact, constitute a concern to "all the citizens" and "all" the spectators. The ritualized laments of tragic closure thus direct the emotional responses of the audience toward resolution in a heightened awareness of community, continuity, and universality.

Euripides' *Andromache*, for instance, moves toward closure with a shared ritual lament, a responsive threnos between the chorus of Thessalian women and the aged Peleus, grandfather of the slain Neoptolemus. This communal lament balances and contrasts with Andromache's isolated lament at the beginning of the play (96–116; cf. 532–34); it marks both the enlargement of the tragic suffering and a cathartic resolution. Collective lament, however, suddenly gives way to individual miracle as Thetis appears as the dea ex machina and promises Peleus immortality in the Isles of the Blest where he will find his son Achilles. The consolation seems individualized and unique; but even here the larger community of mortals is reaffirmed in the goddess's last words (1268–72): "For you must accomplish what has been fated, for this is Zeus' will, and cease your pain over those who have died. For *to all men* this decree has been established by the gods, and all must die."

Aristotle's own favorite model for tragic effects is, of course, Sophocles' *Oedipus Tyrannus*, and this play also lends itself to analysis in terms of the view of catharsis suggested above. It is almost as explicit as the *Hippolytus* in calling attention to the community of shared suffering created by the theater. When the Messenger arrives with the news of the catastrophe within the palace, he addresses the honored elders of Thebes and prepares them for the "grief" (*penthos*) that they will "take upon themselves" when they hear of their king's sufferings (1223–26): "O you who are always in greatest honor in this land, what deeds will you hear, what deeds will you see, and what great grief will you take up if in noble fashion you are still concerned with the house of the Labdacids."[36] The lines effectively introduce the chorus to the climactic events now to be reported. But they also serve the same function for the members of the audience, who, in their sympathetic participation in the action of the play, do indeed "care for the house of the Labdacids" and take upon themselves the "grief" for that house, as if they were the lords of Thebes addressed by the Messenger.

In like manner, at the end of the scene, the Messenger prepares both the real audience of Athenians in the theater and its fictional equivalent—the imaginary audience of Theban elders within the play—for the visual spectacle, just as his opening words prepared them for the verbal narration of the events. In so doing, he also directs them toward the appropriate emotional response to that spectacle, a response of pity (*epoiktisai*): "Yet he [Oedipus] needs strength and a guide, for his sickness is greater than he can bear. He himself will show you. For these gates are opening, and you will soon see a spectacle such as to stir pity even in the one who loathes it" (θέαμα δ' εἰσόψῃ τάχα / τοιοῦτον οἷον καὶ στυγοῦντ' ἐποικτίσαι, 1292– 96). When the doors are then thrown open, the chorus responds with just the kind of emotion that Aristotle suggests. The Messenger had enjoined them to pity, but they respond also with "fear" or "terror": "O suffering *fearful* for men to behold, O *most fearful* sight of all that I have ever come upon" (ὦ δεινὸν ἰδεῖν πάθος ἀνθρώποις, / ὦ δεινότα- τον πάντων ὅσ' ἐγὼ / προσέκυρσ' ἤδη, 1297–99). To this verbal ex- clamation of terror they soon add the physical response of a "shud- der" of fear (1306): τοίαν φρίκην παρέχεις μοι (Such a shudder do you bring upon me). *Shudder* is exactly the word Aristotle himself uses in speaking of the tragic effect of this play, perhaps with this very passage in mind (*Poetics* 14.1453b5, *phrittein kai eleein*).

This shudder of fear affects the play's internal audience, the chor- us of Theban elders, because they recognize the power of the gods and see the sudden, massive reversal in a human life. As the scene continues, however, the terror is resolved into pity as they change their address to Oedipus from "wretched one" to "my friend," "dear one" (*ô tlamon*, 1299; *philos*, 1321). They now sympathize with his suf- fering as they try to understand the reasons behind his self-inflicted pain (1319–21):

κα‍ὶ θαῦμά γ' οὐδὲν ἐν τοσοῖσδε πήμασιν
διπλᾶ σε πενθεῖν καὶ διπλᾶ φορεῖν κακά.

And indeed there is no wonder amid so many woes that you feel double grief (*penthos*) and bear double sufferings.[37]

Viewed in Aristotelian terms, this entire closing movement creates a catharsis, a cleansing release, of the pity and fear that were so violent at the moment of recognition when the chorus first looked with horror on their blinded king. Sophocles gradually channels the cathartic effect into the physical expression of tears, shed both by Oedipus and by his children (1473, 1485).

This weeping within the play also provides a cue for the desired and appropriate response of the audience, their participation in the emotional release in the theater. Whether or not the members of the audience actually join in the weeping, they can join in the emotions it displays. When Oedipus asks Creon to "pity" his children in his last extended speech in the *Tyrannus* (1503–9), he not only shows his own enlargement of concern as he looks beyond his own suffering to the suffering of others. He also enacts that gesture of wider sympathy toward which we as spectators are directed as part of the "pleasure proper to tragedy"; that is, as the appropriate outcome of a successful cathartic experience of a tragedy performance.

LAMENT AS CLOSURE: THE *TROJAN WOMEN*

To return to Euripides, the end of the *Trojan Women* is not only one of tragedy's most extended and moving scenes of ritual lament, it also shows how profoundly Euripides can combine the closure effected by the traditional rites of lamentation with his exploration of the poetics and paradoxes of his mode of tragedy.[38] The play ends with a burial rite for the murdered infant Astyanax, child of Hector and Andromache. The burial of the child in the shield of his father may well be an innovation by Euripides. It heightens the pathos of the long scene of Hecuba's ritual lamentation; and Hecuba addresses this shield both at the beginning and at the end.

Her lament over Astyanax is like the lament over a fallen warrior, which this child will never grow up to be. The shield is a monument of a sort to Hector, but its presence is a reminder of Hector's defeat and the failure of his efforts and sufferings, *ponoi*, to which the shield physically attests. First, Hecuba addresses the dead child (1187–93): "Gone are my endearments, my nurture, and those sleepless nights. . . . What would the Muse-fashioning poet write on your tomb? 'This child, in fear, the Argives once did slay'? Shame on Greece for that epigram. Though you did not, as heir, receive your father's goods, receive this bronze-backed shield, in which you will be buried." She then turns to the shield, and addresses it as if it were the tomb (1194–99): "You who saved the strong right arm of Hector, your best guardian is lost. How sweet the impress that lies upon your strap; and sweet in your orb's well-turned circumference the sweat that often Hector, in the midst of toilsome efforts, dripped from his brow, as he lifted you to his beard." Everything in this ritual is a figure of absence and enacts a paradox of embodied absence.[39] Hecuba herself, as she addresses the shell of Astyanax's body within the hollow circle of the shield, takes the place of the child's parents, for Andromache has just been carried off in Neoptolemus' ship (the opening news of the scene, 1123–35), and Hector is dead. Hecuba uses the language of heroic monumentalization but turns it into the language of female lament. Instead of conferring immortal fame on a great warrior by eulogizing his deeds, she checks the movement toward transcendence by enacting the archetypal role of the *mater dolorosa* over a dead child. The intertextual echo of the Homeric Hecuba's lament over Hector in the *Iliad* deepens this overlay of tragic suffering on epic commemoration. Euripides' Hecuba literally empties out the tokens of epic heroization and converts them into icons of loss and absence.

Hecuba's replacement of Andromache in the funeral rites for Astyanax evokes another incomplete burial of a child. Earlier in the play, Andromache told Hecuba how the latter's daughter, Polyxena, was sacrificed at the tomb of Achilles, an atrocity that had only been hinted at to the mother (620–25). There, acting as Hecuba's surrogate, Andromache covered Polyxena's body with a "robe" (*peplois*, 627) and performed the ritual lament of beating the breast. Here at the end we see the ritual breast beating enacted onstage (cf. 1235ff.); and Hecuba buries Andromache's child, also covering the body with a "robe" (*peplois*, 1143). She is then led off to the ship of her Greek master, as Andromache had been shortly before.

The shield that serves as Astyanax's coffin is also a figure for Hector's absence. The impress of his right arm on the leather strap is the visible symbol of the body that is not there. The sweat that dripped into the shield reminds us both of his mortality and of the failure of those "toilsome efforts" (*ponoi*) from which the sweat flowed. Even the "beard" reminds us of the nonadolescence of Astyanax, of the truncated life cycle of the son who, though buried in the father's shield, will not grow up to be like his father. Euripides here draws on *Iliad* 6 and 22, and possibly also on Sophocles' *Ajax*; but he recasts the traditional threnos into a mood of much greater pathos.

The figures of absence culminate in the closing lyrical exchanges between Hecuba and the chorus about the disappearance of the land and the name of Troy, the absence of the unburied Priam, and the deafness of the gods.[40] "Troy the unfortunate, ceases to exist" (οὐδ' ἔτ' ἔστιν, 1323f.). The cries of lamentation over the city, rather than perpetuating its memory, seem to "wash over it" (—ἔνοσις ἅπασαν— ἔνοσις ἐπικλύζει πόλιν, 1326), thus adding burial or drowning to the other forces of oblivion.[41]

Addressing the shield as if it were a tomb, Hecuba also invokes the commemorative epigram, the monument created by one who works with the Muse, *mousopoios*, the same word that describes the cult song for *Hippolytus* (*Trojan Women* 1189; *Hippolytus* 1428f.). But here the Muse-fashioned work is only an epigram of shame. She returns to this commemorative function of poetry at the end of her lament and again personifies the shield (*Trojan Women* 1221–25): "You, in songs of victory once the mother of myriad trophies, Hector's dear shield, receive your garlands now. For, although you are not subject to death, you will die with this corpse. And yet it would be better far to honor you than those arms of base and clever Odysseus." The metaphorical "mother" fuses family life with war, as the surrogate human mother invests the inanimate weapon with maternity. The trophy of victory is also the tomb of the defeated warrior's son, and the monument itself seems to be involved in his death: θανῇ γὰρ οὐ θανοῦσα σὺν νεκρῷ (For, although you are not subject to death, you will die with this corpse, 1223). The passing on of arms now evokes the debasing of the heroic tradition in the award of Achilles' weapons to the undeserving Odysseus. Hecuba goes even further in these reversals a few lines later, when she calls into question the entire value of commemorative song (1242–50):

> If the god did not overturn our mortal world and enclose it beneath the earth, we would not, when we are gone and vanished [*aphaneis*], be the subject of hymns, giving to the Muses songs for mortals after us. . . . Come, then, and bury the corpse in his miserable tomb. He has such garlands of the dead as he should have. It makes, I think, but little difference to the dead if they get wealthy tomb offerings; these are the empty extravagance of those who are still alive.

As showy funeral rites are reduced to vanity for the living and indifference for the dead, so too the lasting songs of epic fame, Muses and all, become an almost empty tribute and a last, desperately summoned consolation.⁴²

Hecuba is here echoing Helen's reflection in *Iliad* 6 that her sufferings will make her a subject of song for later men (6.356–58). Helen speaks with bitterness, but her remark is at least accepted as an explanation. Euripides' tragic heroine makes a much harsher juxtaposition between the heroic tradition—fame included—and the brutality, vanity, and shame into which her world has disintegrated.⁴³ Unlike Helen's, Hecuba's reflection does not come in a moment of calm and suspension of violence. It stands between a wrenching lament over a dead child and the journey from a destroyed city into slavery (*Trojan Women* 1256ff.).

By adapting this remark of the Homeric Helen to Hecuba's lament, Euripides makes another insertion of tragic sorrow into the tradition of epic commemoration. His version of epic self-reflexivity shows us the process of transforming suffering into tragic art and also suggests that the emotional cost of this transformation is very high. He pushes his audience as close as possible to participating in the anguish of the rites of lamentation; but he simultaneously emphasizes the mimetic quality that this painful ritual acquires in the dramatic art form. By thus exploring the boundary between aesthetic illusion and the emotional reality of an all-too-familiar ritual, he calls into question the pleasure of this form. At the least he makes clear the high emotional price that this paradoxical tragic pleasure exacts. Yet the stylized nature of ritual lament helps to keep the experience both poignant and bearable at the same time.

The technique, as we have observed, is not unique to Euripides. There is a similar divided perspective, overt or at least potential, in the endings of Aeschylus' *Oresteia* and Sophocles' *Ajax, Trachiniae*, and *Electra*. One of the special properties of the dramatic form perfected by the Athenian tragic poets would seem to be just this achievement of full ritual closure, on the one hand, and opening the myths to their problematical dimensions as explanations of the meaning of human life, on the other. Although many tragedies end with their questions about meaning and justice unanswered, the ritual endings provide a feeling of emotional closure; and this need not foreclose the intellectual questioning that the plays stimulate.⁴⁴ Might we see here a characteristic stamp of the Athenian genius, continuing the traditional function of the poet as the voice of communal norms and at the same time transforming the poet's relation to the tradition in decisive ways?[45]

From this perspective we can appreciate afresh why tragedy developed in Athens alone of the Greek city-states. The tragic poet reflects a society whose values had become complex, divided, multiple, a subject of debate and discussion rather than a given. We may think, for instance, of the Mytilenean debate or the Melian dialogue in Thucydides. During the acme of tragedy, Athens in particular experimented with other models for the intellectual's relation to society. It welcomed the traveling Sophists, professional questioners of local norms in unconventional ways. And for a time at least it tolerated the gadfly questioning of Socrates. But Socrates is also the figure for whom Plato, in the next century, creates a specifically antitragic memorial and (in works like the *Crito, Apology*, and *Phaedo*) a non-lamenting "poetry" of death that aims at making tragedy obsolete.

If we look back to the poetry of, say, the Megarian Theognis a couple of generations before the development of tragedy, or even to Pindar, roughly contemporary with tragedy, we see a very different relation between the poet and changing social and economic conditions. Instead of elaborating the existing edifice of the traditional values with increasingly intricate and magnificent structures, as Pindar does, the tragic poet, while drawing on the oral poet's inherited role as spokesman for communal values and the continuities of social and religious forms, also raises the eventuality that these forms are no longer adequate to the difficult questions of life.[46]

Like epic and choral lyric, tragedy depends on its rich poetic heritage from the past, especially the myths and the techniques of mythical narration. It is inconceivable without the prototragic vision of Homer and the use of myth as allusive, multilevel paradigms for events in the present. Yet by removing himself from the performance and by projecting the voice of unified truth into the dialogue and conflict among sharply opposing personas, the tragedian effects a revolutionary change in the conception of the poet's role in society.[47] How Euripides interprets this role we shall see in the following chapters.

Alcestis

3

Cold Delight: Art, Death,

and the Transgression

of Genre

Throughout his oeuvre Euripides plays with the paradoxes of myth and reality, fantasy and realism; but nowhere does he do this more deliciously than in the *Alcestis*. I begin with the famous promise of Admetus to his dying wife (348–54):

σοφῇ δὲ χειρὶ τεκτόνων δέμας τὸ σὸν
εἰκασθὲν ἐν λέκτροισιν ἐκταθήσεται,
ᾧ προσπεσοῦμαι καὶ περιπτύσσων χέρας
ὄνομα καλῶν σὸν τὴν φίλην ἐν ἀγκάλαις
δόξω γυναῖκα καίπερ οὐκ ἔχων ἔχειν
ψυχρὰν μέν, οἶμαι, τέρψιν, ἀλλ' ὅμως βάρος
ψυχῆς ἀπαντλοίην ἄν.

Your form, in likeness fashioned by the clever hand of craftsmen, will lie stretched forth on the bed. On this I shall fall and folding my arms about it, calling your name, I shall seem to hold my dear wife in my embrace, although I hold her not—a cold pleasure, I think; yet so shall I remove the heaviness of my soul.

These lines contain many of the central issues raised by this fascinating and beautiful work, especially its reflections on art and the connections between art, substitution, and death. In their context, the lines show Admetus' intensity of emotion in the moments before his wife's death. His rhetoric, however, magnifies the distance between his dreamy romanticism, almost an aestheticism of grief, and the down-to-earth practicality of the dying woman, whose concern is for the future of her children, not self-centered emotions. Robert Browning's adaptation in *Balaustion's Adventure* catches the mood of unreality and dreamy fantasy:

> A cold delight indeed, but all the same
> So should I lighten of its weight my soul!
> And, wandering my way in dreams perchance,
> Thyself wilt bless me: for, come when they will,
> Even by night our loves are sweet to see.

The passage calls attention to the artificiality of the entire dramatic situation, particularly as Admetus goes on to evoke the magical power of the archpoet, Orpheus, to bring the dead back to life (357–62). Here, however, the fantasy is to be realized after all, and with it the Orphic power to overcome the greatest Necessity of our mortal nature, death itself. Albert Cook has suggestively noted how Admetus' rhetoric "freezes the stiff figures on stage in the irony of an unperceived unnaturalness."[1] I would add that in the course of the play this unnaturalness becomes an artifice whose implications extend beyond what Admetus or any other single character can envision. It embodies a quality of art, the creative, inventive power of daedalic craftmanship which Euripides here, as elsewhere, seems to use as a metaphor for his own poetry.[2] Such a creation will provide "pleasure" through the skill of mimetic "likeness" (*eikasthen*, 349); yet precisely because the work—of words as of hands—is artificial, our pleasure will, to some extent, be "cold pleasure," the pleasure in replication or imitation, not in "reality." This lifelike artifice, however, leads us to question just what reality is—a question that, as Aristophanes exasperatedly observes, is asked somehow or other in nearly every Euripidean play.[3]

The substitution of an art object for a person has a major role in Euripides' lost *Protesilaus*, which closely resembles *Alcestis* in its theme of lovers separated by death, and in a different way in his *Helen*. Substitution lies at the center of the plot of the *Alcestis*, too.[4] The statue is a stage version of the *kolossos*, the image buried in place of a deceased kinsman or kinswoman whose body has not been found.[5] Admetus' statue, shaped "by craftsmen's clever hand," is thus a point of crossing between artistry and ritual commemoration, between the aesthetic and the religious. This dialectic pervades all Euripidean tragedy, and we shall see its distinctively countertragic and paradoxical forms in this play.

The theater, in the civic space beneath the Acropolis, like the plays it contains, demarcates a free space of largely (and perhaps exclusively) male activity set apart from the biological demands of reproduction, nurture, and death that are located inside the house and are tended to primarily by women. In a play whose plot rests on exchanges and substitutions, the fiction-enabling conventions of the theater substitute a story of males defeating death (Apollo, Orpheus, Heracles, and even Admetus) for a story of Necessity's absolute power over a woman in the house (cf. 962ff.). The play moves from the substitution of Alcestis for Admetus to that of Heracles' anonymous prize-woman for Alcestis. To believe in the myth of the play is to reaffirm a social institution whose power of symbolic representation liberates from the most imperious Necessity of our biological nature. Yet this same institution presents these issues not as the absolute triumph of one side or the other but as a conflict and a problem, for the underlying condition of all the play's theatrical fictions is the substitution of art, myth, or fantasy for the inexorable reality, or Necessity, of death.

Euripides brings us perilously close to this deflating view in Admetus' moment of recognition at line 940: "Now I understand." He understands that the substitution of Alcestis' life for his has not purchased a livable human existence: his life is in fact a nonlife (940–61, cf. 272f.). To this extent Euripides suggests that the myth just won't work; and he thus undoes the play's operative fantasy of being able to evade death. But at this point, in a culminating double twist of the irony, Heracles returns to the stage and dispels the gathering clouds of the tragic ending. The discordant figure of earthy appetites, and thus of comedy, defeats Necessity after all.

In a celebrated ode from his *Antigone*, performed only a few years before the *Alcestis*, Sophocles warns that despite its brilliant intellectual achievement, mankind has still devised no remedy against death (360–62). Euripides' play miraculously allows the escape from death that Sophocles leaves as the last residue of untamed Nature. This triumph is doubtless due less to the glory and confidence of Periclean

Athens, then at its height, than to the fact that Euripides put *Alcestis* in place of the satyr play generally presented after the tragic trilogy. The motif of overcoming death is embedded in the myth. Apollo, grateful to Admetus for his hospitable treatment, has granted him the privilege of allowing someone else to die in his stead. Admetus' wife, Alcestis, has offered herself, and the day of her death has now come. The everyday quality of gradual death in the first third of the play is the foil to the miraculous rescue of the heroine by Heracles, who thus rewards Admetus for his (dubious) decison to conceal the truth of his wife's death and receive his old friend as a guest into the house.

When the divine figures exit after the prologue, we enter a tragic human situation: we wait for someone to die (77ff.). But Apollo has also alluded to the arrival of Heracles, the figure of surprise, who will defeat Death "by force" (*bia*, 69). Heracles becomes the bearer of art's victory over death; but his use of "force," rather than Orphic song or persuasion (cf. 357–59, 853), points to a distinctively Heraclean mode of success.

If, as many believe, *Alcestis* did replace the satyr play, Euripides not only combines and confuses comic and tragic moods but also makes this combination the central issue in his play by focusing on the defeat of death's "necessity."[6] He frustrates the generic expectations of the satyr drama by giving us not a playful victory of sexual energy over death but rather a puzzling exploration of "what death means in the context of a genre supposed to celebrate sexual union, where the only character approaching a satyr, reminiscent of the drunken Dionysus, is the drunken Heracles, who often appeared in comedies and satyr plays."[7] The fantasy of escaping death is implied in the opening lines, with their reference to Asclepius, and then taken up wishfully in the parodos (123–31). But the absolute Necessity of death recurs in the last ode as a power greater than even Orpheus or Asclepius (962–72).[8]

This contrast between Necessity and Possibility is embodied onstage in the contrast between Alcestis and Heracles. It also extends by contiguity to the different spatial fields of the two characters. The self-sacrificing wife is totally attached to the inner space of the house, whose biological continuation defines her aims with a completeness and simplicity from which she draws her strength. The boisterous, all-conquering hero, on the other hand, is a restless, wide-ranging traveler seeking temporary shelter and prepared to go even to Hades' "sunless halls" (851f.). For him the house is only a brief stop on his way to Thrace and another of his labors (483ff.). He at once puts Admetus' royal house in its larger context of Thessaly and Pherae (476–80, cf. 508–10), and in touch with central Greece too, as Admetus contemplates a possible reciprocal journey to "Argos' thirsty land" (560, cf. also 481 and 491).

Early in the play the chorus desperately asks for some "resourceful way out of evils" (*poros kakôn*, 213). The word *poros* implies an open, accessible path toward a goal, a clear direction in which passage is possible.[9] Heracles is the mythical embodiment of just such confidence in making his "way," even out of death (cf. *poreuein* in 482f., also 850ff.). He will, in fact, use this same verb, actively, when he has "made a way" for Alcestis "out of the nether halls" (πορεῦσαι νερτέρων ἐκ δωμάτων, 1073). "Of things unexpected the god has found a way" (*poros*) is the chorus's penultimate line in the play (1162).

After the final ode on Necessity, and Admetus' tragic recognition (936–61), the closing section brings the results of Heracles' triumph over Death visibly onstage, almost as a coda of pure wish fulfillment. The dialogue between the two male protagonists here, in a scene of conflict and banter, is a mirror image of the confrontation between the male divinities Death and Apollo in the prologue.[10] In both cases Alcestis' life hangs in the balance. But the fantasy of bringing back life by a contest between males (including the alleged wrestling contest in which Heracles won his prize [1025–33]) contrasts with the biological necessities of birth and death in the background, associated with the woman and the house. Except for Death himself, the figures of life's constricting conditions are all feminine: the Fates, or Moirai, in the prologue (12f., 32–34); Alcestis and the demands she makes of Admetus for her children's sake (280–325); Necessity (Anankê) in the last ode; and the veiled Alcestis in the exodos, still subject to death in the ritual silence that she must maintain (1144–46).[11]

Heracles' victory over Death in an all-male, agonistic setting not only validates the masculine values of hospitality that led to the contest; it also validates the "contest" of the dramatic performance itself, the theatrical activity that can represent an escape from death. The very existence of the play, whose composer, actors, judges, and (possibly) spectators were exclusively male, presupposes a space apart from the female-dominated domestic space, where new life is created and old life is extinguished. This civic space also includes the freedom of the theater, which, thanks to myth and imagination, can stage the defeat of death.

The exodos not only shifts from tragedy to comedy; it also marks a change from the lyric genre of the dirge, or threnos, which belongs particularly to women, to the epinician, or victory song, an exclusively male prerogative.[12] Here the woman is merely an object of exchange between males, and a minor object of exchange at that (cf. 1029–31). In insisting that Admetus receive his veiled prize, Heracles includes him in the specifically male bond of "fellow victor" (νι-κῶντι . . . συννικᾷς, 1103).[13]

While Alcestis is seen only in the intimate space of the house (163–96) or in terms of vertical passage between upper and lower worlds, sunlight and Hades (244ff., 252f.), Heracles introduces the wide geography of his adventures (479ff.). He also redefines Admetus: instead of being a mourner inside the house, as we first see him (199–203), Admetus is seen as the ruler of a broad kingdom and a possible voyager to remote cities (476–85, 510, 559f.). Immediately after his acceptance of Heracles, the chorus praises the wealth and extent of his kingdom (588–96). More important, it also evokes the Orphic magic of Apollo's lyre as he herded Admetus' cattle in the outlying regions of his domain (583–87):

χόρευσε δ᾽ ἀμφὶ σὰν κιθάραν,
Φοῖβε, ποικιλόθριξ
νεβρὸς ὑψικόμων πέραν
βαίνουσ᾽ ἐλατᾶν σφυρῷ κούφῳ,
χαίρουσ᾽ εὔφρονι μολπᾷ.

Around your lyre, Phoebus, the dappled fawn danced with light step, tripping across the high-leafed firs, taking joy in the happy song.

The magic of song, and by extension of poetry and drama, here transforms a constricted place of grief and death into an open, sunny landscape of joy and hope. From total lament and immersion in Hades and the dark streams of Cocytus below (455–59) we pass to a new spatial expansiveness, the result of Admetus "having spread open his house" (δόμον ἀμπετάσας, 597) to welcome a different literary genre, as it were, from another space.

Apollo abandoned the house, and the play, after the prologue to avoid the pollution of death. But his spirit of restorative Olympian art and energy continues through this ode and through the presence of the half-Olympian Heracles, another son of Zeus.[14] Heracles then becomes, rather surprisingly, the incarnation of Orpheus, who is, like Asclepius, by tradition a son of Apollo.

In the early farewell scene Admetus invokes the Orphic victory over death by song as an unreal, rejected possibility in a mood of despair (357–62). Echoing this scene at the play's end, Heracles teasingly assimilates his rescue to the Orpheus myth (1072–74): "If only I had so much force that I could send your wife forth on her way [*poreusai*] from the halls beneath and provide to you this favor." The parallel is all the stronger because Heracles' first resolve to help his friend included an Orpheus-like descent to Hades (850–55): "If I fail in this hunt and Death fails to come to the blood offering, I shall go to the sunless halls of Persephone and her Lord and make my request. And I think I shall bring Alcestis back up, so as to place her in the hands of my host, who received me in his house and did not drive me forth." This shift in the meaning of the Orpheus myth, from a despairing Admetus to a triumphant Heracles, could be read as a token of the transformative power of art—except that Heracles is not Orpheus, and he uses un-Orphic brawn, not song.

Despite his disappearance after the prologue, Apollo, the least domestic of all the gods, returns as an Orphic foil to the biological necessities of the house. He is the father of a death-defeating healer, Asclepius, from whose life the death-laden maternal relation is totally excluded: we hear only of the conflicts between Apollo and his father, Zeus, and with Zeus' craftsmen, the Cyclopes (3ff., 121ff.). Himself named in the same breath as the Orphic magic of restoring life (966ff.), Apollo seems to be defeated by Necessity, only to reemerge triumphant in his onstage representative, Heracles. In the prologue he sponsored Heracles as his surrogate in the battle against Death (64–71), and that scene seems to be recalled in the parallels between the bantering of Apollo and Thanatos in the prologue and Heracles and Admetus in the exodos.

Drama, Euripides seems to say, rather like Socrates at the end of Plato's *Symposium*, can create an intense vision of suffering, loss, and narrowing grief in the tragic mode of the first half of the play; but that same power of mythic representation can also give us the alternative experience: song victorious over grief; expansiveness, freedom, and hope triumphing over constriction and despair; the thrust of vital energy finding its way (*poros*) through the closed doors of Necessity.

Early in the play the chorus prays to the gods, especially Apollo Paian, the Healer, for some "cure," "resourceful passage," "device," or "drug" against death.[15] In a sense the gods do answer (cf. Apollo's foreshadowing in lines 65–71). The device or drug against death of which the chorus despairs, however, is as much the art of the poet as the fabled strength of Heracles, for it is that art, of course, that brings the mythical hero to life in the play before us. To work as "drug" or "remedy" (*pharmakon*, 966; cf. 135) against tragic death, however, the play must also work as "poison," poisoning us with its sadness and its powerful representation of loss and mourning.[16]

Art's ambiguous healing / poison in comic / tragic mimesis is concentrated just at the point when Alcestis' doom seems most inevitable, namely in Admetus' farewell speech (327–68). He promises Alcestis that he will never remarry and so never emerge from his grief and mourning. This speech also contains the play's two most self-referential figures of the power of art: the crafted likeness of Alcestis that Admetus will place in his bed and the myth of Orpheus who will win back his lost beloved through the "enchantments of his song" (ὕμνοισι κηλήσαντα, 359).[17] These two figures work in exactly opposite directions. The "craft" or "skill" (*sophia*) of the artist creates a precise copy of the dead person, fixing her forever as dead and memorializing her absence from the world of the living. There she has a future existence only under the sign of death and absence, as an image or fictional representation of what once was. In the myth of Orpheus, on the other hand, though it is here invoked as a model of what Admetus would like to do but cannot, the dead wife is restored to full presence in the upper world. The statue therefore provides the paradoxical "cold pleasure" of the tragic art, whereas the Orpheus myth prefigures that quality of the "wondrous," the "unhoped for" and the "unbelievable" in the restorative comic surprise of the end.[18] This actualization of the unhoped for in turn reverses the mood of no hope with which the play began.[19]

To signify the end of all the pleasure in his life, Admetus orders the cessation of music in the house and in the kingdom (342–47, 424–31). But the poet will bring back such music through the surrogate, comic Orpheus who causes music once again to resound in these halls (760ff.) The rowdy songs clash with the wails of grief (760–63); but the restoration of music and festivity at the end, with the return of Alcestis, will cancel out that disharmony and make house and kingdom whole once more as a place of joy, feasting, and song (1154–56, cf. 425–31). The victory over death, in other words, transforms the kingdom from a tragic into a comic world.

The statue, then, which some critics have found maudlin or even ridiculous, is a crucial element in the play's representation of its own mimetic power.[20] As a version of the *kolossos*, the statue is the image put in place of a missing corpse. But this motif is an ironical anticipation of the fact that Alcestis will indeed prove to be a missing corpse, a statuelike form that seems to come to life to rob Hades of its prize. Admetus uses the statue to crystallize the impossibility of the life left to him, a life without joy or pleasure, that is, a living death. "You have taken all delight from my life," he tells the dying Alcestis (347), and ever after he will have only the "cold delight" of her image in his bed (353). As an embodiment of mimetic skill or craft (*sophia*, 348f.), however, the statue mediates between art and ritual; and thus it helps to locate the play itself in the shifting ground between rite and mimetic art. The oxymoron of its "cold delight" points to the paradoxes of the tragic pleasure that the play both enacts and, through its unexpected comic ending, also subverts.

As the fabricated double of the deceased, the statue fixes Alcestis forever in the physical form (*demas*, 348) of death. Yet, thanks to the encompassing artful fabrication of the play as a whole, this turns out to be the crystallization of the wrong story, for the play will bring back, on the stage and in life, the "form" or "body" of the living woman (*demas*, 1133), not an artistic or ritual substitute. By implicating the fictional craft of the play itself, the statue nests the central myth within an ever-expanding regress of tales within tales where death is miraculously defeated. Apollo defeats the Fates by the comic device of getting them drunk; his son Asclepius restores the dead to life by his medical arts; Orpheus recovers Eurydice through song; and Protesilaus returns from Hades to his bride, Laodamia, in a myth that has many parallels with *Alcestis*, including the fabrication of a statue of the deceased by the surviving spouse.

Admetus' ritual gesture, then, opens up a sequence of parallel myths that points to the fictionality of the whole situation. If Admetus' statue "is made in the likeness of" Alcestis (cf. *eikasthen*, 349), Heracles' Alcestis at the end also resembles the statue. Though we must believe that the veiled woman at the end is Alcestis, her silence and Admetus' term *demas* (form, body, 1133; cf. 348) also make her, initially, a semblance of the statue, "a replica of his wife in the person of the veiled figure," as Albert Cook says.[21] Admetus is concerned that she might be just a *phasma*, "an apparition from those below" (1127), and he questions the reality of what he sees: it might all be illusion. Thus, even as Euripides negates the tragic tale of death and mourning by the comic finale of bringing back the dead (as in Aristophanes' *Frogs*), he also reveals how close this operation is to the fantasy of making a statue come to life. In this case, the "artful skill" (*sophia*) that fabricates the likeness of the dead form (348f.) also includes the poet's art in fabricating the tale that brings it back to life.

This tension between the death ritual and the mimetic artistry in the statue ramifies into the play's deepest ironies. At one level Euripides proves that his myth is impossible: Admetus, as he himself learns, is destroyed by accepting the gift of another's life for his own (940ff.). At another level the play validates the myth by placing it within a set of analogous tales or exempla of miraculously defeating death. Admetus' acceptance of Alcestis as a gift from Heracles in return for hospitality, in fact, recapitulates the earlier phase of his story in which he accepts the gift of life from Apollo (10ff.).

The relation between the statue commemorating loss and the Orphic rescue myth (348–62) also corresponds to the relation between the epigram-like commemoration of Alcestis among the heroized dead at the end of the last ode and Heracles' actual rescue and restoration of her to the living immediately thereafter. Let Alcestis' grave not be thought of as the mere tomb of the dead, the chorus sings, but rather "let her be honored equally to the gods, an object of reverence to passers-by. And someone stepping aside from the crooked path will say, 'This woman once died for her husband's sake, and now she is a blessed divinity [*daimôn*]. Hail, mistress, and may you grant us good.' Such are the sayings that will address you" (995–1005). In contrast to the privately commissioned art of the statue kept in the intimate bed in the house, this song offers spontaneous ritual commemoration in a public voice and addresses strangers in the totally public space of the highway.

Earlier too, at the moment of her death, the chorus had promised Alcestis' survival in the songs of bards (*mousopoloi*) in the great annual festivals at Sparta and Athens (445–55). The chorus followed that hope of cultic survival with the impossible wish to bring her back (455–59); and, immediately after, Heracles entered (476ff.). Here, in their last ode, the impossibility precedes the ritual commemoration, and here too Heracles enters soon afterward. But in this case that arrival makes the impossible come true and removes the need for a cultic memorial of the absent beloved. This substitution of cult, fame, or epigram for the lost bride is short-circuited by bringing back a "form" that turns out to be the warm, living person. The symbolic evocation of presence becomes superfluous.

By locating his play in the space between ritual and myth, Euripides exploits the full paradoxes of his dramatic form. With the performance of funeral rites a story simply ends, as the chorus says at the beginning (132–35): "For the king everything has been completed. / On every god's altars lie the full blood-dripping sacrifices, / Nor is there any healing of woes." Funeral rites commonly mark the end of tragedies (e.g., in *Ajax, Antigone, Hippolytus, Trojan Women*, and *Oedipus at Colonus*). *Alcestis* begins with death, goes on to the completion of the funeral rites, and then finds a story beyond them.[22]

In the last ode the language of the funeral epigram seems not only to end the story but even to provide its monument, here read proleptically by the passer-by on the road. This choral closure, like Admetus' statue, would fix the myth in a final meaning, an unchanging monument to a woman's remarkable sacrifice and to extraordinary female virtue. The story that the play tells, however, has a very different ending. In fact, by defeating death, it refuses to have an ending. For that nonending to come about, however, the play must break out of the female-dominated house to the realm of male generosity and hospitality, male heroism, and, ultimately, the male-dominated civic art of the theater. The true monument to Alcestis' glory is not the epitaph on the tomb but the play that denies that there is a tomb. Her honor, given in the silent commemoration on the stone, is replaced, in Euripides' final act of substitution, by the honor that he gives her in the enacted commemoration of the play. At the same time, this is a more unstable, polyvalent monument than the epitaph on the stone or the tomb. Its medium is the shifting, invisible tones of the voice, or their absence.

Coming to *Alcestis* after three tragedies on that day of the City Dionysia of 438 B.C., Euripides' audience would have been prepared for the lamentation that dominates the first half of the play. The change from songs of mourning to shouts of festivity would have been as surprising for them as they are for us. The Servant calls attention to the shock of the contrast as the chorus's solemn farewell to Alcestis' corpse fades in our ears (741–46). "There were two kinds of song to hear," the Servant says: one of sorrow, one of joy (760–64). These "two kinds of song" (*dissa melê*) may be taken as the poet's self-conscious comment on mixing tones and genres. If the Servant veers toward the comic side of the "double songs," Admetus enacts the tragic side. He reenters his bereaved house and juxtaposes his memory of the happy wedding song of the past and the present dirge (915–25). In terms of the play's contrasts of domestic and public space, private and civic commemoration, the "double songs" may also refer to the dramatic festival's combination of tragedy and comedy, and more specifically to the tragicomic, pro-satyric hybrid that is the *Alcestis* itself. Tragedies end with funerals, comedies with weddings. The evocation of a marriage ceremony at this play's end exactly reverses the tragic relation of funeral and wedding in lines 915–25.

Even in the comic triumph of its ending, however, the play does not forget its suspension of reality, the magic of its victory over death. When Heracles assures Admetus that the woman is not an apparition (*phasma*) and he not a necromancer (1127f.), Admetus exclaims, "Do I then look upon the wife whom I have been burying?" And Heracles replies, "Yes, know this with certainty; yet I do not *wonder* that you *disbelieve* this *fortune*" (ἀπιστεῖν δ' οὔ σε θαυμάζω τύχῃ, 1130). "Disbelief," "wonder," "fortune" (*apistein, thaumazein, tuchê*): these terms of Heracles apply as much to this tragicomedy as a whole as to the specific situation.

It is significantly the realm of the voice, the area most directly expressive of the play's art world, that calls us back to the sadness and loss with which we began. Lament has been followed by songs of commemoration (445–54, 995–1005), by miraculous Orphic pastoralism (579–87), and by drunken revelry (760–64). Admetus, returning home after the burial and remembering his wedding day, hears the festive *kômos* and wedding song replaced by the ritual lament (*goos*, 915–25). But the last sound that the play impresses on our memory is the zero degree of vocality, the silence of the dead. "She who hears not and sees not" was Admetus' phrase for Alcestis at the moment of her death (τὴν οὐ κλύουσαν οὐδ' ὁρῶσαν, 404). At the end, although he both addresses her and looks upon her (1131–34), she seems still neither to hear nor to see.

In a play where contrasting sounds carry a heavy burden of meaning, the final silence of Alcestis retains the unyielding power of death. The dissonance between the various "double songs" of the play is resolved in the joyful celebration that Admetus can finally decree throughout his kingdom (1154–56). But Alcestis' silence remains, awesome and unassimilated. The gods of death to whom she has been consecrated have a claim that cannot be forgotten. She may not regain her human community and human life until she is cleansed of the pollution of death.

It is only against this power of Necessity—which we may also call reality—that this kind of tragicomedy can have its full effect. This is a lesson that Euripides brings to his later works in this genre. The protagonist who triumphs over death either performs an act of ritual substitution for death (*Helen, Iphigeneia in Tauris*) or else comes close to dying (*Ion*). The *Alcestis* also uses the sacrificial theme, albeit in a gentler and more domesticated form.[23] Even so, the heroine's silent, veiled figure at the end remains sufficient to anchor the play in the harsh Necessity from which it promises and achieves escape. If Heracles, then, is the surrogate of Apollo and Possibility (*poros*), Alcestis herself at the end, despite her resurrection, remains the representative of Death and Necessity (Anankê).

This figure at the end, as Cook suggests, has a statuesque quality that recalls the statue of the farewell scene (348–54).[24] It is primarily the later, novelistic genre that motivates and begins narration (rather than ending it) with the enigmas surrounding a fascinating artwork, as do, for instance, the ancient novels of Achilles Tatius and Longus, and modern novellas like Balzac's *Sarrasine* and *Le Chef d'oeuvre inconnu* or Mérimée's *La Vase étrusque*. The *Alcestis* uses the statue motif primarily as a rhetorical expression of love-in-absence. Nevertheless, its close association with the myth of Orpheus in Admetus' speech and with the central themes of love, death, and substitution justifies considering it more seriously.

The marble statue of the castrato at the end of Balzac's *Sarrasine* is all that survives of the dead lover's passion and creativity. Roland Barthes notes possible affinities with the myth of Pygmalion and then remarks, "Free-standing, penetrable, in short *profound*, the statue in-

vites visitation, exploration, penetration: it implies ideally the plenitude and truth of the *inside* (which is why it is a tragedy that this
inside is empty, castrated)."[25] Admetus' statue, as I have suggested, is
also the locus of an ambiguous mimetic power, containing both the
plenitude of substitution and its emptiness, for the artwork is, after
all, *only* mimesis. In this play both plenitude and emptiness cross in
the mingling of life and death, fantasy and necessity.[26] Desire impels
the statue into being with the infinite power of its Orphic creativity;
but it does so under the sign of death, the emptiness that will make
the statue into a mere phantom, a sign of absence. The statue is thus
emblematic of the entire work, standing as it does at the intersection
of desire, death, art, and absence.

Death in *Alcestis* has the structural function of the nothingness
symbolized by castration in *Sarrasine*. To quote Barthes once more:
"The Sarrasinean aesthetic of the statue is tragic, it risks the fall of
desired plenitude into castrated emptiness, of meaning in outside-
meaning. . . . Passed down along the duplicative chain . . . , the sinister
story of La Zambinella grows distant, no longer exists, save as a
vague, moon-struck enigma, mysterious without being offensive. . . .
As for the final avatar, the passage . . . to written 'representation,' it
recuperates all the preceding copies, but writing extenuates still further the hallucination of the *inside*, for it has no other substance than
the interstice."[27] Because the *Alcestis* is part myth and folktale as well
as "literature," part oral performance as well as "writing," and still in
touch with cultic and ritual commemoration, it can balance that
potential emptiness of the statue and the self-reflexive *mise-en-abîme*
of art-that-"writes"-about-art with an ending that does put the living
woman in place of the statue. It thereby transmutes tragedy not so
much into comedy as into fairy tale, as in related romance forms like
Shakespeare's *Winter's Tale*. But by reminding us that the statuelike
woman *might* be just a *phasma*, it does so only after looking into the
empty mirror of the tragic.

4

Female Death and

Male Tears

ALCESTIS AND THE PROCESS OF DYING

Despite the fantastic circumstances, Alcestis' death unfolds as a "normal" death of a woman in the house: gradual, anticipated, full of pain and also of unexpected family tensions. We observe the inevitable progression as Alcestis makes elaborate preparations; bids tearful farewells to husband, children, and servants; and reveals her most intense emotions before the marriage bed, the center of the woman's life (177–84). The play therefore allows us an extraordinary glimpse of how men and women in classical Athens might be expected to respond to a wife and mother's death in the house. The play begins with the divinities Apollo and Thanatos (Death), but as soon as they exit at line 76, we enter a fully human world and witness the emotional consequences of a death in the family: conflict, escape, denial, and feelings of loss and guilt. The play presents a veritable anthropology of death, a kind of miniature encyclopedia of attitudes and responses, from the heroic self-sacrifice of the wife, which is established at once as the touchstone against which all other reactions to death are measured (cf. 83–85), to the unthinking self-centeredness of the husband and the sense of helpless loss in the children.

The Greek tragedies, we should recall, are not only great works of art; they are also cultural texts, and they were presented before the entire citizenry of Athens at the state festivals. It is legitimate, therefore, to look at this play not just as an autonomous, self-reflective literary and linguistic construct but also as a dense symbolic representation of social behavior, reflective of a culture's way of dealing with a recurrent crisis in human life. We must still be aware of the filter of artistic representation: the play is concerned with telling its story in its own dramatic form, not with being a cultural document. But because Euripides gains much of his dramatic effect by playing his fabulous myth off against a fairly realistically depicted set of cultural practices and attitudes, we can observe how the latter are condensed into clearly defined literary *topoi*, or plot motifs, such as the lament scene, the commemorative ode, and the unexpected rescue.[1] Even in their abbreviated or stylized form, these motifs offer important clues to cultural attitudes.

Of this interaction of social representation and artistic specificity I offer two small examples from what otherwise might appear to be minor details. First, the grave. The lowering of the coffin into the grave is occasionally depicted on the vases used for funerary libations.[2] In the *Alcestis* this scene gains a special emphasis from Admetus' emotional gesture of throwing himself into the grave (albeit shown only in a brief retrospective moment [897–902]). But it also forms part of a gradual depiction of the place of burial from different perspectives and thereby reveals different attitudes and different degrees of emotional involvement in Alcestis' death. The Olympian god Apollo in the prologue does not mention the tomb at all (65–69). Heracles regards the tomb merely as the place of his struggle against Death, and he uses no adjective (845, 1142). The Servant, on the other hand, who has been remembering and grieving for his dead mistress, identifies the burial place to Heracles as the "polished tomb" outside the city gates, implying a conspicuous stone monument in a place of honor (836). But shortly after that, Admetus, returning from the funeral, describes this burial place merely as the "hollow grave" into which he would throw himself in his intense grief (898). The chorus, at the end, in its heroization of Alcestis, firmly denies that the "tomb of your wife" would be merely "the burial mound of the dead who have perished" (νεκρῶν ὡς φθιμένων χῶμα, 995) but rather would be a place of quasi-divine honor (995–1005). Yet the motif becomes more than a means of depicting the responses to Alcestis' death, for Admetus' phrase in line 898, "hollow grave" (*taphros koilê*), as Richard Garner points out, echoes Homer's expression for Hector's grave in the *Iliad* and Sophocles' term for Ajax's in *Ajax*.[3] And so it evokes all the complicated inversions of heroism in this play, implicitly equating Alcestis with the fallen Homeric warrior and, in a further twist of irony, validating the truth of the chorus's vision of a heroized Alcestis in its last ode (995–1005).

The second example concerns dress. The detail of the dress or ornament of the dead (*kosmos*) appear as part of the standard preparations for the burial as the Servant describes them to the inquiring chorus of Thessalian women at the play's beginning (149).[4] Admetus' father, Pheres, enters bearing a *kosmos*, some "ornament" appropriate to the burial, a natural way to motivate his arrival at the funeral, from which he will be so harshly rebuffed. Then, near the very end of the play, the term recurs as Admetus describes the veiled woman whom Heracles has "won" and wants him to keep in his house. Though Admetus cannot see her face because of the veil, he infers that she is young because of "the adornment and dress" (νέα γὰρ, ὡς ἐσθῆτι καὶ κόσμῳ πρέπει, 1050). The clothing and jewelry that were put into the earth as the *kosmos* for the dead now emerge from the grave as the "fitting" adornment of an attractive "young" woman (*prepei*, 1050). Alcestis is not only brought back to life but given back the freshness of youth. Yet the double meaning of *kosmos* (grave ornament and part of female adornment in general) reminds us of the strangeness and ambiguity of the situation. What begins as a prosaic detail of the burial ritual thus becomes the center of two of the play's extraordinary moments surrounding the burial, the son's rejection of his father's presence, and, eventually, the total reversal from funeral to reunion and remarriage.

ORDINARY DEATH

It is striking how rarely Greek literature presents the process of natural death. Warriors die in battle in the epics or in violent circumstances in the tragedies. The *Iliad* recognizes virtually no other death than that in war.[5] The *Odyssey* takes a wider view, for instance in the death of Odysseus' mother (not from illness, as she says, but from longing), but offers little detail (11.197–203). The peaceful death of King Polybus in Sophocles' *Oedipus Tyrannus* is a foil to the violent consequences that this news has for Oedipus himself (941–70, especially 960ff.).

Why should "ordinary" death have so extensive and realistic a treatment in the *Alcestis*? I can only offer some speculations. First of all, the play was probably intended to substitute for the buffoonish satyr drama that each dramatist usually presented after his three tragedies.[6] The experience of death can be made so vivid here because it is going to be overthrown by life. Euripides exploits a double fantasy of escaping death: having someone die in one's place and forcing Death to dislodge his victim. But the effectiveness of the surprise ending depends on our being immersed first in the atmosphere of dying and grieving.

Then, more generally, Euripides is constantly exploring issues of contemporary society by removing the heroic patina of the myths he has inherited. He does this, for example, with marriage in *Medea* and *Andromache*, with war and politics in *Hecuba* and *Trojan Women*, and with vengeance in *Electra* and *Orestes*. The story of Alcestis provides the opportunity to study death in a domestic setting in a similar vein. By placing an indefinite period between the mythical prologue, with Apollo's offer of a substitute victim, and her actual dying, Euripides creates a mood of brooding and anxiety as this house waits for death.[7] By dividing into two—namely Admetus and Heracles—the man who receives the gift of a surrogate victim and the folktale hero who wrestles with Death, Euripides introduces an ironical view of Admetus that enables him to question some of the traditional gender divisions involved in death and dying. Finally, by introducing a long and painful scene of conflict between Admetus and his father, Pheres, Euripides places the situation of dying into the larger context of the extended household, or *oikos*. The introduction of Heracles creates still another set of conflicts: namely, between the duty to mourn and the obligation to receive outsiders under the traditional ties of *xenia*, guest-friendship, between aristocratic males of different cities.[8]

STAGES OF MOURNING

The work of Sigmund Freud (1917) and the more detailed studies of Elisabeth Kubler-Ross (1970) have shown that the experience of death, both by the dying person and by the survivors, is a process with a certain shape and continuity. The Greeks constructed their encounter with death in a similar way and marked the stages of mourning in highly ritualized forms.[9] The *Iliad* depicts in detail how Achilles moves from shock and possibly suicidal grief at Patroclus' death to rage, violent "acting out," eventual relinquishment of the body for the funeral, and some measure of reconciliation or acceptance when he ransoms Hector's body.[10]

Admetus undergoes a similar process; and, I want to suggest, it changes him, although many readers (myself included) will feel that it does not change him enough. To be more precise, the scenic action schematically represents an experience in which a series of events, although long recognized as inevitable, has an effect that Admetus, in his role as mourner, did not anticipate. This unpredictability in turn depicts—in the necessarily condensed, stylized form of Greek drama—the broader social fact that death involves a transitional passage for the survivor as well as for the deceased, a journey whose endpoint cannot be known in advance.

The notion that grieving and weeping hold a therapeutic benefit for the mourner is familiar as early as Homer and finds expression here too, as elsewhere in tragedy.[11] But the play suggests a more subtle form of this "therapy" by showing the changes in Admetus brought about by the actual process of living through the aftermath of Alcestis' death. His responses demonstrate that the grieving process cannot be circumscribed in the external act of a single moment, like making a statue of Alcestis for his bed (348–56), or in a simple external command to his subjects to wear mourning dress and refrain from music (425–31)—a command that Admetus, ironically, does not observe in his own house (cf. 747–72). Grieving, for Admetus, proves to be not the static, vaguely defined future state of a life without festivity (343–47) but rather an experience in time with a rhythm, intensity, and energy of its own.

Admetus' grieving, it must be added, starts out with a load of egotism and selfishness that is probably too heavy to be completely lifted by his experiences. In the same breath, for example, he promises lifelong mourning for his wife and continuing hatred of his mother and father (336–42). The latter sentiment was surely shocking to Euripides' contemporary audience (cf. Aristophanes' use of father beating in the *Clouds*); and this conflict within the family is never resolved within the limits of the play.[12] Nevertheless, Admetus does at least begin to enter the transitional crisis that the grieving process provokes. It is among the further ironies of the play that this whole process nears completion in the closing scene, only to be aborted by the miraculous happy ending. Thus Admetus, far from learning the lessons that this experience has begun to teach him (*arti manthanô*, 940), is encouraged to relapse into his initial selfishness and self-centeredness, once more betraying his wife to honor a guest-friend (1096ff.).

THE FATED DAY: TIME AND MORTALITY

The opening scenes draw their pathos from the approach of the "fated day" as the frame for the hopes and fears of the mortal characters who live in the precious and limited flow of ongoing time.[13] Apollo has saved the house "up to this day" (9) and announces that the awaited end will come "on this day" (20). The chorus knows—we are not told how—that this is the fateful day (*kurion êmar*, 105); and the Servant echoes their words later for Alcestis' own recognition of the same moment (*hêmeran tên kurian*, 158). When Apollo, in the prologue, describes Death as "watching for this day on which she must die" (26), Euripides is invoking the epic and tragic mood of death's inexorability. Death greedily awaits the hour when he may seize his victim.

Death appears as the frozen moment of the "right now" (322) that Alcestis sees terminating the rhythmic succession of days, months, and years (320–22): "For I must die, and that woe is coming not tomorrow, nor the day after; but at once [*autika*] shall I be reckoned among those who no longer exist."[14] To Admetus, however, she holds out the promise that "time" (*chronos*) will "soften" his pain (380), a commonplace echoed, with multiple ironies, by Heracles in the last scene (1085).

The actual experience of dying is acted out by Alcestis in body, emotion, and ritual. Her death is a *nosos*, a disease, that follows a predictable course over time, just as the contemporary medical treatises of Hippocrates teach that it should. Early in the play Apollo refers to Alcestis' dying by the verb *psuchorrhagein* (19f.), "letting the soul break loose" at the final gasp. The Servant repeats the word in the first human account of her condition (143). In the same speech the Servant reports her as "wasting away and being extinguished by disease" (203) and "still breathing a little" (205). The chorus repeats the former phrase as it laments "this best of women, who is being extinguished by disease" (235f.).

However common in real life, this situation, as I noted earlier, is rare in tragedy. The opening scenes of the *Hippolytus*, presented a decade later, show us Phaedra's illness, but this is shrouded in mystery and is not quite a physical illness. Even in a play like Sophocles' *Oedipus at Colonus*, whose protagonist is old and infirm, the actual dying process is kept at a distance. In this miraculous end, in fact, the hero departs "without illness, in no pain" (1663f.). The dying of Euripides' Hippolytus and Sophocles' Heracles in the *Trachinian Women* are, of course, more drawn out, but these are still violent deaths, outside the house.

In Alcestis' case we are shown the physical weakness in her last moments as Admetus asks her to raise her head, and she answers that she would if she had the strength (388f.). "My eye in darkness becomes heavy," she had said just before (385). Euripides exploits the pathos of the scene in the child's cry, "Look, look at her eye[s] and her stretched-out hands" (399). It is assumed that she will die surrounded by her family, even the small children, from whom nothing is hidden.[15]

"TAME DEATH": ALCESTIS' PREPARATIONS

Despite her weakened condition, Alcestis makes the rounds of her house, "stands" before the altar of Hestia, the goddess of the domestic space of the household, and "goes to" all the other altars (162ff.). Prepared and accepting, she takes this final farewell of the ritual life of the house. Then, in her first onstage speech of the play, she makes practical provision for her children's future. She speaks of her death with matter-of-fact simplicity as she makes her last request (280–81):

"Admetus, for you see how matters stand with me, I want to tell you what I wish before I die."[16]

In the following lines she refers to her dying in the same direct, nonmetaphorical way (284f.). She uses metaphor only in the familiar expression, again reflective of the real situation, of "not looking on the light" (282). Closer to the end, she self-consciously marks the division between herself and the living: "You may speak of me as being nothing any longer" (387; cf. 320–22, 381). The stark "I exist no longer" (*ouden eim' eti*) is her final utterance before the last syllable, "farewell" (*chair'*), spoken, we may surmise, with a failing voice (cf. 385, 388f.).

Before this final moment, however, we see Alcestis moving from the ritual gestures of farewell as the final day arrives (158–95) to a moment of lonely horror in her visions of Charon, who seems to embody here the dread that death's approach arouses even in the most self-assured breast (252–64): "I see the two-oared boat in the marsh; the ferryman of corpses, Charon, with his hand on the pole, is already calling me: 'Why do you delay? Hurry up! You are keeping me.' Hastening me along with such remarks, he makes me hurry. . . . Someone is driving me, driving me on—don't you see?—to the hall of the dead, winged, glancing beneath his dark-eyed brows. What will you do? Let me go! Alas, utterly miserable that I am: this is the road on which I go forth." Euripides makes us see the dying person's fear and existential isolation. Charon, or "someone," is forcibly pushing her to join the mass of the dead, the *nekues* (253, 260).[17]

Alcestis' moment of terror stands out against the mythicized visions of death elsewhere in the play. The personified Death (Thanatos) whom Apollo meets in the prologue of *Alcestis* is a rather buffoonish, if determined, figure with whom he can banter in clever repartee. Thanatos carries a knife or sword, but he uses it to consecrate his victim to the underworld, not to cut flesh.[18] Admetus briefly sketches an underworld landscape, with Pluto's dog, Cerberus, and Charon's boat (360f.), but only as a part of his unreal wish for Orpheus' magical voice. Late in the play Heracles, the closest of all the characters to the mythical world, describes Death as wearing a black robe (843) and wanting to drink the bloody offerings by the tomb (844f., 850f.). These are not pleasant features; yet this Death also has "ribs" that Heracles can squeeze with his brawny arms to make him surrender his victim (847–49). Alcestis, however, experiences a place of fearful separation and disorientation where Charon drives her brutally across the horrid marsh to the nameless *nekues*, the lifeless ones, on the other side (252–64).

Only gradually does she come to something like what Philippe Ariès calls "tame death," acceptance and understanding as she reviews her decision to die (280–98) and arranges for her children's future (299ff.).[19] Although she extracts Admetus' promise not to remarry, for the children's sake, she also consoles him by imagining a calmer future life, a time beyond this grief: "Time will soften you," she says, in reply to his despairing cries (380ff., cf. 1085). The peaceful death follows soon after, with her farewells to the children and to Admetus (385–91).

Admetus' experience of death, like Alcestis', has a zigzag or spiral pattern rather than a strictly linear one. Throughout the play he moves between the contradictions of accepting and acquiescing in Alcestis' sacrifice and complaining that his life is now unlivable (cf. 274–78, 382, 386, 391; also the chorus in 228f. and 241). Even so, the new emptiness in his life becomes increasingly clear to him as he actually experiences the house in its bereavement (866ff., 912–25, 939ff.).[20] After moving between emotional cries and a calmer, more rational assessment, he gradually reaches a kind of clarity.[21]

He now has a more raw and realistic grasp of his changed situation, and the measure of the change is the difference between his flowery promise about the statue in the deathbed scene (348ff.) and his wish to throw himself into Alcestis' grave when he returns to the stage after the funeral (895ff.). Early in the play the Servant had told the inquiring chorus, "The funeral ornament is ready with which her husband will bury her" (149). The objective, ritual detail of the "husband" "burying [something] with" Alcestis (*sunthapsei*, 149) has now shifted to a very different emotional register as the husband wants, in effect, to bury himself with his wife (897–99):[22]

τί μ' ἐκώλυσας ῥῖψαι τύμβου
τάφρον ἐς κοίλην καὶ μετ' ἐκείνης
τῆς μέγ' ἀρίστης κεῖσθαι φθίμενον;

Why did you prevent me from throwing myself into the hollow grave of her tomb and from lying there in death with her, by far the best of women?

His intense emotionality here resembles the moments of profound suffering in more traditionally "serious" tragedies: Haemon's suicide and Creon's grief at the end of *Antigone*, Theseus' grief at the death of Phaedra.[23] It also evokes the intensity of female grief which leads to death with the spouse (*sunthanein*): such are the suicides of Euadne in the *Suppliants* of Euripides (however acted out on the stage) and of Deianeira in Sophocles' *Trachiniae*.[24]

Admetus' speech of recognition near the end, "Now I understand" (935ff.), repeats much of the material in his lyrical cries of grief at his reentrance (especially 913–25); but he now has a firmer grasp of what Alcestis' death means (cf. 955ff.). The bed is truly "empty" (945), not filled by the "cold delight" of his floridly promised statue (348ff.). His image of the children at his knees lamenting over their mother's absence may be merely self-pity (947f.), but it also shows him more specifically and concretely aware of their suffering than he had seemed earlier (cf. 265, 388, 404f.). He now sees himself in the very role that Alcestis had occupied early in the play, in the scene pictured by the Servant inside the house (189–91). In fact, the combination of bed and children here, along with the close verbal echo between lines 196 and 950, suggests that he is now reliving that intense feeling of loss and desolation in the *oikos* that Alcestis experienced.[25] Perhaps we are even to think that he really is making good his deathbed promise to be a mother as well as a father to them in her absence (377f.).

In first welcoming Heracles within the house, Admetus essentially denies Alcestis' death. He claims that Alcestis is both living and dead and that the dead woman is an "outsider" in the house (517ff., 532ff.). On the one hand, he allows Heracles to believe that the death lies in the distant future (525f.); on the other, he artificially separates Alcestis from the blood relations of the house (she is the "outsider," 532ff.). This removal of Alcestis' death in both time ("in the future") and space ("outsider") is the (emotionally) logical prelude to his partitioning the house between its mourning and feasting sections.[26] Although we need not interpret these scenes psychologically, his words and acts do, in fact, constitute a denial, which, as Kubler-Ross points out, is one of the early stages in the process of mourning.[27]

In his last scenes with Heracles, however, Admetus is completely overcome by his grief and cannot hold back his tears (1064ff., 1079ff.). He can actually "taste the bitter grief" (1069, repeating the significant

"now," *arti*, from line 940, "Now I understand").[28] He fully acknowledges the sorrow that he had concealed from his friend in the earlier
scene—an emotional education parallel to the intellectual "understanding" of lines 935–61. He now recognizes how essential Alcestis
had been for his basic identity, his view of himself and his life. She
chose not to live in a house empty of her husband (287–89); he finds
the house changed as he reenters it, and he is changed with it.

Although he now repeats many of the lamentations that he ut-
tered just after Alcestis' death (328–434), the mood is different. When
he says how hard it is for him to look upon this bereaved house (911–
14), he brings together in a new way the motifs of sadness and revelry
that had been shockingly combined before (760–72). Previously the
simultaneity of mourning and feasting was merely the factual result
of Admetus' welcoming Heracles into his afflicted house. Now he
combines the antitheses not literally but as an emotional experience,
in his own thoughts, as he juxtaposes the remembered joy of his
wedding with his present sorrow (915–25). In this overlay of the
present by the past, he places the "revelry" (*kômos*) of the marriage
hymn beside the dirge; and the aural change has a visual equivalent in
the juxtaposition of white robes with black (918, 922f.).[29] This past
"revel" (*kômos*) of the wedding in line 918 recalls Admetus' promise—
which he failed to keep—to put an end to revels in the house (343). It
also recalls the feasting of Heracles (748ff.), which the Servant dis-
gustedly labeled a "revel" (*kômos*, 804). Admetus has moved beyond
the divisions in the house implied by those recent revels. In remembering the rites of marriage in the midst of the rites of mourning, he
brings feasting and lamentation together in a more emotionally reflective, complex, and integrated way.

Just before Alcestis' death, Admetus made an elaborate promise
that he would never remarry (328–42). At the end of the play, when he
is still refusing Heracles' request that he take the nameless woman
into the house, he encounters the more realistic demands of what it
means to honor the marriage chamber. The terms of his refusal even
recall Alcestis' sad and solemn rites of farewell at the beginning (cf.
181–88 and 1046f., 1059f.).[30] He now experiences the recognition that
he cannot separate his role as king, friend, and dispenser of hospitality from his concerns as husband, father, and mourner of his
wife.[31] The figure whose arrival initially divided the house now
restores it to health and wholeness. But before that restoration is

complete, Admetus begins to accomplish the reintegration within himself, interiorizing at least some of Alcestis' responsibilities for its inner life (e.g., in recognizing the children's and the servants' suffering in lines 947–49). This being an ironical pro-satyric play, not a tragedy, however, all these developments are cut off and turned around. Admetus betrays his promises just at the moment when he seems to be fulfilling the tragic anagnorisis of learning through suffering.

MALE TEARS

Whether or not Admetus is any more likable at the play's end will probably continue to be a matter of controversy.[32] Euripides could have let him refuse the woman first and then have him rewarded for his new firmness and understanding. Instead, he lets his hero fail the tests that Heracles' gift poses and so once more betray his commitment to Alcestis. Admetus' last speech reverses his earlier decree banning festivity in his kingdom and so recalls the intensity of his previous suffering.[33] His last two lines—the last iambic lines of the play—touch on a contradiction that he does not perceive: "For now we have changed to a way of life better than the previous; for I will not deny that I enjoy good fortune" (νῦν γὰρ μεθηρμόσμεσθα βελτίω βίον / τοῦ πρόσθεν· οὐ γὰρ εὐτυχῶν ἀρνήσομαι, 1157f.). Yet it is precisely the loss of this good fortune that has effected the change. In fact, Admetus has also begun this "change to a better life" by continuing the old one, taking advantage of others' sacrifices and betraying his most solemn promises. On the other hand, this "good fortune" reminds us of the hospitality and generosity that won the god's favor and so made the situation possible in the first place. Euripides, like his hero, seems to have it both ways: he shows us a severely chastened Admetus and an Admetus who is rewarded, a second time, for putting the claims of hospitality first.

The extent of Admetus' resistance to Heracles' offer, however, is significant. It marks a change from the readiness with which he invited Heracles into his house in the previous scene (535ff.). There is still another change toward his guest-friend. Whereas Admetus previously concealed his emotions (540ff.), he now openly displays his tears (1064–69). In the first scene of lamentation, by Alcestis, as the

Servant tells us, "all the coverlet of her bed was drenched with an eye-wetting flood of tears" (πᾶν δὲ δέμνιον / ὀφθαλμοτέγκτῳ δεύεται πλημμυρίδι, 183f.). The hyperbole, in the Aeschylean style (with only three words to line 184), depicts both the Servant's involvement and the emotional expressiveness permitted to women. Admetus here "laments" (*klaei*, 201), but nothing is said of tears. The exaggerated weeping of Alcestis in lines 183–84, however, emphasizes her courage shortly before, when, as the day of death arrives, she remains "without lamenting, without groan" (*aklautos, astenaktos*, 173). Like a heroic warrior too, she does not change color at the approaching woe (173f.). Are we then to view Admetus' tears, like his desire to throw himself into her tomb, as another reversal of gender roles?[34]

To answer this question we must examine male weeping more broadly, especially in the fifth century. The subject has not received much attention, but this play and other supporting evidence suggest an attitude of hesitation, or at least ambivalence, about male weeping.[35] The most manly heroes do not weep, or do so only as the sign of overwhelming catastrophe and as a temporary lapse from their manliness. For a man to weep for himself is to risk feminization.[36]

For the Greeks after Homer, even more sharply than for us, tears were a gendered category. Although men wept, tears were particularly characteristic of women. Women's "love of lamentation" and "love of tears" were a commonplace of Greek thought, often reiterated in tragedy.[37] Like all intense emotions, weeping was associated with the female and with irrationality, and thus required social regulation. According to Plutarch, Solon established for women's expression of grief (*penthesi*) a law that restrained its "disorderly and unbridled quality" (*to atakton kai akolaston, Life of Solon* 21.5). He also restrained "breast beating and lamentation" (*thrênein*) at burials; and Plutarch adds that even in his time the *gunaikonomoi* could punish those who indulged in "unmanly and womanly expressions of emotion in grieving" (ἀνάνδροις καὶ γυναικώδεσι τοῖς περὶ τὰ πένθη πάθεσι).[38]

In Bacchylides' Fifth Ode (probably of 476 B.C.) Heracles is said to weep only once, in pity for Meleager's early death, when he hears the story from the shade in Hades (155–58).[39] At the end of Plato's *Phaedo*, Socrates dismisses the wailing women when he would accomplish his exemplary death of philosophical courage with his male companions, though the companions later prove less stalwart than their master and do weep. In the *Republic*, Plato objects to tragedy because it arouses strong emotions of grief in the audience; and for men to be seen thus by their peers is shameful; it is behavior appropriate to women, not men (*Republic* 10.603e–604e, cf. 3.387e–389e).

Amid the losses of the great plague of Athens that Plutarch relates in his *Life of Pericles* (36.8–9), Pericles did not give in to grief and thereby "betray his pride and his greatness of soul . . . nor was he seen weeping or mourning or present at the tomb of any of his kin," until the death of his last surviving son. Only then, Plutarch continues, was Pericles unable to "endure" (*enkarterein*) or keep his "grandeur of soul" (*to megalopsuchon*); he was overcome by grief when he placed the wreath on his son's head "so that he broke out in wailing and shed abundance of tears, having never done any such thing in any other time of his life." Plutarch regards this restraint, to be sure, as extraordinary, but he also treats it as the sign of Pericles' manly virtues of great-souledness and endurance.

One of tragedy's functions may well have been to display and demonstrate that women's proclivity to excess grief was every bit as bad as it was supposed to be. But, paradoxically, it simultaneously gave expression to that release of tears, including male tears, that the Greeks from Homer on regarded as a "pleasure." Given the Athenian state's careful supervision and restriction of private lamentation at tombs and at funerals, it is even possible, as Nicole Loraux suggests, that the theater served as the area where this "pleasure in lament" could find its expression.[40] Such expression, however, bracketed by the festival occasion and the literary form, was marked as exceptional, as outside the limits of acceptable behavior.[41] A fortiori, male weeping was also suspect. But tragedy can explore the exceptional situations where it is permissible, thereby both validating the norm and also providing the occasion for indulging in its relaxation, at least vicariously. A male audience could enjoy identifying with the cathartic release of tears without suffering the stigma of "womanliness."

In tragedy, and especially in Euripides, male protagonists do weep over heavy misfortunes, their own or others', but the circumstances are usually extreme grief or frustration. Sophocles' Hyllus weeps when he sees the sufferings of his father (*Trachiniae* 795f.). Philoctetes weeps when he awakens on Lemnos and sees the Greek ships that abandoned him sailing away (*Philoctetes* 276–80); and Neoptolemus weeps over his father at Troy and over his loss of Achilles' arms (359f.,

367f.). Polyneices sheds tears at the sight of his father's condition (*Oedipus at Colonus* 1250f., 1253–56), although Oedipus himself takes a bitterly ironical view of this weeping (1356–58). In Euripides, Hippolytus says that he is near or in tears at his father's decree of exile (*Hippolytus* 1070f., 1078f.). Ion weeps at the tale of his mother's sufferings (*Ion* 1369–73). Orestes sheds tears of joy at his reunion with his sister in *Iphigeneia in Tauris* (832f., 862); and in *Orestes* he weeps when he recovers from an attack of his madness (42–44). In the same play Menelaus weeps when he hears of the death of Agamemnon (367f.). In *Phoenissae* Polyneices weeps at his exile when he returns in secret to Thebes (366–68); and in the pathos-filled death scene of the two brothers Eteocles can address his mother only with his tears (1440f.). Finally, in *Iphigeneia in Aulis* Agamemnon weeps in private in the agony of his decision about the sacrifice of his daughter (39–41).

Although weeping over one's own troubles can be a sign of unmanly weakness, it is legitimate for men to weep in compassion for another's woes, although here too there are strong limits. Prometheus is ready to weep for Io but does not actually do so (*Prometheus Vinctus* 637–39). In *Oedipus Tyrannus* Oedipus weeps for his city's tribulations and later for his children (65f., 1485f.). In the first case, however, though Oedipus tells the priest that he shed tears over the suffering of his city, he does not weep onstage. In the second case, Creon calls for restraint (1515). In the *Odyssey* the entire Greek army can weep at Achilles' burial: "There you would not see any of the Argives without tears" (24.61f.). By contrast, in Euripides' *Hecuba*, for example, the old herald, Talthybius, can "wet his eye [with tears]" in pity at Polyxena's death (518–20), but the army only feels "pain" or "woe" (*ponon*, 572), with nothing said of tears. Polymestor weeps in compassion (so he claims) for Hecuba's sufferings (*Hecuba* 953–55), but these are the crocodile tears of a treacherous false friend. Menelaus tells how he responded with tears of pity when he saw his brother weeping, but these tears are not shed in the present moment (*Iphigeneia in Aulis* 476–79).

A large proportion of these male weepers, furthermore, are young and immature, and a significant proportion are old men: Creon at the end of *Antigone* (1261ff.) and *Phoenissae* (1310f.), Peleus in *Andromache* (1200–1220), Amphitryon in *Heracles* (528, 1113f., 1180f.), the old man in Euripides' *Electra* (500–502), Creusa's old servant in *Ion* (940, 967), Cadmus at the end of *Bacchae* (1372f.). As lamentation is a woman's task, male tears, as many of the passages above suggest, are a sign of weakness, defeat, and feminization. Both the vanquished Xerxes at the end of Aeschylus' *Persians* (1026–77) and the crushed Adrastus in Euripides' *Suppliants* (770–836) not only weep but join in an antiphonal lament with women (cf. *Suppliants* 201–23). Xerxes, however, is a defeated barbarian, regal though he is; and in the case of Adrastus, Theseus, exemplar of male nobility and generosity, will lead his friend out of this feminine lament and back to a manly discourse on war (837ff.).[42]

The most unquestionably virile heroes of tragedy regard tears as a loss of masculinity. Tears would thus function as one of the female elements through which tragedy can explore the male's fear of feminization.[43] Tecmessa tells how unwonted were the cries of Ajax, for he considered such wailing to be the sign of a "base and heavy-hearted man" (*Ajax* 319f.). Shortly before, Ajax used the cliché about women's tears when he gruffly told Tecmessa not to weep (579f.). Similarly, in *Trachiniae*, Heracles, weeping in the agony of the robe's poison, feels himself unmanned by his tears, "for no one would ever say that he had seen this man ever doing such a thing before, but without lament I always held out in suffering. But now, alas, from [being] such, I am found out a woman" (1072–75, cf. 1070). It is part of Heracles' tragedy that this hero of masculine endurance confronts in himself the "feminine" condition of physical vulnerability and surrender to pain and lament (cf. also 1046ff., especially 1062ff.). Euripides' Heracles, similarly reduced, says he never thought he would weep (1353–57); and Theseus, leading him back to life, as it were, urges, "Enough of tears" (1394; cf. Sophocles, *Oedipus Tyrannus* 1515).

In the *Helen* Menelaus weeps in frustration when he approaches the palace of Theoclymenus in a somewhat comic scene (455–57), but then he gains in heroic stature and refuses to shed tears to win Theonoe's pity (947–53). Turning to tears, he says, is "female" (*thêlu*), not the part of a man of "action" (*drastêrios*, 991f.). Orestes associates tears with lack of manhood (*anandria*, *Orestes* 1031f.). For King Agamemnon in the *Iphigeneia in Aulis*, weeping is for those of low birth (*dusgeneia*) and is not permitted to the *gennaios* (446–48). Though he envies common men such relief, he himself is "ashamed" of weeping (*aidoumai*, 451–53).

When men do give way to tears, it is often after a struggle to keep them back. When the Atreid kings hear the terrible prophecy in the

Agamemnon, they strike their staffs on the ground and "cannot hold back the tears" (203f.). The Theban elders of the *Antigone*, pitying the heroine, "can no longer hold back the springs of tears" (802f.). Heracles enjoins his son to be "without tears or groans" when he makes the pyre, if he is truly the son of his manly father (*Trachiniae* 1199–1201). At the end of the play, he illustrates his own precept, reversing his earlier surrender to weeping, as he prepares to meet his end in firm, enduring silence (1259–63).[44]

ADMETUS' TEARS: GENDER AND THE "UNIVERSALITY" OF DEATH

We can now return to *Alcestis* and consider the weeping of Admetus in the closing scenes. Through Admetus' prolonged display of grieving and weeping, Euripides explores the places where the rigid dichotomies of male and female behavior in this society collapse and where there is even an overlapping of male and female roles.[45] This blurring of gender roles increases the ironies surrounding Admetus and the ambiguities of his character.

When the Servant tells Heracles that the dead woman is Alcestis, the latter apostrophizes Admetus sympathetically, "O poor man, what a companion you lost" (824). Here the way is prepared for Heracles' role vis-à-vis Admetus in the last scene, the compassionate friend who stands by and offers comfort, permitting, even encouraging, the relief of tears.[46] In the scene with the Servant, Heracles goes on to recall how he noticed the "eye flowing with tears and the shorn head and the face" (826f.). Admetus on that occasion "persuaded" him otherwise, "saying that he was bringing to the tomb a remote family member, an outsider" (827f.). We cannot be sure whether the tearful eye here is Admetus' or the Servant's, and commentators are divided; but Heracles' exclamation in line 824 and the reference to Admetus' "persuading" him (827f.) make it more likely that the tears are in fact Admetus'. It is important, however, that this detail of his weeping is filtered through Heracles' observation and that Admetus is seen as resisting those tears, as his attempted persuasion of Heracles implies.

In the play's final scene that resistance has broken down. Face-to-face with Heracles and the veiled woman, Admetus speaks of his emotions and weeps copiously. Addressing the woman and remarking on her resemblance to Alcestis, he turns back (with characteristic egotism) to his own feelngs: "She stirs up my heart, and from my eyes springs [of tears] have broken forth" (1066f.). Even these tears, however, do not come without resistance. At the beginning of the scene, when Heracles asks Admetus to take the woman in, he replies with a statement about his weeping (1045–48): "Do not remind me of my woes. Seeing this woman in the halls, I would not be able to be without tears [*adakrus einai*]. Do not add illness to me who am already ill, for I am weighted down enough with misfortune." Admetus' resistance here is primarily to the emotional pain that this woman's presence would cause. Yet, given the context (a dialogue with Heracles) and the negative formulation ("I would not be able to be tearless"), he may be implying that these tears too should be resisted. This is the approved male attitude of holding out against tears, but it is a strength of which Admetus feels himself incapable.

Heracles not only acknowledges the need to weep but in fact sanctions it. He sees that Admetus cannot help himself and that he pays no attention to his friend's urging that he "endure." "It is easier to give advice," Admetus says, "than to endure [*karterein*], when you are the sufferer" (1078). Admetus here rejects the traditionally manly role of *karteria* in the face of suffering. Heracles points out, with his characteristic practicality, that "to lament forever" does no good. In the next exchange, however, Heracles seems to sanction tears for a lost beloved (1080f.):

'Αδ. ἔγνωκα καὐτός, ἀλλ' ἔρως τις ἐξάγει.
'Ηρ. τὸ γὰρ φιλῆσαι τὸν θανόντ' ἄγει δάκρυ.

Admetus. I myself also know this, but some desire [longing, *erôs*] leads [me] forth [*exagei*].
Heracles. [Yes,] for loving the one who died leads [forth] the tear.

Heracles' commonplaces in the following lines check Admetus' almost sentimental exaggerations about being "destroyed" and "dead" (1082–86). Even so, his compassionate presence allows Admetus to acknowledge the extent of his "desire" (whether for weeping or for Alcestis, or both).[47] Heracles' repetition of his friend's term "leads forth" (*exagei*, *agei*, 1080f.) now supports him in his emotional response. More restrained than Admetus, he uses the simpler form of the verb and speaks of "a tear" (*dakru*), not "springs" (*pêgai*) of tears (1068). Nevertheless, he virtually gives Admetus permission to weep.

The hyperbole of Admetus' "springs" of tears in line 1068 resembles that of Alcestis' "flood" of weeping in her bedchamber in the play's first extended account of lamentation (183f.). But she is in her bedchamber and in the interior space of the house, which belongs particularly to women. Admetus is standing outside the house, receiving a great hero fresh from a "contest" and a victory, and yet the "feminine" quality of copious weeping elicits no reproach, even from the manly Heracles. We may contrast the admonitions to stop weeping, in the analogous situations, at the end of the *Tyrannus*, the *Heracles*, and the Euripidean *Suppliants*.[48]

Admetus' earlier lamentation takes place within his narrow domestic circle (199–202). It is quite another thing to show his tears to a peer from the exclusively male, public realm of action and heroic behavior, as he does at the end. Admetus, to be sure, is still in the house, or close to it, and not in the more public settings of Socrates or Pericles in the passages from Plato and Plutarch cited above.[49] Yet the presence of Heracles, with his heroic mission (481ff.), his direct address to Admetus as "lord of the Thessalians" (510), and the anticipated reciprocity of guest-friendship in "thirsty Argos" (560), all introduce a degree of self-consciousness about the outside, male, political world.

The greeting between the two kings takes place, necessarily, in the more public area outside the house. "Do I find Admetus in the house?" Heracles asks on his entrance, and the chorus repeats "in the house" in their answer (*en domoisi*, 477–78). For the actual meeting Admetus comes "outside the house" in his role as "ruler of this land," as the chorus announces: καὶ μὴν ὅδ' αὐτὸς τῆσδε κοίρανος χθονὸς / Ἄδμητος ἔξω δωμάτων πορεύεται (And in fact here is the lord of the land himself, Admetus, coming forth outside the house, 507). The greeting between the two men has something of the dignity of a state visit (509):

Ἀδ. χαῖρ' ὦ Διὸς παῖ Περσέως τ' ἀφ' αἵματος.
Ἡρ. Ἄδμητε, καὶ σὺ χαῖρε, Θεσσαλῶν ἄναξ.

Admetus. Hail, O son of Zeus and (descendant) of Perseus' blood.
Heracles. Admetus, hail in turn, Thessalians' lord.

Euripides reinforces the reversals in Admetus' behavior by recalling earlier scenes. Most strikingly, Admetus (1043ff.) makes exactly the same arguments for not receiving the woman that Heracles had made for Admetus' not receiving him as guest (538ff. and 545ff.). His description of his "heavy misfortune" in line 1048 echoes his sympathetic address to his children in lines 404f., but now he is willing to share that personal loss with his guest-friend from outside, including the tears of lines 1047 and 1067f. His statement "Now I understand" (940), unsolicited and arising from a longer experience of loss, sounds less perfunctory and more radical than his acknowledgment of the chorus' remark about "necessity" (420f.): "I understand. This woe has come upon me suddenly. Knowing it, I have long since been worn down."[50] The contrast between "now" (*arti*) in line 940 and "long since" (*palai*) in line 421 also suggests a new grasp of the length of time required really to "learn" about such a loss, although Admetus' "learning" is always clouded by self-pity.[51]

We do not, of course, see what Alcestis may have learned or how the experience of dying will color her future existence. The requirements of ritual (1143–46) and dramatic economy contribute to keeping her silent at the end.[52] The play is called *Alcestis*, but its real center is probably Admetus, and the real concern is male rather than female experience. Alcestis is there as the object of loss but also as a problem: she displays and embodies a heroism that Admetus himself cannot reach. By shifting the focus gradually, but forcefully, from her experience in the house to Admetus and then to Heracles, Euripides moves from female to male emotions in the face of death. The male head of the household need not be a Heracles. In fact, he can weep before Heracles and even find support and consolation for these tears. His experiences become increasingly emotional and internal, not physical; understanding, rather than acting. To our even greater surprise, Euripides works an analogous transformation in the Greek hero of masculine energy par excellence. This Heracles not only vanquishes Death, the ultimate heroic exploit; he is also perceptive of his friend's feelings (cf. 826–28) and expresses compassion for the loss and sympathy for Admetus' need to weep (1081). He thereby enables his weaker comrade (and perhaps those in the audience who identify with him) to have both the tearful grief and the rescued bride.

However much the play seems to open up a space for the woman's experience of death and the woman's feelings, it returns us to the

patriarchal world in which it has its origins. The dubieties of Admetus' character, with its attendant ironies and ambiguities, certainly
allow for a reading subversive of aristocratic patriarchy. But the modern reader's response on these issues is likely to be very different from
the ancient spectator's. This is a gap which ultimately we may not be
able to bridge, but we can at least try to understand.

Although the experience of death by the survivors is an area
where we probably share a great deal of common ground with the
ancients, at least two major differences in cultural behavior emerge
when we look at this play. First, the experience of normal, gradual,
domestic death focuses on the woman. Indeed, the female character
in fifth-century tragedy often serves as the field in which the male
audience can act out its own emotions of grief, fear, anxiety about the
body, or loss of emotional control.[53] Women may have fame or good
repute (*eukleia*), like Phaedra in *Hippolytus*, but they do not have the
honor (*timê*) of men (except, of course, in the extraordinary, hypothetical cases of an Antigone, an Electra, or an Alcestis);[54] and therefore it is legitimate for them to weep, fear, and become emotionally
violent or irrational in ways that the ideals of *sophrosunê, timê,* and
karteria make inhibiting for men. When Medea says that she would
prefer to stand three times in the line of battle than give birth once
(*Medea* 250f.), she is, of course, expressing a realistic concern of
women; but she also reminds the men in the audience (and the
audience may have been *only* men in the fifth century; certainly the
judges were) that it is *also* frightening to stand in the line of battle.[55] In
other words, the feminine persona can express, through female experience, emotions that would be dishonorable for a man to express
openly.

Second, attitudes toward death depend to a great extent on how
the society and the individual regard what comes after death. With
the lack of a strong belief in personal immortality, the Greeks focus
on the world of the living and so define life in terms of its contrasts
with the inevitability of old age and death.[56] This does not necessarily
result in more anxiety about death than a committed Platonist or
a believing Christian might have; but it does, I think, produce a
greater willingness than we would feel to recognize death as an
inseparable part of life. A twentieth-century North American, for
example, would probably be more inclined to define life in terms of
health, happiness, and an anticipated span of years (within limits

given by actuarial tables and medical prognosis), and less inclined to invoke so explicitly death's dark "necessity" as life's defining term. Sophocles' famous Ode on Man contains an implicit definition of man in terms of his domination over nature by intelligence (*Antigone* 332–75) but adds as an essential qualifying part of this definition, "From Hades alone he will bring no means of escape" (361f.).

For all the beauty of its language and the happy ending, the *Alcestis* still draws heavily on this language of tragic inevitability, the "necessity" (*anankê*) of the final ode (962ff.). In this perspective, which tragedy inherits from Homeric epic and which we see reflected in Sophocles' Ode on Man, death is the ultimate defining term of the human condition, male as well as female. It delimits the "portion" (the Homeric *moira* or *aisa*) that the Fates (Moirai) spin out for each of us at birth (cf. *Odyssey* 7.197f., 24.28f.). It separates us definitively from the gods, the "deathless ones" (*athanatoi*), and it makes us what we are: *brotoi, mortales*, beings subject to death. When Admetus regains his wife from death, it is after he has come to recognize, experientially, these conditions of mortality. Their future life together will run its course in the shadow of expected, normal death.[57]

At this point the traditional humanist critic, his work completed, leans back in the comfortable gesture of celebrating universal humanity: male and female are once more joined together after each has experienced the bitterness of death. We have, however, learned to be a little suspicious of what "universality" may conceal. If we want to see male and female differences here bridged under the sign of common mortality, very well; but let us remember that only Alcestis has died, and she appears at the end still robed in the ominous silence of death (1144–46). She has had all the pain of dying; Admetus has had both the joy of lamentation and the joy of always looking on the light of the sun.[58]

5

Admetus' Divided House:

Spatial Dichotomies and

Gender Roles

Alcestis uses death rites and hospitality rites to create a visual concretization and perhaps a critique of Athenian society's sharp division of sexual roles and values. The house, split in its physical substance by the enforced separation of the married pair, is spatially split into a hospitable segment and a grieving segment. In the one there is rowdy feasting and singing, in the other silence and lamentation (760ff., cf. 541ff.). The division between the grieving family's (and servants') quarters and the guests' quarters symbolizes in spatial terms this society's tendency toward gender compartmentalization. To the women belong the biological functions of the house, including the rites that usher a member of the household out of life: lamenting over, washing, and dressing the body for the funeral rituals—a task they still have in Greece and in many other societies.[1] Already associated with pollution through the act of giving birth, women are also expected to deal more directly than men with the pollution of death by washing the corpse;[2] and they have the more expressive role in the formal lament, or *thrênos*, at the funeral.

The values raised by Admetus' decision to invite Heracles are the primarily male-centered values of a shame culture; those raised by the mourning within the house involve marriage and children. Male-centered values are associated with questions of what is shameful, noble, proper, and honorable; the "house" values are associated with the emotional gestures of lamenting and weeping.[3] Euripides, elsewhere sympathetic to women and women's situation in this male-dominated society, takes over a plot whose resolution seems to validate exclusively male privilege; but through the unheroic character of the male protagonist and the ambiguities of the ending he redirects what is largely a male fantasy situation into an ironical exploration of the more problematical areas of private life.[4]

In the background of the gender divisions of tragedy lies some form of the antithesis of war, male, public realm, action, and glory versus domestic life, private realm, passivity, grief, and weeping.[5] This division, which also tends to place the women "inside" and the men "outside," corresponds to the social stereotypes of the time but does not necessarily show the whole truth. There are obviously many exceptions and variations; some, for example, reflecting class differences.[6] Practical reality demands that men and women work together with their complementary skills for the common good of their shared household;[7] but the house also serves as the focus of their differences and their potential polarization. It can thus become a zone for the symbolic projection of "cultural ambiguity," an area in which "boundaries, thresholds and liminality acquire extraordinary significance."[8] Tragedy works with hypothetical situations and poses the extreme positions, where the conflicts will be sharpest. Thus its association of women with the interior space of the house, though doubtless based on social reality, also functions as a complex symbolic construct, part of the society's image representation of itself, its symbolic world picture, or what the French call its "imaginary."

On the far right, one could say, of the dichotomization of the gender role are the "heroic" women: Antigone, Polyxena in the *Hecuba*, Macaria in the *Heracleidai*, Iphigeneia in the *Aulis*. These women come to a swift and violent end, just like male warriors, once their decision is taken; and they conform closely to the model of male heroism, even though, as Nicole Loraux has shown, the female pattern has distinctive features.[9] On the far left are the intense, passionate women who kill men or male children and assert their power over males: Clytaemnestra, Medea, Deianeira, Phaedra. Alcestis belongs to the former pattern but ambiguously combines the traditional female role of devoted wife and mother with elements of male heroism. As we have seen, the play dramatizes this confusion of the stereotypic gender divisions in the area of lament and the treatment of the dead.

In archaic Greece, male heroic death had a carefully coded spatial representation. The warrior, fallen in battle, outside the city and the house, was carried home by his male companions. Once he had been returned to the civic and domestic space, the women, inside, lamented his death and prepared the corpse for burial by the ritual ablutions and by dressing it for the pyre or the tomb (cf. *Iliad* 24.719ff., also 22.509ff.). Sixth-century B.C. Attic black-figure vases illustrate the warrior being carried back to his city after his "noble death" on the field of battle.[10]

Men, of course, died at home too, but the exemplary male death had a public context. The warrior died for his city and was rewarded with honor, fame, and other forms of public recognition (cf. Tyrtaeus 9.22f. West). The man whom death finds at home (*en oikôi*), says Callinus, is neither loved nor missed by the community, whereas the man who dies on the field of battle is mourned by small and great alike, is longed for by the whole people, and is honored like a demigod (1.14–19 West). A woman's death, if noted at all, tended to be in the house (e.g., *Iliad* 6.427f.), caused by grief at the loss of a loved one (like the mother of Odysseus [*Odyssey* 11.171ff.]), and completely lacking in honor (*Odyssey* 15.477ff.).

In life such divisions were probably much less rigid, especially for the working classes. Even in literature there is much crossing over: Homer's Achilles and Sophocles' Philoctetes, for example; each expects the death of his aged father at home. In a famous passage from the *Tyrannus* Oedipus speculates that old King Polybus may have died out of longing for his absent son (969f.); that is, presumably in his house. As far as literary representation is concerned, both Homer and tragedy *tend* to associate women with domestic and private space, and men with martial and political space; and tragedy *tends* to suggest that the crossing of these lines, while not prohibited or even unusual, may be dangerous or may prefigure disorder.[11]

In the funeral practices of mid-fifth-century Athens the separation between public and private became especially sharp with the institution of the public funeral oration and the public burial ground of the *dêmosion sêma* as the place for the men fallen in battle on behalf of their city (Thucydides 2.34.5).[12] Women, to be sure, had an important place in the public rites of mourning, as Thucydides, for example, recognizes (2.34.4, 2.45.2), just as they did in all the civic festivals; but the polis remained suspicious of female lamentation and its intense emotions. Though the women could not fight or die in battle, they produced the city's warriors and gave them to the city for its battles and had a major role in mourning over and burying the dead, as one sees in plays as different as Sophocles' *Antigone* or Euripides' *Suppliants* and *Hecuba*.[13] The actual dying of a woman did not command public attention or public commendation—unless she behaved like a man.[14]

Rather than providing a mirror image of "normal" social conditions, tragedy explores situations where the divisions are blurred and where this blurring produces an in-between zone of destabilized values, disturbing questions, and inversions of the expected or familiar roles. In the *Bacchae* women leave the loom and become victorious warriors and murderous hunters in the wild, mountainous space outside the city. In the *Hecuba* women destroy men by transforming a sheltered interior space into a scene of maenadic carnage such as one might expect on the wild mountainside; and this spatial inversion replicates, in different terms, Clytaemnestra's sacrificial slaughter of her husband in the bath in the *Oresteia*.[15] On the other side, the male's betrayal of the rights of the *oikos* in exchange for public considerations like success in war, honor, or even the safety of the city may also cause disaster, as in Aeschylus' *Agamemnon*, Sophocles' *Antigone*, or Euripides' *Iphigeneia in Aulis*.[16]

These reversals of roles and shifts of boundaries constitute one of the reasons why tragedy has something "to do with Dionysus," the god in whom opposites coalesce, boundaries dissolve, and identity consists in the exposure of a hidden, antithetical double beneath surface unity and clarity.[17] Like comedy, its companion dramatic form at the Dionysiac festivals, tragedy exploits and in turn creates what Mikhail Bakhtin calls a "carnivalesque" situation.[18] Comedy's confusion of gender roles, of course, produces fun rather than fear. In *Lysistrata* and *Ecclesiazusae* Aristophanes uses the comic possibilities of the world turned upside down, a vision so grotesquely impossible and "utopian" (*ou topos*, in "no place") that it can arouse only laughter.[19]

The *Alcestis* explores such issues in the sensitive area of marriage and mourning; and the play's confusion of gender roles creates much of its subtle irony. This irony exists specifically in the multiple perspectives on the characters of Alcestis and Admetus and in the ending. Alcestis' death, for example, which is the center of the action, is both normal and abnormal, both feminine and, in some sense, masculine in its courage. She is a precursor, in the domestic realm, of the nobly self-sacrificing virgins of Euripides' later plays.

On the one hand, Alcestis is the essentially feminine woman. She is cited repeatedly as the model of the ideal wife, the *aristê gunê*. Her death has a distinctively feminine quality too, obviously, because she dies for purely familial reasons, and her chief concern is the well-being of her children, as her last words make clear (280–325).[20] Literally and figuratively, she stays within the limits of the house, which she leaves only for the grave. Unlike Antigone, for example, she has virtually no contact with the public or political realm (cf. *Antigone* 937–43). On the other hand, precisely through this admired female devotion to house and children, Alcestis reaches heroic status and receives the kind of bardic praise traditionally given to male valor (especially 445–54). Echoes of Homeric and epinician poetry in the play consistently associate heroic values with Alcestis rather than Admetus.[21] The physical weakness of her last moments contrasts paradoxically with her role of savior and rescuer by the very fact of this condition. The bardic commemoration of the noble wife who has sacrificed herself for her husband is also an unflattering reflection on Admetus.[22]

Both tragedy and comedy investigate places where the male transgresses into female space (e.g., *Bacchae*, *Thesmophoriazusae*) or the female intrudes upon public space or public action (*Agamemnon*, *Antigone*, *Lysistrata*).[23] The *Alcestis*, with the wife's sacrifice at its center, seems free of such transgressions. Yet, paradoxically, it enacts them in a more complex and subtle form. Alcestis' quintessentially feminine gesture draws to itself the aura of male heroism, whereas the only heroism that the male protagonist can claim is his violation of the grieving domestic space with an inappropriate offer of *xenia*. But this play, looking toward the resolution of conflict and the reunification of the house, keeps the transgressive elements in the background. Thus it suppresses the ritual fact that Admetus' house would be polluted by death and hence a dangerous place into which to invite a guest.[24] Obviously this silence is a necessary enabling fiction of the plot. The suspension of the ritual requirements thus allows the male's impropriety to balance out and even supplant the female's claim to heroic honors.

The paradox of a domestic heroism, then, is both destabilizing and reassuring. It is destabilizing in the enforced passivity and de-heroization of its male protagonist; it is reassuring to a male audience and to the dominantly male values of the society in that it begins and ends with different forms of male fantasies: at the beginning the wife gives her life for her husband; at the end the rescue of Alcestis validates the prowess of a great hero in an exclusively masculine dialogue about the exchange of women. The woman, so eloquent earlier, is now silent and passive.

Our first detailed encounter with the house of Admetus includes the interior space that is the center of Alcestis' life: hearth, altars, bedchamber, storage rooms, and the chests and fabrics they contain (160–88), all the work of women (as also in Homer).[25] This is the image of the secure household that Alcestis, by the sacrifice of her life, will keep unchanged after her death, free of possible disruptions by a second wife and stepmother (cf. 302ff.).

For Admetus, however, the house faces outward as well as inward. Its place in the larger community becomes visible at once in the public mourning that he can command (156, 425, 430; cf. 343–47). At the end he can declare the end of mourning for "citizens in the whole tetrarchy" (1154). The double meaning of the *oikos* for Admetus involves him in the conflict between the obligation to mourn and the obligation to receive a guest-friend. As "ruler of the land" (507, 510), he cannot turn a guest away "from house and city" (*domôn kai poleôs*, 553). He must think about the reputation of his house in the outside world (557, 1057f.) and about his relations with other cities, like Heracles' "thirsty land of Argos" (560).

This different orientation toward the house is particularly clear in the perspectives on the hearth (*hestia*) and its divinities. Alcestis addresses Hestia as a divinity to whom she prays for her children's future happiness in the first item of her reported farewell (162–69). Hestia here is virtually the divinized essence of the woman's role in the inner space of the house.[26] Admetus and other male characters, however, refer to *hestia* as a metonymy for the household into which the king will invite a guest from the outside (545, 750, 1007) and to which the wealth of herds in the surrounding land belongs (588f.). The Servant even uses the related verb *hestiân*, literally, to "receive at the hearth" (765), when speaking of entertaining Heracles. In his parting words to Heracles, Admetus invites him again to "share his hearth" (*hestia*, ξυνέστιος γενοῦ, 1151), once more effacing the claims of the restored wife who stands beside him onstage.

As we first see the house from the sympathetic, if remote, perspective of Apollo, it is the mirror of mortality itself. Within it the mixture of life and death plays about Alcestis and will inexorably be resolved on the side of death.[27] The house is "dearest" to this god, Apollo (23), but he must abandon it lest he be defiled by the "pollution" (*miasma*) of death that it now contains (22). As the Servant describes Alcestis' farewell, we see the house also as the place of marriage, birth, and the nurture of children; domestic work and fellowship; loss and sorrow (158ff.). It is from the house that the children will be married to perpetuate the family (313–18), and it was into this house that Admetus led his new bride. He recalls that image painfully when he reencounters its desolation after Alcestis' death (914ff.).

After Admetus' offer of hospitality, the chorus celebrates the outward reach of the house in hospitality both to man and to god (569–605). It was here, in the forest and pastures on the borders of the city, that Apollo performed the gentle service that won Admetus his second chance at life (569ff.). The household property extends to the slopes of Mount Pelion, where the king's herds are pastured (575ff.), and this part of the household wealth is under the supervision of the husband.[28] Defining the geographical limits of Admetus' power, from its eastern to its western borders and from plains to seashore (590–96), the ode refocuses attention from the inward to the outward orientation of the house, from the female to the male world.[29] Beginning and ending with praise for Admetus' hospitality (569–71, 597–605), the ode correlates this external extension of the power and property of the house with its openness to strangers from the outside.

After this shift of the spatial field to the male realm, the stage action shows only dealings between males. The issues are patriarchal inheritance and its obligations in the scene with Pheres and the reciprocity between males under the ties of guest-friendship in the exchanges between Heracles and Admetus.[30] When Pheres addresses

Admetus, he speaks of "the many-acred fields" that he will "leave" to his son (687f.):

πολλῶν μὲν ἄρχεις, πολυπλέθρους δέ σοι γύας
λείψω· πατρὸς γὰρ ταῦτ' ἐδεξάμην πάρα.

Many are under your rule, and many-acred fields shall I leave to you; for I received the same things from my father.

By contrast, when Alcestis speaks of the "earth" and the city, she associates them with the rooms and the marriage bed to which she bids farewell (248f.):

γαῖά τε καὶ μελάθρων στέγαι
νυμφίδιοί τε κοῖ-
ται πατρίας Ἰωλκοῦ.

O earth and chambered halls and marriage bed of the fatherland, Iolcus.

The return of Alcestis at the play's end symbolically reenacts the beginning of her life with Admetus. The probable stage action of lifting her veil would evoke the *anakalypteria*, the raising of the bride's veil in the marriage ceremony.[31] But in presenting this renewal of marriage not just as her escape from death but also as the gift from Heracles, the scene also visually enacts the economics of Athenian marriage, the exchange of women between males. Heracles has also "won" the woman, as he says, in another all-male exchange, an athletic contest (1025–36, cf. 1102).

The line-by-line debate between Heracles and Admetus at the end (especially 1077–1135) formally echoes their debate over the issue of hospitality in the middle of the play (509–44). Both the athletic contest and guest-friendship are forms of exclusively male honorific competition. Heracles' athletic "contest" at the end is in a sense the continuation of this muted verbal contest with Admetus earlier, and as such it once more exhibits the process of male bonding in an enterprise restricted to men. In both cases this agonistic competition is sublimated into the generosity and harmony of largely masculine institutions—hospitality and athletics, respectively. Thus the competitiveness is subordinated to cooperation and friendship and so ultimately solidifies masculine ties.[32] This ending presents the fantasy of almost limitless masculine power in an all-male world. Guest-friendship between men not only takes precedence over mourning for a woman, it even redeems the loss that her death brings to the house. Heracles' sense of obligation and his physical prowess reunify the house that his entrance and the resultant festivity divided.

Alcestis, of course, expects "gratitude" (*charis*, 299) for her act of self-sacrifice and sets the specific terms that the gratitude should take, namely, Admetus' not remarrying nor giving the children a stepmother (299–307). She also wins fame as a good wife (290–92, 323–25). But she defines her motives in largely negative terms, not wanting to live on without her husband (282–89).[33] Whereas the gift between males belongs to a prescribed code of behavior whose goal is honor, Alcestis refers her gift of her life only to the house, the children, and the bed. Yet her sacrifice is not an exchange analogous to that between the two men in the final scene. Women do not exchange women, and she *gives* rather than *exchanges* herself. In fact, as she observes, her gift is beyond exchange value, "for nothing is of higher value than a life" (301). The echo here of Achilles' famous remark in *Iliad* 9 (401f., 409f.) sets off the particularly feminine nature of her sacrifice.[34] Her willing sacrifice for house, bed, and children, however, stands at the opposite extreme from that Homeric meeting, where the greatest of war heroes are concerned with exchanging women as concubines and where the priceless value of life is the basis for refusing, not accepting, self-sacrifice.

The exodos seems to produce a happy ending, both in the conventional sense (death defeated, marriage regained) and in the sense that the dominant patriarchal order is restored. Indeed, the rift between public and private duties seems healed: the house-dividing violation of the obligations to mourn the dead wife becomes the means of bringing her back to life and restoring the unity of the house. The ending, however, remains one of the most controversial in Euripides because of the ironies just beneath the surface. Admetus behaves like a cad but is rewarded like a hero. (Heracles, the hero par excellence, we may recall, eventually wins both a divine bride and immortality as his reward.) Indeed, Admetus is rewarded in and through the act of betraying the memory of the wife who gave her life for his. We have also witnessed his lack of courage in the face of death and his selfish, if not shocking, disowning of his old father.

On the other side—and there is always an other side to viewing this play—modern readers have sometimes suspected that the posthumous claims and conditions that Alcestis exacts from Admetus in her last speech lessen the sympathy that we feel for her.[35] Viewed in this light, she would illustrate a feature of several of Euripides' earlier plays, which begin with sympathy for the female protagonist, only to render that sympathy dubious or problematical at the end. *Medea, Hippolytus, Hecuba,* and even *Ion* offer analogies, although, of course, the moods and the tragic reversals are very different from those of *Alcestis.* The unattractive features of both protagonists should not be exaggerated, but it is probably right to recognize the ambiguities with which Euripides has surrounded almost every aspect of this play.

Alcestis' silence at the end, whatever its ritual and dramaturgic necessities, is the scenic expression of the lack of total resolution. In contrast to Admetus' effusions to his rescuer in the first part of the play, she has no way of expressing her gratitude to her rescuer. Her silence serves, of course, to keep the focus on the two men; but by muting, perforce, the gratitude of the one rescued, it also keeps the gender roles from becoming symmetrical. We cannot even be sure that Alcestis wants to be brought back.

Alcestis explores the inversion of gender roles not only by giving the heroic act to the woman but also by making Admetus' counter-claim to heroism center on the household. The ambiguity of his heroism corresponds to the ambiguity of his new relation to the house. Heracles' arrival, as a recent critic has remarked, enables Admetus to "trump" Alcestis' implicit feminization of his role by "sealing up the fissure in masculine morale" opened by her assumption of the heroic role.[36] To do this, however, he must open a fissure of a different sort; namely, dividing the *oikos* between mourning for a wife and mother, on the one hand, and receiving a distinguished foreign guest, on the other. The difference of value between Alcestis' self-sacrifice and Admetus' gesture of hospitality gives even greater contrast to the gender roles in the house.[37]

The male and female roles here reverse those of heroic epic or of "epic" tragedies like Aeschylus' *Persians* or *Seven Against Thebes.* The male protagonist remains closely attached to the house while the honorific burial belongs to the woman.[38] The focus of the action is not the warrior's return—dead or wounded, victorious or elated— from the scene of battle but the woman's death in the house and her ceremonial removal from her domestic space to the place of burial outside. This ritualized carrying forth of the corpse, the *ekphora,* forms, in fact, the crucial transitional point between the more or less realistic scenes of domestic loss and the fairy-tale ending (861ff.). Admetus' emotional promise to fashion a statue of his wife for his widower's bed also shows his attachment to domestic space (we may think of the unheroic Paris in Helen's bedroom in *Iliad* 6.313ff.). To give so much attention to the bed is usually the woman's role in tragedy; and in fact, Alcestis has followed the more familiar pattern in explaining why she accepts dying for her husband (175–84).[39]

The conflict between mourning and hospitality within the domestic space may have further implications for the play's representation of male and female roles in marriage. The obligations of masculine relationships are based on a more or less open, visible, and agreed upon set of reciprocities. These are not only highly visible but in fact determine the structure of the events. Apollo gives Admetus the gift of escaping death because Admetus received him generously. Thanatos, laying claim to Alcestis before Apollo, insists on the binding, almost contractual nature of his rights (42–59).[40] Heracles gives Admetus his wife back because Admetus honored the tie of hospitality above all else. Pheres gives Admetus kingship and property in the expectation of receiving care in old age and burial rites at his death (682ff.).

The bond between husband and wife is legally defined and has clearly demarcated obligations (principally the procreation and care of legitimate children and the safeguarding and increase of household property, including proper use of the wife's dowry).[41] But because this relation is confined entirely within the house, its obligations are less visible as public spectacle than the male bonds of guest-friendship. It is only (or primarily) when the marriage breaks down that the obligations have to be rendered tangible and visible in the social spectacle of legal proceedings. The *Medea* dramatizes an analogous situation: the husband's betrayals of oaths and promises bring to light the system of exchanges and obligations, both overt and unspoken, that underlie the day-to-day life of a marriage.[42] These obligations tend to diffuse over time and thus fade in visibility, whereas those of male friendship can be performed in single, sharply focused, even spectacular actions, as is the case with Heracles' gift to Admetus here. Marriage operates within legal obligations that are (and are expected to be) invisible in the normal course of a happy, smoothly running household; male hospitality follows a highly stylized code of behavior that its practitioners need to externalize and reaffirm conspicuously. The *Alcestis*, like the *Medea*, uses remote mythical events to illuminate the often suppressed contracts of the domestic sphere that are overshadowed by the public enactment of male reciprocities.

The contrast between the highly visible and formalized exchange relations between males and the sensational nature of the wife's substitution of herself for her husband in death crystallizes into a single event some of the implicit, more temporally extended obligations of marriage. The extreme situation dramatized in the play externalizes the wife's subordination of her life to the family and her ideal invisibility outside the domestic realm.[43] On the other hand, it also clarifies the husband's obligation to nurture the children (cf. 302– 19, 371–78).

Viewed in a larger perspective, these contrasts may also reflect some ambiguity about values in the aristocratic *oikos*, especially the paradox that whatever wealth the house accumulated within must also be made visible in the outside world through the extravagant displays and highly conspicuous exchanges of gifts that were always part of the aristocratic life-style in early Greece.[44] Through such gift giving noble families established and commemorated their ties to one another. The process is exemplified in the highest, most heroic terms in Glaucus' exchange of his golden armor for the bronze of Diomedes in *Iliad* 6 and has been described at length for the *Odyssey* by Moses Finley.[45]

The *Alcestis* dramatizes some of the tensions in the system, especially those between the centripetal and centrifugal aspects of the household. To the wife belongs the self-enclosing, centripetal aspect of the house, its self-sufficiency and inward-facing direction. With the husband is associated the house's outward-looking face, the establishment of a fame, or *kleos*, visible from afar, and the network of friendships and alliances that reach out to others and are solidified by lavish hospitality. These latter by their very nature must be conspicuous, for their aim is to distinguish this house from others and to create particular bonds between houses. The *Alcestis* projects some of this tension between self-sufficiency and outward extension on the differences between wife and husband, and specifically on the conflict between the private funeral rites for the wife within the house and the elaborate hospitality to a famous *xenos* (guest / stranger) that makes him an intruder into the house at a critical moment. In a democratic polis such practices will arouse suspicion, and this suspicion of lavish display and exchange is perhaps another reason why Euripides presents Admetus' *xenia* in such an ambiguous light. Aristocratic magnanimity is still admired for its grandeur and nobility, and as such is incorporated into the values of the democratic polis; and yet there remains an inherent contradiction with the ethos of democracy.

Making the clash of values into a spectacle for the stage is the business of Greek drama, comic as well as tragic. In *Alcestis*, however, the combination of the funeral and the symposium at the center of the play is particularly shocking, and the chorus openly registers onstage what was probably the reaction of the audience (551f.).[46] Admetus' acceptance of another's death in place of his own saves the house, in one sense, but in another sense it throws into disarray all the relationships around him in the house.[47] The disturbing effects are mirrored in the disruptions of the accustomed divisions in the spatiosexual roles of this society. In a kind of *Verfremdungseffekt* (effect by alienation), these hold up a distorting, caricaturing mirror to the ostensible defeat of death.

If this picture suggests the destabilization of the house of Admetus at this point of its precarious salvation, however, the fairy-tale ending not only resolves these dissonances in the happiest possible way but actually makes them disappear. The emotional acceptance and intense experience of death's "necessity" (965) are canceled out by the unexpected breach of "necessity." The wish fulfillment expunges the destructive consequences of the conflict and of Admetus' failure to live up to his solemn promises to his dead wife. The victory over death and the reestablishment of a disturbed social order through (re-)marriage also shatter the generic limits of tragedy by using the themes of comedy.[48]

After Alcestis' disappearance from the stage, the remaining two-thirds of the play is completely devoted to Admetus. Alcestis is thus doubly displaced. She is (perforce) physically removed from the action, and she is simultaneously removed from the center of the audience's concern. There is even a tertiary displacement as the fullest mourning over her death is, in a way, performed by herself, in the Servant's long account (158–95), so that she thereby fulfills to the end her feminine role in the house. She is then returned to the stage—silent, passive, and in the more familiar feminine role in rescue myths—as the one who is saved (like Danae or Andromeda) by a hero who makes a dangerous journey, defeats a dangerous monster, and wins a victory over Death.

For all of its flirting with tragic form and tragic emotions, then, the *Alcestis* ends in comedy. This is not just a happy ending, but one that shows the social order restored to its "normal" condition after previous inversion. The wife-hero is now silent, submissive, and an object of masculine exchange. The husband, by association with his friend, has regained an aura of dignity, strength, and heroism. But of course this is not comedy. Despite victory, the tone at the end remains solemn. Death is still big. Although, as I have noted, the pollution of death is suppressed, that element surfaces, in displaced form, in the impressive silence of Alcestis at the end and in the necessity of a three-day period to "deconsecrate" her from the powers of the lower world (1143–46):

Αδ. τί γάρ ποθ' ἥδ' ἄναυδος ἕστηκεν γυνή;
Ηρ. οὔπω θέμις σοι τῆσδε προσφωνημάτων
    κλύειν, πρὶν ἂν θεοῖσι τοῖσι νερτέροις
    ἀφαγνίσηται καὶ τρίτον μόλῃ φάος.

Admetus. Why, then, does the woman stand here without speaking?
Heracles. It is not yet lawful for you to hear her address you until she is deconsecrated with respect to the gods below and until the light of the third day comes.

If the play ends with the comic motif of the wedding, this withholding of full reunion makes it the most uncomic wedding imaginable. If the house is restored to wholeness, Heracles' very presence beside Admetus is a reminder of its betrayal. If Admetus regains his marriage, it is at the price of rupturing the equally sacred bond between father and son. The somber mood of the ending, which remains difficult for modern readers (and was probably difficult for ancient readers, too), keeps us in touch with the awesome power of death, and therefore still in the realm of tragedy.

Hippolytus

6

Language, Signs, and
Gender

ASYMMETRIES OF LANGUAGE, VISION, AND DESIRE

The division between male and female worlds takes its most devastating form in the *Hippolytus*. Women are closed into a private world of physical needs and desires in which the sexual division of language works closely with the sexual division of space. Even the Nurse's positive model for communicating with men early in the play, namely consulting doctors, presupposes this barrier (293–96):

> κεἰ μὲν νοσεῖς τι τῶν ἀπορρήτων κακῶν,
> γυναῖκες αἵδε συγκαθιστάναι νόσον.
> εἰ δ᾽ ἔκφορός σοι συμφορὰ πρὸς ἄρσενας
> λέγ᾽, ὡς ἰατροῖς πρᾶγμα μηνυθῇ τόδε.

> But if you are sick with one of those ills not to be spoken of, there are women here, these, to help make your disease subside. But if this misfortune of yours can be brought forth to males, speak, so that this matter can be declared to doctors.

The first two lines suggest that women constitute a separate society, a race apart—like Hesiod's "race of women" (*genos gunaikôn*)—privy to their own secrets and to the "unspoken things" that are not "carried forth" to males.[1]

The situation of women telling male doctors their illnesses is also a piece of social realism on Euripides' part, for the Hippocratic treatise *Diseases of Women* discusses the medical difficulty of treating women who "are ashamed to tell [their illness]" because "it seems shameful to them."[2] Phaedra's "disease," however, veering as it does between the somatic and the emotional, physicality and metaphor, and human and divine causation, expands the medical / ritual aspect of the problem to ever-widening implications for female speech to males. Here men and women can reach one another only through partial, interrupted, or deceitful communications; and the hypothetical situation of lines 293–96 is enacted as a vividly staged event at every major crisis: the revelation of the Nurse to Hippolytus in the next scene, Phaedra's posthumous "speaking" to Theseus from the silent chamber of her suicide, and Artemis' explanation of the truth about Phaedra to Theseus from her superior position above and outside the scenic space as the dea ex machina. In this way the Nurse's potentially helpful model of medical consultation, with its "carrying forth" of female secrets in a gesture of timid exposure, shifts to a negative model of one-sided, concealed, or deceptive hearing and speaking. In particular, her conveyance of Phaedra's secret from the house of Hippolytus and the resultant accusatory letter from Phaedra to Theseus constitute a disastrously aggressive mode of telling women's secrets to men in power.

Hippolytus' "converse" (*homilia*) with Artemis at the beginning is the obverse of that between him and Phaedra. In the case of the goddess there is speech but no vision; in the case of Phaedra there is vision, but they never speak directly to one another. By only hearing, and not seeing, his goddess, Hippolytus maintains her asexual nature and removes a possible discourse of desire, through vision, with her.[3] The intensely sexual woman to whom he never speaks, however, has looked on him with the eyes of desire and heard him all too well, although without seeing him, through the closed doors of the palace (565–600).[4] Phaedra's eye held the outgoing gaze of desire, which seeks its object and is wounded by the erotic power that emanates from the object of desire, from his eye to hers. In rejecting Aphrodite, the goddess of sexuality, for the worship of the chaste Artemis,

Hippolytus idolizes a female figure that he cannot see, and so he cannot be wounded with the power of her erotic glance.

In the prologue this division between hearing and seeing seems to be merely a minor qualification in Hippolytus' knowledge of the divine, an inevitable and unproblematical consequence of his worship of Artemis. The mortal world, however, places different demands on the relations of sight and speech between men and women. His idealized "converse" with a goddess whose body is invisible to him undergoes a total reversal when he encounters the language and the gaze of a woman whose mortal body is "sick" with desire.

When Hippolytus hears of Phaedra's desire from the Nurse, he threatens an ambiguous change from silence to speech, symmetrical with Phaedra's just before: "My tongue has sworn, but unsworn is my mind" (612). As Simon Goldhill remarks, this antithetical formulation reflects a "disjunction between a person's words as external signs and his mind as the inward site of intention and desire."[5] It also raises the question of how to mediate between thought and word when the vehicles of thought—speech or signs—are so unreliable. We swing from the rejection of communication in Phaedra's unspoken desire in the opening scenes to the overdetermination and concretization of language in her silently vocal tablets later, when the message of desire is falsely displaced from her to Hippolytus and is spoken in the mouth of Theseus (883–85).

The Nurse's proposed consultation of doctors in lines 293–96 implies a controlled, rational communication with a helpful end in view and a relation of trust and confidence (at least to a minimal degree) between the speaker and the addressee. But this image of a cooperative, ameliorative communication between male and female is never realized. In her initial attempt to resist her passion Phaedra contemplates a negative relation between male and female discourse. She is concerned that the women's shame in the house and bad tales about women outside will undermine her sons' prestige and hence their opportunities in the public arena (413–23).[6] In the background is the Athenian attitude, enunciated in Pericles' funeral speech, that women should be visible in public as little as possible (Thucydides 2.45.2). Implicit too is the widespread Mediterranean notion that a man loses his honor and thus his social position if shame touches the women of his household.

The destructive effect of male and female communication reaches its climax when the Nurse tells Hippolytus of Phaedra's desire. She has obviously chosen the "male" furthest from any possibility of healing the "disease." Even though he is under oath (cf. 612, 1306), he threatens to breach the confidentiality that the doctors presumably would maintain. Thanks to his self-righteous concern with "purity," the one-sidedness of male communication with women becomes distorted to the point of paranoia. Women, he shouts, should have only wild beasts to associate with them; thus there would be no "passage" (*perân*, 645) within and no passage outward (645–50). He imagines a monstrously exaggerated form of the situation that the Nurse herself described to Phaedra: women enclosed in their private world, dwelling in the midst of things that "cannot be spoken" of safely to anyone except another woman (293). In order to cure Phaedra's disease, the Nurse is willing to have open communication with skilled men; but the effect of this step will only turn Phaedra back to the enigmatic discourse of women's private world: the lying and indirect mode of speaking embodied in the written tablets.

In response to the Nurse's communication of Phaedra's desire, Hippolytus would bar women from all human discourse (645ff.). Phaedra, however, will make another discourse of desire to Theseus, also without seeing him and in silence, but in total persuasiveness, across the barrier of the doors of her chamber (809–11).[7] These unstable relations between language and desire produce asymmetrical disasters: Hippolytus' purely aural communication with Artemis, marking a deficiency or denial of sexuality, avails little beside the all-too-successful communications of Phaedra with Theseus and later of Theseus with Poseidon, both resulting from the urgency of this same sexual force. The collapse of these untenable balances sexualizes language and leads to the total destruction of communication (at least temporarily) in the bull's roar of elemental violence, something no longer commensurate with language (1201–17).

WRITING, CONCEALING, AND REVEALING

The motif of writing calls attention to the way the stage events bring forth the hidden secrets of women from the house to men and unfold the action through the interplay of ambiguous signs in a series of complex, often asymmetrical interchanges between seeing and hearing, various forms of *opsis* and *logos*.[8]

In the *Hippolytus* the association between writing, the female body, (sexual) secrecy, plotting, and revealing what is concealed in the interior space reflects the operation of Euripides' paradoxical art: showing in public, theatrical space matters of the most intense privacy.[9] Aristophanes proves himself an excellent reader of Euripides when he makes male penetration of women's secrets—in this case, religious secrets—the center of the stage action of the *Thesmophoriazusae*.[10] That intrusion into women's rituals acts out on the comic stage the substance of the women's accusations against Euripides and the grounds of their conspiracy—namely, his revelation of their concealed crimes. In an ironic doubling of the theme by the stage events, both parties characteristically prove the charges against them to be correct. The audience sees women, onstage, plotting in secret conspiracies against males (i.e., against Euripides at the Thesmophoria). Euripides displays his arsenal of ingenious devices, intrigues, and disguises to infiltrate these secret meetings and uncover the women's plotting. In order to reveal the hidden essence of Euripides' art—that is, to unmask the truth about Euripides as poet and dramatist—Aristophanes stages a characteristically Euripidean drama and a microcosm of Euripides' dramatic activity; a plot revolving about men—in this case, Euripides himself—who learn and expose women's deadly secrets.

In the *Hippolytus* the search for a hidden truth also extends to men, especially in the scene between Hippolytus and Theseus, where the latter wishes for true speaking among men in the "two voices" of lines 928–31. This motif introduces Theseus' face-to-face accusation of his son (916ff.). Its formulation here is more explicitly intellectualized than in the earlier male-female communications (e.g., 295f.). It is also violently conflictual rather than cooperative. It would require "some terribly skilled Sophist" (*deinos sophistês*), Hippolytus says wistfully, to teach good sense to men (920–21). The discrepancy between wish and actuality in the situation and the irony of the way "good sense" will come to Hippolytus (cf. 730f.) are essential parts of the tragic pattern. For Euripides, the profoundest understanding of human nature comes not from the rationalism of the sophistic move-

ment but from the poet's probing of the emotions and their contradictions, such as those that (thanks to the Nurse) Phaedra, despite
herself, brings forth to men.

When Phaedra opens her deepest secrets to another woman, the
Nurse, Euripides is, of course, revealing those secrets for public scrutiny in the theater. When the gates of the palace open to reveal Phaedra's "hidden grief" (138), the mass (all-male?) audience of thousands
witnesses an intimate encounter between a very private woman and
her confidante. The parallel that the Nurse draws with revealing the
"unspeakable" illnesses of women to male doctors in lines 293–96
also calls attention to this public mode of exploring what a woman
would keep most concealed. A little later, Phaedra herself reflects on
the tension between what she keeps hidden inside and the dangers
of exposure to the public and masculine verbalization outside the
doors (*thuraia*, 395–97). When she makes her resolve of death in
silence after the first stage of her revelation, she repeatedly inter-
twines the themes of female passion, speech, public opinion among
"men" (*andres*), and speaking of concealed things outside (393–97,
407–10).

From privacy and concealment in a discourse only with women,
Phaedra and her Nurse now turn outward "to males," following the
Nurse's model of consulting male doctors (293–96). Yet in the ironic
reversal of sex roles that pervades the play, Hippolytus is inside (or
comes from inside) talking to the Nurse, and Phaedra is now outside.
It is Phaedra who hears without seeing, as Hippolytus did in his
opening address to Artemis (86; cf. 575f.; also the chorus in 585, ἰὰν
μὲν κλύω, σαφὲς δ' οὐκ ἔχω, "I hear a cry but have nothing clear").

This scene precipitates the catastrophe. Its spatial configuration—
Phaedra listening at the gates of the palace to Hippolytus and the
Nurse inside[11]—distills into a powerful (and unusual) scenic experience many of the issues of the play:[12] the crossing between interior and
exterior space, the "bringing forth" of female secrets to males, and
the hearing of words that are liable to crucial misinterpretations.[13]
Phaedra herself vividly enacts the experience that the chorus and
spectators have at the beginning—namely, attending intently to the
"hidden things" about to be "revealed" from within. "Hidden things
stand revealed, and you are destroyed," cries the chorus at Hippolytus' shout from inside the palace (593, τὰ κρυπτὰ γὰρ πέφηνε); and we
recall the chorus's opening lyrics about Phaedra's body wasting away

in "hidden disease" and the Nurse's opening speech on the obscurity of human happiness (138f., 191–97). Like the spectators of this scene, Phaedra witnesses a dialogue that poses a vital problem of interpretation—an interpretation on which depends her life (cf. 593, διὰ δ' ὄλλυσαι).

Enunciating concealed desires parallels the visual movement from interior to exterior scenic space. A few lines later, Hippolytus addresses the "sun's unfolding rays" (601) and exclaims about the "unspeakable sound of words" (602f.). This is the appropriate verbal commentary on what he does onstage: he exits abruptly from the house, laying bare the secrets of the women within. His pleonastic and oxymoronic phrase in line 602, "Such words' unspeakable voice have I heard" (οἵων λόγων ἄρρητον εἰσήκουσ' ὄπα), concretizes speech both as a paradox and as a physical presence whose power the theater explores. The Nurse's instantaneous reaction is the anxious plea, "Keep silence, child, before someone notices your shouting" (σίγησον, ὦ παῖ, πρίν τιν' αἰσθέσθαι βοῆς, 603). This urgent response calls attention to the dramatic tension between what is "spoken," "unspoken," and "unspeakable" (Hippolytus means arrhêton in this last sense in line 602).

Shortly before, in her dialogue with the chorus, hearing, shouting, and silence determine whether or not Phaedra will be "destroyed" (565, 575, 593; cf. 590f.). Language here takes on a double role. On the one hand, it is an objective, factual bearer of information that is spoken or heard (567, 570). On the other hand, it has the power to frighten when it "rushes upon her mind," or *phrenes*: τίς φοβεῖ σε φήμα, γύναι, φρένας ἐπίσσυτος (What report terrifies you, woman, rushing upon your mind? 573f.).[14] Shouting "falls upon the house" and "comes, comes through the gates" (576, 588). Here, addressing Phaedra as *gunai* (woman), the chorus implies the helplessness and peril of a woman when her private speech is carried from "breast" or "thoughts" (*phrenes*) to the public realm "outside." This *phêmê* (report, utterance) is like an attacker from outside, forcing its way into a frightened interior (ἐπίσσυτος φρένας).

At just this point Hippolytus makes his literal rush outside, carrying to the open exterior as a "shouting" the private communication he had promised to hold within his breast (*phrên*, 612).[15] When Phaedra takes decisive action, however, she and Hippolytus exchange their roles of the previous scene: the tablets take the place of Phaedra's voice inside the house, "shouting" their message outside (874–84). The anadiplosis in Theseus' cry, "The tablet shouts, shouts things not to be forgotten" (877), recalls the similar figure in the personification of speech in line 586, "The shouting [of Hippolytus] went, went through the gates."[16]

If Phaedra's first impulse is to cover her secret in silence, Hippolytus moves in just the opposite direction, with equally disastrous results. In his notorious formulation of line 612, "My tongue has sworn, but unsworn is my mind," the mind (*phrên*, also "breast, heart") would elude the social conventions of public discourse. The rare negative adjective modifying *phrên*, *anômotos* (uncommitted to oath, unoathed), both focuses and problematizes the division between private thoughts and public utterance (such as an oath).[17] Euripides had already made Phaedra and her secrets the center of this contrast in the closely parallel formulation "My hand is pure, but my mind [*phrên*] has a polluting stain" (317). In both cases the primary force in the disaster is the disequilibrium between what can be spoken and what lies hidden within the breast. Even verbalizing this disequilibrium contributes to the tragic course of events: the half-knowledge of the Nurse impels her to draw from Phaedra the full revelation; and Hippolytus' threat to break his oath (even though he never actually does) impels Phaedra to her plot of vengeance and self-defense.[18]

WOMEN, SIGNS, AND BEASTS

When Phaedra yields to the Nurse's persuasion and allows the latter to "heal" her disease by magic (478ff.), she is in effect resuming the contrast between male and female in the consultation of doctors in lines 293–96. But now that possible cooperativeness and helpfulness of men toward women change to a more competitive attitude: "Unless we women invent our devices, men would be slow indeed to find them out" (480f.) Phaedra senses all too well the destructive persuasion that this appeal to an irrational hope will have on her; but the Nurse refuses to "close her mouth" and hold back her "words most shameful" (cf. 498–506). Cleverly ignoring Phaedra's plea, she wins her over not by argumentation but by simply going ahead.

When Phaedra thus abandons herself to the irrational hope held

out to her, the Nurse asks for a "sign of the beloved" or a piece of his
clothing (513–15):

δεῖ δ' ἐξ ἐκείνου δή τι τοῦ ποθουμένου
σημεῖον, ἢ πλόκον τιν' ἢ πέπλων ἄπο
λαβεῖν, συνάψαι τ' ἐκ δυοῖν μίαν χάριν.

> I need to take some token [sign] from the one who is desired, either a lock
> of hair or something from his garments, and thus to join from two a
> single joy.[19]

In her long speech just preceding, Phaedra has relied on logical discourse: debating alternatives, setting one idea or value carefully next to another, classifying pleasures as good or bad (373–430).
We have moved from *logos* as rational discourse, in Phaedra's long
speech, to a magical power. Instead of choosing between a discourse
of words with Hippolytus or total silence (her first choice: 244, 271ff.),
Phaedra becomes engaged in an exchange of magical signs, a synec-
dochic substitution of *sêmeion* for *logos* and of an object for a real
person. As a result of this shadowy, in-between discourse of signs, she
neither speaks to Hippolytus nor keeps her love silent. An analogous
transformation of language occurs for Hippolytus. He can fulminate
against women and make long speeches in his own defense, but his
oath to the Nurse also keeps him from full communication with
Theseus (1033, 1060–63); and so he maintains silence about the one
fact that matters.

If the Nurse's request in lines 513–15 moves us (and Phaedra) from
speech to sign, Phaedra's writing does just the reverse. It marks the
intermediate position of the sign as a subverter of both speech and
silence. As her writing now assumes the magical power of seduction
promised by the Nurse, signs become speech. The tablet that "wishes
to signify" becomes the tablet that "wishes to speak": θέλει τι σημῆ-
ναι νέον (857); ἴδω τί λέξαι δέλτος ἥδε μοι θέλει (865). This personification of the speaking tablet joins the intellectualist themes of
testing evidence and making logical inferences to the realm of witchcraft, here an old woman's request for a *sêmeion* from Hippolytus
(513–15).

In the dangerous fluidity between different modes of communication Phaedra's letters move quickly from "signifying" to "fawning,"
"shouting," and even "singing" (865, 877, 879).[20] This protean figura-
tion of the speaking sign ominously develops from a new power

conferred on it by erotic passion. Even the language of Artemis at the end of the play suggests the indirectness with which the troubles of the female body have to be communicated to men. When Artemis describes the Nurse's communication of Phaedra's "disease" to Hippolytus, her verb is not "say" but "signify" (*sêmainein*, ἥ σῷ δι' ὅρκων παιδὶ σημαίνει νόσον, "Phaedra who thanks to [his] oaths signifies her disease to your son," 1306; cf. 295f.). The indirectness of the communication itself is striking. Artemis is telling Theseus about the Nurse telling Phaedra about how Phaedra should tell Hippolytus. But this indirectness only sets off by contrast the excessive power of signification in Phaedra's silently speaking tablets (cf. *sêmainei*, 857).

Women's speech, then, vacillates dangerously between a language of ambiguous erotic signs, on the one hand (the Nurse's magic and Phaedra's written tablets), and a bestial language, on the other.[21] This is not to say that women do not *also* use language and argument (*logoi*) and that these are not just as slippery as men's language and argument. But in Greek tragedy's construction of women, their susceptibility to the force of desire (*eros*) changes argument to magic, as happens in Phaedra's long scene with the Nurse (373–524). Despite what Theseus says about Kypris disturbing young men's minds (967–70), it is Kypris in the mind (and speech) of women that the play reveals, although sexual jealousy and anger have disturbed Theseus' mind, too (cf. 1336f.). The play allows Phaedra a victory of reason and morality over desire, only to make of her the exception that proves the rule: she not only yields to a discourse of magic (503–24) but also uses the deceptive potential of language to manipulate emotions in a false "persuasion" of Theseus (cf. *elenchos*, "testing," 1310–12, 1336f.).

Hippolytus, as we have seen, is the play's strongest advocate of splitting language into gender-defined polarities. He defines women linguistically as subhuman beings who should converse with beasts (645ff.). He regards their lack of control over their bodies' sexual drives as parallel to their lack of a proper human language, whereas his only "converse" with a female figure (Artemis) implies a suprahuman discourse and a mystical but nonvisual, de-eroticized association. This polarization of female language between the bestial and the divine rebounds on Hippolytus himself, destroying the middle ground of speech with men as well as with women, particularly with his father, Theseus. Thus his attempt to deprive women of human speech proves to be a fatal error, for women's speech turns out to be powerful enough to destroy a discourse of truth between males, preventing him from adducing rationally persuasive arguments or evidence to Theseus (925ff., 971f., 1074ff.). Once reliable (i.e., male) discourse breaks down at one point, the whole system becomes endangered, in a kind of domino effect.

The term that implements Hippolytus' exclusion of women from human language is *bestial*, and this undergoes a radical shift of value in its polarizing function. Hippolytus is operating with an implicit equation: male is to female as human is to bestial (cf. 645–48). But the bestial, instead of supporting his hierarchies, becomes the new and spectacular expression of a "successful" communication between the human and the divine that darkens and confounds all the clarity in his world. The bull-monster that Theseus' prayer calls forth from the sea places bestiality on the male side of the equation. Theseus, who is the immediate destroyer of Hippolytus' neat schematizations, had already undermined such sexual dichotomizing by pointing out that erotic instability and passionate violence belong not just to the female but also to "maleness" (*to arsen*, 970).

As the answer to Theseus' address to Poseidon in lines 887–90, the monstrous bull is the manifestation of a divine presence.[22] It is, in fact, the most powerful sign of successful communication in the play, a massive physical demonstration that the invisible gods do "hear" the speech of mortals and manifest their response with irrefutable clarity. In keeping with the directness that attends all the divine "voices" in the play, the bull "speaks" with such a surplus of communicative power that it rends the fabric of reality. It is therefore not only a "sign" (*sêma*) but also a *teras* (1214)—that is, a prodigy, something outside the field of human understanding and normal discourse.[23] This *teras*, although sent by the gods, is also monstrous, or, as the Messenger says, *agrion* (savage). The bestial form establishes the clarity of divine communication but is itself an anomalous fusion of god and beast. And it causes another disruption of hierarchies in the realm of communication, for it totally inverts the communication between earth and heaven that Hippolytus' privileged "converse" with his goddess would seek to establish.[24] That converse sublimates male sexuality into the "untouched meadow," but the communication between Theseus and Poseidon is fraught with male sexuality.

MAGIC, LANGUAGE, LETTERS

In a suggestive chapter of her book on Eros, Anne Carson points out how letters function in the novelistic treatment of love to complicate the ostensible one-to-one relation of eros with the obliquity, deceptiveness, and paradoxes of a triangular situation. Letters are "a means of erotic subterfuge between characters" and "unfold a three-cornered relation."[25] "When letters are read in novels, the immediate consequence is to inject paradox into lovers' emotions (pleasure and pain at once) and into their strategies (now obstructed by an absent presence)." "Letters," she remarks in the next chapter, "make the absent present, and in an exclusive way, as if they were a private code from writer to reader" (p. 99). The letters of Phaedra, however, invert absence and presence. A lover writes to the beloved in order to speak an intense message of love in a secrecy that both the writer and the addressee relish and cherish. Phaedra writes to make public a message of hatred and mutual destruction.

To understand the resonances of these issues for Euripides, it is helpful to look at three other discussions of "writing" (*graphein*) from his time. We must bear in mind that the same word, *graphein*, includes both writing and painting. A fragment of Empedocles (31 B23 Diels-Kranz) describes painters (*grapheis*) as users of "many-colored drugs" (*poluchroa pharmaka*), which they mix in varying amounts to form "images resembling all things" (εἰδέα πᾶσιν ἀλίγκια), including men, women, trees, birds, animals, and even "the long-lived gods, supreme in their honors." For Empedocles the "drugs" that fashion mimetic likeness are the source of *apatê* (deception). This account of painting is in fact a warning against being deceived by "mortal things." Instead, we should heed the truth of his *mythos*, spoken as from a god.

The Sophist Gorgias offers an analogous view of how painters (*grapheis*) fashion a single beautiful body from various colors and forms and thus "give delight to our eyes" (*terpousin tên opsin*, *Helen* 18). Gorgias' analogy, however, is positive in its view of painting. He is referring to the power of language to create "pleasure," "pain," and "desire" (*terpsis, lupê, pothos*) and thereby to effect persuasion in the soul of the spectator and the listener.[26] He too draws an analogy between "drugs" (*pharmaka*) and the artist's skill in his mimetic and persuasive craft (14).[27]

Finally, in an interesting chapter of the *Memorabilia* (3.10), Xeno-phon has Socrates define the art of painting (*graphikê*) as "the figura-tion of visible things" or "the production of likenesses to the things that are seen" (γραφική ἐστιν εἰκασία τῶν ὁρωμένων, 3.10.1). This definition of *graphikê* in turn forms an analogy for seeing the invisible nature of the human soul, the passions and the character of men. We may recall Theseus' wish for the two voices that distinguish the *phrenes* of men, the just from the unjust (*Hippolytus* 925ff.). Socrates puzzles his interlocutor, the famous painter Parrhasius, when he asks about imitating "the character of the soul" (*tês psychês êthos*). Par-rhasius asks, "How, O Socrates, can one imitate what has neither symmetry nor color nor any of those which you just now mentioned and is not at all visible?" (*Memorabilia* 3.10.3). Socrates replies by pointing out that facial expression reflects character and that in de-picting those externally visible expressions the painter, like the sculp-tor (to whom Socrates next turns, 3.10.6ff.), depicts these hidden states of the soul.

There are many issues involved in this last passage, not least the problems that arise from the Greeks' tendency to identify "imita-tion" and "representation." But I cite it in relation to the passages from Empedocles and Gorgias to indicate how deeply for Euripides' contemporaries the art of "inscription" (*graphikê*) implicated the main issues of the *Hippolytus*: discovering our inner being beneath the outer covering of what we seem to be and revealing our actual thoughts and intentions beneath the words, written and spoken, that announce them to others. In these passages, as in *Hippolytus*, *graphikê* embodies an ambiguous and paradoxical relation between surface and depth, appearance and reality, subterfuge and dramatic gesture. In Gorgias too the concern with the aesthetic appeal, the "pleasure" (*terpsis*) that we derive from the "likeness" (*eikasia*), introduces the element of seduction and sexuality. Gorgias' subject is, in fact, the seductive force of persuasion on Helen.

In Euripides' play the concretization of hidden desire into the signs of writing moves language into its ambiguous place between truth and deception. The signifying system of *logos* is most dangerous when it becomes visible as *graphê*, as a tangible sign, or *sêmeion*. The invisibility of the speaker behind the *graphê* produces an asymmetry of communication parallel to the other eye-ear asymmetries and thereby increases the possibility of deception or error. (Plato well appreciates this asymmetry and its dangers in the celebrated myth of the *Phaedrus*; 275d–76c.)[28] Conversely, the tangible rendering of eros and of erotic seduction gives special power to the sign system constituted by *graphê*.

The Nurse cites the *graphai* of older tales, meaning either mythical writings or (more probably) paintings that depict the loves of the gods (451–58). Hippolytus knows of sex only from "hearing it in word and seeing it in *graphê*" (1004), which must be painting, although the reading of books is, in his case, not excluded (cf. 954). The *graphai* cited by the Nurse in lines 451–58 are a figurative double for her own disclosure of seduction to Phaedra: "Galeotto fu il libro . . ." In line 1004 Hippolytus uses these *graphai* as proof of his resistance to such seduction, but he does so just at the moment when Phaedra's *graphê* and its different form of seduction have exercised their full power.

Love and magic have gone together from time immemorial, and Euripides used the combination powerfully three years before in his *Medea*. The *Hippolytus* goes a step beyond the *Medea*, and in a more intellectual direction. Here Euripides associates the primitive love-magic with the power of writing to evoke desire, to make the absent one speak seductively as if present, and to spin a web of fantasied desires around the one to whom the writing is addressed.[29]

When the Nurse promises "incantations and words that cast spells" (ἐπῳδαὶ καὶ λόγοι θελκτήριοι, 478), she invokes an old tradition in which medical treatment is not fully distinguished from magic.[30] These incantations and spells, however, also embody the quasi-magical element in language, that is, the persuasion or seduction that arouses rather than calms desire. The Nurse's *pharmakon* (516) is indeed a poison as well as a medicine, and by its use she eventually breaks down the rational arguments (*logoi*) that Phaedra has been using to check her passion.[31] The Nurse has failed in allopathic measures, rational arguments *against* Phaedra's "disease." She now succeeds (for the moment) with homeopathic magic, joining the irrationality of the love-sickness to the appeal of the irrational, her offer of magical spells or philters.

Euripides' contemporary, Gorgias, compares the power of language to magic, and specifically to erotic magic (*Helen* 10). When Phaedra begs the Nurse to "keep her mouth closed" and not to "let forth words most shameful" (498f.), she recognizes the quasi-magical power of persuasive speech.[32] Words, she knows, possess an irresistible power to "subdue" her soul (cf. 504f.), like the magic power that the Nurse plans to use against Hippolytus (cf. 509f.).[33] At such moments of intense emotion, language is not merely the vehicle of emotion; it becomes a powerful agent in its own right, like the "tyrant logos" (*logos dynastês*) that compels Helen to her crime of passion in Gorgias' *Helen* (8).

Theseus' imprecation, which comes soon after he reads Phaedra's letter, is in effect a magical speech that "sends forth" a destructive supernatural power into human life. "You let forth the curses," Artemis tells him accusingly in line 1324 (ἀρὰς ἐφῆκας). The repetition of this verb reveals the consequences of Phaedra's failure to keep the Nurse from "letting forth the most shameful words" of persuasion and thus revealing her passion for Hippolytus (μὴ μεθήσεις αὖθις αἰσχίστους λόγους, 499). And the effect of Theseus' curse is the supernaturally potent "deep roar" that the monstrous bull "sends forth" in line 1202 (βαρὺν βρόμον μεθῆκεν).[34]

Soon after Theseus' curse, the silent speech of the tablet makes the "dead body present as the clearest witness" (973). Virtually "present" with living force (972), this paradoxically speaking and silent witness obviates the necessity for a "debate with words" (971), as in a civil process or a public trial for murder.[35] The polarized male and female languages suggested both by the Nurse and by Hippolytus (293–96 and 645–48 respectively) now cancel one another out. The intimate, erotically charged female discourse in the house subverts the civic, masculine discourse of the law court. The rational forensic process of sifting evidence collapses before the irrational power of magic to bring a corpse to life and make it speak, like the speaking dead of Odysseus' Nekyia. *Psuchagogein*, the aesthetic "delight" or entertainment brought by the "enchantment" of art or literature, originally meant calling up the shades of the dead, as by magic spells.[36] Hippolytus, Theseus ironically suggests, expects to "conquer his soul" like an enchanter or magician.[37] But the real magic is the emotional power of love. When the catastrophe is complete, Eros is revealed as the magical power that he is (cf. 1274, *thelgei d'Erôs*).

For all of Aphrodite's agency, then, the "magic" of love and persuasion lies not in the supernatural or in witchcraft but in the nature of man, in the power of the passions and the human susceptibility to deception. For Phaedra this magic of language is not only the force of erotic seduction (as it is in the Nurse's speech), it is also the voice of guilt. In separating herself from the unfaithful wives whom she condemns, she wonders how they cannot fear that the very timbers of the house would cry out their crimes (418). But she herself comes to use a quasi-magical, deceptively persuasive voice of retribution and revenge for a sexual injury as her own "speaking" through the tablets accuses and convicts Hippolytus of rape.[38] The deceptive *graphê* now transforms its language of absence into the most effective presence of the play as Theseus' curses assume the power to kill as they issue from his mouth (887–90). It is a further irony, however, that the "evidence" on which Theseus relies is no more reliable than Hippolytus' magically speaking house (cf. 967ff. and 1074ff.).

Hippolytus enters with the line, "Hearing your outcry, Father, I come in haste" (902f.). The "shout" of the father is doubly potent, for it is both a curse and a summons. It calls Hippolytus to the scene so that the imprecatory "shouting" can have its murderous effect (cf. 887–90). Poseidon has "heard" Theseus' outcry in a different sense (1169f.): "O gods and Poseidon, how truly you are my father, since you *heard* my prayers" (*akousas*, 1170). "Voice" then swings still further away from the language of logical inference and legal proceedings in the monster's terrible roar that "fills all the earth" (1215, cf. 692).

When the tragedy is nearly over and the passion is spent, there is a different view of language as a force endowed with supernatural power. Theseus' curse appears as a "bitter gift" from his father, and the king wishes that it had "never come into (his) mouth" (1411f.):

Ἱπ. ὦ δῶρα πατρὸς σοῦ Ποσειδῶνος πικρά.
Θη. ὡς μήποτ' ἐλθεῖν ὤφελ' ἐς τοὐμὸν στόμα.

The fluctuations between too free and too constrained speech in the first half of the play now extend to Theseus. In anger he sent forth his curse all too easily from his mouth (1412); but he cannot take back the "woe destructive" that he "did not hold back in the gates of his mouth" at the critical encounter with Phaedra's ambiguous silent speaking (τόδε μὲν οὐκέτι στόματος ἐν πύλαις καθέξω, 882f.; ὡς μή-ποτ' ἐλθεῖν ὤφελ' ἐς τοὐμὸν στόμα, 1412).

DEMYSTIFICATION AND THE IDEOLOGIES
OF CLASS AND GENDER

In the clear light of reason, writing is just writing: another form of communication, another mode of speaking. Phaedra, in her highly intellectualized meditation on whether or not to die, recognizes writing as merely an orthographic convention, a way of spelling words. Viewed one way, the twofold "shame" or "modesty" (*aidôs*), is a matter of two words "having the same letters" (ταὖτ' ἔχοντε γράμματα, 387).[39] Theseus, a man of action, can scorn Hippolytus' books as "the smoke of many letters" (or writings, 954f.)—an insubstantial construction of the fevered mind (cf. his *bakcheue*, "rage like a bacchant," 954).

On the positive side, the Messenger, after announcing Hippolytus' death, expresses his conviction of Hippolytus' innocence in a sort of reverse hyperbole. He would not believe Hippolytus to be base, he declares, "even if the whole race of women were hanged, and even if one were to *fill the pine wood of Ida* with writings" (καὶ τὴν ἐν Ἴδῃ γραμμάτων πλήσειέ τις / πεύκην, 1253f.). The hypothetical perpetrator of lies is here a vague, nameless "someone" (*tis*); and the "letters" (*grammata*) no longer "speak," shout, or sing (856ff.), but merely take up space. The Messenger's pejorative allusion to the "race of women," with its Hesiodic echoes, also restabilizes discourse into its familiar male-centered form. In place of the society of women talking about men at the beginning of the play, there is now a wholly male exchange, and its subject is the evils of women and their responsibility for the troubles of men.[40]

The familiar commonplace about the evils of women reasserts the social divisions of gender and anticipates that renewal of male bonding to be enacted in the final scene.[41] It also runs parallel to the return of language to its everyday status, now cleansed of the anomalies that (female) writing had created in it. The return of the familiar gender divisions brings clarity back to the world, and with the clarity of gender roles comes clarity of language.

This return to "order" takes place under the sign of the play's most magnificent display of patriarchal authority: a divine father harkens to the cry of his son, who needs to prove his paternity and assert his exclusive sexual rights to his wife and his power over his *oikos*. Conversely, disorder takes the form of the alienation of son and father when a wife's *eros* and *dolos* (desire and craft) displace paternal wrath from female to male victim and call forth paternal vengeance in the shape of monstrous violence against the son. This perverted condition, not surprisingly, brings with it the deafening or blinding of the senses (1215–17) and the obscuring of geographical boundaries as the view across the water toward Athens is blotted out (1207ff.). There is, however, a deeper irony in the fact that what separates the father and the (illegitimate) son is a wife's stratagem to protect the rights of her legitimate children in the public arena of free citizens' right to speech (421–25), that is, the paternal inheritance transmitted and ensured through marriage. And the figure who restores the relation between father and son in the city is a female goddess of the wild and hunting.

By transforming the speaking tablets back to the status of physical objects in nature, pieces of pine wood with scratches on them, the Messenger's hyperbole about filling a region with letters paradoxically demythicizes *logos*. Writing now merely embodies the materiality of the medium that holds the letters, in contrast to the figurative animation of things possessing a magical speech (692, 856ff., 1215). Divested of its magic, language is deflated into a rational medium for communicating truth. Metaphorically reunited with their point of physical origin—the trees—these tablets are returned to the natural order. Outside, in the open, they no longer have the power of deadly "persuasion" (cf. *pithesthai*, 1251).

The Messenger's demystifying materiality of the tablets also brings Theseus' relation with Hippolytus back to a socially approved ground of human feelings: paternal concern and pity for a son. Under the influence of the tablets' message, Theseus contemptuously associated his son with writing as the suspect eccentricity of an abnormal personality (954). Now a humble slave (*doulos*, 1249) can effectively debunk words as a magic power of dangerous persuasion. This apparently simple, instinctive certainty about human character brings us back to earth after Theseus' rhetorical exaggeration about ethereal studies.[42] "I know that he is noble," the Messenger/servant says in line 1254. As in the prologue, a mere slave gives moderating counsel to his aristocratic master.[43]

Everywhere in this work, however, there is a latent ideological thrust behind the play of deceptive appearances and deceptive language. In political ideology, as Fabio Turato suggests, Hippolytus and Phaedra embody, each in a different way, the unified standard of an aristocratic outlook, a monolithic singleness of values: the leisurely pursuits of the *jeunesse dorée*, on the one hand, and the promotion of reputation as the chief goal of life, on the other.[44] But this "nobility" of a simplex value system is fragmented by the plottings of the Nurse, who uses the ignoble rationalism of the sophistic movement to persuade Phaedra and stands ready to use any expedient to achieve her practical aim of saving Phaedra's life (482–506).[45]

A complementary, and more positively oriented, subversion of this aristocratic ideology comes from the opening of the Messenger scene. This little dialogue between the clear-sighted, compassionate slave and the proud, self-righteously punitive king may be a democratic touch, a hint at the self-blindness that accompanies class aspiration and class privileges.[46] The horse-rearing youth who regards himself as "best of men" (*anêr aristos*, 1242) needs a slave to prove that he is "noble" rather than "base" (*esthlos*, 1251; *kakos*, 1254). Hippolytus' ideal was to "enjoy good fortune always with [his] friends, the best men," the youths of the best families (σὺν τοῖς ἀρίστοις εὐτυχεῖν ἀεὶ φίλοις, 1018). Before the action moves beyond the human level with the entrance of Artemis, it is the slave who wins for him, in his "misery" and "ill fortune" (*athlios*, 1261; *dustuchounta*, 1264), what measure of honor and comfort he can now obtain. In the precarious tragic world the boundaries between classes momentarily become as fluid as those between the sexes. Noble birth is not the only source of virtue and strength of character.

Theseus ends the scene by agreeing to have Hippolytus brought before him, out of reverence for the gods and the tie of paternity ("because he is born from me," 1258f.). Although he does not formally acknowledge his slave's advice, the repetitions clearly indicate that the king's change of mind is due to the slave and that he is "using the counsels" of this servant (ἐμοῖς δὲ χρώμενος βουλεύμασιν, 1263). The slave's repeated phrase, "your child" (*ton son paida*), in line 1251 and 1264 also prepares for and reinforces Theseus' yielding. But Theseus' permission is based not so much on compassion as on the more formal criteria of "reverence for the gods" and the inalienable bond of paternity ("because he is born from me," οὕνεκ' ἐστὶν ἐξ ἐμοῦ, 1259). This latter fact especially begins to accomplish in naturalistic human terms what Artemis will do in a burst of divine revelation. Theseus is still deceived by appearances and entangled in the ambiguities of language: he would still reprove Hippolytus "by words and by disasters sent from the gods" (λόγοις τ' ελέγξω δαιμό-νων τε συμφοραῖς, 1267). But it is, again, the slave, eager to "please" his master (σῇ χαρίζεσθαι φρενί, 1262), who first arouses active pity for a "wretched man" (*ton athlion*, 1261f.). He also invokes the norms of civilized behavior: a father should not be "cruel" or "raw" (*ōmos*) to a son whose luck has so turned against him (1264).

Viewed in terms of the gender dichotomies that pervade this play, however, the scene between Theseus and his slave, the Messenger, purchases nobility and innocence for Hippolytus at the price of Phaedra's guilt. It begins to thrust Phaedra back into a role as an exemplar of the mistrust and dissension that women sow among the males who "naturally" belong together.[47] This vindication of the son's nobility by the direct speech of the servant prefigures the father's recognition of his son at the end. It begins the process of overcoming the complications that woman and her deceptive language of signs bring into the all-male world of legal and moral judgments, civic life, athletics, and so on.

The servant is thus an important intermediary between Theseus and Hippolytus. His confidence in Hippolytus not only anticipates the male bonding of the closing scene, but, more important, it validates the masculine ideal of an "instinctive" trust and respect in masculine relations: father and son, servant and lord, fellow hunters, and (by extension) fellow warriors. Thus it redirects and redeems the element of inborn nature (*phusis*) of Hippolytus' first speech (79f.). But the *phusis* that for Hippolytus was a criterion of exclusion (defending his "pure meadow" of chastity) has now become the basis of inclusion, recovering (male) bonds of blood. All of this takes place over Phaedra's dead body.

In Hippolytus' first speech the imagery surrounding his purity evokes the longing for a golden age of a unified, uncomplicated, and unconflicted aristocratic world. This ideal, as Carlo Diano and others suggest, may have overtones of longing for escape from the contagion and physical suffering of the Athenian plague of 429 B.C.[48] But it is also the fantasy of a golden age of sexless reproduction, a world without (female) sexuality or indeed without females at all (see 616–24).[49] In the realm of language Theseus' wish for a voice of pure truth, free of the division between inner being and surface appearance (925–31), is rendered impossible by the dualities of "hand" and "mind," "tongue" and "thought" that stem from the sexual desire of Phaedra and its suppression from language (see lines 317 and 612). Phaedra's desire eventually answers Hippolytus' extreme dichotomizing of gender with the confusion of gender in his suffering at the end and in the survival of his story in girls' marriage rites.[50] Phaedra also answers his rejection of women as part of the "race of mortals" (*broteion genos*, 618) with a common physicality that includes both men and women.

A world polarized between rigid aristocratic simplifications of glory and athletics, on the one hand, and "feminine" deceitfulness and ignoble sophistic expediency, on the other, is doomed to destruction. And so, therefore, is Hippolytus' attempt to create a garden world free of the dualities that begin with gender and sex. In this divided, passionate world of "real" men and women, communication is complex and imperfect, and Phaedra's tablets are the most important representative of this condition. They communicate their powerful message entirely through vision and appearances. They appeal to the strong emotions surrounding the bonds of physical love and procreation with dazzling success (835–51). And, of course, they lie.

Here too, aristocratic simplicity fractures into multiplicities, complexities, and ignoble facts. Noble birth comes up against the inescapable biological fact of Hippolytus' bastardy. The heroic "fame imperishable" turns into a marriage rite based on the memorialization of a woman's passionate and illicit sexual desire.[51] The figure of godlike purity dies, shattered, in the arms of the father who begot him.

As Artemis leaves Hippolytus to his mortal end, the asymmetry of vision that initially qualified their relationship in what seemed a relatively minor way (85f.) now marks the impassable barrier between a dying man and an ever-living goddess (cf. 1437f.). Hippolytus' penultimate utterance (1455), "Pray to have legitimate children such as me," moves back to the realm of wish, but with a painful impossibility, for Hippolytus in effect here acknowledges that he is not a legitimate son.[52] Characteristically locked into the terms of his own discourse, he also forgets that Theseus *has* legitimate children, that they constituted, in fact, one of Phaedra's chief motives for plotting his death (cf. 307–10, 421–27, 717), and that Theseus is now bereft of the wife who bore them (847–51).

7

Theater, Ritual, and

Commemoration

THEATRICAL SELF-CONSCIOUSNESS AND THE BODY

It is one of the ironies of the *Hippolytus* that a play centered on a virginal hero's devotion to mystical worship is all about bodies. Three of the climactic moments of its stage action focus on the body: the showing of Phaedra's sick body from the house after a long scene of puzzlement about what her disease is; the showing of that body as a corpse after Phaedra's suicide; and the carrying in of Hippolytus' broken body for the last scene, his onstage death.

The enactment of mythical narrative through bodies moving, and lying, on the stage is one of the means whereby the tragic poets converted epic and choral storytelling into its characteristically theatrical form. In many of the plays the climax of the spectacle is an injured, moribund, or freshly killed body on the stage.[1] In Euripides' *Heracles* and Sophocles' *Philoctetes*, and in the closing scenes of Sophocles' *Ajax, Trachiniae,* and *Antigone,* the physical suffering of the body is also vital to the theatrical effect. Aristotle observes that the sight of an anguished body either struggling with pain or just after death is a powerful resource. He describes the *pathos* (emotional excitation) that results from "destructive actions, such as deaths in the open and suffering and wounds and suchlike things" (*Poetics* 12.1452b).

In the *Hippolytus*, powerful corporeal imagery promotes a number of complex interactions between language, sexuality, theatricality, ritual, and community. The play moves outward from the intense physicality of Phaedra's world, and its antiworld of Hippolytus, toward the public realm of ritual and the consciousness of the polis. This is a movement from female to male and from private to public discourse. The ending expresses a conception of the community affirmed by the theater and therefore also reflects on the ability of tragedy to deal with the problem of suffering both in individual lives and in the city as a whole.

Woman's suffering, the play suggests, is bound up with her body. And by mirroring Phaedra, as Nicole Loraux has shown, Hippolytus arrives at what the Greeks generally represent as a female experience of the body's vulnerability.[2] What we would describe as the emotional anguish of eros that Phaedra suffers is expressed repeatedly as a direct physical threat to the body and to life itself: Phaedra is "worn down in her body" (131f.), "loosened in her limbs" (199), and finally (in polar contrast to the latter image) has the breath of life stopped by the constriction of the noose (769–72, 779–83). In this gradual expansion of the somatic force of eros, death is the logical result.

This totalizing effect reaches beyond Phaedra to engulf her entire world, thereby revealing the universal power of the source of her "sickness," the divinities of love (cf. 2–4, 447f., 1272–81). When Theseus stands beside her lifeless body, he becomes totally immersed in her all-enveloping cloud of suffering. He feels himself "destroyed" (845f.; cf. 839) and would descend to the darkness of the lower world (836f.). This pain of the house (*algos domôn*, 845) does not lend itself to the masculine remedy of heroic endurance or to formulation in speech; it is "neither endurable nor speakable" (*ou tlêton oude rhêton*, 847).

In expressing his grief, Theseus moves from the (predictable) images of his own destruction and the desolation of his house and children (846f.) to the extremes of upper and lower worlds, to superlatives, and to the all-inclusive geography of generalizations on mortality: the heavenly bodies and the breadth of the sky. "Best of women," he exclaims, "of all those whom the light of the sun and the star-visaged flash of night looks upon" (849–51).[3] Night and day are the basic delimiters of mortal time. The stars of the night sky are a familiar image for vast numbers or infinity (cf. *Iliad* 8.555ff.).

The play contains two scenes of formal lamentation. The lament over Phaedra at the midpoint is centered primarily on the private realm of house and children (cf. Theseus' *algos domôn*, 845; *erêmos oikos*, 847). Hippolytus' death is announced not by women from within the house but by a Messenger to "the lord of the land" (1153), who "brings a tale worthy of concern to you [Theseus] and the citizens, those who inhabit both the city of Athens and the limits of the Troezenian land" (1157–59). The repetition "citizens . . . city" (*politai . . . polis*) reinforces the public framing of Hippolytus' death.[4] The fatal event requires a vast, open landscape and seascape (1173ff.). The lament over him at the end involves "all the citizens" (1462) and a temporal framework that links the present with the remote future (1425–30, 1462–66).

The closing lament looks beyond the personal to the social. This scene is, in fact, an enactment of the social effect of tragedy; it consolidates into a "common grief" (*koinon achos*, 1462) the individual experiences of the separate members of the audience. The communal spirit of this grief—its "many tears" and "tales worthy of lamentation"—places the hero's death into the commemorative tradition of masculine heroism, where loss is framed and distanced by the achievement of lasting glory and its enactment in public ritual.[5]

In its formal design, the tragedy embraces both scenes of lament and thus transforms private grief into public spectacle. But the relationship between the two scenes remains one of ironies and contradictions rather than of progress and symmetry. Aphrodite, in her prologue, marks Hippolytus out for this doom because he is "the only one of the citizens" to declare her "the worst of divinities" and to refuse marriage (12f.).[6] "Only one of the citizens" and "all the citizens" (12 and 1462) frame the definition of Hippolytus as one set apart for special suffering. These terms also frame his problematical relation to the "city," in which marriage remains, after all, central. The institution of marriage that he has rejected (14, 616ff.) will perpetuate his name in the city (1423–30).

Phaedra fell in love with Hippolytus when he visited Athens for initiation into the Mysteries. The Troezenian women are troubled by the news of Phaedra's abstention from "Demeter's grain" because of her "hidden sickness" (131–40). Thus the starting point of the action, both in the causal events before the play has begun and in the unseen action behind the skene as the play is about to begin, involves a partial but curious glimpse of someone involved in "mysteries," a separate world from which the fascinated onlooker is excluded. This is the classic way of falling in love (generally with unhappy results), and it remains an operative pattern from Dante and Petrarch to today.[7]

Phaedra, Aphrodite explains in the prologue, looked on Hippolytus and at once "was held fast in her heart by a passion terrible" (Φαίδρα καρδίαν κατέσχετο / ἔρωτι δεινῷ, 27f.). Love comes through the eyes and spreads to the entire body; and it is appropriately the love goddess herself who tells the tale and expounds the physical workings of her own power. This passage may be echoing the *Homeric Hymn to Aphrodite*, where Zeus turns the tables on the goddess and makes her subject to her own aphroditic effect of desire through the eyes.[8] In Euripides' play, Phaedra founds the temple to Aphrodite in Athens, "feeling a love-passion for someone not in the place" (ἐρῶσ' ἔρωτ' ἔκδημον, 32). The brachyology, reinforced by the paronomasia, expresses the tension between the near and the far characteristic of violent eros. The temple, conspicuously visible, makes tangible a passion which cannot be shown for one who, as *ekdêmos* (out of the country), cannot be seen.

In Euripides' play (as in Seneca's), Hippolytus enters from the broad, undefined space "out of the country" (cf. *ekdêmos*), but he still does not belong to a public world.[9] Even as he stands before the gates of the palace, where Aphrodite's statue is prominent (101), he looks away to the private cultic space of his personal religion, the symbolical "uncut meadow" from which he dedicates a garland to his goddess, the chaste Artemis (73–87).[10] The special "converse" (*homilia*) that he would establish with his goddess in this setting—what Aphrodite in her prologue jealously labels "more than mortal converse" (19)—corresponds to his double removal from the ground of mortal physicality. First, Hippolytus removes the possibility of that exchange through the eyes by which erotic experience comes to men and women (as it did so powerfully to Phaedra). Second, he removes himself mentally from his physical setting to the metaphorical landscape of purity that he associates with religious devotion (cf. 73–87). His combination of the near and the far, the actual and the imagined, soon interacts disastrously with the parallel spatial unrealities stimulated by Phaedra's passion, her impossible longing for his meadows and woods in lines 208–22.[11] These contrasts between wish and reality are closely correlated with the cleavages in the spatial world of the play. Together with the motifs of asymmetrical, restricted, or secretive communication, they give an emotional depth to the intellectualist themes of the deceptiveness of appearances and the deceptiveness of language.

Aphrodite's temple on the Acropolis, by which Phaedra commemorates her love, "looks down upon this land," Theseus' city, the city where the play is being performed (κατόψιον γῆς τῆσδε, 30f.). It takes in the view (available from the Acropolis if not from the theater of Dionysus) across the Saronic Gulf to the scene of the present action in Troezen. It has also "looked down" on the spectacle that inspired Phaedra's love—namely, on the place of Hippolytus' initiation in Athens where Phaedra had seen him (perhaps the Eleusinion in the Agora, though this would not be visible from the presumed site of the temple on the southern slope of the Acropolis), and, figuratively, on the whole course of the action. The spectacle will reach into the future with the founding of another memorial to this "love" in Troezen (*erôs*, 1430).

Aphrodite, the speaker and the remote goddess who herself looks down on the stage from on high, virtually theatricalizes the entire civic space of Athens. She makes the audience the privileged spectators of a cut through time and a synoptic narrowing of space. She thus helps create a visual frame for the audience's perspective, a perspective on the theater as a part of the city. As a goddess with a temple on the Acropolis and as the one who inspired the passions that set the plot into motion, she relates the tragic space (with its X-ray vision of hidden, illicit emotions) to the civic space; but, given the kind of goddess she is, she simultaneously establishes that relation as problematical.

As a recounting of aetiological myth, the play has a place among the monuments of the past, while it simultaneously rearranges those monuments for its own purposes, in its own story. The features of its landscape belong to the remote past but become alive with new relevance to the citizens of the present. Speaking of and through the love goddess in his prologue, the poet creates a wiser, more dispassionate, more helpful monument than Phaedra's temple: the play itself.[12] This metamonument can include the opposite and complementary excesses of its two protagonists. It is dedicated to the love goddess so that others may avoid the sufferings that lie behind that earlier dedication on the Acropolis and its pendant, the rite on Troezen.

The two scenes that follow the prologue dramatize the process by which the passion hidden in the *phrenes* (breast) moves from enclosure to publicity and from privacy to the theatrical space outside the gates of the palace. First, the Nurse gets Phaedra to reveal the secret of her fatal wasting "disease." Having failed in earlier attempts, she tries a "better argument" or "better discourse" (*beltiô logon*, 292), which, as we have seen, consists in the benefit to women of revealing their secret ills to men (293–96). But all her rationalizing is rendered unnecessary by one key word at line 310: "Hippolytus." Like a magical utterance, her "Hippolytus" unlocks Phaedra's secret and sets the revelation inescapably into motion.

The second scene, the dialogue between the Nurse and Hippolytus, further destabilizes the relations between language and space. Phaedra listens, from outside, to the voices of those within. The emotions in the house are not merely spoken in a private conversation but are "shouted," with threatening publicity, to the earth and to the "unfolded" rays of the sun (601–3). "Silence" is the first word of the scene: Phaedra's tense command to the chorus in line 564, "Be silent, women; we are undone." The Nurse's request to Hippolytus for silence (603) echoes Phaedra's request of forty lines before, but now meets refusal, in strong contrast to the chorus's willingness to be silent in lines 565–68.[13] The "unspoken" or "unspeakable" word now risks becoming "a public tale" (*koinos muthos*) to be pronounced "among the multitude" (*en polloisi . . . legein*, 609f.).[14]

At the next crisis, Theseus (played by the same actor who plays Phaedra) stands before the gates to receive another version of the secrets that are being revealed from within. "Alas," the chorus cries. "You are showing forth a word [tale] that is the beginning of woes" (αἰαῖ, κακῶν ἀρχηγὸν ἐκφαίνεις λόγον, 881). The epic phraseology reinforces the shift from a private, domestic event to a public action laden with meaning for the city and its values. "I shall no longer hold down [*kathexô*] in the gates of my mouth," Theseus replies, "this thing of hard passage outward, a woe destructive" (882–85). The motif of bringing forth to the tongue what lies hidden in the "breast" (612) here shifts from Hippolytus to Theseus, from threat to actuality. The consequences of uttering (out-ering) the contents of the *phrên* (breast) are just as destructive as they were feared to be in the previous scene.[15] The victim of this destruction, however, is now Hippolytus rather than Phaedra. The irony of this reversal is all the sharper because Theseus' verb for repressing the outcry, "holding it down" (*katechein*), had described the violent passion that "holds down" the heart of Phaedra in the prologue (*katescheto*, 27).

Theseus' situation, like Phaedra's, dramatizes both the emotional consequences and the theatrical effect of bringing dangerous passions, with their violent social and personal disruptions, from the inside of the *oikos* out into theatrical visibility before the "gates" of the palace represented by the stage front. This unique, public (and possibly all-male) space exposes feminine emotions that would usually reach neither the ears nor eyes of men (295–97; cf. 395f. and *pros andras . . . thuraious*, "to the men outside," 408f.). A self-conscious craftsman sensitive to his audience, Euripides may well have been aware of the disturbing power of releasing and revealing such passions to his audience. He may well have had inklings of the sort of accusations that Aristophanes would level against him a quarter century later (*Frogs* 1049–54):

> *Euripides.* But say, you cross-grained censor of mine, how my Stheneboeas could harm the state.
>
> *Aeschylus.* Full many a noble dame, the wife of a noble citizen, hemlock took,
> And died, unable the shame and sin of your Bellerophon-scenes to brook.
>
> *Euripides.* Was then, I wonder, the tale I told of Phaedra's passionate love untrue?
>
> *Aeschylus.* Not so: but tales of incestuous vice the sacred poet should hide from view,
> Nor ever exhibit and blazon forth on the public stage to the public ken.
> (Trans. B. B. Rogers)

"There is nothing trustworthy in the tongue," Phaedra warns, for the tongue "knows how to advise [or reproach, *nouthetein*] the thoughts of others [literally, thoughts of those outside the doors of the house, *phronêmata thuraia*] but itself acquires most evils for itself" (395–97). This is a rather contorted way of saying that talking is dangerous, and that criticizing others is one thing, but talking too freely about yourself can get you into trouble. The phraseology, however, has the effect of personifying the organ of speech, like the "double voices" of lines 916–31, and associating the dangers of female speech with the women's passage out-of-doors, among "men" (*andres*, 396).[16] When Phaedra's language, through the "silent" tablets, does speak outside, among men, it is more persuasive, and dangerously so, than the face-to-face conversation between males.

In tragedy the language of woman is part of her sexuality and cannot escape being, in some way, eroticized. Her speech is like her "bed" or "body" (cf. 407–10): when it is brought outside the house, to men, it causes shame and trouble.[17] Phaedra's mode of addressing Theseus compounds the ironies inherent in the sexualization of her speaking and her silence. When she breaks this silence, overcoming the traditional inhibitions about speaking of her body to men (cf. 295f.), she plays out the worst cultural stereotype of women. She is revealing a sexually shameful tale about her body ostensibly to defend the honor of her bed, but in fact she is also practicing murderous guile and destructive persuasion, like Aeschylus' Clytaemnestra or Pindar's Hippolyta.[18] Yet she is far from being an evil woman, as the gods know (cf. 1300f.); and the price of her successful persuasion (like Deianeira's in a different way) is her own death.

By leaving her message for Theseus within the gates of the house, Phaedra preempts that "face-to-face" meeting with him that Hippolytus threatened to watch in silence — the meeting when the absent lord of the community ceases to be "away" from it (*ekdêmos*, 659–63; cf. 32). This silent speaking enables her to avoid the appearance of "shaming her bed with respect to men outside" (*andras thuraious*, 408f.; cf. 395f.), that is, losing her reputation of wifely chastity in society. By "unfolding" (864) Phaedra's tablets in the inner chambers within the gates (808–10, cf. 792), Theseus is overcome by the destructive consequences of Phaedra's sexuality. This act of "unfolding" is a victory of female seductiveness, for it negates Hippolytus' attempt to "unfold" the truth of his own nature, now buried under Theseus' "noble words" about Phaedra (984f.).[19] With this reversal Hippolytus changes from accuser to accused. Instead of being the champion of open speech and face-to-face encounter among "men outside" or among the "strangers" who constitute the eyes and ears of society (408f., cf. 660–63), he becomes the deceiver and brazen liar (cf. 916–42). His own ambivalence and vacillation between promises to conceal and threats of revealing (cf. 604–12, 656–60) turn back against him, thanks to Phaedra's unhesitating decisiveness about speaking, her last act in life and in the play (716–31).

Hippolytus' threat at the critical moment to keep silence but to watch Phaedra's looks in Theseus' presence (660–62) contributes to the fateful change of Phaedra's love to hate. When he threatens to look on her face with watchful eyes, he sets up an antaphroditic inversion of Phaedra looking at him in silence and dedicating her temple to her secret love for one who is out of her presence (*ekdêmos*, 27–32).

Defeated by her lies, Hippolytus leaves Troezen, "unfolding his hands" to the gods in an oath of his innocence (1190–93). The gesture is an ironical echo of his cry to the sun's unfolding rays when he first hears of Phaedra's love from the Nurse in line 601. It brings no reply from celestial Zeus. Instead, as Hippolytus takes the whip "into his hands" (ἐς χεῖρας, 1194; cf. ἀναπτύξας χέρας, "unfolding his hands," 1190), the answer comes from the fearful "roar from the earth like Zeus' thunder" (1201). This sound destroys both sight and hearing (1202, 1205–17). Air and space change to entrapment as Hippolytus, in a mirror image of Phaedra's death by the noose, is "enfolded" (literally, "enwoven") into his reins (ἡνίαισιν ἐμπλακείς, 1236) and caught in an entangling constriction that is "hard to be unfolded."[20] The following ode on Eros' airy flight over the earth and "all that the sun beholds" (1274–81) sets off this inversion from open landscape to fatal constriction.

As we moved from Phaedra to Hippolytus, the spatial field changed from intimate secrets in private space to increasingly open vistas, culminating in the Troezenian shore and the bull's attack. But Hippolytus' catastrophe returns us to enclosure. The shore where Hippolytus takes his accustomed ride, and which his hunting companions address sadly as a part of civic space (*poliêtis aktê*, 1126), soon becomes only the border of a wild sea that blots out the familiar landmarks, the places by which the city relates to other cities and to its own past (cf. 1197, 1198–1200, 1205–9).[21]

For Phaedra, concerned with how she is seen or shown and still concealing her love, time is a mirror that reveals base men for what they are (428–30).[22] Applied to Hippolytus, the image follows the play's inversions of visible and invisible (1078f.): "Would that I could stand and look at myself, how I weep at the evils that I am suffering." Hippolytus is unable to show to others the self that he thinks he "really" is. His mirror can only reflect a self-enclosed and self-defined view of "himself" back to himself. The object he sees is his lamentation over the injustice done to him.

Hippolytus' last action on the stage is to cover his face (1458). This powerful stage effect harks back to the early scenes of Phaedra's concealment (cf. 243) and also to the generalizations of the Nurse about the hiddenness of the true goals of life (cf. 194).[23] This circular movement as much continues Phaedra's (and Aphrodite's) triumph as it vindicates Hippolytus. Only when his face is turned away from the public space of the orchestra to its covering in death and to the gates of Hades that he sees open before him (1447) can his inner spirit or mind (*phrên*) become visible to the one spectator to whom it most matters. Theseus, with an exclamation of grief, now calls Hippolytus' *phrên* "pious and noble" (οἴμοι φρενὸς σῆς εὐσεβοῦς τε κἀγαθῆς, 1454). It is among the ironies surrounding the problem of discerning a person's *phrenes* that the words echo Phaedra's speech at the point when she is still resolved to die in noble silence, believing that "a just and noble mind" is the only worthy object of struggle (γνώμην δικαίαν κἀγαθήν, 427).

Viewed in relation to his mistaken certainty about himself in his speech about the mirror (1078f., above), Hippolytus' last gesture also continues his self-delusion. His goddess descends from Olympus to earth "to reveal [Hippolytus'] just spirit, so that he might die with honor" (ἐκδεῖξαι φρένα... δικαίαν, ὡς ὑπ' εὐκλείας θάνῃ, 1298f.). But something about that "spirit" (*phrên*) remains veiled, unrevealed, even in its moment of fullest glory. By repeating Phaedra's initial gesture of covering the face, Hippolytus remains identified with the female and stands far from the full radiance of conspicuous martial glory or the masculine fame of the noble death that Artemis' "death with glory" might suggest (1299).

The goddess who used Phaedra, however, does not attempt so much for her. Her sole hope for death with honor lay in the silence about her passion, which the cult of Aphrodite will totally refuse (1429f.). Euripides' ending, unlike Seneca's and Racine's, makes little attempt to give Phaedra a heroism that somehow parallels Hippoly-tus'. Artemis' brief epitaph is only a small step in that direction (1300f.). Phaedra's "nobility," like her "glory," remains ambiguous (*gennaiotês, eukleia*; cf. 717–21 and 1300f.). In Seneca's play, Phaedra's memory remains a disturbing presence, something that Theseus cannot simply forget or leave to Artemis (Diana) to accommodate.[24] The Senecan Theseus can curse her but not entirely forget her, and the play ends with her burial as well as Hippolytus' (*Phaedra* 1279–80): "As for her, let the earth press on her when she is buried and let the soil lie heavy on her unholy head." Euripides' Artemis mentions Phaedra, but her gift of cultic commemoration for Hippolytus suc-cessfully effaces her presence.

"A COMMON GRIEF FOR ALL THE CITIZENS"?

The next, and last, step in the vindication of Hippolytus is the exten-sion of private grief to the public realm, as "a common grief for all the citizens" (1462). After so much has been kept disastrously hidden, this epilogue gathers the entire citizenry in the theatrical inclusiveness of a pity which all have experienced and all have a right to share. It claims the theater's ability to open private grief and destructive in-wardness to the public, communal space where those passions, by the fact of their theatrical exposure and representation, work some good for the very realm that the hero rejected. Yet the communal sorrow is strangely at odds with Hippolytus' own rejection of the communal realm of "citizens" (cf. 1016–20). The discrepancy keeps open the difference between the tragic content of the myth repre-sented and the social context of the theater.

This inclusion of the entire polis in grief for Hippolytus reverses his disgrace in the eyes of the king and father who had shouted to the polis his outrage at what he took to be his son's crime inside the house (*iô polis*, 884). In refuting the charges against him, Hippolytus had taken an oath that he should be *apolis*, without a city, if the accu-sations were true (1029–32).[25] The Messenger announced the news of his death as "a tale worthy of concern [*merimna*] to the citi-zens" (1157–59). At the end, however, he is a subject of "concern" (*merimna*)—that is, an object of praise in song—to maidens approach-ing marriage (*mousopoios merimna*, 1428–30). The language evokes the praise poetry of Greek lyric, especially the odes for victorious athletes.[26] In tragedy the honor that the community gives to such heroes is shot through with ironies. This male hero receives a place in the female part of the marriage rites, so that his recognition by his father is balanced by the various forms of feminization that attend his life story as we see its completion in the final scene.[27] A cultic role in the women's side of marriage is an unexpected change from the male chorus's song at Hippolytus' fatal departure from the city for the seashore (1131–41, and note the theme of marriage in lines 1140f.). Even so, to have a share in the Muses as a *mousopoios merimna* is to be a part of the continuing traditions and the social memory of what, despite the power of Phaedra's writing, is still an oral culture.

Superficially, then, the breach between public and private, between male and female space, seems to be closing. The Messenger's opening declaration that Hippolytus' death is a matter of civic concern (1157–59) seems to be vindicated in the chorus's "common grief for all the citizens" (1462). Tears are shared in public, and grief embraces both domestic and civic spaces. This civic lament in theatrical space supersedes both the privacy of Theseus' lament over Phaedra and the mythical remoteness of the grieving sisters of Phaethon in the second stasimon (737–42).[28] Outpourings of personal sorrow are not to be left uncontrolled.[29] As we move from the domestic and natural worlds, respectively, to the city, we also move toward a more restrained, ritualized expression of grief.

The "amber-lit flash of tears" for Phaethon belongs to a remote, unreal setting of river and ocean, far from the cities of men. This is a grief unmitigated by the civic forms of commemoration—whether in the form of ritual, story, or song—and unrestrained by the control of social norms. It remains inarticulate (there are only tears, no words), futile, part of nature's beauty and strangeness, but not human.[30] The tears over Phaedra were shed in the context of the domestic woes of the house (852–55); the tears that the Troezenian girls will bestow as a metaphorical fruit of grief for Hippolytus to pluck (1427) belong to the domestic context of marriage. Artemis, who reports this ritual grief as a consolation for Hippolytus, herself cannot weep (1437–39).[31] But the tears that end the play, though in the future, belong to citizens and to the city's memory (1465f.).

This ending holds out a possible alternative view of the story told about Hippolytus. Instead of a tale of intrigue inside the house, characterized by the interior, female "hidden grief" of Phaedra (*krupton penthos*, 138f.), it is a public myth and a public sorrow appropriate to the death of a hero. It belongs among the "tales deserving grief" of "great men," the last words of the play.[32] Instead of the dangerous female privacy of festering, isolated, asocial passion, Hippolytus' story moves to the public space of the polis and to visible, communal gestures. This change is appropriate to the theater, with its public context and its dramatization of masculine endurance and a grief "for all the citizens." Hence the play's last word, *katechousin* (hold out, prevail), now refers to the long continuity of the public voice in the city and the communal memory, in contrast to the verb's earlier meaning, the required suppression of a shameful *logos* into silence or oblivion (cf. 27, 883).[33]

But the picture is not quite so neat. Hippolytus' death during the characteristically male action of driving a chariot turns into the feminine experience of the vulnerability and penetrability of the body.[34] Phaedra acts out the masculine heroic ethos of dying for the sake of fame, or *eukleia*.[35] This confusion of sexual roles also questions the gender-specific nature of morally colored terms such as *noble, glorious, manly*, and *brave* (*gennaios, eukleês, andreios*). When Artemis from on high "reveals" the truth to Theseus (1288f., 1298f.), she would make him "conceal" his body in the underworld, like Phaedra (1290–94). The goddess's suggestion that he leave life by an "upward flight" (*ptênos anô*, 1292) pictures the suicide of this hypermasculine hero in the generally female form of death by hanging, like Phaedra's, which he had described as leaping off to Hades like a bird (828f.). Instead of winning glory, Theseus risks acquiring "shame," *aischynê*, Phaedra's chief concern in the first part of the play (1291).

Hippolytus' closing gesture of covering his face is part of his downward journey to Hades (1447), not the upward movement to the heavens associated with *kleos*.[36] He asks for what would be a manly death by the spear (1375), but his end is overdetermined as female suffering. His death agonies repeat Phaedra's cries in the pains of love at the beginning of the play, and he reenacts her initial impulse toward interiority and secrecy. Even as they imitate one another—and because they imitate one another—male and female remain disastrously polarized. The collapse of sexual differentiation produces chaos for the house, the community, and the realm of moral action generally.[37]

If I am guilty, Hippolytus had sworn, "may I perish without glory and without name" (1028). Thanks to Artemis, this self-curse is finally averted; but the "name" that Hippolytus does receive at the end is as ambiguous as the "glory" of Phaedra with which it is interwoven (1428–30):

ἀεὶ δὲ μουσοποιὸς ἐς σὲ παρθένων
ἔσται μέριμνα, κοὐκ ἀνώνυμος πεσὼν
ἔρως ὁ Φαίδρας ἐς σὲ σιγηθήσεται.

Always will there be for you the Muse-fashioned care of maidens, nor will the passion of Phaedra, having fallen upon you, be without name and kept in silence.

Nearly every word of Artemis' prophecy has an ironic undercurrent. The "Muse-fashioned concern" harks back to the song of the hunter chorus at Hippolytus' departure (1135ff. and 1157). But this song at the end is of maidens, not men. Remaining among maidens, *parthenoi*, in the marginal realm of Artemis, Hippolytus has failed to cross the divide from adolescence to full manhood.[38] The terms of his fame, furthermore, are negative: "not nameless," "not kept in silence."[39] What lives on is not the resounding fame in the "hearing" of men (*kleos*) but the "nonsilence" of a woman's eros.

The litotes of the "nonsilence" and the "not unnamed love," then, carries an undertone of the triumph of a woman's vengeful "silent" speech and perhaps of Hippolytus' own ambivalence about the silence imposed by his oath. The afterglow of his life's achievement comes to be constituted of everything that he has abjured (cf. 1423–27 and 14, ἀναίνεται δὲ λέκτρα κοὐ ψαύει γάμων, "He refuses the bed and does not touch marriage"). Artemis' compensation even enables Phaedra to possess him forever in a kind of posthumous eros.[40] But Phaedra's quasi victory is not free of ambiguities. She had twice accepted death in order to keep her love silent (cf. 310, 352, 710–22). At the end she is joined forever with Hippolytus in a public "naming" of her love (*erôs*), whose most important feature is its "nonsilence" (κοὐκ ἀνώνυμος . . . σιγηθήσεται, 1429f.).

The Homeric warrior receives a *sêma*, a conspicuous marker or tomb, to commemorate the martial glory that will survive him.[41] What is *episêmos*, marked out as conspicuous, for Hippolytus on the prominent hill of Athens is the temple of the goddess of love (30–33), about whom the Servant admonishes him early in the play (88ff.).

Aphrodite has a temple at the city's summit and a statue before the house, in the presence of which she is declared "conspicuous" (*episêmos*) among mortals (101–3). The commemoration that Hippolytus receives both in the marriage rites at the end and in the temple at the beginning, moreover, is given him not for what he does but for what is done to him. The active role comes from Phaedra, from her female passion of eros. Hippolytus is only its passive, unwilling object.

Phaedra's part in the foundation of the temple is anomalous in still another respect. If we follow the manuscript reading, Phaedra "named it as established because of Hippolytus" (or "over Hippolytus"), yet no one but Phaedra and Aphrodite need necessarily know that the temple is built in Hippolytus' name—from his point of view a dubious honor.[42] Thus the "naming" of this monument too is interwoven with silence. A woman's relation to the public discourse of the city, even in the realm of Aphrodite, must remain problematical. The counterpart to this ambiguous "naming the temple for [or after] Hippolytus" in Phaedra's tragedy is the "nonsilence" that attends her love at the end (1429f.).[43]

A woman's virtue, according to Pericles, consists in being talked about as little as possible, for good or for ill (Thucydides 2.45.2). Once her love is revealed (596), Phaedra's name is not spoken again by any human character in the play. (In fact, her name is mentioned only six times in the tragedy, as against fourteen occurrences of "Hippolytus.") When Artemis announces the marriage rites at the end, it is to compensate and commemorate Hippolytus, not Phaedra. Whatever reading is adopted in line 33, the city's monument to Aphrodite is named for Hippolytus, but Phaedra receives only the ambiguous "nonsilence" about her eros.

Despite his earlier grief over Phaedra, Theseus has not a word to say about her in the last third of the play. He does not even take up Artemis' correction of Hippolytus about the "third" victim of Aphrodite's revenge in lines 1403f. (where the suppression of Phaedra's name is particularly striking).[44] In his last speech Theseus invokes the "glorious" (*kleina*) territory of Athens to lament his loss (1459–61):

ὦ κλείν' Ἀθηνῶν Παλλάδος θ' ὁρίσματα,
οἵου στερήσεσθ' ἀνδρός. ὦ τλήμων ἐγώ,
ὡς πολλά, Κύπρι, σῶν κακῶν μεμνήσομαι.

O glorious boundaries of Athens and of Pallas Athena,[45] of what a man are you deprived. O miserable me, long shall I remember, Kypris, your evils.

These lines carry all the more weight because they are the last utterance of the only conventionally heroic personage in the play, and they associate Hippolytus with the "glory" of the civic realm and the language of the polis. In stating Athens' loss, Theseus calls Hippolytus *anêr*. Yet what the king "remembers," in the first-person verb, is the power of the goddess, that is, the realm of sexuality that blocked Hippolytus' passage to manhood (cf. *anêr*, 1460). Through its contents—Aphrodite's destructive power—Theseus' "remembrance" both parallels and completes the irony of Artemis' promise of commemoration for the "passion of Phaedra" in lines 1429f.

In one sense Hippolytus does become a man: he proves his endurance in meeting death bravely, like a warrior (*karterei . . . kekarterêtai*; "Endure . . . My enduring has been completed," 1456f.). By conferring on his killer the "purity" that he had so narrowly sought in his unbalanced way of life, he also achieves, at a new human level, his most cherished value.[46] This extension of his purity to a male relationship contrasts with his previous involvement with Artemis and brings Hippolytus as close as he will get to the masculine world of the polis.

Hippolytus' absolution of Theseus also reverses the moral direction set by the gods. Artemis will take her revenge on Aphrodite by killing "a mortal most dear to her" (1420–22). For a moment Hippolytus overreaches mortal limits and wishes that men could curse the gods.[47] But in the human world he chooses not to perpetuate the gods' cycle of anger, vengeance, and retaliation, with its cost in undeserved human suffering. Instead, he and Theseus together enact the efficacy of those institutions by which a civilized community deals with crimes of bloodshed.[48] When Artemis departs, we return from a primitive world of blood revenge to the legal and religious procedures of the polis, from the unrestrained emotions of the gods' childlike narcissism to consideration for others and the rule of law. The fact that Hippolytus seals his promise by an oath to "Artemis who conquers by the bow" (1451), the very instrument of her future vengeance through an innocent mortal (1422), stresses the contrast between divine law and human law. It may also suggest that Hippolytus, with perhaps merciful innocence, still does not fully understand what his goddess is. Artemis can offer only a remote cult of marriage and indirect punishment of the agent of the disaster, both apart from the civic sphere. With Theseus and the chorus Hippolytus enters the areas of legal regulation and civic commemoration.

On the personal level, however, Hippolytus' recovery of what he regards as his privileged relation to "purity" appears in the same negative construction as his fame. In the latter case his story is "not unnamed in silence"; in the former, he is to leave his killer's hand "not impure" (*ouk anagnos*, 1448). If Euripides, then, uses the female as the fundamentally Other, he concomitantly presents the traditional male heroism as alienated from itself. The ambiguity of Phaedra's mixture of disgrace and nobility revealed by Artemis near the play's end (1300f.) is matched by the ambiguity of Hippolytus' feminized heroization, by the passivity of his role in the events that bring him honor, and by the privacy of the area in which he shows his "nobility" and his "endurance" (*gennaiotês, karteria*, 1452, 1456f.).[49]

Yet these negative formulations of Hippolytus' honor, by defamiliarizing his form of *kleos*, intimate a new kind of heroism, one that Euripides will explore further in his *Heracles*. The private world, personal ties, and the quality of feelings among men become more important than deeds of physical prowess. Although this male emotional bonding has the civic realm as its background (1462f.), Euripides nevertheless makes fully visible the distance between these more inward values and the traditional heroism embodied in Theseus, champion of Athens and defender of law and order against outlaws and monsters (974–80).

HEROIC FAME AND TRAGIC GRIEF

In the epic the appropriate response to tales of woe is *terpsis*, joy or pleasure. Euripides frequently calls attention to the Homeric paradox of "taking joy" in lamentation.[50] At the end of *Hippolytus* this paradoxical affinity between "joy in tears" and aesthetic pleasure contains a characteristically Euripidean self-consciousness about the theatrical effect. Because the tears of future brides commemorate Hippolytus and Phaedra (1425–28), even the marriage ritual appears as an extension of the suffering dramatized in the play.[51] Despite his woman-hating, sex-denying ways, this prudish youth is forced to a sympathetic recognition, at least on the level of cultic symbolism, of the anxiety and pain that young girls experience in marriage, for this ceremony is as much a ritual of mourning and separation for them as it is a ritual of joyful reintegration and reincorporation.[52] Comedy, of course, handles a concluding marriage ritual in exactly the opposite way, as in Aristophanes' *Peace* or *Birds*.

In contrast to this remote and problematical marriage ritual stands the immediate theatrical catharsis of shared, communal mourning. Indirectly Euripides establishes these communal tears as the proper theatrical response. Instead of the remote grandeur of epic or choral narratives (such as occur in the paeans and victory odes of Pindar and Bacchylides, and indeed in the Phaethon ode of this play), the theater presents men and women with whom its audience can sympathize directly, emotionally, and communally. The *koinon achos* (common grief) is the emotion proper to a theater that has become conscious of itself as a uniquely communal form, even when its characters are royal personages of the heroic age. Personal grief is lifted from the level of individual response to the level of self-consciously communal reaction.

In making the reunion of father and son the climactic point of intense feeling between males, Euripides is drawing on the greatest scenes in the literary tradition. Behind him stand the closing books of the *Iliad*, especially the displaced father-son meeting of Priam and Achilles in book 24 and the reunions of Odysseus with his son and father in *Odyssey* 16 and 24, respectively. By combining the reunion of father and son with communal lamentation, Euripides blends intense personal emotion with the approved heroic models of masculine behavior. The newfound closeness between father and son, then, becomes the occasion for the bonding of citizens *qua* citizens, for this scene re-creates the past as both public myth and as emotionally involving (male) experience. But, as in the law courts and assembly, that bonding, however deeply rooted in the emotional response of pity, fear, and sympathy, does not exclude intellectual evaluation and moral judgment. The theatrical frame of the spectacle and the dialogical presentation of all the events encourage an intellectual distancing and a spirit of critical alertness.

This intellectual spirit, however, is only a small part of the tragic effect. When heroic narrative became part of the democratic city-state, it helped create and instill a common moral and emotional sensibility. Tragedy not only strengthened and deepened this communal sensibility but also increasingly examined its parameters, the contiguous and contrasting areas of experience in the polis: athletics and public life, sexuality and politics, paternity and citizenship, loyalty to the household and the responsibilities of civic action. Sophocles raises these issues by dramatizing conflicts such as those between the family's care for its dead and the political integrity of the city in the *Antigone*, or by exploring the clash between the destructive, antisocial traits of great men and women and their contributions to the society as a whole: such are Ajax, Philoctetes, Heracles in the *Trachiniae*, Electra, and Oedipus in the *Coloneus*. Euripides uses the somewhat more indirect technique of exploring the tensions between ritual forms (including their origins) and the contents of a given rite (as here in the combination of marriage and mourning for Hippolytus).

These closing rituals present a glaring anomaly. Theseus' Troezen finds room to declare as "a common grief for all the citizens" the death of a man who deliberately refused to identify with the concerns of citizens. The generosity of the mourning ritual can reach out to grieve over a social misfit.[53] But this generosity has no place for Phaedra, who is referred to only briefly by Artemis.[54]

For all her preoccupation with her personal emotional life, Phaedra, Minoan princess though she is, conveys a far greater sense of what it means to be the citizen of a polis than Hippolytus does. Contemplating the effects of compromising herself, she recognizes the dangers and responsibilities of participating in the *ekklesia* and wishes that her children "may dwell in the city of glorious Athens free, flourishing in the right to open speech" (*parrhêsia* 421f.). Hippolytus, on the other hand, wants nothing more than "ever to be happy with his dear friends of the best families" (1018). For him competition means participation in the Panhellenic, not the civic, "contests," avoiding the "dangers" of being ruler of a city (1016–19). Throughout this section of his defense (1013–21) he invokes an apolitical quietism or withdrawal (*apragmosynê*) that Theseus, traditionally the energetic founder-hero and also an embodiment of Athenian activism, can hardly be expected to approve.[55] By contrast, Phaedra acknowledges the competitive spirit of the polis: she is sensitive to how a mother's shame harms a son's *parrhêsia* and *eukleia* (426f., 717). Is it an accidental irony that Theseus, addressing the "glorious boundaries" of Athens (or Athena) in his closing words (1460), echoes Phaedra's reference to "glorious Athens" in line 423? Hippolytus never utters a patriotic sentiment of this nature.

This closing commemoration of the youth's death as a "public" grief, however, may be less communal than the transmitted (and usually accepted) text suggests. Do we know for certain that the chorus of Troezenian women, speaking for the city as a whole, pronounces this public lament? There is evidence for two choral groups in the play: the regular women's chorus just mentioned and also a (doubtless smaller) chorus of Hippolytus' hunter companions.[56] These latter enter with the hero in his dedicatory song to Artemis in the first scene (58ff.). They also share with the female chorus the shock and dismay at his exile shortly before the news of the disaster (1102–52). Is it possible that these young men reenter with the "servants" (*dmôes*, 1358) who carry in the shattered form at line 1342?[57] Given the ease with which the manuscripts confuse the attribution of parts and the rarity of double choruses, it is possible that this attribution of the final lyrics was lost in transmission (cf. the still unresolved problem of the final lyrics of the *Trachiniae*).[58]

Suppose, then, that the hunter chorus, and not the female chorus, pronounces the closing tribute. In that case, these lines would not be an objective statement of the city's view but rather an indication of loyalty and trust by Hippolytus' own followers—important, to be sure, but definitely a partial perspective. If this is so, the tensions in the hero's relation to the city, civic space, and civic ritual remain taut to the very end.

INDIVIDUAL AND COMMUNITY IN EURIPIDES

As these last points imply, the balance between the public and the private in Euripides is nearly always fraught with tension. The *Bacchae* is perhaps the most striking example, with its dramatization of the doom of the royal house of Thebes, on the one hand, and its brilliant psychological portrait of neurotic repression, on the other. Sophocles and Euripides differ markedly in this regard. Euripides' characters have personal lives less closely defined by the framework of the house or city to which they belong. This autonomy of the personal enables Euripides to create such relatively marginal figures as Hippolytus, Medea, Electra, Ion, and even Andromache, Helen, Heracles (of the *Heracles Mad*), and Orestes and Iphigeneia (of the *Iphigeneia in Tauris*)—figures whose peculiar nature and interest for the audience develop apart from a communal context. Euripides has no dearth of tragic figures whose tragic situation is inseparable from the sufferings of their city, as is the case for the protagonists of the *Suppliants*, *Trojan Women*, *Hecuba*, *Phoenissae*, and *Iphigeneia in Aulis*. Where he focuses the suffering on the female figures, however, as he does in these later plays, the image of the polis that they embody is the polis captured, in ruins, or riven by inner conflict.

It is instructive to compare the ending of the *Hippolytus* with comparable scenes by Sophocles—particularly the endings of the *Trachiniae* and the *Philoctetes*. Like Euripides, Sophocles ends with a private meeting of two male protagonists, around whom, directly or indirectly, hovers divine presence or divine pronouncement. But in the two Sophoclean endings the personal intimacy is far less important than the divinely established destiny, its meaning for the community, and the heroic past and future.[59] The same is true for the ending of the *Ajax*, where funeral ritual reintegrates the protagonist into the heroic community; and for the finale of the *Oedipus at Colonus*, where the private suffering of Oedipus' daughters, though not disregarded, is kept subordinate to the future blessings for Athens and the imminent doom of Thebes.[60]

The *Trachiniae* also concentrates on the father-son relation at the end; but it focuses far more strongly than does the *Hippolytus* on the formal authority of the father in the house (*Trachiniae* 1220ff.), on the expectations of heroic behavior and the hero's relation to the heroic tradition, and on the ever-problematical relation of the action to the justice of Zeus (1275–79).[61] In like manner, the *Philoctetes* looks beyond the personal bond between Philoctetes and Neoptolemus to the public dimension of the action in the hero's return to Troy and to the "great destiny" (*megalê moira*) that the hero is to fulfill in the history of his people. The *Antigone* also ends with a powerful father-son scene of sorts as Creon returns to the stage carrying the body of his son. Here too the destruction that takes place within his *oikos* involves the city through the king's (unsuccessful) role as mediator between the natural and supernatural orders, the upper and lower worlds.

Euripides' ending stays closer to the personal but keeps the personal in a problematic relation to the public realm of both city and cult. The closing tableau of the father's and the citizens' lament seems a far more authentic and satisfying ritualizing response to suffering than the cult founded by Artemis in Troezen. Is Euripides suggesting that the official cultic forms, deriving as they do from the remote Olympians, no longer address the emotional core of suffering as effectively as the catharsis brought by the tragic spectacle? Is the public affirmation of sadness in the play's closing lines really appropriate to a marginal, privatistic dropout like Hippolytus? Does he really belong among "the great men" to be mourned by "all the citizens"? Does not Artemis' gift of marriage songs to enshrine Phaedra's eros only memorialize the violence, bitterness, and mistrust that make human relations into failures and lives into tragedy?

Euripides' ending, to be sure, allows for a certain continuum of feeling between the personal and the civic, between the father's mourning in the house and the mourning among all the citizens. As the austere Artemis departs, the act of mourning moves from distant, anonymous brides to the theatrical here and now, the actual people present onstage, the actors and chorus who have been directly touched by the deaths in the house. The tears too change from a metaphorical "fruit" to a ritual "beating" in sorrow (1427 and 1462f.). Consolation now becomes an immediate communication, within the framework of house, community, and, of course, theater.[62]

At the same time, the shifting between present and remote future, between emotional lyricism and gnomic generality, and between Athens and Troezen reminds us that the events we have witnessed have a universal as well as a local significance. In viewing these events as the work (in part) of divinities whose power extends over the whole world, we also see them as the local manifestations of something much larger.[63] We become the spectators not only of Athenian and Troezenian myth but of the human condition in its tragic dimension. Through its tragic theater, among its other cultural achievements, Athens lays claim to being "the education of Greece," in Pericles' idealizing view (Thucydides 2.41.1). It can absorb and recast, in simultaneously Athenian and Panhellenic form, the myths of other communities. Thus the local, uniquely Athenian "contests" of plays in the competitions at the City Dionysia can contain the "Hellenic contests" (*Hellenikoi agônes*) in which Hippolytus finds an alternative to civic life (1016). This competition is at the center of Athenian civic life, but it also applies Panhellenic myths to the personal struggles and sufferings involved in being human. The Athenian play itself becomes a *Hellenikos agôn*, a contest that has meaning for all of Greece, and "an education for Greece."

In a fragment of the lost *Alexander*, the chorus's phrase at the end of the *Hippolytus*, "*koinon achos*," refers to the death that comes to all men (fragment 46 Nauck): πάντων τὸ θανεῖν· τὸ δὲ κοινὸν ἄχος / μετρίως ἀλγεῖν σοφία μέλεται (Dying comes to all. But wisdom practises moderation in the pain of the common woe). Through the experience of this "common woe" in the tragic spectacle, the individual spectator participates in the "community" of all who suffer mortality, and he thereby experiences the brotherhood and the solace of grief contained in the poetic tradition.

As in the weeping of Odysseus at Demodocus' songs of Troy or in the meeting between Priam and Achilles in the last book of the *Iliad*, tears shed in the memory of suffering are the universal bond between men—and women too, if the female chorus does, in fact, speak the closing section. To create this bond, private, concealed suffering must become the "common grief" shared in public.[64] The mortal spectators are made conscious of their solidarity as *deiloisi brotoisi* (miserable mortals). The dry eyes of Artemis (1437f.), in contrast with the citizens' lamentations, define the mortal condition.[65] This very absence of expressive grief in the goddess constitutes the sign of tragedy's unifying emotional effect on its human audience. This ending also reflects on the means by which men can grasp their condition through symbolical representation. The bonding in a shared experience of grief and its release in tears belong both to the tragic chorus and to the theatrical audience as an enactment of the unifying effect of tragedy on the polis. In this way the universal "delight in weeping" in epic, kept at a distance by the third-person narration, becomes the mixed, complex theatrical experience of common grief for an Athenian youth, performed live by an Athenian citizen chorus before their fellow Athenians.

This mourning brings together the three spatial realms of house, city, and the remote, nonhuman world of nature and the gods. The universe over which Aphrodite and Eros rule (1–5, 447–50, 1272–82) is full of mortal tears (cf. 738ff.)—tears that a goddess cannot shed. When viewed against the private mourning for Phaedra in the house at the midpoint of the play and the remote lament of Phaethon's sisters, beyond the limits of civic time and space (737–42), the "common grief for all the citizens" at the end performs its socially reintegrative function for the city by reestablishing the bond between father and son.[66] The two generations in the male line are placed together before the city as a whole, in reparation for the divisions that female passion has brought to the patriarchal household.[67]

Such a reading, however, remains within the terms of the theater as defined by Euripides' society—a theater whose audience was (probably) the male citizenry of the polis. This ending rigidifies the sexual and spatial dichotomies between male and female and restores a familiar, male-centered status quo.[68] The woman is back in her familiar place as the outsider, foreigner, or intruder. Father and son (even the illegitimate son) are reunited in their common victimage by chaotic and chaos-inducing female desire; and the woman, with her passions of love or grief, remains the necessarily excluded third term.

The reconciliation and farewell between father and son and the mourning of male "citizens" belong to a grief that can be kept within the frame of civic order and so lifted to a healing beyond tragedy. By contrast, Theseus' lament for Phaedra (817ff.) or the Heliades' for Phaethon (732ff.) is left in the realm of the limitless and the inconsolable. In both cases the images evoked belong to a remote, uncontrollable world of wild nature or the underworld, a world that is the negation of the bounded, controllable realm of the polis. If, as Nicole Loraux suggests, the grief of women is dangerous to the city,[69] the shared grief of father and son, like that of brothers and fellow warriors in *Ajax* or of hero companions at the end of *Heracles*, however painful it may be at the moment, has in view a healing of previous divisions in the city or the house.[70] Just as the male-focused ending encloses this grief in the frame of civic lament, so Artemis' promise of the rite at Troezen encloses female eros and its dangerous goddess, Aphrodite, in the civic frame of marriage, where it is kept within the limits of a state institution (1423–30).

Beneath the common grief of all the citizens in the masculine realm of public discourse, then, lies the still-unhealed fragmentation of the city's life into male and female experiences. For the young man there are athletics and male companions unfettered by civic or familial responsibilities; for the young woman, preparations for marriage; for the adult man, the ties of male kinship, the civic realm, and politics; for the adult woman, house and marriage. For the youth, there is the father who pities and forgives;[71] for the woman, far from home and parents (cf. 752–66), there is only the Nurse, who misjudges and betrays. Her goddess, Aphrodite, should be the unifying element between the pairs, but here she sets them into discord rather than bringing harmony. Aphrodite's enemy, Artemis, does little better: she reinforces the division between god and mortal and perpetuates enmity among the gods (1420–22, 1437f.).

It is revealing to compare the father-son scene at the end of the *Hippolytus* with the father-daughter scene at the end of the *Bacchae*. In the later play the masculine law and order of the polis have been overthrown by emotional violence closely associated with the female. The palace and the royal house are figuratively, and perhaps also literally, in ruins. The members of the royal family are either destroyed or soon to be dispersed in exile. Agave is never again to look on the Theban mountain of her murderous revels; Cadmus is to return to the barbarian world from which he founded Thebes. The gesture of solidarity here is between the weaker and more marginal segments of the city: the old man and the woman, the one having given up his power, the other never having possessed it.

Sophocles, on the other hand, does not permit so massive a destruction of the civic and patriarchal order. Even in the *Antigone*, where female resistance to male civic authority generates a divisive and destructive conflict, the father-son bond is, in a sense, reaffirmed by Creon's appearance with Haemon's body and by the concluding remarks of the chorus of the male elders, the embodiments of a still-living voice of civic authority and civic life. The *Trachiniae*, *Oedipus Tyrannus*, *Electra*, and *Oedipus at Colonus*, for all the suffering of the protagonist and his or her house, all end with the patriarchal succession ensured. In many Euripidean plays, however, the burden of grief and loss shifts from adult males to women and old men (as in the *Andromache*, *Trojan Women*, *Hecuba*, and *Bacchae*). The solidarity of communal lamentation seems to offer less comfort; and the image of the community itself changes from inclusion, strength, and continuity to exile, fragmentation, and uncertainty.

Euripides has perhaps already experimented with the technique in the destruction of Jason at the end of the *Medea*; but there, as in the *Hippolytus*, the disaster is more individual and familial than communal. In the *Hippolytus*, at any rate, theatrical community and civic community remain strong, and the latter is reinforced by the stage presence of Athens' founder to the very end. As in the *Medea*, *Heracles*, and *Bacchae*, the community of the theater is asserted in the face of a universally recognized threat. In all four cases, in different ways, this threat is female passion, hatred, or irrationality, that has access to supernatural destructive power.

8

Confusion and Concealment:

Vision, Hope, and Tragic

Knowledge

Deducing hidden causes and invisible truths that lie beneath the surface phenomena of the visible world was a major intellectual concern of the late fifth century. It is the unifying theme among authors as different as Anaxagoras and the Atomists, Hippocrates, and Thucydides; and it recurs as a concern of tragedy, most notably in Sophocles' *Oedipus Tyrannus*.[1] The *Hippolytus* has an important place in this intellectual debate. Its contribution is characteristically Euripidean: to demonstrate the role of the passions—especially sexual desire, jealousy, and sexually motivated anger, hatred, and vindictiveness—in leading otherwise intelligent, noble, and high-minded people to mistake appearance for reality, falsehood for truth. And, as is generally the case in tragedy's version of the problem of knowledge, such a mistake is not just a theoretical or abstract issue. It has the gravest consequences for the lives of men and women. As Phaedra says and the play demonstrates, the wrong kind of discourse about passions "destroys the well-settled cities and homes of mortals" (486ff.).

The quality of being hidden defines the important realities in the human world depicted in the *Hippolytus*, the motives of men and women and the goals of their actions. The hidden "disease" of love directs Phaedra's movements and sets the tragic events into motion. Immediately before the palace doors open to reveal that disease, the Nurse generalizes on the woes of mortals, which she traces to ignorance of what lies hidden (*kruptei*, 192) in Hades. Our sufferings (*ponoi*, 190), she implies, are due to mistaken or impossible loves: we are *duserôtes* (194) because we lack clear signs about the end of life and the hereafter (cf. *apodeixis*, a "showing forth," 197).

Ironically, bringing "the hidden" into the light produces further deception.[2] The play begins with a movement from the house, where Phaedra keeps her disease "hidden" (138ff.), to the "bright light" and sky, which are among the Nurse's first words as the palace doors open to reveal the lovesick queen (178ff.). The Nurse's first speech, noted above, points back to ignorance, darkness, and the underworld (191–97). Hippolytus returns to the stage with an invocation to the unfolding rays of the sun (601) and soon makes his disastrous threat to bring into the light what his tongue had promised to conceal (604–14, cf. 656–63). Phaedra reluctantly emerges from the house, only to return to her chamber for the constriction of death by the noose (776–86) and a "bitter housekeeping" (πικρὸν τόδ' οἰκούρημα, 787). Hippolytus, for all his love of the out-of-doors and devotion to the "heavenly" Artemis (59, cf. 67), has the dark doors of Hades awaiting him and is trapped in the deadly "bondage" of his own reins (1236ff., cf. 1225 and 1246). The pure setting of his devotion to his "celestial goddess" (59ff., 67–72, 75–78) is obliterated by a landscape where chthonic darkness blots out the light of the sky (1205–8, cf. 1215–17). Like Phaedra, he dies with a closing gesture of "covering" or concealing (cf. 1458 and 712).

In the interchanges of roles and suffering between the two protagonists, the motif of concealment shifts from the world of Phaedra to that of Hippolytus. As Hippolytus goes into exile a condemned man, justice seems overturned, and the chorus of his fellow hunters laments its perversion. The gods' concern for us, the hunting companions say, when it comes to their minds (*phrenes*), removes pain; but the companions are troubled when they behold the flux in human fortunes (1104–10). This attempt to make sense of suffering also passes through an act of concealing, for the chorus here says that it "hides understanding, intelligence, by hope" (ξύνεσιν δέ τιν' ἐλπίδι κεύθων, 1105). This condensed and difficult phrase (discussed more fully below) may mean that the chorus believes in the gods' concern for men, even in the midst of men's changing fortunes. When men allow this "understanding" to be submerged in the "hope" that human life (because of the gods' concern) would be happier than it in fact is, however, they are dismayed at what they see; namely, life's unpredictable shifts from joy to sorrow. Alternatively, this phrase could be taken more closely in conjunction with the following sentence, in a concessive sense: the gods' concern for men, coming to the chorus's thoughts or mind (*phrenes*), removes pain; but the chorus is disturbed by seeing the flux of human fortunes even though it enwraps (hides or buries) in hope its understanding about the gods' concern.

The two possible interpretations, then, may be paraphrased roughly as follows: (1) I am disturbed when I witness the instability of human fortunes, and thus I keep my understanding about the gods' concern for us hidden, submerged, in the hope that the gods can really make our lives less painful and our well-being less precarious; or (2) although I keep my understanding of the gods' concern for us enclosed, protectively "hidden," in the "hope" that this knowledge permits me to have, I am nevertheless disturbed when I witness such sudden changes in human fortunes as this unexpected disaster of Hippolytus.

Translators generally impute a more or less optimistic meaning to the "concealment" of hope:

"So I have a secret hope / of someone, a God, who is wise and plans" (David Grene).

"Yet that hid hope in some all guiding Mind / falters" (F. L. Lucas).

"Sed intelligentiam aliquam divinae providentiae dum *opinor possidere* rursus deficio" (Theobaldus Fix, in the Didot edition).

Whatever translation one adopts, "concealing" (*keuthein*) casts a shadow over hope in the gods. "Hiding in hope," far from conveying confident "faith" (as *elpis* is sometimes mistranslated), implies fragility, helplessness, uncertainty, and doubt in the confrontation of wish and reality.[3] Such "hope" is either a false expectation (the result of a discrepancy between wish and reality) or a self-deception (the result of truth's inaccessibility and men's willingness to acquiesce in "mere" hope and therefore in their own condition or ignorance). The chorus's gnomic utterance at the very end of the play reminds us of how precarious hope in fact is, for they sing of the grief that has come to the citizens "contrary to our hope," "without our expecting it" (*a-elptôs*, 1463). The fact that Euripides uses a similar generalization about what is *aelpton* to conclude five other plays only reinforces the point about how unreliable and dangerous *elpis* appears to him and his contemporaries.

The mood of uncertainty is taken up by the response of the women in the antistrophe, and they pray for an easy acceptance of change and a spirit "untouched by suffering" when they contemplate Hippolytus' present situation (1111–19). But the hunting companions in the next strophe, after the sight of something so "contrary to hope" or "expectation," have minds (*phrên*) no longer "pure" (1120): οὐκέτι γὰρ καθαρὰν φρέν' ἔχω, παρὰ δ' ἐλπίδ' ἃ λεύσσω (For no longer do I have a pure mind, but what I behold is contrary to hope).[4]

Theseus' wish for the two voices in lines 925–32 gives an intellectualized definition to the issue of seeing through the outer surface to the hidden inner face of reality. But in the plot and stage action the issue is played out more concretely and emotionally in the physical area of Phaedra's body. In the first scene the condition of this body is the hidden object of knowledge. The emergence of Phaedra's person from the palace, through the gates (170), is surrounded by suspenseful expectation and curiosity about her body: "In what respect has the queen's body been injured, changed in its color?" the chorus asks (174ff.): τί δεδήληται / δέμας ἀλλόχροον βασιλείας. The visible surface of the body (-χροον) conceals a mystery hidden beneath.

In the following scene Phaedra would hide her face from the Nurse (*krupson, kruptei*, 243, 245) while the tears run from her eyes. Her form or face is subjected to the curious vision of others, but her own gaze is inward, toward her thoughts, or *gnômê*, and toward the shame she feels. Thus when she asks the Nurse to cover her head, she shifts from the physical role of the eyes as the place of tears to the eyes as the locus of an inner vision, the mental organ that perceives her shame (243–49):

Nurse, once more cover my head,
For I am ashamed at what I have spoken.
Cover [me]. A tears comes forth from my eyes [*kat'ossôn*],
And my sight [eye, *omma*] is turned toward shame.
For to be upright in one's resolve [*gnômê*] gives pain.
Madness is a woe. Yet it is better, if one does not have that resolve, to perish.

The Nurse's reply, "I cover; but will death not cover up my body?" (κρύπτω . . . καλύψει, 25off.), returns us to the physical meaning of concealing and the motif of the body (*sôma*). But concealment and death also recall her opening lines on the hiddenness of life's ultimate meaning (191–97). Phaedra's gestures and the Nurse's generalities begin to build up a view of truth as something wrapped in secrecy and hidden behind an obscuring surface. This pattern gradually establishes concealment or obscurity as the condition of human knowledge about life's meaning, about the individual heart, or about what words say.

Hippolytus' first scene has an effect exactly the opposite of Phaedra's. His dedication of the garland from the "untouched meadow" stakes out his place in the open countryside (73–81). This landscape of virginity, with all its ambiguities, is a symbolic projection of his own self-image.[5] His place within it, both enacted and confirmed by his dedication, seems secure. He locates himself in a shelter that (so far, at least) is free from tension with a concealed interior. His language too asserts a simplicity and clarity of belonging. It exudes confidence about definition and boundary and establishes his firm directness in his ritual approach to his goddess. "I bring" and "do you receive" (φέρω, δέξαι, 74 and 83) delineate the gestural simplicity of this, his first act in the play. Phaedra's relation to divinities and ritual acts, by contrast, is obscure, mysterious, or misleading (cf. 135–60). Her opening commands to her servants, in contrast to the certainty of Hippolytus, are followed by expressions of physical and emotional dissolution and distress. "The fastenings of my limbs are loosed," she tells her attendants, "and the headdress upon me is heavy to bear" (199 and 201).

Hippolytus marks out the parameters of his "meadow" in a sharp succession of positive and negative qualifications. He excludes shepherds and iron but allows the bee. He refuses what is acquired by teaching but accepts the gifts of innate nature. He permits those who are "moderate" or "chaste" (*sôphrones*) but debars the "base" or "evil" (*kakoi*). His well-marked temporal succession of past and present tenses reinforces the definiteness of temporal beside spatial boundaries (cf. ἦλθέ πω, διέρχεται, εἴληχε). His own special prerogatives in this meadow are firmly, even arrogantly, set forth by a powerful verbal gesture of exclusion: "To me alone of mortals does this privilege belong" (μόνῳ γάρ ἐστι τοῦτ' ἐμοὶ γέρας βροτῶν, 84).

In this special "association" (*homilia*) with his goddess (85), Hippolytus sets out from a point of certain knowledge and clear boundaries. Yet this knowledge has a dangerous asymmetry: the truth that mortal vision could convey about the goddess is obscured by a nonseeing of her "eye" (*omma*). He would associate with Artemis, he tells her, "hearing your voice but not seeing your eye [i.e., face]" (κλύων μὲν αὐδήν, ὄμμα δ᾽ οὐχ ὁρῶν τὸ σόν, 86).[6] Artemis' eye, unlike Phaedra's in line 246 (cited above), is the outward gaze, the eye that is seen by others. It is objective rather than subjective; but its inwardness is problematical. One who sees this outward-looking eye has no certainty of penetrating to any knowledge of the "thought" or "mind" (*phrên*) within.

Just how limited is mortals' knowledge of the gods becomes evident at the end. Artemis, whom Hippolytus still cannot see (though she sees him, 1391–5), takes easy leave of their "association" (1441). Her eyes are untroubled by tears; her "seeing" remains unclouded, unaffected by emotions: "I see [you], but it is not lawful for me to shed tears from my eyes" (ὁρῶ· κατ᾽ ὄσσων δ᾽ οὐ θέμις βαλεῖν δάκρυ, 1396).[7] His eyes are full of the "darkness" that marks mortality in its ultimate form (1444): "Alas, darkness is now reaching me, [covering] over my eyes" (αἰαῖ, κατ᾽ ὄσσων κιγχάνει μ᾽ ἤδη σκότος). What he "sees" is the blackness of death, the "gates of those below" (ὄλωλα καὶ δὴ νερτέρων ὁρῶ πύλας, 1447).

The meaning of Hippolytus' more-than-mortal "converse" with Artemis (19) emerges more clearly by contrast with the "dearest converse" between Phaedra and Theseus, over which the latter mourns in lines 836–51 (τῆς σῆς στερηθεὶς φιλτάτης ὁμιλίας, 838). Theseus sees his children made orphans, himself "destroyed," and his house bereft (845–51). This "converse" (838) contains just those elements that Hippolytus' "converse" with Artemis excludes: an implicit aspiration toward the divine that would evade the two defining terms of the mortal condition, sexual procreation and death (cf. Hesiod, *Theogony* 603–12). Whereas Artemis' converse with Hippolytus proves to be something that she can leave "easily" (1441), Theseus' loss of his most loved converse blots out the light of life (836–39): "To the gloom beneath the earth, beneath the earth, in darkness, would I change my dwelling, dying, miserable that I am, deprived of your dearest converse. For you destroyed rather than perished yourself."

When he refers to his now-orphaned children a few lines later, he connects death and procreation (847–51): "The house is deserted, the children bereft. Woe, woe, you left [us], left us, you, the best of all the women whom the radiance of the sun and the star-visaged gleam of night look upon." His combination of sunlight and starry night is a rhetorical figure for the totality of the world; but the combination also expresses the play's tragic shift from light to darkness, upper to lower world, aspiration toward divinity and the inexorability of death for mortals.[8] Theseus' address to the absent Phaedra just after lamenting the loss of his "dearest converse" in line 838, "You destroyed rather than perished yourself" (839), has a meaning that he learns only at the play's end (cf. 1403, 1433).

Despite his emphasis on purely aural association in line 86, Hippolytus has not entirely escaped erotic impressions that come through the eyes.[9] Defending his purity against Theseus' accusation, he claims to know of love only by "hearing it in word and seeing it in painting" (1004).[10] Hearing and seeing here stand in complementation rather than contrast, for this is the realm of mortal limitations, not the specialness of the divine *homilia* (converse) that Hippolytus describes in line 86. In "seeing" the painted forms of eros, "untouched" though he is (*athiktos*, 1002) by the thing itself, Hippolytus at least acknowledges the way eros comes through the eyes. That knowledge is combined, significantly, with the motif of *graphê* (painting, but also writing), the medium through which Phaedra will respond to his invulnerable purity (cf. 1002) and destroy it. Her *graphê* gives him the appearance of uncontrollable sexual appetite. It "paints" a picture of Hippolytus that is exactly antithetical to the one Hippolytus paints for Theseus: Hippolytus' relation to the *graphê* (painting) of love is, he says, one of innocence and purity (1002–6). Both as writing and as painting, *graphê* destroys the deeroticizing, nonvisual distance that Hippolytus keeps between himself and the object of his "converse."

A few lines later, in defending himself against possible motives for his alleged attack on Phaedra, Hippolytus gives first place to the "beauty of her body" (1009f.): πότερον τὸ τῆσδε σῶμα ἐκαλλιστεύετο / πασῶν γυναικῶν (Or was her body distinguished in beauty beyond all other women's?)

The problematical "body" of Phaedra, a private concern of women in the house at the beginning, now returns, in an explicitly erotic sense, in a quasi-forensic and quasi-public debate between males, an object of struggle and enmity in a life-and-death contest. This is the only place where Hippolytus acknowledges Phaedra's "body" as an erotic object. He means to dismiss that eroticism by the rhetorical question; but his language recalls Theseus' different relation to that body, expressed in that very different form of rhetorical emotionality in lines 849–51. In fact, his phrase "most beautiful in body of all women" (1009ff.) is a reminder of Theseus' lament for the "best of women" (cf. ἐκαλλιστεύετο / πασῶν γυναικῶν, 1009f.; and γυναικῶν ἀρίστα, 849).[11]

The word Hippolytus uses for *body* here is not *demas* but *sôma*. *Sôma* is the marked rather than the unmarked term, and in this play it is used always of the body dead, about to die, or badly injured.[12] His past tense, "was excellent in beauty," underlines the fact that this vulnerable body is no longer living. Unwittingly, but insensitively, he also exacerbates Theseus' grief for a beloved wife who is now only a *sôma*. Just seven lines before, he described his own body, hitherto both physically and sexually intact, as a *hagnon demas* (pure body, 1003). Unknowingly, he echoes the phrase that the chorus in the parode uses of Phaedra's body (δέμας ἁγνόν, 138). But Phaedra's *demas* is "pure" here as a result of her "impure" desires, the miasmic feeling of having an interior "pollution" (φρήν δ' ἔχει μίασμά τι, 317).[13]

By her initial act of "purification" Phaedra begins the process of transforming her *demas* into *sôma*. Instead of cultic purity, she enters the impurity of death. In the scenes with Theseus and Hippolytus we witness the power exerted by that *sôma* on the stage, where it was wheeled out, as from the interior of the house, on the *ekkyklema*, "a bitter spectacle" (809ff., cf. 856ff.). Thus on every level our visual experience of Phaedra's body, both in life and in death, makes the body and its purity the source of contradictions and conflicts beyond Hippolytus' knowledge or control.

Longing for the "converse" with a remote and invisible goddess, Hippolytus rejects the goddess whose statue (*agalma*) stands before him, tangibly, at the gates of his palace (101): τήνδ' ἡ πύλαισι σαῖς ἐφέστηκεν Κύπρις. It is characteristic of the mystical in his character to prefer the remote to the immediate, the invisible to the material, the far to the near. When the Servant then appeals to Aphrodite not to hear (*kluein*) Hippolytus' words (119), he establishes a communication with the divine that is exactly the opposite of Hippolytus' with

Artemis: Artemis is heard but unseen, whereas Aphrodite is seen but (as the Servant prays) should not hear.

Aphrodite, however, has both seen and heard all too well. The love goddess uses the power she exercises through vision—the eroticized vision to which she subjects Phaedra (24ff.)—to punish one who "falls upon what is bigger than mortal converse" (19).[14] Extolling the power of Aphrodite later, the Nurse tells Phaedra of complaisant husbands who know of their wives' infidelity but "seem not to see" it (νοσοῦνθ' ὁρῶντας λέκτρα μὴ δοκεῖν ὁρᾶν, 463).

Beyond Hippolytus' uncut meadow, then, lies a realm where seeing and hearing stand in more complicated, paradoxical, and precarious relations than he imagines. The force of eros that results in Phaedra's written tablets blurs the distinction between seeing and hearing. That distinction is completely swept away by a later aural product of this eros, the bull's roar from the sea. This monstrous sound, emanating from celestial and chthonic spaces together (1201–5), overpowers both the hearing and the vision of Hippolytus and his entourage (1215–17).[15]

All the characters' attempts at flight or purity, with their implicit aspiration toward transcending bodily nature, are subverted by the essential elements of the mortal condition in its physicality: constrictions by the seasonal rhythms of the earth in the need for "Demeter's grain," sexuality, and death.[16] Phaedra's body, once famed for its beauty (as line 1009 might also imply), is now a dead body because of her attempt to keep it "pure" (136). And it inspires in Theseus the grief and anger that lead to the murderous, fatal smashing of the body of Hippolytus (*sôma*, 1353). Far from being impermeable to the demands of mortal corporeality, Hippolytus' body, like Phaedra's, becomes the site whereon is enacted, in the unique, physical form of dramatic representation, mortals' subjection to pain and death.[17] The other route by which a mortal attains divinity—the godlike eternity of fame—is also entangled with physicality, as it proves to be dependent on the eros of a woman (1429ff.). Finally, as a bastard, Hippolytus faces an even more basic contradiction in his physical being. His claim to aristocratic *gennaiotês*, or nobility, stands in constant contradiction with a given of his existence, a prenatal circumstance over which he has no control.

Earlier too, the traditional male "glory" or "honor" was involved in the confusions of familiar sexual categories created by the passion of Phaedra and the extreme rejection of sexuality in the "purity" of Hippolytus.[18] Phaedra's speech of lines 411–30, which wins her the chorus's praise for *sôphrosynê* and their assurance that she has won "noble repute" (*doxa esthlê*, 432), shifts between the traditional dichotomies of city and house to reveal to men the uncomfortable truth that their standing in the public realm of the city depends on the behavior of their wives in the private realm of the *oikos*. In this way Phaedra shows the power and danger implicit in female sexuality and therefore the need for men to control it. For her, as for Aeschylus' Clytaemnestra, Sophocles' Deianeira, and Euripides' Helen, a woman's sexual transgression or sexual jealousy spreads its destructive force outward from the house to the community as a whole. Homer's Helen is the prototype, as Aeschylus fully recognizes (see *Agamemnon* 403ff., 684ff.). In *Hippolytus* a woman's passion produces "a common grief for all the citizens" (1462).

The dangers of this situation are already intimated on the microcosmic level of language in Phaedra's speech beginning on line 412. Scholars have repeatedly discussed the first half of this great *rhesis* (373–430), with its notorious problem of the double pleasures or double forms of shame (385–87), but have paid relatively little attention to the second half, lines 395–430.[19] This passage powerfully formulates a major issue of Greek and other Mediterranean societies: the power that women's sexuality wields over men through the shame that they can bring to the house, to the man's career, and thus to the whole community. When Herodotus traces the Greeks' wars against barbarians to the love affairs of women, he gives a lighter version of the same concerns, although his accounts of Gyges and, later, of the wife of Masistes are more serious exempla (Herodotus 1.8–13, 9.108–13).

Phaedra here moves with dangerous fluency from the heroic to the domestic, from the ideals of masculine *aretê* to the specific preoccupations of women in the house. As in *Alcestis*, the familiar divisions between male and female roles become blurred. From her personal concerns, as a woman, with overcoming her passion and gaining a good reputation among men (395–410) she passes to a general gnomic utterance on the distinction between "the noble" and "the base" (using masculine adjectives in lines 411ff.). After this she adapts Achilles' heroic ideal about truth and honest appearances to her own situation (413ff.): "I hate women who are sound-minded [chaste] in words, but in secret possess daring that is not noble" (413ff.; cf. *Iliad* 9.312ff.). The Homeric echo stands out sharply against her specifically female and domestic preoccupation with illicit love, husband, and house (415–21). Concluding with the "children to whom she has given birth," she intensifies this incongruity between her context and the male heroic code.

The theme of "disgracing" husband and children—a point several times taken up by Theseus in the latter half of the play—leads her into the public and largely masculine field where that "disgrace" counts most. Whereas the king's son competes only in athletics (1016–20), Phaedra is thinking about "competition" (ἁμιλλᾶσθαι) among males in the polis. Her most explicit reference to masculine activities directly follows her reference to her motherhood. After uttering her fears about being "caught shaming her husband and children," she wishes them free speech (*parrhêsia*) in the city of "glorious Athens" (420–23). The reference is to the confidence to make speeches in public debates of the assembly, in which only male citizens participate. This is the civic realm that the king's son rejects. Her phrase "city of glorious Athens" (πόλιν κλεινῶν Ἀθηνῶν, 422ff.), in fact, recurs in the mouth of King Theseus, who speaks with full civic authority, at the play's end (1460f.): "O Athens' and Pallas Athena's *glorious* boundaries, what a man have you lost" (ὦ κλείν' Ἀθηνῶν Παλλάδος θ' ὁρίσματα).[20]

"Even if a man has a bold heart" (literally, "bold entrails or guts," θρασύσπλαγχνος, 428), Phaedra says, he is "enslaved" by the shame attaching to his mother or father (424–27). In her concern for the civic context of her sons' future, she gives a new and unexpected turn to the disparity between surface and depth that focuses on the body, specifically the female body. Her closing generalization is an even more striking mixture of male and female spheres. She compares time's revealing of base men to a mirror reflecting a young girl's features (428–30). Here she moves us back to the female sphere, even though her immediate reference is the reputation of men in civic life. The abruptness in the transition from political reputation to the boudoir takes us by surprise, but it also points up her intensely personal and feminine interpretation of what it means to "be seen" among the base.[21] This is her closing phrase (παρ' οἷσι μήποτ' ὀφθείην ἐγώ, 430). The contrast of grammatical genders in the simile reflects the crossing of sex roles in Phaedra's speech. The would-be handmaid to the girl, holding the mirror, is the masculine *chronos*, time. Those among whom Phaedra would not be seen are not the women with whom she compared herself in lines 414ff. but the masculine *kakoi* (base men), generalized from the κακοὺς θνητῶν of line 428 (base of mortals).

The grammatical juxtapositions of masculine and feminine forms throughout this passage (411–30) become active dramatic elements in the manner that Phaedra chooses to resolve her moral dilemma. She does, in one sense, preserve her *eukleia* (good repute, 1299; cf. *eukleeis*, 433, 717); but later, Artemis will point out the anomalous juxtaposition of *oistros*, the gadfly sting of female sexual desire (like Io's in the *Prometheus*), and her nobility, or *gennaiotês*. The latter is also the male virtue claimed for Hippolytus in the father-son embrace at the end (1452, 1455). There is an analogous crossing over into the masculine realm in the characteristically female mode of her death. A woman's death by hanging, surrounded by lies and trickery (1310–12), Phaedra's is nevertheless also a death by "force" and a "wrestling of hand" (βιαίως θανοῦσα . . . / σᾶς χειρὸς πάλαισμα μελέας, 813–15).[22]

As the play develops, these themes move from the house outward to the city. The wooden beams of the house become the wooden tablets of Phaedra's lie that reach out from the interior to the "eye" of Zeus and to the depths of Poseidon's sea to destroy Hippolytus (886ff.). The question of knowing the "guts" and thoughts of a man (424ff.) moves from a domestic to a juridical context where the issues are life and death (925–31). Though the question in this latter passage is still framed in the generalizing vocabulary of the sophistic movement, the issues are far from abstract or theoretical, for the speaker holds the power of life and death and will exercise it in accordance with his view of the hidden disposition (*phrên*) that he is examining.

What Phaedra says of time's revealing base men in lines 428–30 also evolves thematically as she reveals her "hidden" disease in the course of the play. The motif will be taken up by Hippolytus himself in his frustration and self-pity at not being able to display his true, inner self (*phrên*) to his accuser, Theseus (1078). His "witnesses" are (ironically) silent, like his accuser (1076ff.). His wished-for mirror, unlike Phaedra's "mirror of time," reflects only his suffering, and that back to himself alone (1078ff.).[23] Overwhelmed by what Phaedra has revealed, Theseus will not wait for time to change his opinion about the moral state of Hippolytus' *phrên* (cf. 1051, 1322). When Artemis vindicates Hippolytus, too late, she "displays" or "shows" his *phrên* as "just" (*ekdeixai*, 1298; 427, 925–31). What for the goddess is a cool, intellectual "demonstration" (another meaning of *ekdeixai*) is agonizing pain for the mortal victims. Aphrodite's mode of showing her truth to mortals, as we shall see, is no gentler to its human recipients (*deixô*, 9 and 42).

Just as we seem to be emerging into the light of truth, Artemis' language pulls us back toward the concealment practised in the first part of the play: Theseus, like Phaedra, should "cover his body in shame" in the underworld (1290ff.: πῶς οὐχ ὑπὸ γῆς τάρταρα κρύπτεις / δέμας αἰσχυνθείς). Although *demas* is the direct object of *krupteis* (cover the body), the collocation δέμας αἰσχυνθείς in line 1291 recalls Phaedra's plight of being "shamed in respect to body." Shattered and near death, Hippolytus is now carried onstage with the cry, "Alas, alas, ill-fated I am, from my unjust father, by unjust curses [literally, oracles] have I been torn apart in my body" (1348ff.). The mangled body visible and audible on the stage is now a spectacle that reveals the consequences of incorrect judgment about the hidden, invisible *phrên*. The injured body recalls Phaedra's concealed love sickness in the first part of the play. But in Hippolytus' case the injury to the body is fully apparent on the outside, and not a mysterious feminine ailment within (cf. 293–96).

In the prologue, Aphrodite makes an ominous promise to "show the truth of this tale" (*deixô*, 9) and to "show" (*deixô*) the love of Phaedra to Theseus (42). Phaedra's "showing," however reluctant, fulfills the goddess's plan, though in a way slightly different from Aphrodite's description, for Phaedra herself, and not the goddess, will "make the matter visible" to Theseus (42).[24] When she does eventually bring forth to men the hidden disease of her body (293–96), it is not to cure the illness in a cooperative and sympathetic confidence with a male doctor but rather to let the disease rage with a violence that only seems to confirm the stereotypes about female passion, deception, and destructiveness (cf. 628–33).

In a world where exterior and interior correspond, face-to-face meeting is a guarantee of honest and honorable behavior. In the *Phoenissae*, for example, Jocasta tries to reconcile her warring sons with the gnomic statement "Whenever a friend [or kin, *philos*], angry at a friend, meets him and gives eye to eye, then alone can one consider what he is coming for" (461–63). Polyneices' *exordium*, "The tale of truth is simple, and justice needs no elaborate interpretings" (469ff.), continues this hope of a simple correspondence of word and thing, appearance and actuality. In the *Hippolytus* the tragedy of both protagonists revolves about the loss of any such correspondence. Phaedra's vivid concern with face-to-face meeting eventually results in the powerfully persuasive form of its negation, the writing that creates a semblance of truth but speaks a falsehood (*pseudeis muthoi*, 1288; *pseudeis graphai*, 1311) that prevails over the face-to-face discourse between father and son.

Phaedra's delaying tactics to maintain her "concealment" and the way her secret "appears" or "is shown" provide the chief interest for the first stage of the plot. The momentum of the second part increases when what she is concerned to conceal is not the guilty passion per se (cf. 138) but rather the "shameful deeds" or "unjust acts" which she had earlier refused (409–14). At the first great crisis of the action Phaedra stations herself at the gates to hear the "cry" that "comes through the gate" (588); and, as a result, "what is hidden is made revealed" (the chorus, at 593). She clarifies the new situation as she calls upon "some god" to "appear" as her helper or companion in "unjust deeds" (πάρεδρος ἢ συνεργὸς ἀδίκων ἔργων, 676). In her last iambic speech, some forty lines later, she openly acknowledges the "unjust deeds" that will protect her good name, repeating the imagery of face-to-face confrontation of the earlier scene: "Never will I shame my Cretan house, nor shall I come to Theseus' face [*es prosô-pon Thêseôs*, 720] under accusation of unjust deeds because of one mere life."[25] These "unjust deeds" (in the deliberately loose syntax of the phrase) reach beyond the accusation of adultery in the previous remarks about "looking into the face" (e.g., 416) to a more ominous crime, implicit in the "one life" at the end. The decisive result of this scene at the palace gate is Hippolytus' decision to rupture the correspondence between word and thought. When he proclaims, "My tongue has sworn, but unsworn is my mind" (*phrên*, 612), he treats the tongue merely as an external organ of speech that no longer contains or conceals what lies in the inward organ of thought, the *phrên* that is unbound by the oath. That rupture of correspondence between speech and thought is what destroys him (916ff., 1074ff.).

The play's permutations of this rupture are various: word and deed, tongue and thought, falsehood and truth, appearances and reality, outside and inside, writing and speech, hearing and seeing.[26]

As the last pair indicates, however, the dichotomies are unstable, and the terms shift to opposite sides of the contrast. When Theseus sees the body of Phaedra, for instance, and reads the tablets, receiving her last "words" through his organs of sight, he is taken in by false appearances. Autopsy, which fifth-century thinkers regard as the surest and clearest proof, is here deceptive.[27]

The parallelism between Hippolytus' asymmetrical hearing but not seeing Artemis and Phaedra's hearing but not seeing Hippolytus at the gates of the palace joins the two protagonists in a complementary susceptibility to self-deception. Hippolytus is deceived about his self-righteous superiority to Phaedra, for vision (appearances) and speech will both prove to be on her side, fatally for him. Phaedra is deceived about Hippolytus, for, in a double twist of irony, he does not break his oath, and his tongue and his mind do remain in harmony. This parallelism between the two protagonists also establishes a tragic continuity between the opposite ends of the spectrum of human aspirations.[28] Hippolytus yearns for a more than mortal association with a goddess by denying the eroticizing vision that comes through the eyes (86), the subject of the ode to Eros, the first stasimon (525–27). Phaedra, who is too much a prey to the power of vision, falls in love with Hippolytus. Totally subjected to the needs and weaknesses of her body, she rushes to meet her mortal end in Hades before her time (cf. 828ff.). Both figures respond to a one-sided perception: words without sight for Hippolytus, sight without words for Phaedra. Both embody opposite but parallel forms of tragic ignorance. In a fearful disintegration of differences, the total denial of sexuality and the total subjection to sexuality conduce to misapprehending reality and, of course, converge for the destruction of both sides.

Theseus' arrival before the gates of the palace (790ff.) pushes these destructive movements to their next crisis. Like Phaedra in the previous scene, he hears a terrible cry from within (776ff., 790ff.). Like the other two protagonists, he is involved in an asymmetrical communication as Phaedra's tablets speak and shout without their speaker being visible, for she has gone off *aphantos* (made unseen) to Hades (828). The deceptive message of the tablets throws "clarity" (*to saphes*) into confusion and predetermines Theseus' error in the wish for "clear evidence" about the just or unjust voice (925–31).

The gates that it is Theseus' special prerogative to enter refuse to open. He has to use his marital and regal authority to gain entrance (729ff., 806–10).[29] Once inside, he finds the silent tablets that "shout." Now the homecoming traveler who has been so eager to be received into the house seeks "flight" outside (877ff.). The sheltered place inside, forbidden to all but the legitimate spouse and king in its sanctity, now seems to turn inside out as its shame reaches even to the heavens, where it "dishonors the holy eye of Zeus" (885ff.). In the intricate weaving together of sexuality, the body, speech, and knowledge, Theseus' disorientation takes the threefold form of flight from a desired interior, the "speech" of the silent tablets, and the anomalously synaesthetic "seeing" of a "song" of woe ("What a song, alas, did I behold, making utterance in the writings," 880ff.).

Theseus' arrival and passage through the gates to the inner chamber of Phaedra open up a gateway to Hades. His cries of grief, drawing on the previous allusions to the myths of Phaethon, Cephalus, and Semele, enlarge the domestic tragedy of private suffering to its mythic dimensions as a large-scale cataclysm of cosmic darkness engulfing the light (cf. 836–51, 1121–25, 1444).[30] In his grief he will transform the brightness of day into a confusion of light and sunless darkness (836ff., 849–51; cf. 885ff.). He will, furthermore, make his own mouth a metaphorical gateway of doom for Hippolytus (882ff.). What comes forth is "something of hard passage," *dusekperaton*, a "woe destructive" (882ff.). The motif of difficult crossing recalls the ill-omened crossing of Phaedra's Cretan ship to Athens in the preceding ode (752–63) and her passage to Hades here (828ff.). It also points ahead to the failure of Hippolytus, tangled in his reins, to pass through the darkness that surrounds him on the Troezenian shore, far outside the palace.[31]

The careful description of Hippolytus' crash belongs to the outer world of his beloved horse racing. Phaedra had longingly contemplated this world when she was fully bound to the interior, domestic space of her confined life and hidden desires (228–35). The speech of women that Hippolytus would have enclosed and isolated within the house (645ff.) now proves to have an immense geographical reach. It upsets all the hopes of the proud and expert athlete, whose race ends in defeat, not victory. We may compare the similar account of racing, also ending in death, in Sophocles' *Electra*.[32]

The correspondences and tensions between the domestic and celestial zones and between female enclosure and male heroic aspiration are here extreme, for Hippolytus' fatal entrapment in the reins of his horses echoes both the entrapment of Phaedra in her noose inside the house and the fall of Phaethon in the previous ode. Like Hippolytus, Phaethon was an adolescent who failed to reach maturity; he crashed to his death from a high place in the sky, blasted by Zeus' thunderbolt after losing control of the flaming chariot of his father, Helios, the sun god.[33] Praised as the "brightest star of Athena" (1122) as he leaves the stage, Hippolytus perishes when something from the earth (chthonios, 1201) strikes and obliterates the sky (1205–9). The physical details of his crash reinforce this fall from high to low. He is initially high up on the vehicle, with his companions "below the chariot" (huph' harmatos, 1195), and he "falls" (piptei) in a way that leaves little life in his body (1246f.). The bull hurled forth from the sea totally confuses the relation between high and low. It "trips up" the horses (esphêle, 1232) just as Aphrodite threatened to "trip up" (sphallô, 6) Hippolytus for aspiring to a "greater than mortal association" with a goddess (19).[34]

The overturned chariot and the unfinished race constitute a powerful visual representation of Hippolytus' tragic life story. In losing this last and most crucial race of his life, he makes a circular return to his starting point in the play (cf. 1447 and 101). In his anomalous male purity, he does not run the course of life to its goal but returns to his starting point, as he had prayed for in the beginning: "May I round the course to the end of my life, just as I have begun" (87).[35] There is an implicit critique of his failed generational passage in this metaphor, for the male athletic competition that his language evokes should be only a temporary stage, to be supplanted by a fully adult, masculine role as citizen, husband, and warrior.

In a culture obsessed by the desire for lucidity, by the identification of knowledge and vision, and by clarity of definition in language, space, status, gender, and social roles, tragedy asserts the recalcitrant ambiguity and interconnectedness of everything human. Hippolytus explores the cruel discrepancies between such desires for distinctions and the tragic view of the human condition. The inherent ambiguities of language and communication are the model for the ambiguities of the human condition, located precariously between dependence on the perishable body and aspirations toward imperishable divinity. Vision is the means of reaching truth and making sharp distinctions between the different areas of reality. But vision also inspires the irresistible eros, rooted in the body, that sweeps away distinctions and confuses roles, status, and spatial limits. Desire for Hippolytus enters Phaedra's body through the eyes (24–33). Hippolytus rejects the silent but prominently visible image of divinity before his house (101) in favor of a celestial goddess whom he can hear but cannot see (86).

Around and in opposition to the unstable, asymmetrical nature of Hippolytus' *homilia* (converse) with Artemis cluster the precarious limits and boundaries between mortality and divinity that form the core of this tragedy and so much of Greek tragedy. At the same time, this intersection of speaking, hearing, and seeing is also the model for the interchanges and reversals between the deceptive surface of the body (especially the female body), the deceptiveness of words (especially in the concretized, visual form of the written word), and the passage between inner and outer space, with its concomitant motif of concealment and obscurity. At the end of his life Hippolytus finds the knowledge that Aphrodite said he lacked in the prologue (56ff.): "He does not know that the gates of Hades stand open, and that he is looking upon this light for the last time."

While the linear progression of his life has come to its final point, the formal effect of repetition marks the circularity of a life story fixated at the stage of the adolescent and the *parthenos*.[36] Hippolytus' own words now echo the last statement of his enemy goddess from the prologue: "Alas, the darkness now reaches down over my eyes" (αἰαῖ, κατ' ὄσσων κιγχάνει μ' ἤδη σκότος, 1444; cf. 56ff., above). Now, after he has been idealized as an almost celestial luminary (1121), he experiences the "dark" that awaits all mortals (1444; cf. 836ff., 849–51). Through what the eyes see, he comes to full knowledge of his mortality. Instead of the light of day and life there is the darkness that lies behind and below (cf. also 849–51). This is also the knowledge that the Nurse early in the play had described as enwrapped in the mists of darkness (191–97). This darkness, at both the beginning and the end, defines the conditions under which knowledge is possible for mortals. It is tragic knowledge. This means that it is achieved not by soaring over the mists (732ff.) but by entering the darkness.

Hecuba

9

Golden Armor and

Servile Robes: Heroism and

Metamorphosis

A feeling of impermanence and instability pervades the *Hecuba*. Its plot depends on events of a temporary and transitional nature, the enforced delay of the victorious Greek army in the Thracian Cherso-nese on its return from Troy to Greece. As the spatial setting lies between Asia and Greece, so the temporal setting is the interstitial period between the capture of Troy and the homeward return—or, in terms of the Epic Cycle, between the *Sack of Troy* and the *Returns*.[1] Ghosts dominate the opening of the play. The prologue is spoken by the ghost of Hecuba's youngest son, Polydorus, who was murdered by his treacherous Thracian host, King Polymestor; and the ghost of Achilles demands the sacrifice of Hecuba's daughter Polyxena in return for releasing the winds that will let the fleet sail home. To this setting belongs another kind of change as well: the peak of heroism is past, and what remains is the decline. The great feat of Troy's capture is over. Achilles is only a shade. He and his son, Neoptolemus, are distinctly marked as remnants, traces of a lost grandeur. It is a mood that the post-Trojan War dramas frequently cultivate: we may think of Euripides' *Andromache*, not far removed in date from the *Hecuba*, and his *Troades, Helen, Iphigeneia in Tauris,* and *Orestes*; and also of Sophocles' *Philoctetes* and his lost *Polyxena*.[2]

As often in his plays, Euripides expresses change through the motif of clothing. In this play dress reflects the main themes of suffering, mutability, and revenge. Change is both individual and social, and the motif of clothing draws the two levels together. In particular, the place of clothing in rituals like supplication, burial, and sacrifice links psychological and cultural meanings. Clothing has a special significance for gender roles because its manufacture and care are the work of women, and thus it involves the functions of women in society. On the individual level, change takes the form primarily of the mutability of fortune; on the social level, it is evident in the degeneration of heroic behavior. The two areas work together not only to depict the moral decline in this postwar world but also to show how a corrupt society and brutalizing conditions deform even a noble nature, as the pitiable *mater dolorosa* becomes a monster of vengeful hatred.

Because Hecuba is a queen and the leader of a group of women, her metamorphosis involves larger social categories. Through the collective nature of her vengeance and, as we shall see, its association with bacchantic ritual, her onstage transformation also enacts the metamorphosis of female submissiveness and helplessness into murderous fury. By combining personal change and cultural decline with the fabulous, mythical motif of metamorphosis and with evocations of maenadic ritual, Euripides goes beyond the familiar tragic topos of mutability of fortune to explore psychological and cultural identity, the questions of who or what is the real Hecuba and whether a stable definition of female character is possible.[3] Masculine identity is no less problematical; and here the traditional heroism, particularly as it appears in the *Iliad*, is a constant point of reference. The Homeric Achilles' singleness of purpose is transmuted into the inexorability of a bloodthirsty ghost, and the Homeric Odysseus' resilient adaptability is turned into treacherous shiftiness and mendacity. Though it is far from being a mere political allegory, the play casts into mythical terms and into gender conflicts the moral degeneration in the Hellenic world analyzed in Thucydides' history of the Peloponnesian War.

The heroic past makes a spectacular appearance in the play in the chorus's account of Achilles' ghost in the parode: "He appears with golden arms" as he "strides to his tomb" and "holds back the sea-traversing ships" (τύμβου δ᾽ ἐπιβὰς / οἶσθ᾽ ὅτε χρυσέοις ἐφάνη σὺν ὅπλοις, / τὰς ποντοπόρους δ' ἔσχε σχεδίας, 109–11). In the prologue the shade of Polydorus had said merely that Achilles "appeared above his tomb" (ὑπὲρ τύμβου φανείς, 37). The chorus embellishes this epiphany with the visual detail of the "golden arms." The addition belongs to the lyrical style, obviously, and to the epic world;[4] but it also marks this event as something beyond the reach of the lesser men whom we encounter in the play. We feel at once the discrepancy between this sudden, terrible flash of radiance from a past era and from beyond the grave and the wrangling of the meaner survivors, which is vividly described (116ff.).

Achilles' tomb is the play's most conspicuous landmark. But instead of being the site of immortal glory, as it is in the epic world, it is here the site of bloody human sacrifice and a murderous epiphany. For Odysseus, giving lasting honor to the warrior's tomb is the major reason for sacrificing Polyxena (315–20). This would-be place of heroic glory at the beginning is answered by the "tomb" of the long-suffering Trojan queen at the end (*tumbos*, 1271). In Polymestor's prophecy, Hecuba will become a "sign for sailors" in the shape of a "wretched bitch" (1273); that is, the spit of land known as Cynossema (the sign of the bitch). Unlike the "far-seen marker" (*sêma*) that Hector imagines as the monument of a warrior's "glory imperishable" in the *Iliad* (7.86–91), the *sêma* that Hecuba will become belongs to bestial metamorphosis, shame, and monstrosity. It will preserve her "name" for infamy, not glory (1270–73):

Εκ. θανοῦσα δ' ἢ ζῶσ' ἐνθάδ' ἐκπλήσω πότμον;
Πο. θανοῦσα· τύμβῳ δ' ὄνομα σῷ κεκλήσεται . . .
Εκ. μορφῆς ἐπῳδὸν μή τι τῆς ἐμῆς ἐρεῖς;
Πο. κυνὸς ταλαίνης σῆμα, ναυτίλοις τέκμαρ.

Hecuba. Dead or living will I fulfil my doom?
Polymestor. Dead, and your tomb will have as its name . . .
Hecuba. Do you mean something called after my form?
Polymestor. . . . Will be called "the wretched bitch's sign," a landmark [*sêma*] for sailors.

In contrast to the warrior's concern with the lasting memory of his name, on which Odysseus places such emphasis (317–20), Hecuba dismisses her future reputation (1274): "No care to me, as long as you pay me the just punishment" (*dikê*, 1274).[5]

As in the *Iphigeneia in Aulis*, to which the subject matter of this play is a sequel of sorts, the golden, god-fashioned armor is the touchstone by which we can measure the unheroic nature of this fallen world (*IA* 1071ff., *Hecuba* 109–11). Gold evokes both the divine ancestry and the near divinity of this greatest of the heroes.[6] Achilles' armor also has the impenetrability and permanence of the heroized warrior. In the world of this play, however, the chief characters wear clothing that can be torn and have bodies that will suffer wounds.

Aside from this reference to Achilles' armor, gold in the play is associated with the degeneration of heroic values. Early in the play it is combined with the horror of the slaughter of Polyxena, the gold of whose necklace will be stained with the black blood from her slit throat (150–53).[7] The actual death scene repeats the same combination of black blood and gold: Neoptolemus pours a libation of wine (*choas*, 529) from an "all-gold goblet" (*depas panchruson*, 527f.) and soon afterward pours the terrible "libation" (*choas*, 535) of "the girl's unmixed black blood" (μέλαν / κόρης ἀκραιφνὲς αἷμα, 536f.) Of gold too is the sword with which he makes the sacrificial slash across her throat (*amphichruson phasganon*, 543). In the ode of foreboding for their own fate that follows, the Trojan women describe the destructive radiance of Helen's beauty as illuminated by the sun's golden rays (635–37). In the following ode, the third stasimon, the chorus's deep gaze into the "infinite rays of the golden mirror" in the apparent safety of the bedroom (925ff.) contrasts with the imminent invasion of Greek warriors, to which their husbands' eyes are closed (921f.). The combination of gold and approaching violence depicts the precariousness of the peaceful moment and the vulnerability as well as the allure of women's beauty. The gold of Troy is, of course, the motive for Polymestor's murder of Polydorus; and it then serves, appropriately, to bait the trap that brings his punishment and Hecuba's revenge.[8]

As the discontinuities in the motif of gold indicate, change here is radical, coerced, and irrational. Its most visible and wrenching effects are the massive destruction of individual and communal life. Hecuba herself becomes the exemplar of the mutability of fortune, a marker to sailors amid the sea's dangers, but also, as even the Greek herald Talthybius compassionately observes, a warning to all men of the uncertainty of prosperity: this queen of the "gold-rich Phrygians" (ἄνασσα τῶν πολυχρύσων Φρυγῶν) is now a homeless, childless old slave woman prostrate on the earth (491–96).[9] In the prologue the shade of her son Polydorus places her present misfortunes under the familiar sign of the *ephêmeros*, the creature whose life is defined by the vicissitudes that a single day can bring.[10] These are the last words that the son addresses to his mother in the prologue (55–58):

ὦ μῆτερ, ἥτις ἐκ τυραννικῶν δόμων
δούλειον ἦμαρ εἶδες, ὡς πράσσεις κακῶς
ὅσονπερ εὖ ποτ᾽· ἀντισηκώσας δέ σε
φθείρει θεῶν τις τῆς πάροιθ᾽ εὐπραξίας.

O Mother, how from royal house you came to see the day of slavery, how ill you fare, as once you fared well; some god destroys you, balancing out your previous prosperity.

In the cycle of good and bad fortune or the counterbalancing of happiness by misfortune (as Polydorus' *antisêkôsas* suggests), Hecuba has passed from her happiness to "the most wretched of mortals," as the chorus will call her later (720f.). This reversibility of happiness is writ large in the transformation of Troy from a great city to a heap of smouldering ashes, a change of which the play reminds us again and again. The motif of smoke in particular calls attention to this reduction of solid substance to the ethereal, evanescent trace that survives.[11]

With the destruction of their city, the women of Troy are changed, collectively, from free women to slaves. Of the individual changes, the harshest is Polyxena's exchange of the expected bed of a prince for that of a slave (349–66, cf. 551f.). Yet by her voluntary death she will retain "always" the stability of her inward nobility and thus prove the truth of her royal birth and nurture. Such is the constancy of the truly noble person, as Hecuba says in her eulogy over her (592–602): οὐδὲ συμφορᾶς ὕπο / φύσιν διέφθειρ᾽, ἀλλὰ χρηστός ἐστ᾽ ἀεί (Nor by disaster did she corrupt her nature, but is noble always, 597f.; cf. also 579–82).[12] Yet just this resistance to change, through fidelity to an innate nobility of nature, is the foil to the change that takes place in Hecuba as she moves from maternal tenderness to terrifying vengefulness.[13] This contrast between mother and daughter, change and fixity, may enhance rather than mitigate the sense of degeneration. As Polyxena herself says, death is perhaps the easier fate (349ff.). The price of staying alive is brutalization.

This inner, spiritual change in Hecuba has its objective correlative in the external, physical change that Polymestor prophesies in the closing scene: she will become a bitch with fiery eyes and then will be fixed in the sea as a marker for sailors (1265–73).[14] Hecuba herself calls this fate "a transformation of [her] shape" (μορφῆς τῆς ἐμῆς μετά-στασιν, 1266); and a few lines later she perhaps hints at something magical, using the striking phrase μορφῆς ἐπῳδὸν . . . τῆς ἐμῆς (literally, "something sung upon or about my form," 1272). The word *metastasis* here is relatively rare in tragedy. It occurs only five times in the extant tragic corpus.[15] It implies not just "change" of shape but also the mutability of mortal fortunes.[16]

Another form of bestial metamorphosis awaits Hecuba's enemy, the treacherous Thracian king, Polymestor. Having violated both the justice of men and the laws of the gods (as Hecuba says, 1234–37; cf. 714f., 852f.), he is expelled from human society to a desert island (1284f.). The desert island may be only a threat, but it nevertheless makes the point that this man has placed himself beyond the pale of humanity.[17] Earlier in the play, Polymestor underwent a more vivid, if figurative, metamorphosis into a bestial monster in one of the play's most powerful scenes. After Hecuba had executed her vengeance, he returned to the stage blinded and crawling on all fours, like a wild creature of the mountains (1058f.). Like a wild beast too, he would hunt down his enemies and sate himself on their flesh and bones (1073f.).[18]

This bestialization of Polymestor not only enacts metamorphosis before our eyes; it also moves us still further from the world of Achillean and Iliadic heroism. Instead we enter the shifting realm of the *Odyssey*, with its protagonist of many turns. Polymestor's blindness and vengeful cries evoke the blinded, enraged Polyphemus (cf. *Odyssey* 9.395ff.).[19] His cannibalistic fury (1073f.) may well be modeled on the Cyclops' gory thoughts of revenge, themselves a repetition of his horrible feasting (9.458–60):

τῷ κε οἱ ἐγκέφαλός γε διὰ σπέος ἄλλυδις ἄλλῃ
θεινομένου ῥαίοιτο πρὸς οὔδεϊ, κὰδ δέ κ᾿ ἐμὸν κῆρ
λωφήσειε κακῶν, τά μοι οὐτίδανος πόρεν Οὖτις.

Thus, as he is dashed here and there around the cave, his brain would be splattered on the ground, and then would my heart find rest from the woes that No-good Nobody gave me.

The similarities between Polymestor and Polyphemus also extend to the structure of the respective episodes. When Agamemnon is summoned by the cries of the stricken Thracian (1109–19), we are reminded of *Odyssey* 9.399–408, the summoning of the Cyclops by Polyphemus' cries. But if Polymestor "becomes" the Cyclops, Hecuba paradoxically becomes his vanquisher, Odysseus. The Homeric Odysseus' clever foresight in giving his name as Outis (Noman) to forestall the monster's vengeance has a parallel in Hecuba's prearranged complicity with Agamemnon to prepare the way for scot-free vengeance (726–904). In both cases, though in very different ways, planning, deception, and foresight preempt a monster's counterattack and thus ensure that justice is served. In both cases the plotter obtains a just revenge for the murder of his or her own (a child in Hecuba's case, companions in Odysseus'). In both cases the vengeful punishment is meted out for the savage violation of the rights of guest-friendship. Both episodes conclude with the motifs of prophecy and with the threat of delayed vengeance from the gods (cf. *Odyssey* 9.507–36, and *Hecuba* 1259ff.).

Hecuba's epic model for her revenge is thus the "guile" (*mêtis* or *dolos*, 884) of her other enemy, Odysseus, whose cruelty, calculation, and indifference are apparent in the first episode. Is it another reflection on the instability of this war-torn, debased world that her *dolos* of just vengeance echoes the *metis* of a hated enemy? Or are we to see here another twist of Hecuba's tragedy—that in avenging the death of one child her plotting recalls the man most responsible for the death of another? Or is this similarity-in-opposites to be regarded as the result of the spread of indiscriminate violence, a lowest common denominator of human nature to which both sides are reduced as the ripples of war's violence move outward? These are not mutually exclusive alternatives; they indicate the skill with which Euripides uses the resources of his literary tradition.

Hecuba's tragedy, as we have observed, ends with metamorphosis. It began, however, with another situation of unstable identity, the appearance of Polydorus' shade in the prologue. He too occupies an unsettled state. A Trojan, he had been sent for safekeeping to Thrace. Murdered, he now belongs to the world below, but he has been allowed to visit the upper world. He appears onstage, made visible to us, the audience, as he had appeared in a dream to Hecuba (69ff.; cf. 54 and 702–8). He is dead, but his body is unburied, "cast forth" (*ekblêtos*, 699; cf. 781), and thus he cannot find the complete quiescence of the dead. His body has been made subject to the restless ebb and flow of the sea (26ff., especially 28–30: κεῖμαι δ’ ἐπ’ ἀκταῖς, ἄλλοτ’ ἐν πόντου σάλῳ, / πολλοῖς διαύλοις κυμάτων φορούμενος, / ἄκλαυτος ἄταφος);[20] and, recovered on the shore, between sea and land, it is not immediately recognized (656–702). His mother's cry of recognition that her fearful dreams have proven true (703–9) harks back to the prologue and formally links this anagnorisis with the role of Polydorus' shade there.[21]

The outer covering of Polydorus' body does not soften the cruelty of its exposed condition: it is described as γυμνωθέν, "made naked" (679). The enfolding garments (peploi), by which Agamemnon can tell that this is not a Greek (734f.), are presumably the remnants of the clothing still clinging to the corpse, although one might assume that it was nude when it washed up from the sea.[22] In any case, these robes remind us that this body was deprived of its proper human covering in death (cf. 30, 679) and is thus a victim of crimes against both human and divine laws.[23]

In the retributive justice of the play, however, the killer is also suspended figuratively between the upper and lower worlds, for in his pain and confusion he would leap to the heavens or plunge into Hades' dark abyss (1099–1106). Like Polydorus, Polymestor is "carried about" without apparent direction (1075, φέρομαι; cf. φορού- μενος of Polydorus' sea-tossed body, 29). He even compares himself to a ship making for land (1079–82), harking back, with poetic justice, to the sea similes of Polydorus' corpse in the prologue.

Polydorus' body links him to the other major Trojan victims. Both he and Hecuba experience the instability of the body's physical state, by metamorphosis in the one case, by exposure and nonburial in the other. In both cases this instability expresses the loss of per- sonal autonomy in the victimage that follows war. Polydorus resem- bles Hecuba through the motif of marine transformation in subjec- tion to external physical force. But his fate is also connected with the fates of his two sisters. When Polyxena was led off to her sacrificial death, she bade farewell to both Polydorus and Cassandra (426–28), whereupon Hecuba expressed her doubts that he was still alive (429). The servant then discovers Polydorus' body when she goes to the shore for the water with which to perform the funerary ablutions for Polyxena (658ff., cf. 609ff.). Hecuba, overwhelmed by this additional blow, asks whether the body is that of Polyxena or Cassandra (671ff.).

The second movement in the action begins with bodies. But now the cycle of violence passes from the sacrificial killing of Polyxena to the betrayal and murder of Polydorus. Agamemnon enters with the query, "Why, Hecuba, do you delay to bury your child?" meaning Polyxena (726f.). She then explains Polydorus' murder and asks to defer the burial of Polyxena until she can bring her children's bodies together. The two siblings are a "double care to their mother," and she will bury them with a "single fire" (μιᾷ φλογί, / δισσὴ μέριμνα μητρί, 894–97; cf. 1051 and also 45). The play ends with a reference back to this scene: Agamemnon commands Hecuba to look after the two bodies of her children, brought together as one by the phrase *diptuchous nekrous* (the twofold corpses, 1287f.; cf. 897, 1051). The play begins with the murder of Polydorus, but Hecuba's revenge for this crime is bracketed by the burial of Polyxena.[24]

The motif of the "two bodies" serves as the signpost of increasing violence. In the prologue Polydorus stresses Hecuba's double loss of children (45f.); but the full significance of line 45, "The mother will see two corpses of two children" (*duoin de paidoin duo nekrô*), emerges only later. The coupling of Hecuba's two children in lines 45 and 897 not only depicts the double suffering of the *mater dolorosa* but also hints at a parallel with the two children of Polymestor. In lines 891–97, in fact, the doubleness of Hecuba's loss follows immediately upon the first allusion to Polymestor's children as part of the revenge she is now plotting. When that revenge is complete, his children, like hers, will be but "bodies of twofold children" (*paidôn dissôn sômata*, 1051).

Clothing is both the covering that can conceal the true form beneath its folds and the sign of an external status or dignity that violence can suddenly strip away. I have already noted how it expresses the sufferings of Hecuba's murdered children, Polydorus and Polyxena. Indeed, on the Attic stage in general clothing has an important symbolic and expressive function. From Xerxes' tearing his robes at the end of the *Persians* to Pentheus' dressing as a maenad in the *Bacchae*, it gives visual enactment to catastrophic changes in status.[25] Euripides in particular is the master of rags, reversals, and sudden revelations, as Aristophanes amusingly shows in *Acharnians* and *Thesmophoriazusae* and plays like the *Telephus* and *Helen* amply illustrate.

When Hecuba begs Odysseus for her daughter's life in the first episode, she reminds him of the time when he was in her power. At that time he came to Troy disguised in ugly rags, as a spy for the army

(Ἰλίου κατάσκοπος / δυσχλαινίᾳ τ᾽ ἄμορφος, 239f.). He then supplicated her, "so that his hand was dead with numbness in [her] robes,"
as he says himself, with vivid recollection of the occasion (ὥστ᾽
ἐνθανεῖν γε σοῖς πέπλοισι χεῖρ᾽ ἐμήν, 246). Now she is the suppliant,
but her supplication is futile. This world has no place for the reverence, reciprocity, and pity (aidôs, charis, oiktos) that a suppliant should
arouse (cf. 254f., 275–78, 285f.). Unlike her mother, however, Polyxena
refuses to plead and instead proudly assures Odysseus that he need
not "hide his hand beneath his garment" (huph' heimatos, 342). Unlike
her conqueror and master, she will not invoke Zeus as god of suppliants to beg for her life (342–45).[26]

This moving scene ends with Polyxena leaving the stage for her
sacrificial death. She asks Odysseus to cover her head with his robes
(amphitheis kara peplois, 432), to spare her the sight of seeing her
mother's tears. Hecuba echoes her daughter's gesture in the next
scene when the herald, Talthybius, finds her, as the chorus says, "all
enclosed in her robes" (sugkeklêmenê peplois, 487), lying on the earth,
prostrate in her grief (cf. Polyxena's "covering her head in her robes,"
432). Hecuba's gesture here pinpoints a critical moment in her transformation. In between these two scenes, the chorus sings the first
stasimon, in which they weave the peplos of Athena at the Pan-
athenaeic Festival as the mark of their future slavery, working their
masters' looms (466–72).

The climax of the play's first half, the slaughter of Polyxena,
reverses some of the abject misery associated with the peplos but
moves the pathos in a new direction. The Herald's narrative makes
the peplos the focus of the sacrificial (and implicitly sexual) violence
to which the girl submits and also of her dignity in the face of that
violence. In the pathetic courage of her voluntary death, she tears
open her peplos to expose her body to the knife (558ff.). This uncovering both contrasts with and fulfills the covering of her head in line 432
as she surrendered her life to Odysseus. As the blood pours out of the
fatal wound (Euripides does not spare us the details), she is still
careful to cover, even in death, what must be hidden from men's eyes
(567–70). Even her killers, in awe and admiration, honor her with the
funeral adornment of a peplos (578). The nakedness of her brother's
corpse, by contrast, shows his murderer's utter disregard for the sanctities that constitute civilized life. To that extent the Greeks are better
than the barbarians, but the comparison does them little honor.

In the *Hecuba*, as also in the *Medea* and *Bacchae*, the dramatic structure has the form of a sudden reversal of the weak and ostensibly powerless in the second half of the play. The motif of the garments helps to articulate that change. The looms that denoted female enslavement in the early portion of the action (363f., 470f.) return as part of the Trojan women's plot of revenge. They are able to get Polymestor's children into their clutches by the device of praising the weavings and robes of the Thracian women (1152–54). Thus an apparent expression of solidarity among women in the submissiveness of female labor turns into an act of murderous rebellion against the patriarchal family, the killing of sons and the overpowering of a powerful king and father. Hecuba thus makes good her promise to a dubious Agamemnon that women's guile and numbers can overcome male strength (*arsenôn kratos*, 883f.).

Early in the play suppliant gestures associated with robes marked the total subjection and powerlessness of women. Now the women's robes conceal the daggers with which they kill Polymestor's sons (λαβοῦσαι φάσγαν᾽ ἐκ πέπλων ποθὲν / κεντοῦσι παῖδας, "taking daggers from somewhere out of their robes, they stab the boys," 1161). This use of concealment and guile completes the first part of Hecuba's plan, in which she leads Polymestor to think that she and her women might have valuables hidden "inside [their] robes" (πέπλων ἐντὸς ἢ κρύψασ᾽ ἔχεις, 1013). The motif of concealment in robes thus undergoes a massive reversal that mirrors the structure of the play. Instead of total female passivity under crushing sorrow and male violence (cf. 432, 487, and above), "concealment in robes" comes to reflect the unexpected resourcefulness, energy, and murderous violence in the erstwhile victims. Citing the example of the Danaids and the Lemnian women, Hecuba had reassured Agamemnon that feminine wiles could defeat "male strength" (883f.) and thus execute vengeance on Polymestor (886f.). Thus the peplos, the sign of women's domesticity, modesty, and obedience to male authority, reveals this hidden other side of the female in tragedy—the sudden, terrible release of murderous, vengeful power. No wonder Polymestor compares these women to "Bacchants of Hades" (1077).

In this transformation of the Trojan women the motif of clothing undergoes another shift. Beneath apparent change lies a hidden constant of personal identity, a potentially monstrous being whose "true" nature is now unveiled. The process is analogous to the *Bac-*

chae's vision of the theriomorphic beside the Olympian Dionysus or to Pentheus' transformation, effected by a change of dress, into a maenad and thence into a hunted beast.[27] Here, as elsewhere, clothing focuses such contrasts and interchanges between outward appearance and inner being, physical form and true character.[28] In the *Hecuba* female clothing reveals its secret of hidden violence, just as the characteristically female interior space (the Trojan women's tent and, later, Clytaemnestra's chamber) becomes the scene of the defeat of male strength. Yet there is an element of instability even in this climactic display of what women may hide within. The mythical metamorphosis of Hecuba at the end both literalizes and continues the inner changes that this woman of sorrows undergoes. Both Hecubas—the helplessly protective mother and the determined, efficient avenger—lie beneath the covering of her torn robes of mourning.

The other transformations in the play are perhaps simpler, but they are necessary to complete the process whereby a hidden inner nature, for good or ill, is laid bare. Polymestor's figurative transformation into the Homeric Cyclops, as we have seen, makes visible the inner monstrosity that lies just beneath the surface of his hypocritical pieties. Having peered well beneath this veneer, Hecuba will not look him in the eyes (968–75).[29]

Polydorus' body was changed by the sea to the point of near unrecognizability. Sent out of Troy because he was too young to bear arms (14f.), fixed in the transitional state between child and adult, he is also, as we see him in the prologue, somewhere between wandering shade and buried corpse. Yet even in his helplessness his journey from Hades to the world above reminds us that the weak have a form of power. The gods of the lower world, at least, are merciful; and this sea-damaged body, from which the shade cannot break completely free despite the cleavage of death (28–31), becomes the evidence that convicts the Thracian king of his crime and sets into motion the terrible justice that avenges it.

Polyxena, finally, like her mother, passes from regal honor to slavery. Yet by her act of uncovering and then concealing her young, vulnerable, beautiful body, she shows that a noble nature, even amid such massive reversals of fortune, can remain true to itself. In the paradoxes and reversals of coverings and concealments in this play, the torn robe that exposes this tender body shows the new and moving heroism of a mere girl who is *psuchên aristê* (noblest in spirit,

580). The only other individual to receive this epithet is Achilles, the great epic warrior of the golden armor (110) and the traditional bearer of the title *aristos*, as he is here, too (134): "the best of the Danaans" (*ton ariston Danaôn pantôn*).[30] Polyxena's "heroism," however, holds the bitter paradox of resting on female submission to male violence.[31]

The play ends not with the constancy of such unexpected and unpredictable nobility but with the transformation and enslavement that have turned all these lives upside down. The only thing that is unyieldingly "hard" in this world of flux and metamorphosis is the brutal force of "necessity." Polymestor uses the word in his cruel prophecy of the death of Cassandra, the last of Hecuba's surviving children (1275); and the play ends with the words "harsh necessity" (στερρὰ γὰρ ἀνάγκη, 1295; cf. 1241). Agamemnon's closing commands about the imminent sea voyage (1283ff., echoed in the chorus's obedience, 1293f.) also remind us of the beginning of the massive change in these women's lives on the night of Troy's fall, as they described it in the third stasimon (905ff., especially 937–41). This "harsh necessity," as the chorus says in their closing lament, effects the final transformation amid all these shifting conditions. It fixes the Trojan matrons forever in their new life as slaves; they, like Hecuba, will change no more from this final form.[32]

10

Violence and the Other:

Greek, Female, and

Barbarian

Like Medea, whose story is almost a mirror image of hers, Hecuba is both female and barbarian. In both respects she occupies the place of the Other; and upon this Other (as in the *Medea*, too) are projected both the doing and the suffering of particularly horrible violence. Euripides may have been willing to risk the play's somewhat disjointed structure, on which criticism has generally focused, to explore the interconnections between war, monstrosity, barbarian violence, women, and the erotic atmosphere of Polyxena's sacrifice.[1] These interconnections include the relation between the violence done *to* the Trojan women by Greeks in the first half of the play and the violence done *by* the Trojan women to the Thracian Polymestor in the second half.

Women's suffering in war, female vengeance, and the contrasts of Greek and barbarian are not entirely symmetrical. The first is a harsh fact of ancient life; the other two are (at least in part) constructions of the imaginary, projections or forms of symbolic representation and conceptualization. But their close interrelation in this play forms a disturbing commentary both on war and on male-female relations in the polis. To project a larger-than-life image of Greek (especially Athenian) social practice, the play combines the familiar Greek polarity of marriage versus war with the Greek analogy between marriage and sacrifice; and it explores the otherness of the female by combining it (as in the *Medea*) with the otherness of the barbarian.

Both the Trojans and the Thracians, to be sure, are barbarians— that is, non-Greeks with whom the Greeks have complex political dealings. Both horrify the "civilized" Greeks by combining brutality, cruelty, and guile. But there are important differences between them. Euripides' Trojans belong to a great polis, already made sympathetic by the *Iliad*, and which the Greeks have battled as an equal. The Thracians possess at least the rudiments of civilization: they farm a rich land (8f.) and have some kind of military organization (1089). Yet the play never mentions a city, only the "house" (*domoi*) where Polymestor was supposed to protect Polydorus. The sphere of his rule is a "land" (*chôra* or *chthôn*), not a city (770f.). His people are devoted to warfare and horses.[2] From Euripides' contemporaries on to Livy, Horace, and Ovid, the Thracians are notorious for their warlike violence, lack of self-control, unreliability in oaths, and drunkenness.[3] Obviously Polymestor has to be civilized enough so that we feel outrage at his betrayal of a solemn trust. But Euripides can also draw on the cultural stereotype of the Thracian barbarian to depict the villainous side of his character and thus motivate our initial sympathy for Hecuba.

The Trojans resemble Greeks in their political institutions. In other plays, too, notably *Andromache* and *Trojan Women*, Trojan victims are not only sympathetically presented but are even morally superior to their Greek captors.[4] Trojan women attract Greek men (albeit fatally); and in the *Hecuba* they even compare their sufferings in war with those of Greek women (649–56).[5] Their dress often bears a resemblance to Greek clothing, while Thracian dress never does. The women of Troy perform their toilette in a manner recognizably Greek (923–27) and wear a peplos to bed, "like a Dorian girl" (933f.).[6] When Hecuba confides to Agamemnon her plot against Polymestor, the Greek king, speaking to the Trojan woman, refers to the Thracian as "a barbarian" (*phôta barbaron*, 877). And when Agamemnon speaks of *to barbaron* in general as a synonym for uncontrolled violence, he is addressing the enraged Polymestor, whom he tells to "expel the barbarian element [*to barbaron*] from his heart" so that he can state his case coherently (1129).

The play rings the changes on these shifting ties among the

three groups. Trojans and Thracians have an old relation of guest-friendship, which Polymestor's betrayal changes to hatred. Agamemnon, bound by military alliance to the Thracians, works secretly as an ally of the Trojan queen. He and Hecuba have the pivotal roles, for both are involved in a three-way bond among Greek, Trojan, and Thracian, with surprising reversals in each case.

The locale not only makes possible this three-way interaction, it also deepens the play's moral consciousness. The Thracian Chersonese, though important and familiar to Athenians from at least the sixth century (cf. Herodotus 6.34ff.), is also remote enough to function symbolically as a kind of moral no-man's land, a world where all morality is endangered. The audience seems to be at the fringes of civilization, with the smouldering ruins of a great city in the background and the bloody sacrifice of a Trojan virgin in the foreground. Here, as in the Taurian Chersonese of a later play, *Iphigeneia in Tauris*, the savagery of human sacrifice can be practised, but by Greeks, not barbarians. The conclusion of the Trojan War, far from ending violence, permits betrayal, releases bloodlust, and promotes an ethos of seeking an eye for an eye.[7]

The death of Polyxena, which dominates the first half of the play, is a strong enactment of the violence and violation that war brings to women. Her fate is decided by the all-male "army of the Hellenes" (117f.). Though the decision is hotly debated, the outcome is virtually a foregone conclusion (cf. 40–44). This community, unlike that of Aeschylus' *Agamemnon* or Euripides' *Iphigeneia in Aulis*, is not shaken apart by such an action; nor do we witness prolonged conflict, doubt, and agony over the decision as we do in the other plays. Indeed, we may wonder if Euripides is reflecting pessimistically on his own city when he has the "two sons of Theseus, scions of Athens, . . . with one mind agree to crown Achilles' tomb with the [girl's] pale blood" (123–27).[8]

The details of the sacrifice are highly eroticized, following the pattern of the sacrifice of Agamemnon's own daughter, Iphigeneia, at the beginning of the war.[9] Polyxena's naked body, about to be pierced and bloodied by the sacrificial knife, is viewed from the perspective of the masculine gaze (558ff.).[10] When she rips open her robe from shoulder to navel to reveal the usually covered portion of a young girl's body, the assembled soldiery is watching to see her given in death to Achilles. To these exclusively male spectators she "showed her breasts and chest most lovely, like a statue's" (μαστούς τ' ἔδειξε στέρνα θ' ὡς ἀγάλματος / κάλλιστα, 560f.). Euripides' own audience, we should recall, may have been entirely male; the judges, in any case, certainly were.

War here displaces erotic into destructive energy, an insight that haunts Greek and Roman reflections on war from the *Iliad* on to Herodotus, Euripides' own *Helen* and *Iphigeneia in Aulis*, and Virgil's *Aeneid*.[11] The play shows two forms of sexual violation, Polyxena's sacrifice and Cassandra's sexual enslavement (824ff.), and they are analogues of one another—allomorphs, one could say. The two daughters are, in fact, brought together explicitly in the parode (126–30). Polyxena knows that the alternative to her sacrificial death includes sexual servitude (365f., cf. 351–53). While Polyxena's sacrifice is central to the present dramatic situation, in the background is another, more general eroticization of the violence of war, developed in the third stasimon (905–52)—the last full ode that the chorus sings in the play.[12] This ode begins with the women's lament over the city's violation: Troy is no longer among the inviolable cities; it is "shorn of its crown of towers" (910f.) and defiled by the "stain" (*kêlis*) of the fire and smoke of the attackers. The image of the city "shorn of its crown of towers" immediately establishes the analogy between the (figurative) rape of the city and the actual violation of its women. Euripides here draws on the Homeric analogy between breaking the *krêdemnon* (veil) of the city's towers and tearing the *krêdemnon* that protects a matron's chastity.[13]

This analogy moves from figure to reality as the chorus takes us into the intimate space of their bedchambers where they undress and prepare to lie with their husbands on the night of Troy's fall. In this long and detailed description of a woman's boudoir (914–41), fully in the manner of Euripides' domestic realism, we see the horrors of war from a uniquely female perspective.[14] We may be reminded of the contrast between warriors and women in Aeschylus' *Seven Against Thebes*, but Euripides' mood is intimate rather than martial. The Trojan women are in their bedchambers, indeed in bed, not on the city walls. They reveal their sexual vulnerability as they tell how at the shout of the attack they each leap up, leaving the intimacy of the bed (λέχη φίλια, 933, possibly with erotic connotations), "wearing a single shift, like a Dorian maid," and are not even able to supplicate

Artemis (933–36). Here, as in the case of Polyxena, the categories of virgin (cf. *kora*, 934) and married woman are thrown into disarray. Though seen in their sexual role as married women, they nevertheless compare themselves to a maiden, and they would take refuge with the goddess who protects virginity and is particularly concerned with girls in their transitional state between maidenhood and marriage. But what awaits them is not the (sanctioned) loss of virginity but the loss of the chastity of marriage.

This violation is, in fact, immediately invoked as the chorus continues, "I am led away toward the sea's passage, seeing my husband dead, as I look back toward the city" (937–38). The deaths of the husbands for whom the singers were adorning themselves earlier seal their fate as a sexual commodity to be enjoyed by a new possessor.[15] The sexual theme, however, goes still a stage further in the epode as the chorus curses Helen and the marriage that has destroyed their city (943–52).

The dynamics of the plot consist in the abrupt reversal of the female from victim to agent, a pattern that Euripides uses (in different ways) in *Medea, Ion,* and *Bacchae.* In this way the violence in the martial realm, outside, moves within, to the interior space of women's domain. One of Polyxena's functions in the play is to make this reversal as sharp as possible by enacting the role of helpless, if noble, submission to male violence. She also helps to connect martial with sexual violence. She thus introduces into this remote setting themes associated with the *oikos* that will become important at the play's end.

Commentators generally single out Polyxena as the one bright spot in the darkness of the action.[16] In an otherwise admirable book on Euripides, André Rivier, for example, calls the dying Polyxena "only the image of a perfect body, falling under the knife of the priest, without losing anything of the purity of its forms, of the harmony and decency of its marvelous nudity. The blood that spurts from her throat speaks to us not of cruelty nor of nothingness, but it underlines the radiance of this transfigured flesh, beautiful as palpitating marble."[17] Even critics who recognize the horror of the scene succumb to its alluring mixture of reverence and the personal nobility of the victim.[18] These modern critics fall into Euripides' trap. They confound the admiration that we are supposed to feel for the victim with the circumstances of her killing. Like Iphigeneia in the *Aulis*, with whom she is often compared, Polyxena proves to be the ideal victim: she makes no appeal to her suppliant status, offers no resistance (342–45), and submissively acquiesces in serving and enhancing with her body the honor of a warrior.

Talthybius, the herald who narrates the death scene, is sympathetic to both Polyxena and Hecuba. But even his sympathy shows something insidious. His report suggests an interpretation of the human sacrifice that elides its brutality. Commentators tend to take Talthybius' point of view and emphasize the nobility of Polyxena's self-chosen end at the climax of the scene (553–75). But the very mention of Polyxena's "modestly hiding what should be hidden from men's eyes" calls attention to the sexual violation that lurks behind the ritual violence. At the same time these details suggest the sexual violation that Polyxena has escaped, a fate the other women of Troy, including her sister, Cassandra, cannot avoid.[19] They thus make the reasons for her choice all the clearer, though they do not lessen its nobility.

The pathos of Polyxena's death scene is all the greater because it draws on the deep associations of marriage and death that run throughout Greek culture. For the young bride marriage is a rite of passage involving loss and separation. The primary mythical exemplar of marriage from the girl's point of view is the Maiden, Kore or Persephone, who literally suffers sexual violence sanctioned by Father Zeus and makes a forced descent to the underworld. The girl who dies young is the "bride of Hades";[20] and Polyxena herself laments that it is as "a nonbride, without marriage song," that she will "lie in Hades' house" (416, 418; cf. 612). Like a bride, the virgin Polyxena submits to male violence (however muted) in the name of a social order dominated by masculine authority. The myth of the Danaids, as Marcel Detienne reminds us, reveals violence as the necessary complement to the fructifying sexual union of marriage, in the Greek view.[21]

In Greek tragedy particularly, marriage and death are interlocking phenomena. In Euripides' *Iphigeneia in Aulis*, the girl's engagement in marriage to Achilles is a ruse for the sacrifice to which she is destined as the victim. In the *Medea* another kind of ruse transforms a bride's wedding into a horrible funeral.[22] Euripides' *Alcestis* and *Helen* and Sophocles' *Trachiniae* and *Antigone* also offer close parallels for the intertwining of marriage and death, especially sacrificial death.[23] Marriage and sacrificial killing go together as model acts of the civilized city; but here, as elsewhere in tragedy, that combination marks the contradictions and tensions that exist within the social order, as disturbing parts of what most members of the audience would prefer to see as the seamless fabric of civilized life.[24]

The interchangeability of marriage and sacrifice is a logical consequence of this total subjugation of women in a world where they are either slaves or concubines, or both. The exchange of women between men in marriage under the patriarchal order of the city is here replaced by the exchange of women between men through human sacrifice. The military society of the camp and of the martial assembly displaces marriage into the transgressive form of human sacrifice, only to reveal the affinity between the two.

The women are the most visible (though of course not the only) victims of the new amorality. Hecuba's attempts to change the assembly's decision and assert her maternal claim to her daughter's life are brutally shunted aside (cf. 90f., 141–43). Supplication in the past may have saved her from death, and for enslavement (289f., 301f.). Now that plea is ineffectual (288–90). She is not even allowed to join her daughter in death (391–408). In place of the bond between mother and daughter, Odysseus maintains the right of the all-male society of warriors to give the bodies of its women to the best men as a reward for valor and a mark of honor (306–20). Hecuba may invoke a universalizing law (799ff.), but to gain her revenge she has to work on and through Agamemnon and by ad hominem arguments.

The motifs of marriage and sacrifice come into particularly close proximity through the metaphor of the heifer (*moschos*, 206f., 526). This is a familiar metaphor for a young girl approaching marriage;[25] but the heifer is also, as here, the beast for the sacrifice. In the anticipations of this sacrificial slaughter early in the play, Polyxena is implicitly compared to a young spotted doe bloodied by a wolf (90f.) and to a foal taken away from its mother (141f.).[26] Both are images associated with marriageable girls. The second of the two heifer metaphors, in fact, introduces the account of Polyxena's sacrificial death and plays on the double inversion. The "leaping heifer" separated from her mother and placed among the "select young men" (525f.) is not the bride (as the imagery, in a different context, might lead the audience to think) but the sacrificial victim. The blood that is to be gathered in a basin and poured out in ritual libation (535f.) is not that of a real heifer but "the black blood, unmixed, of a girl" (536f.). The conventional images here become horribly literal.[27]

In her last onstage scene, Polyxena allows herself to be led away because she prefers the "bed" of Hades to the bed of a slave. "I was nurtured," she says, "amid noble hopes as a bride for kings" (351f.). And so now she announces her resolve to Odysseus: "No bought slave from somewhere will stain my bed that in time before was deemed worthy of kings" (365f.). Her use of "stain" or "defile" (*chrainein*, 366) evokes sexual violation and prepares for the sexual connotations of the sacrificial act later.[28] Instead of such a base union, she will "place her body next to Hades'" (368), a phrase suggestive of the convention by which a girl who dies unmarried is the bride of Hades.

By this choice, first, of Hades and freedom rather than sexual union with a slave, and, later, of voluntary surrender to the sword rather than violence and (implicitly) sexual violation, she remains an ambiguous *parthenos*. She is, of course, intact sexually, as a *parthenos* should be. Yet the substitutions—the bloody wound in place of defloration, sacrifice on Achilles' tomb in place of marriage—leave her virgin status anomalous. As the mark of her sacrificial death, the blood seals her unmarried condition; but blood is also closely associated with the biological changes that define a girl's passage from *parthenos* to *gunê*.[29] Her anomalous situation perhaps accounts for the elaborate physical description in lines 558–70, for, as commentators observe, so detailed an account of the female body is unusual for this period.[30]

When Talthybius tells how Polyxena showed her breasts "like a statue" (559f.), the image of artistic beauty, tinged perhaps by the religiosity also associated with the statue or *agalma*, keeps the scene at a certain aesthetic distance. Such is the effect to which Rivier is responding when he extols "the purity of [her body's] forms, the harmony and decency of its marvelous nudity."[31] Showing the breasts can have an erotic nuance, as in Helen's gesture (in a very different situation) in *Andromache*, line 629. But Talthybius' description also echoes Polyxena's appeal to Hecuba's maternal breasts in line 424 (cf. 424, ὦ στέρνα μαστοί θ᾽ οἵ μ᾽ ἐθρέψαθ᾽ ἡδέως and 560, μαστούς τ᾽ ἔδειξε στέρνα θ᾽). Thus it conveys both the pathetic helplessness of a young girl leaving her mother and the continuity between the violation of the girl and the violence done to the mother (cf. also 405–8).

Euripides' rhetoric here disturbs by shifting between the distanced aesthetic contemplation of a beautiful object and the emotional involvement of pity and pathos. In harsh contrast to this generalized beauty of Polyxena's form are the specific parts of the body into which Neoptolemus thrusts his weapon in the next lines: throat, windpipe, blood, and breath. The details bring home to us the corporeal reality of Polyxena; she is not a statue but a human sacrificial victim. The distancing suggested in the statue image is even more sharply reduced later when Hecuba begs Agamemnon for help: "Pity us, and standing away, like a painter [*grapheus*], look at me and behold what sufferings I have" (807f.). Now the art object's effect has definitively shifted from pleasure to pity and horror. Even the aesthetic distance is intended to enhance involvement. The simile of the painter beholding at a distance a scene of suffering can also suggest the mixture of pain and pleasure of the tragic spectacle as a whole.[32] If so, Euripides' self-conscious poetics subtly remind us once more how the tragic paradox makes a pleasurable spectacle of the most painful suffering.

These contradictions surface in the sacrifice itself, where the ambivalence of the killer, Neoptolemus, clashes with the brutal directness of the slash that ends the girl's life: ὁ δ' οὐ θέλων τε καὶ θέλων οἴκτῳ κόρης / τέμνει σιδήρῳ πνεύματος διαρροάς (And he, both unwilling and yet willing, out of pity for the girl, cut with the iron [knife] the passage of her breathing, 566f.). Neoptolemus' "pity for the girl" continues to cue the audience toward sympathy for Polyxena. Yet the starkness of the next clause, introducing the honors that the army heaps on her corpse, quietly but firmly sets into relief what has happened to a living being (571): "When she let forth her breathing at the slash that brought death . . ." (ἐπεὶ δ' ἀφῆκε πνεῦμα θανασίμῳ σφαγῇ). The repetition of the word *pneuma* (breath) from line 567 keeps in the foreground the physical violence of ending a life.[33]

The choice of Neoptolemus as the wielder of the sacrificial knife (223f., 523ff.) is traditional;[34] but Euripides uses the detail to intensify the brutality of the killing, reminding us that Neoptolemus is also the one who killed Priam at his altar (a hint at sacrificial slaying), as Euripides takes care to inform us early in the play (23f.): "[Priam] himself falls at the god-built altar, slaughtered by the murderous son of Achilles." The contrast between the two decorative adjectives, "god-built" and "murderous" (*theodmêtos*, 23; *miaiphonos*, 24), though they are spoken by a hostile witness, prepares us for the literally sacrificial violence to come, with the altar replaced by the tomb.

The contrast between Polyxena's acquiescence and Hecuba's almost demonic skill and resourcefulness in gaining revenge shows women polarized between two extremes: the submissive virgins, Polyxena and Cassandra, and the dangerous mothers who avenge their children, Hecuba and, later, Clytaemnestra. The polarity between submission and power pervades the play. It is acted out before our eyes in the two aspects of Hecuba, the desperate suppliant and the demonic avenger.[35] To prove that she can succeed in her vengeance, Hecuba cites the examples of the Danaids and the Lemnian women, women who kill husbands (886f.). The latter, in the famous central ode of Aeschylus' *Libation Bearers*, are the example par excellence of women as figures of monstrosity (*Choephoroe* 631–45).[36] Polymestor in fact bitterly echoes that ode at the end of his speech of defense (1177–82): "Not to stretch out lengthy words, if anyone of men of times past has spoken ill of women or if there is anyone to do so in the present or in the future, I will sum them all up and declare: Such a race neither sea nor earth nurtures, and he who encounters it understands this well." The phrase "men of times past" is probably an explicit allusion to Aeschylus (cf. *Choephoroe* 585–88).

Like Hecuba and her fellow captives, the Danaids and the Lemnian women embody collective female violence. When Agamemnon asks Hecuba how women will overcome men, she answers, "Terrible is a massed group [*plêthos*] of women, and with their guile hard to fight against" (884). "Mass" and "guile" (*plêthos* and *dolos*) supply the want of physical strength. Hecuba's promise to Agamemnon is made good (so to speak) when her victim, Polymestor, tells how "the mass of women" held him down to blind him with their pins (*plêthei gunaikôn*, 1167). Just as the women are about to execute their vengeance, the chorus boasts that an "unwarlike hand" will destroy their enemy (*apolemôi cheiri*, 1034).

The women's sudden change from fondling the boys to murdering them is evocative of another form of collective female violence, the maenads' sudden change from Golden Age bliss to savagery in the *Bacchae* (689–78). That scene, to be sure, would not be written for some twenty years, but the pattern of maenadic violence was suffi-

180

Euripides

and the Poetics

of Sorrow

ciently established in myth and art to serve as a model for the Trojan women here. Polymestor in fact calls his Trojan attackers "Bacchants of Hades" (1076).[37] In both cases the domesticity (real or feigned) of women's weaving changes abruptly to horrible bloodshed, and the change reveals the hidden intensity of female violence.[38] The Trojan women's turnabout from quasi-maternal solicitude (1157) to murder, though premeditated, resembles in its suddenness the maenads' shift from suckling wild beasts to warfare and again reverses the traditional female role (*Bacchae* 701, 723ff., 734ff.). The maternal violence of the *Hecuba*, one might say, is a trial run for the more terrible and more literally maternal violence of the *Bacchae*.

"Will you take a sword in your aged hand and kill a barbarian man?" So Agamemnon incredulously questions Hecuba about her wish for vengeance (876f.). Though Polymestor is a man "most hard to combat" (*dusmachôtatos*, 1055), he is vulnerable to women who are *dusmachoi* in their own way (884). Female violence does not need the sword or the drugs that Agamemnon mentions in line 878. Its distinctive character emerges in the overdetermined form of bestiality and bacchantic madness in Polymestor's description of the women (884). "Women destroyed me, captive women," he cries; "terrible, terrible are the things we suffered" (1094f.). And then, more calmly: "Hecuba destroyed me with the captive women—no, not destroyed, but something greater" (1120). And finally, when Agamemnon decides against him: "Alas, I am defeated by a woman, then, and submit to punishment from those baser than a female slave" (1252f.). Disbelieving Hecuba's ability to execute her vengeance, Agamemnon called the captive women the "prey of the Greeks" (*Hellênôn agran*, 881); but in their revenge they themselves become the predatory beasts (1077–79, cf. 1072–75).

As in the *Bacchae*, the reversals between victim and agent also involve an interchange of human and beast in sacrifice. The sacrifice of a human in place of a beast (cf. 260f.) is answered by a transformation of human murderers into their bestial equivalent. Polymestor becomes a four-footed beast raging to sate itself on human flesh (1056–60, 1071f.). The Trojan women are octopi—creatures emblematic of trickery—that snatch at human hands and feet (1162–64).[39] Hecuba, finally, will become a doglike monster (1271–73).[40]

The collective violence of the women, however, finds its strongest image in the scene of Dionysiac *sparagmos* that Polymestor evokes.

He imagines Hecuba and her companions as Bacchants, not of Dionysus but of Hades, celebrants of a grisly perversion of ritual as they "divide up" his children as "sacrificial victims" and as "a bloody feasting for dogs, and as [flesh] savagely cast forth on the mountains" (1075–78):

ποῖ πᾷ φέρομαι τέκν' ἔρημα λιπὼν
Βάκχαις "Αιδα διαμοιρᾶσαι
σφακτά, κυσίν τε φοινίαν δαῖτ' ἀνή—
μερόν τ' ὄρειον ἐκβολάν.[41]

The imagery of dismemberment, cannibalism, and sacrificial slaughter echoes, with obvious "poetic justice," the cries of Hecuba as she learned of Polymestor's murder of her son (716–20):

ὡς διεμοιράσω
χρόα, σιδαρέῳ τεμὼν φασγάνῳ
μέλεα τοῦδε παιδὸς οὐδ' ᾤκτισας.

How you divided up the flesh, with iron sword cleaving the limbs of this child, and showed no pity.

She significantly repeats the rather rare verb *diamoirân*, "divide up" (as a sacrificial victim), "rend apart," that she used of Polymestor's murder of her son.[42] This association of female collective violence with the mountains also collapses the familiar distinction between the women's interior, domestic space and the wild outside; the former proves, paradoxically, to be just as savage as the latter.

Hecuba's vengeance against Polymestor is continuous with the sacrificial violence against Polyxena. In both cases there is a chilling contrast of physical intimacy and brutal bloodshed (546–80 and 1148–71), and in both cases bodies are made "bare" or defenseless for slaughter (558–65; cf. γυμνόν μ' ἔθηκαν, 1156, of Polymestor's weapons). Polymestor's cries in lines 1075–79, however, suggests a monstrous expansion of that perverted rite. No longer in the community (minimal as it is) or under the control of men, the captive women are, for the moment, wild Bacchants who rend and "divide" male children as sacrificial meat and then leave the remains on the mountain for dogs and beasts. The progression from child murder to a bacchantic, Fury-like sparagmos and devouring of human flesh is also an implicit commentary on the real barbarism hidden beneath the claims of heroic honor in war.

By presenting the sacrifice of the daughter as a narrative directed primarily at her mother, Euripides brings together the two areas of war's violence against women: the highly eroticized blood sacrifice of the virgin and the helplessness and enslavement of the older woman. As in the case of Aeschylus' Clytaemnestra and Euripides' own Medea, however, the mother's rage and grief prove to be far from ineffectual. Subjected she may be, but Hecuba's anger cannot be brought under the control of those who have power over her. It operates under the aegis of male authority and legalism (Agamemnon's consent), but it soon takes its own direction into the realm of the demonic and the monstrous.

This movement from martial sacrifice to the hints of bacchantic *sparagmos* in Hecuba's revenge is simultaneously a movement from a fantasy of total male control to a nightmare of invincible female violence. The blinding of Polymestor also suggests symbolical castration, particularly when combined with the destruction of his two male children.[43] The *Medea* uses a very similar pattern: Medea starts out with her domestic pleas and her subjection to the male rulers of the land, first King Creon of Corinth and then King Aegeus of Athens. But at the end she also murders two male children and unleashes her own personal power in the magical poisons and the dragon-borne chariot.[44] Like Medea, Hecuba overcomes male strength and attacks a man where he is most vulnerable to the female, in his need for children (especially sons) to continue his line. And like Clytaemnestra in Aeschylus' *Agamemnon* (an important text in the background of this play), Hecuba also takes revenge for children who have been made the instruments of the war games and power plays of the male generals and politicians.[45]

Euripides complicates the mother's revenge by making it depend on the sexual servitude of her other daughter, Cassandra, who proves to be Hecuba's strongest argument in winning Agamemnon's help. But because Cassandra's victimage so closely parallels Polyxena's, Hecuba's use of Cassandra deepens her own degradation. The Greeks use Polyxena's body as an offering to Achilles to express gratitude to (and win favor from) his ghost. Hecuba uses Cassandra's body to win Agamemnon's gratitude and favor, close upon the army's respect for Polyxena because she gave her body willingly to the sacrificial knife. Here, in both love and war, the principle of reciprocity, denoted by *charis*, is involved (cf. 830), but *charis* is successful only for base or murderous ends.[46]

Although Cassandra never physically appears in the play, she has an important place beside her two murdered siblings. Polyxena addresses her last farewells to Cassandra as well as to Polydorus (426–28). Later, after the sacrifice, the servant sent to the shore to fetch water for Polyxena's funerary libations finds the body of Polydorus. When she reports this wrenching news, Hecuba asks if it is the body of Cassandra (676f.).[47] In this latter scene the deaths of all three children are, prophetically, joined together; and in all three cases the body is the focus of the dramatic power.

To win Agamemnon's support for her revenge, Hecuba falls back on the "gratitude" (*charis*) that he owes both her and Cassandra for "the dearest embraces in bed" (830).[48] In the lines that follow, Hecuba goes on to use *charis* in a slightly different but related meaning, as the joy or pleasure of sex: "From the dark and its nocturnal spells [*philtra*] there comes the greatest joy [*charis*] to mortals" (831f.). Some recent editors delete these two lines, which occur in the manuscripts but have one or two (easily correctable) textual problems and are familiar from various late anthologies.[49] We would doubtless be more comfortable without them. If they are genuine, they are not alien to Hecuba's desperation in attempting to link as closely as possible the two kinds of *charis*, the sexual joy or pleasure that Agamemnon has in Cassandra and the consequent gratitude that he should feel toward Hecuba. The point is not lost on Agamemnon, for in his reply he acknowledges the claims of justice but also raises as an objection the fear that he may seem to his army to be acting out of "gratitude" or "favor" toward Cassandra (*Kassandras charin*, 855).

There is no reason to doubt that Agamemnon is genuinely moved by pity and justice, in contrast with the coldly practical and legalistic Odysseus. In fact, the repetition of the phrase αἰδέσθητί με, "Respect my supplication," from Hecuba's supplication of Odysseus (286 and 806) reminds us of that previous scene. But the shift from law to sex within Hecuba's appeal to Agamemnon in lines 799–832 not only lays bare the moral bankruptcy of this world; it also confirms the sexual dynamics behind the war itself.

Paradoxically, Hecuba's success, moving as she does from law to sex, clarifies the helplessness of law. Neither religion nor the traditional sanctities can do much to check the cycles of violence that the war has released. In the absence of divine intervention, the prophetic role frequently assigned to the deus ex machina in the exodos is taken by the raging, frustrated, blinded barbarian murderer.[50] The only viable source of law is the Greek army, but it is unruly, bloodthirsty, and corrupted by demagogues who appeal to its basest instincts (cf. 131–40).[51]

Polyxena's sacrifice was a public act, done in the open space before the entire army in the clear light of day. Hecuba's acts of murder and mutilation belong to the dark, private space of the captive women. In tragedy this offstage space, often representing the interior of the house or palace, functions as the space of the irrational or the aspects of personality that are hidden, dark, and fearful. It is often the place of female sexuality, deceit, and revenge. Here Hecuba's unseen violence answers a crime that is "unspeakable, unnamable, unholy, unendurable" (714f.). She begins by preparing the interior space for its grim work. She reassures Agamemnon that her revenge plot will succeed with the line "These enclosures [of the tent, *stegai*] conceal a crowd of women" (880). When she puts her plot into action, she lures Polymestor into the tent with a disingenuous statement about the safety of these enclosures (1014–19):

> Hecuba. The chambers [*stegai*] of the captive women are set apart.
>
> Polymestor. Is it safe inside, and are there no men?
>
> Hecuba. No men of the Achaeans are within, only us women, alone. Come then into the house [*es oikous*].

By this false security of the proffered chambers Hecuba avenges the murderous betrayal of a child in what should have been a safe shelter (cf. 1212, 1224f.).

The association of these private interiors of the women with deception and trickery has already been established by a small but important detail earlier in the play. In order to adorn the body of Polyxena for burial, Hecuba has recourse to the jewelry of "her companions inside the tent" (616), which, though they are now slaves and captives, they have "concealed from their masters" as a "theft from their own homes" (εἴ τις τοὺς νεωστὶ δεσπότας / λαθοῦσ' ἔχει τι κλέμμα τῶν αὐτῆς δόμων, 617f.). Even though this "stealing" (cf.

klemma, 618) is, in a sense, of their own property, the motif associates the interior of the tent with the resources of female guile (cf. 884). This is the first hint of the women's skill as deceivers, but when they next employ deceit it will be not for the benign purpose of piously celebrating a funeral.

The bait for Hecuba's trap is not only the gold hidden within the women's private quarters; there is much more gold, according to Hecuba's ploy, in the private "chambers" of Troy's female goddess, in the *stegai* of Athena (1009). The same word, *stegai*, is used for the Trojan captives' tent only a few lines later (1016). When Hecuba describes the supposed treasure as "the ancient caverns of the Priamids' gold" (χρυσοῦ παλαιαὶ Πριαμιδῶν κατώρυχες, 1002), she overdetermines this association of female plotting, interior space, and concealment, especially as *Priamidôn* can also mean "the women of Troy." Polymestor makes the motif of concealment explicit when he rephrases Hecuba's line later, while denouncing her plot, and calls the alleged treasure "the Priamids' hidden coffers" (κεκρυμμένας θήκας Πριαμιδῶν, 1146f.).[52]

Polymestor's blind raging enacts before us, in the "real" world of this drama, the part of the "mythical" Cyclops of Homer's *Odyssey* (1056–82).[53] Hecuba's victory imitates the crafty vengeance of her Greek enemy, Odysseus, in his famous attack on the Cyclops. Like Odysseus, she practises guile—*dolos* or *mêtis*—to blind a monstrous enemy and take revenge for the murder of her own. Soon after that she suffers the literal change of identity, fulfilling Polymestor's prophecy of her transformation into a sea monster—a bitch with fiery eyes (1265ff.).[54] As her desire for vengeance destroys her character, Hecuba begins to approximate her barbarian and bestial antagonist, Polymestor. The opposites become twins. His animality is acted out externally (1056–59, 1070–72); hers is shown inwardly and then reflected by the metamorphosis, as a symbolic projection of the inner change that we have seen developing throughout the play.

The blurring of the distinction between victim and agent that has already been adumbrated between Agamemnon and Hecuba in a common subjection to necessity (864ff.) now extends to Hecuba and Polymestor, but at a more bestial level.[55] Although the two murderers exchange the roles of agent and victim, deceiver and deceived, they remain impenetrable to one another's pain. When Polymestor grieves over his dead sons and his blinded eyes (1255), Hecuba replies,

"You feel pain. What then? Do you not think that I feel pain for my child?" (1256). Such reciprocity of feeling, like other forms of reciprocity in the play, has no place in this world. He can answer only with the taunting, "Do you rejoice in doing outrage [*hubrizein*] to me, you evil-doer?" (1257).

The most fearful metamorphosis of the play, then, is not the future change in Hecuba but the way the two enemies come to resemble one another in the present. As Hecuba moves from just avenger to monster, she will become literally a stranger to herself; she becomes one with her own hatred, trickery, and murderousness. We may recall her invocation of the Lemnian women and the Danaids as women capable of murderous deeds with whom she compares herself (886f.). Her metamorphosis signifies not just the loss of control over her body but also the loss of control over her hatred and violence. When vengefulness thus gets out of control, it overrides all other considerations, including the loss of her humanity: "This is of no concern, as long as you pay the penalty to me," is her reply to Polymestor's prophecy that she will be fixed forever in the form of a dog (1274).[56] The situation is a mythicized equivalent of Thucydides' account of the degrading transformations of character and language in the Corcyrean revolt (especially 3.82.1 and 83.1).

In this world of undifferentiated violence, the distinction between Greek and barbarian so fundamental to Greek moral values in the fifth century becomes attenuated. In the later stages of the Peloponnesian War, for example, Euripides and Thucydides both associated the violence of war with the barbarization that reached within Greece. Euripides presents a Trojan mother, Andromache, accusing the Greeks of "inventing barbarian evils" in killing her child (ὦ βάρβαρ' ἐξευρόντες Ἕλληνες κακά, *Trojan Women* 764).[57] Thucydides registers horror at the Thracian mercenaries who in 413 B.C. cut down all the children in a school in the Boeotian town of Mycalessus (7.29.4). In fact, he singles out the Thracians for their bloodthirstiness: "The race of the Thracians, like the most murderous of the barbarian peoples, when it becomes emboldened, is murderous in the extreme" (*phonikôtaton*, 7.29.4).[58] War confuses not only the categories of civilized and barbarian but also, as we have seen, those of human and animal, justice and revenge, the normal and the monstrous.

In the last section of the play the Greeks are on the sidelines. They are technically in control, but the fulcrum of power has shifted to the barbarians and their thirst for bloody vengeance. The Greeks are distanced, horrified, protected by the screen of their power. But they are also inseparable participants, and their fate is drawn into that of the barbarians. At the end the issue ceases to involve Greeks at all; it becomes a conflict between the two barbarians, Hecuba and Polymestor.

This final struggle reveals the complementary dangers of the barbarian character: the savagery and cruelty of Polymestor and the wiliness, vengefulness, and trickery of Hecuba. There is a wily cruelty in Polymestor, too: he keeps probing for the places where he can hurt Hecuba until he finally hits on the prophecy about Cassandra's murder, the detail that will cause her the greatest possible pain.

The play closes with Polymestor's prophecy of the bloody events in Argos. Again like the Homeric Cyclops, he would mar his enemy's success by telling a prophecy of future suffering that he knows from his special relation to divinity (cf. 1267).[59] His scene of violence shifts from the Chersonese back to the center of Greece as he foretells Agamemnon's own death by his "bitter housekeeper" (1277, 1279).[60] The audience realizes, as Agamemnon does not, that he is watching his own story played out in this wild, un-Grecian setting.

This remote setting reflects back to the king of the Greek heartland the other side of Hecuba's own story. Not only is his fate in Argos the continuation of the sufferings of the Trojan queen; it is also a fearful mirror image of her story, translated into Greek terms. Back in Greece, Clytaemnestra will play the role of Hecuba, as Iphigeneia has already played that of Polyxena, and Agamemnon himself will become Polymestor.[61] Like Polymestor, he will be the powerful male who suffers bloody wounds at the hands of a woman in an interior space to which female plotting, vengeful cunning, and persuasion have lured him. The echo of Aeschylus' *Agamemnon* also reminds us that Agamemnon had already played the role Odysseus plays here by sacrificing a young girl to the spirit of war in the rites at Aulis, and also thus appeasing a wrathful deity who withheld a sailing wind.[62] Euripides prepares us for this identification in Polymestor's offstage cry at his children's death, "Alas, once more" (ὤμοι μάλ' αὖθις, 1037). He exactly repeats Agamemnon's offstage cry when he is struck his death blow by Clytaemnestra in *Agamemnon* (1345).

By being drawn literally and figuratively into both the tone and the substance of the struggle between the Thracian and the Trojan murders, Agamemnon once more calls attention to the permeability of the barrier between Greek and barbarian. In expanding into a three-way struggle this brutal conflict between an insatiably vengeful old woman and a brutal, treacherous barbarian king, Euripides is showing to the Greeks the barbarization that is going on among them, even in Greece itself (cf. Thucydides 3.82f.). Through Polymestor's prophecy, the quarrels in Troy will, in fact, extend to Greece, which is inevitably engulfed in the barbarization of human relations that we have witnessed on this distant Thracian shore.

This last scene completes Agamemnon's shifting position between distance and involvement. Asked to "stand at a distance like a painter" to see Hecuba's "woes" (*kaka*) clearly (807f.), he finds himself increasingly drawn into these woes. A little later Hecuba invokes as "perhaps foreign to the argument" (τοῦ λόγου ξένον, 824) what is actually its most relevant point, the presence of Cassandra at Agamemnon's "side," in the bed of love (826, 829). That direct, carnal proximity pulls him, albeit reluctantly, from the sidelines into Hecuba's revenge plot (cf. 850–63). In the last scene, he is ostensibly to "serve as judge of another's woes" (τἀλλότρια κρίνειν κακά, 1240), and he is supposedly duty bound not to "drive these away" to someone else (ἀπώσασθαι, 1242). But these "foreign woes" very soon migrate to his own house (1277, 1290f.). He then orders the ally whom he regarded as a friend and as having a "common" (*koinon*) interest with the army (858–60) to be dragged "out of the way" and "cast forth" to a desert island (ἐκποδών, ἐκβαλεῖτε, 1282, 1285).

Agamemnon shares the moral blindness of the now physically blinded Polymestor, who is not only a perverted deus ex machina and a form of the tricked, blinded Cyclops of the *Odyssey* but also a brutalized, almost parodistic version of the blind seer of truth in the *Oedipus Tyrannus*.[63] Blinding himself to the horror of the coming events, Agamemnon is also blind to the gods' possible role in human affairs in the one area where it has most often been invoked, the winds. He ends the play with a command to the Trojan women, now firmly back in their place as captives, to return to their tents and prepare to follow their "masters" back to Greece (1288f.). He then speaks his last lines (1289–92): "For I see these favoring winds that send us homeward [*pros oikon*]. May it be well for us as we sail homeward, and may we see all well in our house [*ta en domois*], leaving behind these sufferings." Throughout the play the suspension of the winds had been in the hands of the ghost of Achilles or some undefined god; and it was to obtain those winds that would send them "home" (*pros oikon*, 37) that the army had sacrificed Polyxena.[64] But now Agamemnon, seeing the winds, is silent about gods or Achilles' shade.

The winds that are conveying Agamemnon to his "house" (*oikos*, 1290) are also bringing him to the "bitter housekeeper" (*oikouros pikra*) of Polymestor's prophecy just fifteen lines earlier, who will kill both him and Cassandra (1277). Agamemnon's voyage "home" (1277, 1290f.) is the retributive mirror image of the Trojan women's loss of their home in the first stasimon (444ff.) and the destruction of a house by marriage in the third (946–49). It thus suggests a continuing pattern of retributive justice invisible to the participants. It is part of Agamemnon's blindness that the danger lies not in the sea but in the opposite quarter. "Home," *oikos* or *domos*, carries dark connotations throughout the latter half of the play. The reference to Agamemnon's own house is all the more ominous because it reminds us of the treachery and murder that Polymestor committed in his *domoi* (cf. 995, 1134, 1212, 1245), as well as of the women's terrible revenge inside.

Through the ironies of this ending, the *Hecuba*, like the *Bacchae*, though less obviously, reverses its perspective on the action.[65] Polymestor's Dionysiac prophecy (1267) functions in a manner analogous to Dionysus' theatrical magic of masking, unmasking, and disguising. It dissolves the barrier between actor and participant, self and other, not only for the mythical King Agamemnon but also for the contemporary audience. The community of spectators watching the play doubtless wanted to see itself as the humane, pitying audience that Hecuba was trying to create for her suffering. But the members of this Athenian audience of the war years, as Thucydides' Mytilenean and Melian debates indicate, also knew that they were citizens of a powerful state involved in an increasingly ruthless struggle.

Agamemnon's silencing of Polymestor (1282–86) projects into the orchestra and the stage action the Athenian spectators' own wish and need to suppress this voice of recognition. In this way they could banish their own violence and savagery to an imaginary desert island far from Athens and continue to sit in godlike removal and judgment on barbarians, as Agamemnon does up to line 1275. But for them, as for Agamemnon, the theatrical space imaginatively located the horrors and the violence not in the far-off Chersonese but in their own city, and in their own hearts. They too, in watching these savage, brutal barbarians, were really watching themselves.[66]

11

Law and Universals

The *Hecuba* is typically Euripidean in the way it combines large and complex matters of current intellectual debate with the intense emotions of a mother's loss of her children in what has rightly been called a concentration-camp world.[1] *Mythos* and *logos*, mythic and rational thought, although not necessarily opposed, are juxtaposed in a powerful and unexpected way. Far from destroying the power of tragic myth by intellectualism and abstraction, as Nietzsche claims, Euripides creates a remarkable new kind of tragedy that brings together the mythical elements of prophecy, metamorphosis, and monstrosity with debates on law, punishment, justice, friendship, and moral universals.[2]

In a succession of three scenes Hecuba tries to persuade a ruler who holds the power of life and death. In the first she hopes to influence Odysseus to save the life of her daughter Polyxena. In the second, she would persuade Agamemnon to aid her in her revenge against Polymestor, the villainous king who has murdered her son Polydorus. In the third, she confronts Polymestor in a quasi-juridical situation, defending herself before Agamemnon, the judge, for her bitter vengeance on a Greek ally. The association between the first two scenes is formally marked by the repetition of the suppliant entreaty, "show reverence to me" (αἰδέσθητί με), both to Odysseus and to Agamemnon (286 and 806), though with very different results.[3]

Hecuba's meeting with Odysseus is the first face-to-face encounter between a Greek and a Trojan. It shows us the world in which Hecuba now lives; she is completely subject to the conquerors and destroyers of her city. It also introduces us to the moral corruption of the Greeks. This is a society in which *charis*—gratitude or, more broadly, the obligations of reciprocity and civilized exchange—is forgotten or sophistically evaded.[4] In return for having saved Odysseus' life at Troy, Hecuba will receive her own life—but nothing more. Instead, Odysseus argues that it is more important to show *charis* to a dead warrior by sacrificing the virgin Polyxena. The basis for this decision is the practical expedient of keeping the city strong by offering the highest rewards of honor to its best fighters (303–20, 326–31). Odysseus also uses this point to reinforce the division between Greek and barbarian and thereby to answer Hecuba's appeal to an "equal law" (*isos nomos*), extending to both slave and free in the matter of shedding human blood (290ff.).

This scene marks Hecuba's first effort to cut across the barriers of power and status through universally accepted norms of behavior, in this case the horror of human sacrifice (260) and the injunction against dragging suppliants, especially women, from the altar and killing them (cf. 288–90). By rejecting her plea, Odysseus is implicitly placing the expedient "decree," or *psêphos*, of the assembly (259) above a widely accepted *nomos* of religious usage. At the same time, his reaffirmation of the right to sacrifice Polyxena gives a quasi-religious authority to the bloodshed of war. War and the killing done in its name virtually assume the status of a religious ritual. This sanction for war is enacted mimetically in the ritual slaughter of a girl in behalf of the army's bloodiest warrior. The state can command the sacrifice of its innocent young and, as Odysseus argues, can exalt such killing in the name of glory, or *timê*.

The second scene, the exchange between Hecuba and Agamemnon, occurs at approximately the midpoint of the play. Hecuba intensifies her appeal to a universally recognized "law" by associating it with the power of the gods (798–807):

ἡμεῖς μὲν οὖν δοῦλοί τε κἀσθενεῖς ἴσως.
ἀλλ' οἱ θεοὶ σθένουσι χὠ κείνων κρατῶν

νόμος. νόμῳ γὰρ τοὺς θεοὺς ἡγούμεθα
καὶ ζῶμεν ἄδικα καὶ δίκαι' ὡρισμένοι·
ὃς ἐς σ' ἀνελθὼν εἰ διαφθαρήσεται
καὶ μὴ δίκην δώσουσιν οἵτινες ξένους
κτείνουσιν ἢ θεῶν ἱερὰ τολμῶσιν φέρειν,
οὐκ ἔστιν οὐδὲν τῶν ἐν ἀνθρώποισι σῶν.
ταῦτ' οὖν ἐν αἰσχρῷ θέμενος αἰδέσθητί με,
οἴκτιρον ἡμᾶς.

We are slaves and weak, perhaps; but the gods are strong and so is the law
that rules over them. For by law we believe in the gods and live having
established notions of what is just and unjust. If this [law], coming before
you, is destroyed and if those who kill their guest-friends or dare to
pillage the shrines of the gods are unpunished, then nothing in human
affairs is secure. Holding these things as shameful, show reverence to me;
pity us.

I shall return to this passage later. For the moment, let me point out
some differences between this appeal to "law" and that in the scene
with Odysseus (266ff.). First, Hecuba combines the human force of
law with the divine. Second, she is implicitly answering Odysseus'
separation of Greek and barbarian (328ff.) by including both in a
generalizing "we" (e.g., 800f.), followed by the generalizing "who-
ever" and "mankind" (*anthrôpoi*, 805). In line 290 she had said only
"you." But over against this appeal to law as a moral imperative of
universal validity is the change in its content. In the first passage
(266ff.) she was trying to save a life; here she is planning to kill in an
act of retributive justice.

In her long plea to Agamemnon, Hecuba appeals initially to the
punishment of impiety (*anhosion*, 790, 792; cf. *hosia*, 788), which
includes Polymestor's violation of the rights of guest-friendship and
burial (791–97).[5] Agamemnon's response is to turn away (812). When
he finally responds, it is clear that he is moved chiefly by the point
that Hecuba raised only as a last resort, "something perhaps foreign to the argument," as she called it (ἴσως μὲν τοῦ λόγου ξένον
τόδε, 824), namely Cassandra and sex. Harking back to Hecuba's
opening words, Agamemnon asserts his concern for pity, pious regard for supplication, and justice (850–53; cf. 788–92, 801–5). We
can accept his moral sincerity, but he devotes ten lines of his fourteen-
line speech (850–63) to excusing himself to the army for placing
his personal erotic attachment above the pragmatic issue of support-

ing a "friend" (Polymestor) against an "enemy" (Hecuba and the Trojans).

The third and final scene of Hecuba's pleading differs from the previous two in that it is a triangular debate, with Agamemnon as the arbitrator between Hecuba and the now blinded and childless Polymestor. This scene, like the first, is structured as a *hamilla logôn* (formal debate), but it has a juridical character that is lacking in the previous scenes. Agamemnon is determined to "render a just judgment" (*krinein dikaiôs*, 1131); and this will rest on whether Polymestor's motives are personal, and therefore reprehensible, or political, deriving from his "friendship" with the Greeks, and therefore pardonable. A related issue is whether or not Greek standards of ethical behavior—loosely speaking, *nomoi*—also apply to barbarians.

The issue of Greek versus barbarian frames the debate. Agamemnon begins his instructions to Polymestor with the exhortation, "Cast out the barbarian element from your heart and speak" (ἐκβαλὼν δὲ καρδίας τὸ βάρβαρον / λέγε, 1129f.). He concludes with the decision that what is "shameful to the Greeks" (αἰσχρὸν τοῖσιν Ἕλλησιν) is the standard by which the Thracian king will be judged (1248, cf. 1199f.). In condemning Polymestor, Agamemnon is implicitly validating Hecuba's appeal to reverence toward guests, even though this rests on the supposed superiority of Greek over barbarian values rather than on an ethical principle that could apply to all humankind (1247f.; cf. 805, 902–4). Nevertheless, this is a step in the direction of the universalizing meaning of Hecuba's dictum on *nomos* in lines 798–805, particularly as she is also a barbarian; but it is not the same thing as a principle of divine law.

Agamemnon goes on, however, addressing Polymestor, "If I judge that you committed no injustice, how will I escape blame?" (1249). The basis of this blame seems to be a universal ethical criterion of what is "shameful" or "noble" (*aischron, kalon*, 1248, 1250f.). But his statement may also remind us that Agamemnon is not a completely impartial judge looking only for *to dikaion*. His first reaction to Hecuba's plea had been a general willingness to help "for the sake of the gods and of justice" (*to dikaion*, 852f.), as long as he "did not seem to the army" to be acting "out of favor to Cassandra" (855). When he speaks of "avoiding blame" in condemning Polymestor at the end, therefore, we are reminded that earlier, too, he ranked his standing in his group above any abstract principles of justice or morality. We are reminded also of Odysseus' blunt refusal of Hecuba's offer of her life for Polyxena's so that he could still give due *charis* to Achilles' shade and "avoid blame" from the army (383f.). The parallel brings together the slaughter of one daughter, Polyxena, and the forced concubinage of another, Cassandra. In the movement from Odysseus to Agamemnon principle does ultimately win out over pragmatism, but the victory is much entangled in the parallel ironies of the situation: Agamemnon's persuasion by sex and selfishness rather than pure principles of justice when he accepts Hecuba's entreaty (824ff.), and Odysseus' narrow interpretation of the reciprocity due to guest-friendship when he rejects Hecuba's plea for her daughter's life (299–302).

By arguing that the good of mankind depends on justice (805), Hecuba makes a universal morality central to her appeal to law (*nomos*) in lines 799–805. This issue pervades the entire play. The situation itself raises the question of universal law, for it involves the interaction of three different peoples. These three peoples, in fact, represent the three ethnographic groupings with which (as we also see in Herodotus) the Greeks are most familiar: the Greeks themselves; the civilized barbarians of the non-Greek world, such as the Persians, Lydians, Egyptians, and (as here) the Trojans; and the less civilized peoples on the remoter fringes, such as the Scythians and (as here) the Thracians. By combining the dichotomies of Greek and barbarian with those of freeman and slave, friend and enemy, male and female, strong and weak, Euripides forces us to think about values that may cut across these divisions of class, race, or gender.

The play works out these polarities in two different but complementary ways. On the one hand, the distinctions seem to break down, and opposites collapse into one another. Agamemnon, for example, as Hecuba demonstrates, is no more free, or no less a slave, than the captive queen (864ff.). The parallelism between the Greeks' killing of Polyxena, the Thracian Polymestor's killing of Polydorus, and Hecuba's killing of the two sons of Polymestor undermines the distinction between Greek and barbarian and makes us question the repeated assertions of the Greeks' ethical superiority to them.

On the other hand, Euripides puts universalizing morals into the mouths of his characters, only to show how questionable these norms are when applied to the speakers themselves. This is a world in which men and women cannot live up to the moral principles that they affirm. Or, from a wider point of view, the societies depicted in the play are not ready for the high ethical standards that the play itself envisages. This gap between ideal and practice is most marked in the case of the chief protagonist, Hecuba, but it extends to the moral ambivalence or outright hypocrisy of other characters such as Odysseus, Agamemnon, and Polymestor. Only Polyxena shows a nobility and moral honesty that remains untarnished.[6] But of course she disappears early in the action as a victim of the bloodthirstiness of the warrior spirit.

By the last quarter of the fifth century, Greek intellectuals were familiar with notions of cultural relativity and the problems of universal principles. The ethnographic writings of Herodotus, Hecataeus, and the early Hippocratic authors show how different societies define opposite forms of behavior as "lawful" (e.g., burying versus eating a deceased relative). The Sophists were exploring the bases of morality in society and giving prominence to the antithesis between "nature" (*phusis*) and "convention" (*nomos*) in forming social norms and to the "unwritten laws" (*agraphoi nomoi*) in maintaining social cohesion. Even the conservative Pindar could speculate on the all-powerful force of "convention," *Nomos*, king of men and gods alike (fragment 152 Bowra = 169 Snell-Maehler). Euripides staged a celebrated debate on the importance of written law as the hallmark of democratic government in *The Suppliants*, not far removed in date from the *Hecuba*. And the *nomos-phusis* antithesis touched almost every major author from the middle of the century on.[7] The Sophists Hippias and Antiphon, among others, explored notions of universally valid, "natural" laws that apply across cultural or racial boundaries and are binding on all men equally.[8]

In his scrutiny of the conventional value systems of his city, Euripides repeatedly questions the division between slave and free, Greek and barbarian. He often develops the paradox of the slave who has a nobler nature than his master.[9] His barbarians are sometimes more civilized than his Greeks. In a famous passage from *Iphigeneia in Tauris*, for instance, the barbarian King Thoas is horrified when he learns of Orestes' matricide: "By Apollo," he exclaims, "not even among barbarians would one dare such a deed" (1174). In the *Bacchae* the god Dionysus, disguised as a Lydian devotee of the bacchantic rites, defends the worth of barbarian customs (*nomoi*)—in this case the Asians' worship of Dionysus—against the Theban Pentheus' charge that the barbarians are inferior to the Greeks in intelligence. "No," the disguised Dionysus replies, "in this matter they are more intelligent; but their custom laws [*nomoi*] are different" (483f.).

A century or so before Euripides, Heraclitus had already posited "the one divine law" as the source of all human law (22 B114 Diels-Kranz).[10] By the middle of the fifth century it was widely believed that laws involving religious matters or pollution, such as matricide, supplication, burial, and the guest-host relationship, are god-given and applicable to all humankind. This view underlies Antigone's defense of the "unwritten laws" pertaining to burial and also the chorus in *Oedipus Tyrannus* on the laws that are begotten on Olympus (*Antigone* 450–60, *Oedipus Tyrannus* 863–72).[11]

In this period too, "law" or "laws" (*nomos, nomoi*) could imply a universally valid moral principle of right and justice. Euripides' Odysseus in the *Cyclops* instructs the rude monster on the "law for mortals" that prescribes the proper treatment of suppliants (299–303). His *Suppliants* twice uses the expression "the law of the Panhellenes" to describe the broad validity of the rites of burial (526, 671). The *Orestes* too, speaking of the universal abhorrence of matricide, uses the expression "the common law of the Greeks" (τὸν κοινὸν Ἑλλήνων νόμον, 494ff.). The chorus of the *Medea* would ally itself with "the laws of mortals" to dissuade the heroine from killing her children (νόμοις βροτῶν ξυλλαμβάνουσα, *Medea* 811–13); and these "laws of mortals" recur a number of times elsewhere in Euripides.[12] The so-called Anonymus Iamblichi, generally thought to belong to the end of the fifth century, seeks to establish "law and justice" (νόμος καὶ τὸ δίκαιον) as the firmly fixed rulers over human life, "bound strongly in place by nature" (6.1). There is no man so strong, the treatise goes on, "who would be able to dissolve the law that is common and advantageous for all" (7.15).[13] Early in the fourth century Xenophon had Socrates speak of "law" or "laws" given by the gods which "no man can avoid," such as the prohibition against incest (*Memorabilia* 4.4.20f.). In all these passages, and in classical Greek usage generally, *nomoi* refers to prescriptive "norms" that direct or enjoin a certain type of (moral) behavior or action.[14]

In the opposite direction, anthropocentric and rationalistic theorists of human progress such as Democritus and cynical thinkers such as Critias held that *nomos* is a purely human creation, a necessary survival mechanism for society, but of no absolute or universal value. Cynical relativists such as Plato's Callicles and Thrasymachus of the *Gorgias* and *Republic* and the thinkers referred to by Antiphon the Sophist drew the conclusion that one should therefore follow "nature" (*phusis*) or the "necessities of nature" (*anankai phuseôs*)—that is, amoral impulses and desires—whenever one can get away with it.[15] The ethnographers, such as Herodotus and the author of the Hippocratic *Airs, Waters, Places*, also contributed to the view that *nomoi*—custom laws, social norms—are valid for each society individually but without universal significance.

Euripides is familiar with both relativistic views of *nomos*. In the *Hippolytus*, for example, Aphrodite seems to embody one of the "necessities of nature," the irresistible compulsion of the sexual drive. The Nurse names the goddess to vindicate the claims of an amoral "nature" against social "convention," urging Phaedra to satisfy her illicit desire for her stepson (433–81). In the more positive, normative view, *nomos* may be relative to each society but is necessary for its survival and is binding on all its members. Euripides draws on this current of ideas in his own "ethnographic" plays such as the Taurian *Iphigeneia* and *Helen*.[16]

With this background in mind, we can take a closer look at the central scene of the *Hecuba* and at the role of Hecuba's verses on *nomos* quoted above (798–805). Hecuba's legal defense against Polymestor is two-pronged. First, she must show that he did violate laws that apply to both Greeks and barbarians and free and slave; that is, laws that have a universal, or at least very wide, significance. Second, she must show that in killing her son Polymestor did not act as a "friend" (*philos*) to the Greeks. The two arguments are closely related, for, as Agamemnon points out when Hecuba first requests his help, Polymestor's injustice against a Trojan would appear irrelevant to the Greek army because the Thracian is a friend (*philos*) while the Trojan is a foe (*echthros*, 858–63). Persuading Agamemnon thus requires a principle powerful enough to counteract this practical reality. Euripides complicates the situation by giving the moral superiority to the enemies of the Greeks and by making the Greek leader sympathetic to these enemies. On the other hand, Agamemnon, as we have observed, fulfills the demands of justice largely for personal and unworthy motives; and the Greek side also includes the amoral pragmatist Odysseus.

Hecuba's first line of argument, her appeal to *nomos* in lines 798–805, is not without its ambiguities, as we shall soon see.[17] But she can obviously strengthen her case if she can invoke the law that is recognized as both universally applicable to all men and sanctioned by the gods. She also knows that Agamemnon has sufficient moral sensitivity to find this argument appealing even if not definitive. She thus fuses *dikê* as retribution with a broader and more abstract principle of "what is just" (*to dikaion*), without which, as she says, nothing in human life is safe (805). Her examples are the universally recognized crimes of killing guests and sacking the shrines of the gods (803–5). She prepares the way for this universalizing argument just before her lines on *nomos*. Here she calls Polymestor an outlaw in the eyes of the gods, "a host most impious," one who "fears neither those above nor those below" (790f.), a violator of the rights of guest-friendship and burial (792–97).

Agamemnon seems to acknowledge that Hecuba's *nomos* is more than just "convention," for he accepts her plea "for the sake of the gods and the principle of justice" (*to dikaion*, 852f.). The broad ethical significance of this *nomos* also leaves its stamp on the rest of the action. When Hecuba finally lures Polymestor inside the tent for her terrible revenge, the chorus sings of "what is owed to Justice [Dikê] and to the gods" (1029f.).

Agamemnon's initial response to value terms such as *law, justice,* and *nobility* is a rather flaccid statement of willingness to help; but he immediately qualifies Hecuba's moral absolutes by the expediencies of the situation. "Greatest light of the Hellenes" he may be (841), but his chief concern is how he will appear to his army (854). The division between *philos* and *echthros* poses a serious obstacle (858–61): "The army considers this man [Polymestor] as a friend [*philios*], the one dead as an enemy [*echthros*]; but if this latter here [Polydorus] is a friend [*philos*] to you, this is something apart and not a common concern to the army [οὐ κοινὸν στρατῷ]." Hecuba removes this problem with a generalization that goes in a direction just the opposite of that on *nomos* in lines 798–805, for she here reflects cynically that no one is free; and among the limits on this freedom are *nomoi*, now understood not as a universal law validated by the gods but as a circumstance of mortal life, the "decrees of laws" in one's individual city (*nomôn graphai*, 866). Shortly before, the chorus reflected on how the "necessities" established by *nomoi* make people exchange friend for foe, and vice versa (846–49). These plural *nomoi*, as the contingencies that limit human freedom or the "decrees of laws" in individual cities, seem to be distinguished from the singular *nomos* of lines 798–805 and so reinforce its universal force.

Hecuba's statement on *nomos* in lines 798–805 would be intelligible to her audience most simply as advocacy of the centrality of the "unwritten laws," the universal human regard for suppliancy, guest-friendship, and burial that are the foundations of civilization. Such sanctities are recognized by all and are felt to be of divine origin and defended by the gods.[18] This argument, then, would have a function analogous to that of "justice and reverence" in the myth of the *Protagoras* (322c–d)—that is, a social principle that is necessary if men are to cooperate and survive in communal living. We recall that she has just described the impious Polymestor as one who "feared neither those above or those below" (791f.). Yet her statement "For by *nomos* we believe in the gods and live defining what is just and unjust" is disturbing both in its sense and in its dramatic function. Her argument is, in fact, complete in the previous sentence. But she overdetermines the divine power of *nomos* and thereby adds a note of exaggeration; perhaps, we think, she does protest too much. The statement on law, in other words, has to be viewed in its dramatic function.

Understood as an appeal to divine law, the phrase "For by law we believe in the gods" might mean that the divine law that rules even the gods makes us believe in gods. That is, humankind's very worship of the gods would itself be an emanation of the universal, divine law. As commentators point out, however, the fifth-century connotation of the phrase "by law we believe in the gods" (νόμῳ τοὺς θεοὺς ἡγούμεθα) suggests the skeptical vein of sophistic thinking. Insofar as this rational view of religious worship can be localized in a specific theory, it seems to be of the more benign Protagorean rather than the more cynical Critian type.[19]

Hecuba, then, may be hinting at the Protagorean relativizing of religious belief: the existence of the gods depends entirely on social convention ("it is by *nomos* that we believe in gods"). Yet she does not draw the destructive conclusion that *nomoi* are therefore of limited validity or that the gods are only a clever device used by rulers to keep their subjects in check (Critias 88B 25 Diels-Kranz). Instead, she skips over the problem of multiple, relative *nomoi* among the different societies and races of humankind and turns to a single unifying *nomos* as a stable moral principle, without which "nothing is safe" (805). But she exploits a certain ambiguity in the notion of *nomos* (universal law, relativistic custom law).[20] This hint of ambiguity prepares us for her betrayal of the very principle that she here affirms so nobly.

Given our suspicions about the extent of Hecuba's commitment to justice in the abstract, we may wonder whether this hint of sophistic relativism is not to be taken more seriously—that is, as a reflection of the moral ambiguity of Hecuba's position. To be sure, the appeal to a universal law of moral action is not entirely foreign to her concerns: she is after all, pursuing justice, assuming the identification of vengeance with justice, as the range of Greek *dikê* permits. Yet, viewed in the most cynical light, such a law is itself only an instrument toward her revenge, one more weapon in her arsenal against the man who killed her son. In this case, as Gordon Kirkwood suggested some forty years ago, we see here the meeting of two Hecubas, the noble sufferer of the first half of the play, whose vengeance rests on an unassailable moral right (the "law" of lines 798– 805), and a Hecuba who will do anything to obtain her revenge.[21] This latter, unscrupulous Hecuba can thus turn abruptly from law to persuasion and sex, from the divine to the all too human.

There are, perhaps, further hints of this instrumental attitude toward *nomos* in the concern with "strength" and "weakness" that leads up to Hecuba's praise of "law" (*astheneis*, 798; *sthenousi*, 799). This passage recalls the beginning of the scene, her silent deliberation on her own weakness as a slave and her reflections on whether or not to supplicate Agamemnon (741; cf. 749; οὐκ ἂν δυναίμην, "I would not have the power").

Some of the ironies in her appeal to law have more to do with the condition of the world around her than with her own lust for vengeance. Her claim that without respect for law "nothing is safe among men," for example, stands out bitterly in a world where so many basic human rights have been trampled. She is calling on

Agamemnon to enforce a kind of law that he has himself violated by sacrificing his own daughter.

What is at stake here, as in much of late fifth-century literature, is the thinness of the line between civilization and savagery and the ease with which morality and its safeguards can be swept away—even in the name of law and justice themselves.[22] Without something like Hecuba's all-pervasive *nomos*, men would relapse into the precivilized condition of Protagoras' myth, or the "Wild Men" of Pherecrates' comedy of that name,[23] or the rude selfishness of Euripides' own version of the Odyssean Cyclops. The Thracian Polymestor is a good candidate for such an incompletely civilized man. The Thracians themselves seem to vacillate; sometimes they are an agricultural society, and sometimes a race of horsemen devoted to the god of war (cf. 6 and 1089f.).

The universality of Hecuba's *nomos*, then, sets off the moral disintegration of every part of the world in which she lives. Here we see Greeks behaving little better than the barbarians whom they have conquered and over whom they vaunt their moral superiority. This is the lesson of Thucydides as he describes the moral degeneration in the Corcyrean revolution, in which men "carried to still more extravagant lengths the invention of new devices, both by the extreme ingenuity of their attacks and the monstrousness of their revenges" (3.82.1).[24] Both Greeks and Thracians kill innocent children; both have violated human and divine laws. The Thracian ruler has killed a guest for gold; the Greek conquerors have sacrificed the murdered guest's sister, equally innocent, to honor a dead warrior. At an earlier stage of the war, the Greek chief sacrificed his daughter to the war. We are reminded of this remoter violation by the prophecy of Clytaemnestra's future vengeance in the play's closing lines, and also by the motif of sacrificing a virgin at an altar to end a god-sent period of windless calm. The impiety of Polyxena's sacrifice is reinforced by the parallelism with Neoptolemus' killing of Priam at the altar (cf. 23ff. and 118ff.). It is not accidental that the same warrior, Achilles' son, Neoptolemus, is appointed to cut Polyxena's throat (223f., 523ff.).

If Hecuba's universal law seems to be overcoming the strong division between Greek and barbarian established early in the action (cf. 291–95, 326–31), that division later collapses in another, far more dangerous way as Greek and barbarian show more similarities than differences. On the other hand, the play never forgets the hard fact of this division, particularly as war has made the Trojans the slaves of the victorious Greeks.[25]

Agamemnon's final sentence of condemnation against Polymestor boasts of the Greeks' moral superiority: the crime of killing a guest may be easy for a barbarian, but for a Greek it is a deed of shame (1247f.). Yet the Greeks, including the speaker, have committed deeds just as shameful. And in any case, Agamemnon is not speaking entirely out of considerations of moral absolutes, for we have seen how it is eros rather than *nomos* that wins him over to Hecuba's cause.

To appreciate the complexities of Hecuba's appeal to the universal law in lines 798–805, we must examine the scenes that lead into and follow that speech. This scene begins with the remarkable stage device of a quadruple aside, an effect unique in extant Greek drama. Agamemnon enters with the direct address "Hecuba," offers to help in the burial of Polyxena, and then steps back in amazement when he sees the new corpse outside the tent (726–35). Everything in his opening lines demands a reply, particularly as his tone is one of sympathetic concern. But Hecuba answers him not with "Agamemnon," as one would expect, but with a syntactically contorted self-address (736–38):

δύστην', ἐμαυτὴν γὰρ λέγω λέγουσα σέ,
Ἑκάβη, τί δράσω; πότερα προσπέσω γόνυ
Ἀγαμέμνονος τοῦδ' ἢ φέρω σιγῇ κακά;

O you unfortunate, for in saying "you," I mean myself, Hecuba—what shall I do: Shall I fall in supplication at the feet of Agamemnon here, or shall I bear my woes in silence?[26]

By naming herself "unfortunate," she is naming a different Hecuba, one who will no longer be the savior or mourner of a child but the avenger of a child. While Agamemnon stands before her in perplexity, she speaks four asides, each deliberating on whether she should use formal supplication to enlist his aid in her vengeance. Only when she satisfies herself that his help is indispensable (749–51) does she utter the long-awaited vocative, "Agamemnon," nearly thirty lines after his opening "Hecuba" (752 and 726).

By stressing the host-guest relation between Polymestor and his victim (774, 791f.), Hecuba makes Polymestor a criminal in the eyes of the gods and thus leads logically into the universalizing terms of the law that she elaborates a few lines later (798–805). Yet her use of "punisher" (*timôros*) in line 790 also echoes her own concern with "revenge" (*timôrein*) in her aside at the beginning of the scene (749). When she introduces her appeal to *nomos*, therefore, by dwelling on the contrast between the "weakness" of slaves like herself and the "strength" of the gods and of the "law that rules over them" (799–801), she also indicates that this appeal is part of her strategy to bridge the gap between slave and free, friend and enemy, that she saw as an obstacle to her suppliancy at the beginning of the scene: "But if (Agamemnon) should drive me from his knees, considering me both a slave and an enemy, I would only be adding to my pain" (741f.).

To win Agamemnon's help she must break down the barrier of slavery, enmity, and barbarism that separates them. The division by social status, political allegiance, and race is compounded by gender and age differences. Once she has convinced Agamemnon of the validity of her ends, she must also remove his objections to the means, resolving his doubts about the capacity of "old women" (*graiai*, 877) and "females" in general to conquer "males" (καὶ πῶς γυναιξὶν ἀρσένων ἔσται κράτος, 883; cf. τὸ θῆλυ, 885).

These considerations do not necessarily diminish the value of Hecuba's divinely sanctioned law in absolute terms, but they do suggest a confusion of ends and means. A high moral principle cannot escape being transformed into an instrument of revenge. When her speech is viewed as a whole, her "law" stands alongside persuasion (*peithô*), which she also regards as quasi divine. Persuasion too, she says, has the same universal power over "mortals" and "mankind" (*thnêtois*, 814; *anthrôpois*, 816). Even though she is presumably addressing these lines to herself,[27] she still allows persuasion to displace law and the gods, for if the gods are powerful and nomos rules over them, she says, persuasion is "the only sovereign over mankind" (816).

Hecuba ends her speech with still another moral universal: "It belongs to a man of nobility [*esthlos*] to serve justice *everywhere* and *always* to harm bad men" (844f.). Her extreme flattery of Agamemnon immediately before, however, undermines the initial impression of disinterested moralism (841–43): "O master, greatest light to the Greeks, be persuaded. Offer your hand to an old woman, for vengeance, even if she is nothing—do so anyway." The key phrase, "Offer your hand for vengeance" (παράσχες χεῖρα . . . τιμωρόν), suggests that "serving justice everywhere" and "always harming bad men" are less important to Hecuba than getting revenge.

The chorus now comments on how "laws" (*nomoi*), here plural and in a relative sense, impose their "necessities" on mortals, forcing them to treat their worst enemies as friends and vice versa (846–49). They may be thinking of how Hecuba agonized with herself at the opening of the scene about whether or not to turn for help to one of her bitterest enemies (741f., 745f.). In any case, these *nomoi* subject men and women to the contingencies and external circumstances of events. The chorus's remark thus applies to Agamemnon, who will be helping an "enemy" against a "friend," at least in the eyes of the army (858–60). Hecuba soon makes explicit this application to Agamemnon: he is unfree, subject to circumstances and chance no less than a slave. In speaking here of the "decrees of laws" (*nomôn graphai*, 866), she uses *nomoi* in a relativizing sense, laws as the creations of men which infringe upon other men's freedom of choice and action. Far from being able to work with the gods for a broad moral purpose, men here are entirely trapped in the material conditions of their mortality, all "slaves" to some circumstance or other.

In her earlier appeal to *nomos* in lines 798–805, Hecuba would bridge the gap between free and slave by a moral principle that includes all men equally. She had argued along similar lines in her earlier supplication to Odysseus (291f.). Those passages claim justice as the right even of slaves. Hecuba now bridges the gap between slave and free from below, as it were. All men, she suggests, are slaves, even those who are ostensibly free. Going even further, she promises to "free from fear" (869) this man whom she has just called "the greatest light of Hellas" (841). Agamemnon's initial response to her suppliant gesture was the offer of her freedom (754f.). She has now reversed the role of master and slave; and she has revealed a hidden enslavement even for the luminous king of the victorious army.

When Agamemnon is satisfied that agreeing to help Hecuba will not diminish his standing before the army, he turns from principles to means. How, he asks, will women be able to overcome men (876–94)? Reassured on this score too, he once more turns to the circumstances of the moment, the fact that the gods have sent no wind and the army must stay where it is in any case. "So be it," he says; "for if the army could sail, I could not have granted you this favor" (898f.). Moral principle is here reduced to convenience, even if the circumstances of the convenience are supposedly determined by the gods.

This emphasis on circumstances also casts doubt on the moral generality that forms Agamemnon's last words in the scene (902–4):

γένοιτο δ' εὖ πως· πᾶσι γὰρ κοινὸν τόδε,
ἰδίᾳ θ' ἑκάστῳ καὶ πόλει, τὸν μὲν κακὸν
κακόν τι πάσχειν, τὸν δὲ χρηστὸν εὐτυχεῖν.

May all be well. For this is common to all, both to each one privately and to the city, for the base man to suffer something base and for the noble to enjoy good fortune.

His statement recalls Hecuba's shortly before (844f.): "It belongs to a noble man to serve justice and everywhere *to harm the base* always" (τοὺς κακοὺς δρᾶν πανταχοῦ κακῶς ἀεί, 845). But Agamemnon waters down Hecuba's gnomic statement by turning it from active to passive (from *drân kakôs*, "harming the base," to *kakon ti paschein*, their "suffering harm"). Doing or acting, *dran*, as Bruno Snell long ago pointed out,[28] is an essential element of the tragic situation; it is the necessity to choose action. By recasting Hecuba's phrase into the passive—not *dran kakôs* but *kakon paschein*—Agamemnon attenuates the element of the moral will. The same effect appears in the feeble hope "May it somehow [*pôs*] be well."

Agamemnon allies himself with Hecuba by implicitly including her in "all men" who have a "common" concern with morality (902). The term *common* (*koinon*) also points up some of the ironies that undercut the assertion of moral principle here. Forty lines earlier he used the word in a much narrower sense: the political definition of *philia* that excluded anything "common" between the Greek army and the private affairs of Hecuba (860), since he must not seem to be showing "favor" (*charis*) to Cassandra, an *echthros*, over a *philos* like Polymestor.[29] The change, of course, is brought about by Hecuba's erotic persuasion. Thus here, as throughout the entire scene, the expansion of the horizon of value terms from group interests to universal issues of justice has narrow and selfish motivations.

The principle that Agamemnon endorses here as the "common concern of all"—that the base suffer and the noble prosper (902–4)—flies in the face of what Hecuba has so bitterly experienced. In the opening scene the chorus laments that she is indeed a noble person

who has had the worst possible fortune, while base men like Odysseus have prospered (98ff.). The truth of this statement is intensified
by the suffering of the play's noblest figure, Polyxena. Agamemnon's
formulation in lines 902–4, that the suffering of the bad and the
prosperity of the good are "common both to each individual in
private and to the city" (*polis*), reminds us that Hecuba's claims can
be only as a "private" individual because she now has no city and is,
as she said at the beginning of her speech, *apolis* (811).

Polymestor's entrance on the stage, after the choral ode, takes up
these last words of Agamemnon and confirms their meaninglessness
(956f.): "Nothing is to be believed, not even reputation, nor is it
possible for the one who fares well not to fare badly." Polymestor's
world is one of pure circumstance, the "fortune" (*tychê*) through
which "faring well" can suddenly turn into "faring ill"—as he will
soon see. For him, however, unlike Hecuba, there is no moral principle or divine causation behind such fluctuations of fortune. It is
therefore appropriate that the traitorous Thracian should begin by
stating that "nothing is believable" or "trustworthy" (*piston*), for he
has shown himself to be in no way *pistos*, as Hecuba says later in
defense of her vengeance (1234).

As Hecuba continues to weave her net of guile around Polymestor, the language of conventional morality becomes the language of
deception. She invokes the *nomos* that a woman does not look directly at a man (968–75). This *nomos* is not the divinely sanctioned law
of lines 798–805 but a minor item in a code of behavior governing the
details of daily life. Here it serves as a clever excuse for shielding her
eyes so that she can conceal from her victim the fierce hatred that
her glance might betray.[30] When Hecuba leads Polymestor on with
her alleged secret about the hidden gold, he names her his "friend"
(*philê*) and then generalizes, "In what way could he who fares well
help his friends who are not faring well?" (984f.). The lines recall the
discussion about the good or ill fortune of the good or bad man
between Agamemnon and Hecuba in the previous scene; but these
conventional pieties are now only a screen for greed, on the one
hand, and murderous vengeance, on the other.

That earlier discourse is recalled again in the very different mood
of the chorus's pronouncement as Polymestor is screaming with pain
and anger (1085f.): "You wretch, evils hard to bear have been done to
you; but to one who has done shameful things, terrible things are the

penalty." Hecuba and Agamemnon's rather bland generalizations about the base man suffering something bad are here intensified and realized in vivid and horrible form. The neutral *kakon* or *kakôs* of the earlier scene (844f., 903f.) has become *aischra* or *deina*; and there is no mention now of success or good fortune for the good man.

The final scene of the play is the formal debate, or *hamilla logôn*, between Hecuba and Polymestor, with Agamemnon sitting in judgment. The moral generalizations about right action continue, but there are a number of ironical twists. Hecuba, for instance, opens her defense with a dictum about good words matching good actions (1188–91). But, of course, she has been the chief manipulator of language, especially deceitful language. In her peroration she urges Agamemnon to "do no benefit" (*eu dran*) to one who is not reverent, trustworthy, pure, or just (1234f.). As one who has violated all the sacred bonds between men (what is trustworthy and just) and among gods (what is reverent, holy, or ritually pure), Polymestor deserves only harshness from men.[31] She is harking back to Agamemnon's own generalization at the end of her scene of supplication, that "the evil man should suffer evil, the decent man should have good fortune" (903f.). But once more she gives specific and energetic form to what for Agamemnon was vague generality. She also omits the positive side of Agamemnon's dictum, good fortune for the good man. Pushing Agamemnon beyond his feeble pieties, she forces upon him the moral choice that he has tried to sidestep. "If you help this man," she says, "you will appear base" (*kakos*, 1233). She thus compels Agamemnon to choose between the expediency of helping allies and a commitment to moral values. Agamemnon's reluctance to help her in their first scene rested upon how it would appear to his army (854–56). Here Hecuba turns this argument back upon Agamemnon, but in a broader moral sense.

Agamemnon's closing judgment seems to place the principle of justice above the ties of friendship, or *philia* (1250f.): "Since you had the boldness [*etolmas*] to do things that are not noble, endure [*tlêthi*] things that are not friendly." Polymestor then cries out that he is defeated by a woman and a slave and is being punished by those who are "baser" (*kakiones*, 1252f.), to which Hecuba rejoins, "Is this then not justly so, if you did base things?" (1254). The value terms *phila*, *kala*, *kakos*, and *kaka* are obviously being used here in several ways.

Justice and right seem to be winning out over the more material considerations of alliance (friendship) and rank or status (*kakos* in the sense of base or ignoble or low on the social scale). Yet the terms for *justice* ring at least a little hollow as they come from Agamemnon's mouth, for we have seen him persuaded at least as much by his sexual relationship with Cassandra as by the absolute morality of Hecuba's case. When he rejects Polymestor's claims to *philia* in favor of Hecuba's claims to *dikê*, therefore, we recall that there is another kind of *philia* in the background: namely, the tie to Cassandra and the *philas euphronas* and *philtata aspasmata* ("dear nights, dearest embraces," 828f.) of Cassandra's bed that Hecuba had used to persuade him.

One of Hecuba's points against Polymestor's self-defense is that "the barbarian race could not be friendly [*philon*] to the Greeks" (1199–1201). But of course she is just as much a barbarian as Polymestor; and her hidden trump card is her equally barbarian daughter who is *philê* in a special way. The arguments go through many twists and turns, but the underlying circumstances at nearly every point undercut at least some of the claims to universally valid moral principles on both sides. There is no question that Hecuba's cause is just and that she has our sympathy. But Euripides does not let us forget that she is using rather than following abstract principles of justice.

The discrepancy between the ideal of justice and its violent realization would perhaps be less sharp had not Hecuba herself claimed the authority of a divinely sanctioned and universally applicable "law" for her situation. In this way, while we cannot claim that Euripides is introducing a full-blown notion of natural law, he does raise issues that go beyond the conventional Greek morality that one does harm to one's enemy and good to one's friends. Arthur Adkins, for example, argues that both Hecuba and Agamemnon are proceeding on the premise that it is acceptable to kill a guest if one is doing it as a favor (*charis*) to a friend, or *philos*. In that case, all that Hecuba has to do is to show that Polymestor is not truly a *philos* to the Greeks. Hecuba does, of course, make this argument (1199–1201), but it is not the major part of her case. Her speech on law and the gods had already created a far wider frame for these issues. Agamemnon himself, in accepting her as suppliant, had also accepted "justice" and "the gods" as the underlying moral basis for this action (851–54). At the end of that pivotal scene, Agamemnon redefined the exclusiveness of *philos-echthros* obligations in a way that generalized the "common" element of shared concern from the Greek army to "all men" (858–63 and 902–4, see above). Yet as the generalizations about moral principles are bandied back and forth, Hecuba's appeal to the absolute morality of her case proves to be her weakest point.

Hecuba therefore undertakes to prove that Polymestor is not a *philos*, not because she accepts his premise (i.e., that killing Polydorus was justified as a favor from one *philos* to another) but because she has no other choice. As she knows, this is a world where expediency comes first. She knows from her first encounter with Agamemnon that appeals to law, piety, justice, and goodness are less effective than appeals to sex and the power to persuade (*erôs* and *peithô*). And her earlier encounter with Odysseus taught her that appeals to suppliant rights, gratitude, and the gods are of no avail. Adkins reads the play as normative of Greek values in the fifth century; I am arguing for reading it as a devastating critique of a world that has lost touch with basic moral values and with a language that could articulate them. Hence the recurrent insistence on doing or suffering evil and the repetition of value words such as *kalos*, *philos*, and *esthlos* show a progressive relativization of moral terminology. Euripides has made this relativization particularly disturbing by having us measure it against Hecuba's appeal to a universal law for men and gods in lines 798–805.

Adkins's reading would center the play on the exclusiveness and self-interest associated with the terms *philos* and *echthros*. A *philos* is one who helps or benefits the interests of the group; an *echthros* is one who harms or hinders those interests.[32] As we have seen, Agamemnon begins with this position (858–63) but (for somewhat dubious reasons) moves beyond it (cf. 902–4, and the discussion above). One can easily find in Euripides endorsements of the kind of traditional morality that Adkins suggests for this play. There is, for instance, the principle stated by the old servant in *Ion*, who urges Creusa to poison the suspected interloper: "Whenever one wants to do harm to an enemy there is no law [*nomos*] that stands in the way" (*Ion* 1046f.). In our play, however, Hecuba's statement about *nomos* enunciates a higher level of morality; indeed, one that is too high both for the speaker and for those around her.

The ugliest aspect of this situation is Polymestor's expectation that he could win his case. In Athenian political debates of that period, arguments for expediency over morality did win, as we see from the Mytilenean and Melian debates in Thucydides.[33] Euripides cleverly creates a situation where the standards of public policy in the assembly confront the standards of private justice in the law courts. To put it differently, Polymestor tries to confuse a deliberative debate and bouleutic oratory with judicial debate and dicastic oratory. The former, as I have noted, regularly puts aside the moral issues of right and wrong and considers only self-interest, advantage, or expediency. The possibility of confusion is rendered all the easier because Agamemnon is acting both as a judge in a court of law and as a political and military leader looking out for the advantage of his army and its allies (cf. 854–63). The situation, however, sets into relief the contradictions between the two types of moral standards. One hopes that these discrepancies disturbed at least some members of the audience. Certainly the contradictions between public morality and justice, both private and universal, would be very much alive for Plato, a very young child at the time of the *Hecuba*, who would try to reconcile them in the ideal, philosopher-governed city of the *Republic*.

To return to our play, Hecuba does succeed, after all, in both the public and private sides of the issue. Agamemnon rules that Polymestor did not behave as "friend" to the Greeks in murdering his Trojan guest-friend but acted for his own personal advantage, and that the laws of Greek morality apply to barbarians. Hecuba thus does break through the exclusivity of *philoi-echthroi* relations to larger moral considerations of piety, trust, and justice in her peroration before Agamemnon (1234–37). The chorus at this point gives strong approval to her speech in a generalization about "worthy deeds" (*chrê-sta pragmata*) finding the impulse of worthy words "for mortals" (1238f.). We are, of course, on Hecuba's side, and we join the chorus in approving her claims on justice, piety, and trust. Yet we cannot forget the hypocrisy of the judge in this case and his earlier concern with public opinion. Particularly when Agamemnon's last words in rendering his decision are *ta mê phila*, "things that are not friendly" or "not shared by friends," we cannot forget that a personal *philia* qualifies his objective devotion to justice in the abstract.

In the *Hecuba* Euripides holds out the possibility of universal moral laws, but he also shows us a world not yet ready for them. Despite hints of the gods in the background, men, left to their own devices, produce wanton slaughter, the destruction of young life, violent revenge, and madness. The human community offers little of secure moral value. The army of the Greeks is violent, bloodthirsty, and corrupted by demagogues who appeal to its basest instincts. The city of Troy is destroyed. The king of remote Thrace reveals his savagery beneath his veneer of civilized behavior (1056ff.) and receives his appropriate punishment in being banished to a desert island (1284–86). His end resembles that of the morally ineducable man in Plato's myth of *Protagoras*, one who does not partake of justice and reverence. Of such a person Protagoras says, "Let him be killed as being a disease of the city if he cannot share in justice and reverence" (*Protagoras* 322d). One wonders if Euripides had been hearing or reading the famous Sophist. In any case, Polymestor clearly lacks the basic civilized values that make a human community possible, and so he is left without any community. Curiously, his Thracian subjects do not protest, even though he calls on his "warlike people" (1089f.). Are they too disorganized to oppose the order of a Greek general?

The society to which Agamemnon is returning does not offer much to offset the moral bankruptcy of his army's political institutions. Polymestor's final prophecy of the "bloody bath" that awaits Agamemnon in Argos (1281) reveals to the audience what Agamemnon himself does not recognize—namely, that the cycle of violence does not end with Troy, Hecuba, or Polyxena, but will work itself out in his own palace. For behind the sacrifice of the virgin Polyxena, of course, lies the sacrifice of the virgin Iphigeneia, also killed at the altar in response to the lack of winds. The murderous violence of Troy and Thrace continues, in mimetic repetition, into Greece. Here Clytaemnestra takes over the role of Hecuba, and Agamemnon that of Polymestor: a fiercely angry mother lures a warrior into her interior realm for a terrible revenge.

Rather than extending the civilizing norms from the Greeks to the barbarians, the play shows us Greeks drawn into collusion with a barbarian's revenge—a characteristically barbarian revenge in its use of guile, flattery, bodily mutilation, and the killing of children. In the closing lines Agamemnon virtually descends to Hecuba's level. He wrangles with an enraged barbarian and stifles by force the prophecy of the "murderous bath" that awaits him in Argos (1281).

Man's recognition of a divinely sanctioned law that may transcend the play's bloody divisions between Greek and barbarian is, for Euripides, a hope that the "real" world—the human world reflected in this play—cannot sustain. The ideal, however, is in the air, as Euripides' many statements about law and the unwritten laws in this and other plays show, and it will not be forgotten. It returns, with stronger philosophical arguments and with a greater hope of realization, in Plato, Aristotle, and the Stoics.[34] And it comes to fruition centuries later in the Roman conception of the *ius gentium* and the modern notions of natural law.

12

The Problem of the Gods

The most difficult problem in the interpretation of Euripidean tragedy is deciphering the role and meaning of the gods. The difficulties
raised by the onstage appearance of divinities in plays like the *Hippolytus*, *Heracles*, and *Bacchae* are notorious. The use of the deus ex
machina in plays like *Electra*, *Ion*, the two *Iphigeneias*, and *Orestes*
complicates rather than resolves the moral questions of the action.
Plays in which the gods are in the background and make no direct
appearance or intervention, like the *Medea* or the *Hecuba*, might seem
to be freer of such problems. In fact, the opposite is the case.[1]

Always a dramatist—and an original and inventive dramatist—
Euripides is interested in the range and diversity of religious experience.[2] Thus the Hecuba who in our play associates the gods with
moral laws (799–805) can, in the *Trojan Women*, invoke Zeus as an
impersonal "necessity of nature," a kind of cosmic force operating
remotely and mysteriously in human affairs (886). Euripides can also
imagine the intensely private, almost mystical relation between a
mortal and a particular goddess, such as that between Hippolytus
and Artemis in the *Hippolytus*; or he can speculate on divinity as a
principle of moral purity, as it is for Theonoe in the *Helen* (cf. 865–72),
with her "great temple of justice in her nature" (1002f.). Or he can

directly attack the baser aspect of the traditional anthropomorphic myths through the vengeful cruelty of Hera in the *Heracles* (cf. 847ff.), only to have his hero himself turn his back on this view of the gods in the name of a higher morality (*Heracles* 1340–46).[3]

We have seen how a famous ode from *Hippolytus* presents the chorus of Hippolytus' hunting companions as torn by conflict between their pious hope in the "gods' care" for mortals and their agonized questioning of the randomness of human suffering as they "look on the fortunes of mortals" (1104–1110), especially the misfortunes right before their eyes.[4] Here the attempt to resolve the discrepancy between the comfort of pious belief and the actuality of meaningless suffering produces a deep spiritual malaise. And within *Hecuba* even an enemy, the herald Talthybius, looking upon Hecuba's reversals, wonders whether Zeus or chance governs human life (488–91, with the generally accepted deletion of line 490). Writing in the age of the sophistic questioning of traditional values, Euripides may well here be reflecting the troubled mood of his contemporaries, or at least those who were touched by the contemporary rationalistic currents and were also earnest, decent citizens committed to the state religion and concerned to make moral, intellectual, and spiritual sense of their world.

Because Euripides' gods appear not only as an independent reality in the world but also as features of personal belief and attitudes that define the emotional and moral makeup of his characters, no single generalization or categorization will be adequate. Euripides often constructs his action in such a way that arguments for and against divine justice are equally possible. His concern, then, seems to be less with shaping a conclusive theology than with creating an interlocking structure of events, attitudes, and supernatural forces that makes us deeply question the moral nature of the universe and our role within it.

The dominant situation in the first part of the *Hecuba* is a supernatural demand for a human sacrifice. But, as in Euripides' other sacrifice plays, human sacrifice is as much a reflection on a corrupt human world as it is an indictment of gods who demand human blood. The suffering that the gods here require from the innocent and immature—not, that is, from the mature, manly warriors of the Homeric type—is the sign of a world from which heroism has disappeared or is displaced to unexpected areas and paradoxical situations among those whose lives would normally have no contact with the heroic world.[5]

Euripides, to be sure, often presents the gods as independently existing beings who have complex, anthropomorphic relations among one another in ordering the human world. Such is the quarrel between Aphrodite and Artemis in the *Hippolytus* (especially 1416–23), or the divine assembly that will decide Helen's fate in *Helen* (878ff.), or the new collaboration of Athena and Poseidon in the prologue to the *Trojan Women*. But he never loses sight of the meaning of the gods as a mirror in which man views his own nature, and especially his moral nature. Although it may be an exaggeration to claim that the gods are "an essentially human problem," as Fernand Chapouthier does,[6] it is fair to say that the way different figures invoke and describe the gods is as much a comment on their individual characters as an attempt to sketch a coherent theology. The gods (inter alia) provide a large and independent domain in which characters' actions reveal their most constant and basic values. In the *Hippolytus*, for example, the male protagonist's manner of addressing Artemis and Aphrodite at once establishes his values, and with them the strengths and weaknesses of his personality. And in the *Bacchae*, all the main characters reveal and enact their underlying natures by the ways they understand Dionysus.[7]

In the *Hecuba* the strongest instance of this use of the gods as a mirror of individual moral character is the entrance of Polymestor (953ff.). This man, who has shockingly outraged both divine and human law, has as virtually his first words onstage a generalization about the moral chaos of the world. One cannot trust in anything, he says, for "the gods themselves mix everything up . . . so that it is through ignorance that we revere them" (ὡς ἀγνωσίᾳ / σέβωμεν αὐτούς, 957–60). We realize at once that we are dealing with a man for whom religious sanctions have no meaning. He is simply lacking in moral awareness, and these opening statements about the gods show us this deficiency of a criminal personality. He projects his own moral disorder upon the gods. It is appropriate, then, that this sociopathic, homicidal figure is finally cast completely outside human society, to a desert island (1284ff.). Given the fact that the delay in the sailing winds that makes Hecuba's vengeance possible *may* have something to do with the gods, Polymestor's confident belief in the random movements of the gods is comparable to Jocasta's dismissal of oracles in the *Oedipus Tyrannus.*

The amoral, Machiavellian politician Odysseus makes virtually no mention of the gods (the allusion to Persephone in line 136 hardly counts) but argues for martial honor as a socially useful principle, even if it involves the barbarous practice of human sacrifice (306ff.). He sees no religious dimension at all in obeying the command of Achilles' ghost. He insists drily only on the practical results of the deed, keeping the Greek state strong by honoring the best warriors (306–31). He may follow the outward forms of piety (cf. 342–45), but he honors these more in the letter than in the spirit. Hence he will accept Hecuba's supplication only in the most limited, legalistic sense: her life in exchange for his, and nothing more (301f.). In lines 342–45 it is significantly Polyxena, not Odysseus, who refers to the efficacy of the suppliant gesture and to "Zeus, god of suppliants."

The chorus, with the piety born of desperation, urges Hecuba to use her suppliant status, go the temples, and "call on the gods of the heavens and the gods below the earth" (145–53). As the women of the chorus reflect on their city's suffering in the second stasimon, they blame Helen's "private folly" (641ff.) and trace the cycle of events back to the quarrel of the three goddesses and the judgment of Paris (644–49). At the end of the third stasimon they return to Helen, curse her, and call her marriage the "woe from some avenging spirit" (*alastor*, 947f.).

In neither case do the women give much emphasis to divine causation. When they do blame the gods in a general way, they are often only expressing their helplessness and resignation about "life" or "chance" (*tuchê*), a recurrent theme in the play, as in Euripides generally. Thus their immediate response to the messenger's account of Polyxena's death is to attribute their own and Troy's suffering to "necessity from the gods" (θεῶν ἀνάγκαισιν, 584).[8] Their closing comment on the action, however, as they are being led away to slavery, is "harsh necessity," with nothing said about the gods (στερρὰ γὰρ ἀνάγκη, 1295). We may recall also Polymestor's bare *"anankê"* in his prophecy of Cassandra's death.

As women who have led sheltered lives, the members of the chorus have conventional views of the gods; and they have no means of self-protection other than the traditional sanctions against the violation of suppliants, to which Hecuba too makes appeal (287–90). They gloat over Polymestor's punishment as the triumph of "Justice and the gods" (1028). Yet they are not interested in probing more deeply into the questions of divine justice. Even when they look back as far as the judgment of Paris (644ff.), they close the stasimon with the very human reflection that in Greece too a girl is weeping in bereavement at home or a mother is tearing her cheeks in the mourning ritual for a dead son (647–57). In this respect they are very different from an Aeschylean chorus.

Hecuba herself is, as one would expect, the most complex of all the characters in her view of the gods. Her tragedy circumscribes the arc from her appeals to traditional piety in the first half of the play (e.g., 287ff., mentioned above) to the horrible, if justified, vengeance that she exacts from the murderer of her son. She pronounces one of Euripides' fullest and most celebrated declarations of moral principles deriving from the divine order in her appeal to *nomos* in lines 799–805 but has no scruples about shifting the grounds of her appeal to Agamemnon's infatuation with Cassandra.[9]

Agamemnon pays lip service to punishing the criminal, but he is more concerned with keeping up appearances and avoiding "being slandered" before the Greek army (854–63).[10] When he pronounces his final judgment against Polymestor and in favor of Hecuba, he validates her peroration, calling Polymestor a man "neither pious nor trustworthy to those to whom he should have been, nor holy, nor just" (1234f., cf. 852f.). But his ulterior motives and Odysseus' amoral expediency have undercut any commitment to the moral and religious values implied by these verses. This is, after all, a society that permits human sacrifice, betrays the most sacred laws of civilized life, and seems almost completely incapable of noble, disinterested moral action for its own sake.

The prologue informs us at once that the son of Achilles, the warrior whose honor is the central motif of the first half of the play, has slaughtered Priam at the "god-built altars" (23f.), a foreshadowing of the human sacrifice to come, also at an altar, and with the same slayer (534ff.).[11] Hecuba's appeals to the sanctities of the suppliant and to the horror of human sacrifice have no effect (cf. 145ff., 260ff., 287ff.). For these reasons, among others, scholars consider this play among the darkest of Euripides' works. Like the *Trojan Women*, it asks what Gunther Zuntz calls "the desperate question which is at the heart of all of Euripides' works; . . . how is man to live in a godless world?"[12]

Remote as the gods are in this play, there are several places where they do seem to intervene in human affairs. Yet the relation among these passages only brings out their remoteness and obscurity. Their absence seems almost Sophoclean and is certainly in striking contrast with Euripides' approach to the same material a decade or so later in the *Trojan Women*.[13]

In the prologue, first of all, the shade of Polydorus explains how he has "requested of the gods in power below to obtain burial and come into [his] mother's hands" (48f.). These chthonic gods have allowed him to visit the upper world, where he brings to Hecuba her disquieting nocturnal visions (cf. 68ff.). In due course, his body does come into her hands for burial (657ff.). To this extent the gods are merciful.[14] But these are only the gods of the lower world, and what they grant is burial (which is properly what lies in their power), and not, for instance, the salvation of the child for which Hecuba prays to them soon after. The recovery of Polydorus' corpse is obviously essential for uncovering Polymestor's crime and thus for bringing him to justice.[15] But Euripides presents it only within the limited framework of the chthonic intervention promised in the prologue, not as part of a broader scheme of divine justice.[16]

Addressing Hecuba herself in his last lines, Polydorus suggests that "some one of the gods" may be causing her present suffering, to counterbalance her previous good fortune (57f.). This appeal to the traditional notion of the gods' envy puts the question of theodicy into the foreground, but it hardly suggests a satisfactory solution. Earlier in the prologue, in fact, Polydorus attributes the suffering of the play's most innocent and pathetic victim, Polyxena, to a remote, impersonal "destiny" (43f.): ἡ πεπρωμένη δ' ἄγει / θανεῖν ἀδελφὴν τῷδ' ἐμὴν ἐν ἤματι. Later, after the discovery of Polydorus' body, the chorus attributes Hecuba's terrible suffering to some "divinity" of her ill fortune (720f.): "O poor woman, how whatever divinity [*daimon*] that is heavy upon you has made you most suffering of mortals."

Speaking from the other side of the division between life and death, Polydorus can describe this murder with a certain distance and objectivity. Hecuba, however, views these divine dispositions with the raw grief of a mother. Thus, when Odysseus announces the girl's impending sacrifice, Hecuba gives the bitterest possible interpretation to the gods' role in human life. She refers not to some vague "god," as did Polydorus' shade (*theôn tis*, 58), but incriminates Zeus himself. He did not permit her to die, as she would have liked, but has kept her alive so that she may witness sufferings of which each is worse than the last (232f.): οὐδ᾽ ὤλεσέν με Ζεύς, τρέφει δ᾽ ὅπως ὁρῶ / κακῶν κάκ᾽ ἄλλα μείζον᾽ ἡ τάλαιν᾽ ἐγώ. So, too, Hecuba's plea for "some god" to come as helper (163f.) will not be heeded.

After the failure of her intense prayers for the lives of her children, she does not again pray to the gods, even though, as we have seen, she invokes the gods as principles of justice in her appeal to Agamemnon (799ff.; cf. 1234ff.). Once having decided on revenge, she does not expect divine aid. The powers she invokes are Kypris (825ff.), as an allegorization of sex, and Peitho, the true "tyrant for men" (816ff.). The chorus, at the moment of Polymestor's punishment, combines Justice, as a personified force, with the gods (τὸ ὑπέγγυον Δίκᾳ καὶ θεοῖσιν, "what is held under debt to Justice and the gods," 1028f.); but for Hecuba herself *dike* is human rather than divine justice. Impiety and disregard for the gods bulk large in Hecuba's initial accusation of Polymestor (790–92); and Agamemnon agrees to help her "for the sake of the gods and justice" (θεῶν θ᾽ οὕνεκ᾽ ... καὶ τοῦ δικαίου, 852f.; cf. 1234f.). But the gods disappear from his final judgment (1240–54).

The first stage in Hecuba's just revenge is often interpreted as owing something to divine aid. Her revenge is possible, as Agamemnon allows, because "the god is not sending the favorable winds" (οὐ γὰρ ἵησ᾽ οὐρίους πνοὰς θεός, 900). The suspension of the winds by a "god" is all the more striking because hitherto the agent of the calm has been the shade of Achilles (cf. 37–39, 109–115). The Messenger, in fact, quotes verbatim the prayer to Achilles to "release" the ships as Neoptolemus slaughters Polyxena and pours out her blood as an offering to the shade (538–41). Agamemnon's allusion to divine collaboration, then, is vague and full of contradictions and reflects his own feeble commitment to morality. He will aid the cause of justice if it brings him no inconvenience, and his help depends on such an external contingency as the winds. At the same time, the passage can be read ironically as a hint of a remote divine justice working in ways beyond Agamemnon's understanding. This justice, in fact, as Polymestor's closing prophecy suggests, works precisely through the moral blindness of Agamemnon. The two possibilities are by no means mutually exclusive. In fact, taken together, they show Euripides using the gods simultaneously to raise the problem of a moral world order and to reveal human character: men show what they are in the way they speak of the gods.[17]

Closely connected with this passage is the closing scene of the play. After Polymestor's terrible prophecies about Hecuba's transformation and the murder of Cassandra and Agamemnon in Argos, the latter announces that he sees "the favorable winds [blowing] homeward" (καὶ γὰρ πνοὰς / πρὸς οἶκον ἤδη τάσδε πομπίμους ὁρῶ, 1289f.). The echo of line 900 is important and intentional. Euripides is again raising the possibility that divine powers are somewhere in the background and will eventually punish the Greeks for the atrocities they have committed at Troy.[18] On closer inspection, however, divine intervention is as obscure and ambiguous as it was in the previous passage. The only future sufferers here are Cassandra, who is a totally innocent victim, and Agamemnon, who is guilty, to be sure, as the leader of the army, but within the framework of the play has been the gentlest of the Greeks. The chief agents of Hecuba's sufferings have been Odysseus, the strongest sponsor of sacrificing Polyxena (131ff.), and the two sons of Theseus, from Athens (123f.), who do not appear in the play.

At the end Agamemnon says nothing of the gods, as he had in line 900; he says only, "I see the winds." If the gods are working in the background, then, they are working in mysterious ways. Agamemnon is totally blind to them. He "sees" the material aspect of the world, but not the invisible powers, possibly moral powers, beyond that. The only one to have any vision of these powers is the most unworthy possible vehicle of the gods' will, the greedy and treacherous Polymestor. Claiming Dionysus, "prophet to the Thracians," as his authority, he is a parody of the deus ex machina and so a problematical figure to offer assurances of divine justice.[19] The prophecies that he announces are given not to implement justice but to compensate for his helplessness and to encompass his own revenge against those who have punished his crime.

The agency of Dionysus is part of a pattern of bacchic motifs evident throughout the play.[20] Cassandra is described repeatedly as subject to bacchantic madness (121, 676f.; cf. 827); but this "Bacchant" is a helpless and innocent victim, and Hecuba will sing a "bacchic tune" of dirges over another daughter's body (684–87). More powerful still is the description of the Trojan women as Bacchants when they attack Polymestor and his sons. He calls them "Bacchants of Hades" (1077), and his account of their deed, in wild lyrics, makes it resemble a Dionysiac *sparagmos* (1078ff.).[21] The collective nature of this female attack also connects it with maenadic violence (cf. 1156ff., especially the "multitude of women," *plêthos gunaikôn*, 1167). These Dionysiac elements, however, like Polymestor's Dionysiac prophecy at the end, though in the service of justice, are deeply imbued by the all-too-human passions of violent revenge. If Hecuba looks and acts like a maenad, she is driven by cold-blooded calculation, not Dionysiac inspiration. What may have been literal in the divine punishment of the Thracian Lycurgus has become figurative in the wholly human punishment of the Thracian Polymestor.[22]

The mention of other divinities in the play gives as little clear assurance of divine justice. The chorus's prayer to Artemis at the fall of Troy was unsuccessful (935f.). In the first stasimon, in fact, they speculate anxiously on their future toil as slaves in this goddess's shrine on Delos (458ff.). Hecuba lures Polymestor to his doom by the promise of treasure hidden by a black stone near Athena's temple at Troy (1008f.). Yet it is not the goddess who is avenging her city's ruin, but the human plotter who is enlisting the goddess's name in her own scheme of vengeance. Hecuba may relish using a sacred place to punish a man who has trampled on divine and human laws. Yet this reference to Athena's temple among what is now a heap of smoking ruins (cf. 476–78, 823, 1215) may also remind us of the goddess's refusal to defend her city (cf. *Iliad* 6.297–311). Athena, like Artemis, is a divinity whose festivals the Trojan women will adorn as slaves (466ff.; cf. 458ff.).

The gods, to be sure, are not forgotten at the end. The suspension of the winds has *something* to do with supernatural forces, even if we do not know exactly what they are. The winds' return may be due to powers greater than the shade of Achilles (cf. 900). Even after the appeasement of Achilles' shade, the winds hold off long enough to allow Hecuba to work her hard justice on Polymestor. And the lower gods' granting of Polydorus' request for burial does eventually bring about justice. Even so, we cannot say that the good are rewarded, as Agamemnon would have it in his superficial pietism of lines 902–4; yet evil does seem to be punished. Evil, in fact, seems to contain the seeds of its own self-destruction. Reenacting his earlier greed for Trojan gold, Polymestor makes his vice into the instrument of his own punishment. In trapping him, Hecuba cleverly brings together the gold stolen from Polydorus (994) and the lure of still more gold at Troy (1002, 1009). The appearance of Polydorus' shade in the prologue at least raises the possibility of just and merciful gods, in the lower if not in the upper world. The disposition of the cosmos into its several zones of divine control in the opening lines can imply a hierarchical world order that is reconcilable with divine justice (ἵν' Ἅιδης χωρὶς ᾤκισται θεῶν, "where Hades has been set to dwell apart from the gods," 2).

The broader reaches of the action, leading back to Paris and Helen and forward to Agamemnon and Clytaemnestra in Mycenae, could be made to imply something like an Aeschylean pattern of retributive justice extending from one crime to another. The echoes of the *Oresteia* and the sacrifice of a maiden to obtain favorable winds, now from Troy back to Greece, certainly leave room for speculation about some kind of poetic justice hidden from the participants but visible to us the spectators in our godlike overview of the events. But Euripides does not develop such reflections at any length.[23] The justice that lies in the future is glimpsed only as part of the intended cruelty and revenge of Polymestor against Hecuba. Polymestor gloatingly reports these prophecies not in the name of justice but to inflict pain on his enemies. His main target is not the Greek general but the bereaved Trojan mother, via another innocent victim, her last surviving child, Cassandra.[24]

The one person for whom the chorus prays for a *failed* voyage "home" (*eis oikon*, 952), namely Helen, has (so far as this play indicates) an ultimately happy return over the sea (950–52):

ἂν μήτε πέλαγος ἅλιον ἀπαγάγοι πάλιν,
μήτε πατρῷον ἵκοιτ' ἐς οἶκον.

As for her, may the sea's flood not carry her back again, and may she not arrive at her paternal home.

We are reminded of the Trojan women's bitterness in the previous ode about the beautiful Helen's safe crossing of the sea as Paris' bride (ἅλιον ἐπ' οἶδμα ναυστολήσων / Ἑλένας ἐπὶ λέκτρα, "to sail upon the sea's swell to Helen's bed," 634f.).[25] In sharp contrast with the chorus's impotent prayer against Helen's return here in the third stasimon stands their lament, in the same ode, over their own sea voyage into slavery (937–41):

ἄγομαι δὲ θανόντ' ἰδοῦσ' ἀκοίταν
τὸν ἐμὸν ἅλιον ἐπὶ πέλαγος,
πόλιν τ' ἀποσκοποῦσ', ἐπεὶ νόστιμον
ναῦς ἐκίνησεν πόδα καί μ' ἀπὸ γᾶς
ὥρισεν Ἰλιάδος.

I am led away upon the sea's flood, seeing my husband killed, looking back to my city, when the ship made its journey home and set me apart from the land of Troy.

This cruel discrepancy between the two crossings of the sea is underlined by the similar phrasing for the Trojan women's journey over the sea into captivity and the prayer for Helen's nonreturn across the sea (ἄγομαι . . . ἅλιον ἐπὶ πέλαγος in 937f., and μήτε πέλαγος ἅλιον ἀπαγάγοι in 950). The verbal echo depicts the frustrations of the chorus's demand for justice and, by implication, the refusal of the gods to hear their prayers (cf. 935).[26] It may be part of a hidden divine plan that the guilty Helen's happy "return" (940) to her ancestral "house" (*oikos*, 952) is to be answered by the doom of Agamemnon's return to his (*oikos*, 1277 and 1290). Yet the sea passage that awaits Hecuba (cf. ποντία νοτίς, 1259), according to Polymestor's prophecy, holds no relief or recompense for her suffering. There are intimations of divine justice at work in the movements of the sea that cast Polydorus' body ashore to reveal his murderer, but the only gods mentioned are the nameless ones who "have their strength below," the chthonic deities whom Polydorus supplicated for proper burial (49f.).[27]

Whatever justice from the gods Euripides intimates, then, is qualified by their remoteness and their inscrutability. What he does show us is the blindness of men: the physical blindness of the justly and savagely punished Polymestor; the moral blindness of the Greek king and general, who renders a just judgment but for dubious, compromised motives; and the pathetically failed hopes of the chorus for the punishment of Helen. In such a world the human actors are left alone, to work out their own solutions to the evil and degradation around them. Men's and women's bad moral dispositions—whether the result of innate character (in the case of Polymestor) or circumstances (in the case of Hecuba)—are the chief determinant of the suffering that we see enacted before us: the murders, betrayals, rape, and enslavement that follow in the wake of war.

The gods, invisible and anonymous, *may* be viewed as creating the circumstances that favor this process of retributive justice, but Euripides leaves the question open. Here, as elsewhere, he does not give us an unambiguous theology. For those who die a painful death in innocence, like Polydorus or Polymestor's children, or in nobility and generosity of spirit, like Polyxena, there may be vengeance, but there is no palliation of suffering. The gods below may help Polydorus obtain burial, but while he and his family still live, they seem indifferent.

It is characteristic of the mood of *Hecuba* that Euripides presents this remoteness of the gods not primarily as a theological problem but from the perspective of the human victims. Virgil, one of antiquity's most sensitive and attentive readers of Euripides' Trojan plays, found the epic equivalent of these distant tragic gods. When the Greek attack lays bare the vulnerable city of Troy, the halls resound with the wailing of the women, but their cries arouse no compassion in the heavens: "ferit aurea sidera clamor" (Their cries strike the golden heavens, *Aeneid* 2.488). When we do see the gods, it is an ugly and fearful sight, and one that has its origins as much in Euripides as in Homer: "apparent dirae facies inimicaque Troiae / numina magna deum" (The dread forms appear and the great powers of the gods unfriendly to Troy, *Aeneid* 2.622f.).

The obscurity of the gods in *Hecuba* has the effect of throwing the problem of violence back into the human world, but without any hope of resolving the sacrificial crisis.[28] Eventually the wrongdoers' own baser passions will lead them to destruction. The Greek world will both continue and reenact the violence that we have seen here in Thrace and further back at Troy. The second stasimon, about Helen and Paris, ends with the bitter reflection that the Greek girl or mother in Sparta will be tearing hair and skin in the mourning rites just as the Trojan women have been doing in the Chersonese (650–57).

Unresolved violence has the instability of the sea and the strangeness and disorientation of mythic metamorphosis. But at the same time, the terrible sameness of cyclical repetition encircles Hecuba, Polymestor, and Agamemnon. This is perhaps Euripides' way of saying that evil creates its own constricted and self-destructive world. The large spaces framing the action—the distances between Hades and the upper world; the sea between Troy and Greece; the triangle of Priam's palace, the Thracian tomb of Achilles, and the palace of Agamemnon—all shrink into the dangerous enclosures of the Trojan women's tents and their later equivalent in Mycenae. The cruel, greedy, and treacherous Thracian king will be removed to a desert island. Hecuba, victorious in her terrible revenge, will be frozen into canine shape as a landmark for sailors. And for Agamemnon an obscure doom, waiting, like Polymestor's, in a woman's chambers, adds a quiet, brooding horror to the outrages of the last scene.

13

Conclusion: Euripides'
Songs of Sorrow

Alcestis, *Hippolytus*, and *Hecuba* reveal different facets of Euripides' mind and art, but despite the differences they have certain features in common. The *Alcestis* is a domestic tragicomedy with a mixture of fairy-tale atmosphere and intense personal suffering that in the extant plays reappears again only in the *Helen* some two decades later. The *Hippolytus* explores the nature of passion, the problems of communication and language, and the emotional and moral pitfalls of intense aspiration and one-sided devotion to an ideal. While each work in different ways allows a certain measure of grandeur and nobility to its protagonists, the *Hecuba* takes a more problematic view of human nature and leaves our sympathies much more divided. It combines the pathos of terrible suffering in war with a steady degeneration to vengeful plotting and ugly violence. Except for the innocent Polyxena, victim of a bloodthirsty warrior's ghost, no figure in the play is left untarnished.

In all three plays, a major female character challenges the predominantly masculine center of power and authority and in some way questions the limits of that power. Alcestis forces her husband to confront the gap between the value that he attaches to family ties and affections and the honorific exchanges of guest-friendship that belong to the outward-facing world of male prerogatives. Phaedra's erotic passion invades the garden world of idealized purity that Hippolytus would create with his virginal huntress-goddess, Artemis, and shatters its defenses by opening it up to the power of Aphrodite that he has rejected (both for himself and others) so absolutely. In the process, Phaedra also releases the suppressed violence and hatred that fuel Hippolytus' total rejection of Aphrodite. Hecuba begins as a helpless victim, a mourning mother who sees her remaining children taken from her one by one in the aftermath of the war that has already destroyed her city. But submission changes to vengeful energy at the last outrage. As Phaedra uses Theseus as the instrument of her vengeful self-defense, so Hecuba uses Agamemnon and indirectly involves the Greek army in her terrible, if justified, revenge.

In all three cases the women are impelled to their actions by their intense emotional commitment to house and family. Alcestis and Phaedra both try to ensure their children's future; and each is prepared to sacrifice her life in the process, although in diametrically opposite ways. Hecuba will stop at nothing, including her own self-abasement, to punish the murderer of her son. In all three plays too, the energy, commitment, and force of the female protagonists overshadow the male figures, who in any case are so ambiguous in their virtues that they arouse very divided sympathies in modern readers and critics, as they probably did in the original audiences.

Euripides' way of using the female protagonists as a challenge to the largely male world of public life, civic affairs, and even domestic authority pervades Greek tragedy, from Aeschylus' Clytaemnestra to Sophocles' Deianeira and Antigone. Euripides leaves us with an even greater and more problematic disequilibrium because so few of his male characters can reaffirm heroic or communal values as can Aeschylus' Athena (in *Eumenides*) or Sophocles' Ajax and Heracles (in *Ajax* and *Trachiniae*). Two other features of these plays enhance Euripides' decentering effect: the depiction of extreme emotional states (Phaedra's desperate passion, Hecuba's virulent hatred) and the lack of a clear moral governance of the world by the gods.

Aphrodite in the *Hippolytus* comes as close as a Greek divinity can to being a personification of emotional forces or Freudian instincts; and her wrath, like the revenge of Dionysus in the *Bacchae*, enacts the return of the repressed part of the emotional life. The excess of aphroditic power in Phaedra works to avenge its deficiency in Hippolytus. But the divinities of the *Hippolytus* are more than mere allegories of the passions or their lack. Artemis' promise of future revenge (1420–22) suggests a world order whose very nature is a conflictual ebb and flow of forces that can never be reconciled. The dying Hippolytus "does not go gentle into that dark night," and his impulse to curse the gods (1415) shows that mortals are not necessarily reconciled to the suffering that the nature of the world seems to require of them.

Euripides' gods are in some ways just; but their way of ensuring justice, at least in the plays written at this phase of his career, is to use the destructive impulses of men and women. The resulting justice, as is often the case in Greek tragedy, is retributive rather than restorative. The lighter atmosphere of *Alcestis* does not allow these problems the scope that they have in the other two tragedies, but the conflict among the gods in *Hippolytus* and the virtual absence of the gods from *Hecuba* throw the human world back entirely upon the passions of the human protagonists, with little restraint from a coherent moral order. As we have seen in *Hecuba*, the appeal to a universal moral law is itself co-opted into the scheme of single-minded vengeance.

These plays, however, achieve more than psychological depth or a cynical exposé of human corruption and amorality or the incrimination of the existential condition of humankind projected upon the gods; they also examine the conflicts and contradictions between different values and areas of life. In particular, the working out of these conflicts reveals an interconnectedness among the different parts of life that the individual characters' partial, fragmented perspectives necessarily obscure. The gods are not just a convenient way of beginning or ending the play or a piece of outmoded, creaking machinery; they place the issues into a universalizing perspective and display the latent relations and reciprocal forces among the parts of this tragic world. The absolute, one-sided worship of an Artemis means the anger of an Aphrodite; the total surrender of one's being to revenge, however justified, is a state of brutality that the gods can foresee, albeit through an unworthy vehicle of that vision (*Hecuba* 1265–84).

In *Alcestis*, the figure of Thanatos in the prologue, for all the banter and dark humor in the exchanges with Apollo, dramatizes the inexorability of death in the human condition and thus creates the asymmetry between the situations of Alcestis and Admetus on which the meaning of the play hinges. In *Hippolytus*, Aphrodite dooms the protagonist as much by the fact of her existence in his world as by the details of her plot. In *Hecuba*, the shade of Polydorus, thanks to the dispensation of the gods of the lower world, can unfold the secrets of the past and claim the rights of the dead that set the revenge plot in motion.

It is not easy to evaluate the degree of Euripides' sympathy for women. His female characters are neither wholly idealized nor wholly demonized. They are the center of powerful and complex emotions, and, like many tragic figures, they struggle with painful choices at crises that threaten them with the destruction of what they value most. Like the other tragedians, he emphasizes the destructiveness of female passion; but he is equally emphatic about the violence, greed, callousness, and immorality of the male characters. Indeed, the women, despite all their emotional excesses, often come off as more admirable, and certainly as more interesting, than their male counterparts. Phaedra wins an ambiguous admiration even from the hostile Artemis (*Hippolytus* 1301f.); and ultimately even Hecuba's just, if horrible, vengefulness is nobler and more sympathetic than Agamemnon's shallow expediency.

From Aristophanes on, Euripides has been stereotyped as the playwright who excels in intensive psychological portraits of desperate women. Like all stereotypes, this one contains some truth; but Euripides is also a dramatist who perceives the sharp divisions between male and female experience that are part of his social reality. In the closed inner world of female space Phaedra's "disease" of eros secretly grows in her veiled body; and from her closed, silent chamber emanate the false, folded tablets that achieve her revenge and protect her domestic honor as the mother of her children. In *Hecuba* the intensity of the mother's vengeance follows from women's connection with children, birth, ritual lamentation, and the details of funerary rites. The exasperation of her suffering is directly related to her concern for her children and her involvement in the sacrificial marriage / death of her daughter. Her success in attaining her revenge depends on using the erotic attraction of another daughter, Agamemnon's concubine, Cassandra. The sexual subjection of both Polyxena and Cassandra reveals women as helpless victims of male violence and self-aggrandizement in both sex and war; and

Hecuba, like Phaedra and Medea, is able to turn this dependence on males to her own purposes.

Hecuba's revenge, like Phaedra's, is of a characteristically "feminine" nature, as Greek tragedy tends to construct the feminine: it depends on guile, enclosure, and the readiness of women to conspire with one another against men. Yet it succeeds because it is so unexpected. Ironically, men's underestimation of women is the latter's best weapon. The Dionysian reversal from enfeeblement to unforeseen collective violence emerges as a kind of nightmare vision of feminine justice, appropriate to a barbarian, perhaps; and yet this violence, once released, cannot be contained within the barbarian world, as the continuing Dionysian prophecies of the barbarian Polymestor show.[1] Agamemnon would brush aside any threats from his "bitter housekeeper" in Greece (*Hecuba* 1277), just as he would banish the murderous prophet to a desert island in Thrace. But this stifled prophetic vision from the realm of the god reveals the dark truth that blinded Polymestor and to which Agamemnon is figuratively blind as well.

The *Hecuba* anticipates the *Bacchae* in the way in which the realm of Dionysus contains a potential in human behavior that the men in power in the city would either deny or suppress. In both plays Dionysian disguise conceals the possibility that women can release the repressed violence of their invisible emotional life; and in both cases the god's epiphany, as it were, takes the form of the sudden display of this violence in its full horror.[2] In the *Bacchae* and in the *Hecuba*, as also in the *Hippolytus* and *Medea*, this violence works outward from the domestic space of the house, particularly in some relation to children. The *Bacchae*, of course, goes much further than the *Hecuba* in tracing the spread of this violence from the women inside the house into the city as a whole, and it goes far beyond *Hecuba* in identifying a latent kinship with this violence in the king himself; but the seeds are already there in the early play, particularly in the king's refusal to recognize in his own realm what he has seen in the barbarian world around him. Hecuba, of course, can succeed only with Agamemnon's complicity. Only in the *Bacchae* are women able to sustain a face-to-face confrontation with the male martial and political authority of the city, probably because Dionysus is actually present among them and has infiltrated the king's palace and person.[3]

Hecuba's status as a barbarian keeps her monstrous revenge in the realm of the "other," and so helps Agamemnon to compartmentalize her behavior within this remote corner of the Greek world. Yet the otherness of women is inherent in the separateness of the spatial world they occupy, whether in Greece or in the Troad. The inner chambers of Clytaemnestra in the heart of the Argive palace or of Phaedra in the dominions of Athens are as potentially deadly and guileful as the Trojan women's tents in Thrace. The *Medea* brings female and barbarian violence even within Athens, city of culture and the arts. The chorus sings one of Euripides' most beautiful odes, praising Athens as the home of wisdom and the Muses, at just the point when the Colchian enchantress has secured this city as the refuge for the revenge she is plotting (*Medea* 824–65). Her vengeance, like Hecuba's and Phaedra's in different ways, combines female conspiracy, domestic intrigue, and children, and unfolds in a closed inner chamber with a horrible mangling of flesh (*Medea* 1136–1223).

As Nicole Loraux and Froma Zeitlin have shown, that interior space of women also serves as the correlative of an enhanced sensitivity to somatic experience—the penetrability and vulnerability of the body in disease, injury, and painful death.[4] It is in the chambers within the house that Alcestis' wasting away in death and its terrors are directly experienced by the male spectator of her suffering. The aftermath of this experience henceforth divides his house between the largely female involvement with children, marriage, and death and the largely male prerogatives of receiving noble guests in heroic hospitality. Only the fantasy solution of a warrior hero's irresistible valor solves the problem, but even here the power of death lingers in the veiled and silent presence of the woman in the last scene.

Although Euripides is exploiting traditional elements in the depiction of women, from Homer's Helen and Circe and Hesiod's Pandora on to Aeschylus' Clytaemnestra and Sophocles' Deianeira, he is also conscious of rewriting aspects of the tradition, particularly in his expository prologues and aetiological epilogues.[5] In engrafting his own vision of human psychology and divine intervention on the monuments from the past, he calls attention to his unique artistry and innovation. Thus the *Hippolytus* has its own version of the foundation of the temple of Aphrodite at Athens and the cult of Hippolytus at Troezen, and the *Hecuba* tells how the promontory of Cynossema is associated with Hecuba. The *Alcestis* has its own self-reflexive comments on how the fame of its heroine survives through the ages in the songs of poets (445–54, cf. 989–1005). Euripides thereby places his own play in the sequence of commemorative songs that challenge death by surviving through fame. But he also distances himself from this ritual commemoration by *Alcestis'* surprise ending, which effectively replaces the funeral monument with the play that enacts a literal defeat of death as part of its story. His account of Hecuba's metamorphosis is a μορφῆς ἐπῳδόν, a difficult phrase that might imply a "song composed upon" another tale, thus combining a personal vision of the myth with a recognition of its past forms and the creation of a new, more disquieting kind of monument. Monument and metamorphosis here come together in the poet's insight into the way the new medium of tragedy refashions the old myths.

In the *Heracles* Euripides can project an image of his chorus as the servant of the Muses, growing old in the company of their songs (*Heracles* 673–86). He thus implicitly claims for his work a continuing place in the great traditions of the past and in the songs and festivals of his community, as his praise of Alcestis in the first stasimon of that play implies (*Alcestis* 445–54). At the same time, that tradition is changed as it is refracted through the new medium; and the new perspective transforms the traditions as much as it perpetuates them: hence the bitter ironies in the rites that keep alive the memory of Hippolytus' sufferings at Troezen. The play itself, then, with all its ironies and paradoxes, becomes a new kind of monument. It is a source of less stable, more polyvalent meanings than those of the past, in part because it commemorates the female violence enacted in hidden places. Hence the love of Phaedra "will not be kept in silence" (*Hippolytus* 1430) beside the new brides' ritual honoring of Hippolytus; and the truth of Hecuba's monstrosity will remain written upon the face of nature.

Drawing on the traditions of ritual lament and choral song, Euripides' tragedies are in a sense songs of sorrow—sorrow for the suffering that seems an inevitable part of being human, and sorrow for the hatred, bitterness, folly, and error that make life even harder than it need be. They are also songs of the sorrows that would otherwise be hidden away, uncommemorated because they are endured in the privacy of the secret world where the larger part of Athenian women's lives unfolds. As we have seen, Euripides calls attention to his crossing of the boundaries between public and private space as he opens the chambers of Alcestis, Phaedra, and Hecuba to the public view of the theater.

As the end of the *Hippolytus* reveals, however, the sorrow that is thereby revealed can, thanks to the tragic form, be shared in communal lament where it is clarified and exposed, for good or ill, as a "common grief for all the citizens." That is perhaps the best that the tragic poet can do: to help us connect with the suffering of our fellow men and women. Whether this enlargement and refinement of our sympathies only conduce to the audience's acceptance of the status quo in resigned acknowledgment of "harsh necessity" (*Hecuba* 1295) or whether it actually was meant to produce real change is something that we cannot know. Literature has many uses and many meanings, and arguments for a conservative, liberal, or revolutionary Euripides can probably all be extracted from the plays.[6]

If Euripidean tragedy sometimes invites us to adopt the cold and remote perspective of the gods, like that of Artemis at the end of the *Hippolytus*, it also more warmly engages and directs our emotions through the sympathetic responses of the chorus. The chorus helps to transform the image of community from abstraction or impersonal collectivity to affective identification. It thus encourages the formation of the community of the theater, the audience's sense of its role as involved spectators of events of which they feel a part. Individual members of an audience will, of course, identify with one or another of the protagonists; but, as the choral close of *Hippolytus* suggests, the chorus can sometimes provide at least a model for a collective emotion, a surge of feeling, doubtless enhanced by the now-lost musical accompaniment, that can sweep over the assembled multitude and add an affective component to the moral judgments that the action has also required us to make.

The end of the *Hecuba*, on the other hand, raises the question of what happens when even that community of shared feeling is eroded by the "harsh necessity" of all-engulfing violence. The assembled Greeks whom the chorus describes in the parode are carried along by the murderous desires of a warrior's ghost and the persuasions of Odysseus' cold calculations of military efficiency (107–40). A little later, however, this bloodthirsty crowd of warriors is moved to pity and admiration at the noble death of an innocent girl, the only truly heroic act in the play, and even the Messenger weeps when reporting the details (518–20, 571–82). Although the scene is only narrated, not seen, and the tender emotions are soon left behind in the killings and maiming that follow, it momentarily provides an alternative, more compassionate model of spectator response.

The Athenian spectators, identifying with their experience in the law courts, would presumably endorse Agamemnon's decision to acquit Hecuba. But where human justice has either to condemn or to pardon, the mysterious mechanism of metamorphosis, beyond human logic or agency, exacts a punishment of another kind. The brutalization of Hecuba is now a fact, recorded in the physical shape of our world, just as the future punishment of her accomplice, judge, and conqueror is fixed in the mythical and literary tradition, which is here projected into the form of Dionysian prophecy. Beyond the judgment of a human court, both the criminal and the punisher are joined in a common fate; both Polymestor and Hecuba are in different ways expelled from the community of civilized men and women. But then that same community of civilized people depicted here—that is, the victorious army of Greeks—enforces the "harsh necessity" that leads off the enslaved Trojan women as the spoils of war.

This play, unlike *Hippolytus*, offers no overt word of comfort, nor does it suggest that any is possible; but it at least provides a long view forward into a time when what happened in this remote barbarian land will, mutatis mutandis, be reenacted in Greece, with Greek protagonists. It is not accidental that this vision of Agamemnon's reversal of roles from victor to victim and from spectator to participant comes from Dionysus (*Hecuba* 1267), the god who also presides over the tragic festival and the instability and deceptiveness of appearances that tragedy depicts.[7] Yet the shift of perspective in the Dionysian fluidity of boundaries can apply to the audience as well as to the actors. Talthybius' narrative of Polyxena's sacrifice virtually creates a miniature theatrical spectacle: the anonymous mass of the army looks upon the scene with almost voyeuristic fascination, as one would look on a beautiful statue (*Hecuba* 560f.). But this is a spectacle that refuses to stand still and in its own way fights back and fashions its own terms for being viewed. By her dying act of covering her body as she falls, Polyxena in fact asserts that she is not a spectacle, not just an object to be enjoyed by the (male) viewer, but a feeling human being with emotions of shame and vulnerability. Looking at her shames the army, the first level of spectators, as it shames us, the spectators in the audience. We are forced to recognize that the art work reaches beyond its purely aesthetic effect of stimulating pleasure, like the beautiful statue (560f.). Instead, the paradoxical tragic spectacle re-presents the consciousness and the helpless suffering of a dying victim whose pain becomes our own.

Here, as throughout the play, the audience is forced to shift its sympathies from the victorious Greek warriors to the enslaved barbarian women. In the *Erechtheus* and *Children of Heracles* of approximately the same time, the sacrificed virgin who goes willingly to her death is an Athenian princess whose noble end exemplifies Athenian patriotism. In *Hecuba*, however, the noble victim is a barbarian captive from a city conquered by Greeks. At the end the audience sees another barbarian, the enraged Thracian king with his bloodied eyes, suddenly changed from being judged to pronouncing a prophetic sentence of his own (*Hecuba* 1259–81). To be sure, the stichomythic form of Polymestor's prophecy separates it from the solemnity and dignity of a full oracular speech by a deus ex machina and emphasizes its involvement in the passions of the present moment. Nevertheless, the brutal murderer is now the mouthpiece of a divine perspective that takes in the future drama of Agamemnon now beginning to unfold—a drama that will both continue and repeat the old.

Notes

Abbreviations

Allen: Allen, Thomas W., ed. *Homeri Opera*, vol. 5. Oxford Classical Texts. Oxford: Clarendon Press, 1912.

Austin: Austin, Colin, ed. *Nova Fragmenta Euripidea in Papyris Reperta*. Berlin: De Gruyter, 1968.

Davies: Davies, Malcolm, ed. *Poetarum Graecorum Melicorum Fragmenta*, vol. 1. Oxford: Clarendon Press, 1991.

Diels-Kranz: Diels, Hermann, and Walter Kranz, eds. *Die Fragmente der Vorsokratiker.* 6th ed., 3 vols. Berlin: De Gruyter, 1951–52.

LSJ: Liddell, H. G., Robert Scott, and H. S. Jones, eds. *Greek-English Lexicon.* 9th ed. Oxford: Clarendon Press, 1925–40.

Merkelbach-West: Merkelbach, Rudolf, and M. L. West, eds. *Fragmenta Hesiodea*. Oxford: Clarendon Press, 1967.

Nauck: Nauck, Augustus, ed. *Tragicorum Graecorum Fragmenta.* 2d ed. Leipzig: Teubner, 1889.

OCT: Oxford Classical Text(s).

Page: Page, D. L., ed. *Poetae Melici Graeci*. Oxford: Clarendon Press, 1962.

Radt: Radt, Stefan, ed. *Tragicorum Graecorum Fragmenta.* Vol. 3, *Aeschylus*; vol. 4, *Sophocles.* Göttingen: Vandenhoeck and Ruprecht, 1985, 1977.

Abbreviations   Snell-Maehler: Maehler, Hervicus, post B. Snell, ed. *Pindari Carmina*. Pars II,
    Fragmenta. 4th ed. Leipzig: Teubner, 1975.

West: West, M. L., ed. *Iambi et Elegi Graeci*. 2 vols. Oxford: Clarendon Press,
    1971–72.

1. Introduction

1. On the changing fortunes of *Hecuba* over the centuries, see Heath (1987) 43ff., especially 55.

2. For discussion, see below, chapter 3.

3. Devereux (1985) 15f., 17f.

4. Goldhill (1990) 101, citing especially the scholion on Aristophanes, *Acharnians* 504; and Isocrates, *De Pace* 82.

5. For this aspect of tragedy, see Vernant and Vidal-Naquet (1990) 29ff., 264ff., 330ff. Goldhill (1990) provides an excellent statement of the balance between tragedy's normative and transgressive currents. I have developed some of the implications of this approach in C. Segal (1981b) chaps. 2, 3, and passim; and (1986a) 21–74, especially 45ff., 63ff.

6. For example, Aristophanes, *Acharnians* 634–40.

7. For this aspect of tragic commemoration, see Pucci (1977) 181ff.; C. Segal (1982a) 334ff., 345ff., (1992b) 108f.; also chapters 2, 3, and 7, below.

8. Barthes (1986) 38–39.

9. On the problem of self-reflexivity and breaking the dramatic illusion, see C. Segal (1982a) chap. 7; Easterling (1991) 55f. In a sophisticated form like Euripidean tragedy, as in Shakespearean tragedy, many levels of meaning are possible, and dramatic illusion can coexist with literary self-consciousness, although the latter, obviously, does not have the extreme form of the parabasis of Old Comedy, where the poet directly addresses his audience. Tragic self-reflexivity is obviously far subtler and less direct.

10. See the useful caveats of Easterling (1987); and below, chapter 5.

11. See Schaps (1982) passim. On the parallelism of war for men and marriage for women, see Loraux (1981) = (1989) 29ff.

12. Slater (1968) deserves credit for calling attention to this phenomenon in a broad cultural context, but many aspects of his psychosocial interpretation, though suggestive, are highly questionable. One should remember that not all the women of Greek tragedy are bad, and one should not assume that all male-female relations are abysmal; see Easterling (1987) passim; Gould (1980) 49ff.

13. See, for example, Slater (1968); Foley (1981b); Zeitlin (1985a); Seaford (1987), (1990); Loraux (1985); and C. Segal (1992c).

14. See C. Segal (1981b) 81ff., (1986a) 57f.

15. For the interior localization of Medea's dangerous power, see *Medea* 894ff., 950ff., 969ff., 1137, 1143.

16. See C. Segal (1982a) 205f.

17. On other adaptations of the betrayal plot in *Iphigeneia in Tauris*, especially of *Oresteia*, see Caldwell (1973–74) passim. For this technique in Euripides, see also Burnett (1971) 205–12.

2. *Euripides' Muse of Sorrows and the Artifice of Tragic Pleasure*

1. We may think especially of the "comedy of innocence" drama in the *bouphonia* where the ox to be sacrificed supposedly assents to its slaughter by finding the sacrificial knife and agreeing to its own death; see Burkert (1983) 136–43, and the references cited there; also Easterling (1988) passim.

2. Searle (1969) 22ff.

3. I do not mean that the plays constitute a worship of Dionysus in a formal sense. There is obviously a big difference between going to a temple of the god and going to the theater. But they do form part of a celebration which is, in the broad sense, religious and therefore features heavily ritualized elements. Seaford (1989) 87 argues for the generally "positive role which ritual tends to play in Homer as opposed to the negative role it tends to play in tragedy."

4. On the implicit self-reflexivity in the chorus's question in this ode, see Henrichs (forthcoming).

5. For the problem of specific and traditional in the occasional nature of archaic poetry, see Gentili (1988) 115ff.; Burnett (1983) 3ff.; Rösler (1984) 200–202; Nagy (1990) 339ff.

6. See Herington (1985) 113ff.; also Nagy (1989) 66–68, with a more historical emphasis.

7. *Heracles* 673ff., and see further discussion below.

8. On tragedy's techniques for claiming a voice of civic authority, see C. Segal (1992b) 85ff.; also Goff (1990) 117; and, in general, Meier (1990) 87ff.

9. Alexiou (1974), Danforth (1982) passim.

10. I do not mean to endorse the theories of William Ridgeway or some of the Cambridge ritualists about tragedy's origins from choruses or songs about dying heroes or gods, but only to call attention to the importance of ritual lament in the formal structure of tragedy.

11. See *Frogs* 1309–63; cf. Euripides, *Heracles* 348ff.; *Trojan Women* 511ff.; *Helen* 168ff., 1107ff.

12. See Aeschylus, frag. 277 in Hugh Lloyd-Jones's appendix to the Loeb Classical Library *Aeschylus*, ed. Herbert Weir Smyth (Cambridge, Mass.:

Harvard University Press, 1971), 556–62; also Sophocles, *Ajax* 333ff. See, in general, Reinhardt (1979) 11f.

13. For this aspect of the tragic performance, see Stanford (1983) chaps. 1 and 3. Speaking of the emotional effect of drama, Easterling (1988) 109 observes, "I do not think we can rule out the possibility that some sequences of words, music and actions could be felt to have exceptional power, something that went beyond the fictive world of the drama and was able to effect the world of the audience for good or ill."

14. On the contrasting songs, see Perdicoyianni (1992) 94.

15. See Pucci (1980) 32–45.

16. For the contrast of festivity, especially in song and dance, and war, see *Iliad* 3.393 and 15.508; see Schadewaldt (1966) 63f. It is interesting that the joy of song finds no place in Hesiod's contrast of the just and unjust cities in *Works and Days* 225–47.

17. See Loraux (1990) 21; also below, chapter 4.

18. For an important discussion of this passage, see Pucci (1980) 25ff.; also Gentili (1988) 41.

19. See Hesiod, *Theogony* 52ff.; Homer, *Odyssey* 4.594–98.

20. Sophocles, *Trachiniae* 1–3; see Diano (1968) 215–69; also Pucci (1980) 28ff.

21. For the dramatic function of these shifts in the function of song, see Parry (1978) 159ff.; Foley (1985) 149f., 183f. For the implicit poetics of the ode, see Walsh (1984) 116ff.

22. Herington (1985), especially 118–29 and 140ff.

23. See C. Segal (1986a) 79ff., (1992b) 87ff.

24. See Foley (1985) 255ff.; C. Segal (1982a) 318ff., 345, and (1992b) 108–10.

25. For recent surveys of the problem, see Goldhill (1986) 48–56; Conacher (1987) 48–56. On the lack of resolution, see Goldhill (1984) 277–83.

26. *Ajax* 1393ff. On the tensions surrounding the ritual at the end, see C. Segal (1981b) 138–46, 150f., and the references cited there; Easterling (1988) 97f.

27. These lines have many difficulties; I follow the texts of Jebb (1893) and Lloyd-Jones and Wilson (1990), but read τόδε in the last line to make translation possible.

28. On the play's reference to Ajax's future cultic status, see Burian (1974).

29. See C. Segal (1970a), and chapter 7, below, for further discussion. Cf. Pindar's self-conscious monumentalization of the athletic victor in *Nemean* 6.28–30. He "directs his glorious wind of words" toward the victor and then generalizes, "For men who are gone, songs and tales attend [preserve] their lovely deeds."

30. Sophocles' *Oedipus at Colonus* is a partial exception, but even this play

says little about immortal fame for Oedipus and shifts at the end from the hero to the daughters and the future suffering in Thebes.

31. See Golden (1992) 31ff., drawing on Nussbaum (1986) 390f.

32. See *Politics* 8.1339a50ff., especially 1341a21–26 and 1341b33–42a17, where Aristotle discusses the emotional excitement produced in an audience by the orgiastic quality of flute music. The traditional view, that catharsis refers to audience response, was powerfully stated by Jacob Bernays (1857), reprinted in Barnes, Scholfield, and Sorabji (1978) 154–65, especially 156ff., although his medical interpretation of catharsis remains controversial. Bernays also brought to bear the passage cited above from the *Politics*. For further discussion and bibliography, see Keesey (1978–79); Barnes, Scholfield, and Sorabji (1978) 188; Golden (1992) 5–18; Rorty (1992b) 12–15; Lear (1992); and Janko (1992), especially 346f.

33. See Keesey (1978–79) 202f.; Halliwell (1986) 198; also Halliwell in Kennedy (1989) 163f.; Golden (1992) 37; Else (1967) 439: "The great virtue, but also the great vice, of 'catharsis' in modern interpretation has been its incurable vagueness."

34. On weeping as a response to the tragic events, see below, chapter 4.

35. *To philanthrôpon* has the specific meaning "moral sentiment" but also includes the wider meaning of "a general feeling of sympathy with our fellow men"; see Stinton (1975) 238, n. 2; Moles (1984) 328, 334; see also Halliwell (1986) 219, with n. 25; Heath (1987) 66, and further references in n. 133; Carey (1988) passim, especially 134f.

36. For other aspects of this scene, see C. Segal (1986a) 97–99, and (1993b) chap. 11.

37. With Jebb (1893) and other editors, I prefer to stay closer to the manuscript, reading φορεῖν in line 1320, rather than θροεῖν with Lloyd-Jones and Wilson (1990).

38. For a sensitive analysis of this scene in a Derridean perspective, see Pucci (1977) 182–84.

39. I borrow this phrase from the fine study by Cole (1985) 9ff.

40. See lines 1312f., 1320ff.; cf. also 1277–81.

41. For drowning and burial in the obliteration of the monumental works of men, see Poseidon and Apollo's destruction of the Achaean seawall in *Iliad* 12.17–34; see Ford (1992) 139–71. Cf. the imagery of flooding and oblivion in Pindar, *Isthmian* 5.48ff., where Aegina is "set upright" by the "much-destroying storm of Zeus" at the Battle of Salamis, in contrast to the silence that must "drench" boasting—a silence about ill fame that might attach to those of the Greeks who did not fight but medized.

42. Similarly, in the farewell between Clytaemnestra and Iphigeneia in *Iphigeneia in Aulis* 1440–44, a mother's grief undercuts heroic monumentalization.

43. On this passage, see Gregory (1991) 177, who, however, interprets it more positively than I do (see my review, C. Segal [1993a]).

44. On the open-endedness of some tragic endings, from a perspective of narrative rather than ritual or emotional effect, see Roberts (1988).

45. For the Athenian spirit of synthesis and innovation, see Else (1965) chap. 2; and Herington (1985) chaps. 4 and 6. I would not want to minimize the innovative spirit of Peisistratus in reorganizing the Athenian festivals, but the tendencies may have been already present in the culture.

46. Pindar's elaboration, of course, may contain much that is fresh and original in renewing or defending aristocratic values in changing times; see Kurke (1991) 255f., 259f., and (1992) passim, especially 107ff.

47. Tragedy also has many continuities with the oral tradition, as is argued in Havelock (1982) 261–313. But the situation of drama is, I believe, far more complex than Havelock allows; see C. Segal (1982a), especially 266, with n. 6 (now in Segal [1987] 263–98); also C. Segal (1986a) 76ff.

3. Cold Delight: Art, Death, and Transgression of Genre

1. Cook (1971) 97.

2. Such metaphors are familiar from Pindar; see especially *Olympian* 6.1ff., *Pythian* 6.7ff. and 7.1ff., *Nemean* 5.1ff; see C. Segal (1986a) 156f. For Euripides, see, e.g., *Hecuba* 807f., 836–40; *Andromeda* frag. 125 in Nauck (1889). See, in general, Franco (1984).

3. See Aristophanes, *Frogs* 1082; and Euripides, frag. 638 Nauck.

4. For Euripides' *Protesilaus* (frags. 647–57 Nauck) and its similarities to *Alcestis*, see Dale (1954) 79, on lines 348–54; Franco (1984) 134f. Substitution in *Alcestis* is closely linked to the themes of exchange and reciprocity and the importance of *charis* (favor, gratitude, kindness): see, inter alia, Bergson (1985) 14f. From the point of view of the play's implicit poetics, it is, I think, more helpful to focus on substitution rather than repayment, as does, e.g., Burnett (1965) in E. Segal (1983) 258. On the importance of substitution in the play on a number of levels, see Bassi (1989) 24f.

5. See "La catégorie psychologique du double," in Vernant (1985a) 325–38, especially 326f., 332; also Franco (1984) 133ff.

6. The question of the "satyric" versus "tragic" tone remains controversial. For good recent discussions, see Von Fritz (1962) 263f., 312–21; Rohdich (1968) 23ff.; Seidensticker (1982) 129ff.; Riemer (1989) 1–5. For the earlier literature, see Lesky (1925) 84ff.

7. Cook (1971) 95.

8. There is probably a deliberate recall of Asclepius in the first ode: cf. *monos d'an*, line 123, of Asclepius, and *monas d'out'*, line 972, of Necessity; cf.

also 127f. and 985f.; and note Alcestis' "abrupt doom" (*apotomos moros*, in 118f.) and Necessity's "abrupt" or "stern" temper (*apotomon lêma*, in 981).

9. See Detienne and Vernant (1974) 149ff. (English trans. 1991, 151ff.).

10. The parallel extends also to the scene between Admetus and Pheres, on which see Burnett (1971) 42f.

11. On the ritual necessity of Alcestis' silence at the end, see Betts (1965) 181–82; Parker (1983) 37, n. 17, and 329, n. 10. Riemer (1989) 100–103 gives a useful review of the earlier literature.

12. On the epinician elements in the scene, see Garner (1988), especially 66ff.

13. This solidification of an all-male world apart from the house becomes even stronger if one compares the scene with Agamemnon's subjection to Clytaemnestra in the carpet scene of Aeschylus' *Agamemnon*, which has striking verbal parallels with our passage (*Agamemnon* 941ff., and *Alcestis* 1105ff.).

14. It is interesting to note the shift from the opening matronymic for Heracles (505) to the emphatic patronymics later (1119f., 1136f.).

15. The terms are *akos, poros, mêchanê*, and *pharmakon* (135, 213, 221; cf. 966ff.).

16. This double meaning of *pharmakon* in relation to the art of writing has become celebrated through Derrida (1972) 87f.

17. Euripides seems to be using a version of the Orpheus myth in which the bard succeeds in bringing his Eurydice back from death; see C. Segal (1989) 17–19, 155ff.

18. For the *thauma anelpiston*, "the marvel unhoped for," see 1123; cf. 1130, 1134, 1160. For the motifs of wonder and unbelief in the happy ending, see also Rohdich (1968) 43, with n. 62.

19. For the absence of "hope" (*elpis*), see lines 132, 146; cf. also *poros* in 213 and 1162.

20. Barnes (1964–65), in Wilson (1968) 28, finds "a ridiculous quality" in the statue speech, whereas Burnett (1965), in E. Segal (1983) 261, calls Admetus' promise "positive, delicately stated, and filled with a powerful meaning." Beye (1959) 114 calls the statue motif "ludicrous," citing Dindorf's judgment (*inventum valde absurdum*). For further discussion and citations, see Franco (1984) 131; Seidensticker (1982) 144f.; Burnett (1971) 36f.

21. Cook (1971) 97.

22. The rhythm of the latter half of *Alcestis* is, in fact, determined by the step-by-step performance of the funeral rites: 618f., 740–46, 862–925. On tragedy and funerary ritual, see above, chapter 2, and below, chapters 4 and 8.

23. For the importance of the sacrificial motif in *Alcestis*, in a positive perspective, see Burnett (1971) 22–27.

24. Cook (1971) 97.

25. Barthes (1974) 208.

26. Euripides uses a similar constellation of elements some twenty years later in his *Helen*, where the cloud image of the heroine also raises analogous questions of art, death, and the perception of reality; see C. Segal (1971) = (1986a) 227ff., 263ff.

27. Barthes (1974) 208.

4. *Female Death and Male Tears*

1. On Euripides' tendency to compose in terms of such more or less isolated motifs, see Seeck (1985) 157ff.

2. For the lowering of the coffin into the grave, see the Athenian black-figure loutrophoros by the Sappho-painter (Athens, Nat. Mus. 450): Kurtz and Boardman (1971) pl. 36; also Shapiro (1991) 634, with fig. 4.

3. Garner (1988) 64, citing *Iliad* 24.797, and *Ajax* 1165 and 1403. For still a further set of associations, see Seaford (1986) 57f., apropos of Deianeira's *koila demnia* in Sophocles, *Trachiniae* 901.

4. Compare the *agalmata* (adornments) that Hecuba places over the body of Astyanax in *Trojan Women* 1218–20.

5. See Loraux (1982) 32f. There are a few exceptions, e.g., Achilles' anticipation of Peleus' death from old age in *Iliad* 24; cf. also Andromache's lament over Hector in *Iliad* 24.743–45.

6. That *Alcestis* is a substitute for a satyr play is the consensus of modern scholars and probably the view of ancient scholars as well (Hypothesis II, ad fin.): see Lesky (1925) 84–86; Dale (1954) xviii ff.; Seidensticker (1982) 129ff., 137ff.; and Conacher (1984) 73f. Occasional arguments are proposed for its being a regular tragic offering; e.g., most recently by Riemer (1989), with a useful review of earlier scholarship, see pp. 1–5; see also Lesky (1983) 209; and Von Fritz (1962) 263f., 312–21.

7. See Lesky (1925) 55.

8. See Rosenmeyer (1963) 235f.

9. See, for example, Garland (1985) 13–20; Alexiou (1974) 4–10, 25–33; Danforth (1982) 35–56.

10. The concern of literary work with the mourning process is already well established in the Near Eastern epic tradition in the *Epic of Gilgamesh*, where the hero's grief for Enkidu has many similarities with Achilles' for Patroclus. See, for example, Beye (1987) 36.

11. See Diano (1968) 245ff.; Pucci (1977) 168ff.

12. For Hesiod, "insulting with harsh words an aged parent on the woeful threshold of old age" stands beside adultery and crimes against orphaned

children as sure to bring Zeus' anger and punishment (*Works and Days* 331f.). Thury (1988) 199–206 ingeniously tries to argue that an Athenian audience would have accepted Admetus' treatment of his father as part of his transference of his family loyalties to his wife, as a matter of generational conflict that would be readily understood, and as a reflection of a conflict between *nomos* and *phusis*. These elements, to be sure, may be mitigating factors, and Admetus' response to Pheres must be kept within the limits of acceptable behavior since he is clearly not a villain nor to be imagined as obviously in the wrong. On the other hand, it is an exaggeration to claim, as Thury does (p. 205), that Alcestis "practically demands from Admetus that he hate and reject his father." Nothing in Alcestis' criticism in lines 290–92 justifies the extreme response of Admetus (toward *both* parents) in lines 338f., though these latter lines are understandable as part of the extreme emotionality of this speech. His gratuitous insult of Pheres in lines 636–39 and refusal of *gêrotrophia* and burial in 662–65 would also be disturbing, as the chorus's intervention at 673f. indicates. Thury (p. 202) overlooks this passage when she says that "Admetus' attitude is clearly not shocking to the chorus." Nor is the legal situation so clearly on Admetus' side as Thury claims (pp. 199–201); see *contra* Lacey (1968) 116f.

13. For the "fated" or "pitiless" day of doom (*aisimon êmar, morsimon êmar, nêlees êmar*), see, e.g., *Iliad* 11.484, 11.587, 15.613, 21.100, 22.212; *Odyssey* 16.280. Cf. also the reflections on the coming "day" of Troy's destruction in *Iliad* 4.164, 6.448, 21.111, etc.; and the famous passage in Lucretius, *De Rerum Natura* 3.898f., on death as the "single hostile day" (*una dies infesta*) that takes away all of life's joys. For man as *ephêmeros*, the creature defined by the vicissitudes of the single day, see Fränkel (1946) passim; Wankel (1983) 129.

14. I adopt what I think is the most plausible meaning for line 321, where, despite the efforts of interpreters, the manuscripts' "to the third day of the month" gives no satisfactory sense. Diggle (1984) plausibly regards *mênos* as corrupt.

15. Compare the deathbed scene in Lucretius 3.466–69 of the family members gathered around the bed of the dying person.

16. For parallels to this last wish of the dying person, see Seeck (1985) 51ff.

17. For the "nameless dead," see also Hesiod, *Works and Days* 154. The reality of Charon for the fifth-century imagination is indicated also in the depiction of this figure, with his bark, next to the tomb on the white-ground lekythoi of the late fifth century. On these vases, however, Charon is a rather mild human figure, not a terrifying ogre, and has none of the horrific aspect that so disturbs Alcestis here; see Shapiro (1991) 649–50, with fig. 21. The Charon of Aristophanes' *Frogs* 180–209 also has nothing particularly terrifying about him. Possibly the tragic context, even in a pro-satyric play, can allow the expression of anxieties that must be repressed in the objects used in

cult. On the scene of Alcestis' vision of Charon, there are good remarks in Lesky (1925) 74ff.; Nielsen (1976) 96; Rosenmeyer (1963) 212 and 225; and Von Fritz (1962) 304.

18. "Murderous Hades," against whom the chorus invokes Apollo later in the play (225), seems more ominous but gets no details. Hesiod describes a harsh Death, of "iron heart" and "pitiless breast," but even he is not a figure of utter terror (*Theogony* 758–66). For the truly horrifying face of death, the demonic image of sheer terror, the Greeks use the female figure of Gorgo, the petrifying mask of death; see Ramnoux (1986) 50–54; Vernant (1985a) passim, and (1989) 117–29; Loraux and Kahn-Lyotard (1981). The threat of her appearance from the depths of Hades after the visions of heroes and heroines fills Odysseus with "green fear" and terminates his exploration of Hades (*Odyssey* 11.633–35). Seeck (1985) 32 suggests that the notion of Thanatos who consecrates the dying person to death may have been Euripides' own invention. On the traditional representations of Death, see Grillone (1974–75) 39f., with n. 1.

19. For the calm and acceptance of "tame death," see Ariès (1982) chap. 1, especially 13–22.

20. See Burnett (1965), in E. Segal (1983) 266.

21. For this juxtaposition of intense emotion and logical argumentation, compare lines 380ff. with 420ff., and 895ff. with 935ff. See, in general, Rosenmeyer (1963) 225f.; and Seeck (1985) 40–44; both point out Greek drama's tendency to present different aspects of an emotional situation sequentially in separate scenes.

22. On the dramatic function of this *kosmos* (funerary ornament) in the play, see above.

23. *Antigone* 1240–43, 1306–11, 1328–33; *Hippolytus* 836–39. Cf. also Adrastus' wish that he "had died with" (*sunthanein*) the Seven who fell at Thebes (Euripides, *Suppliants* 769). The motif of togetherness in death later becomes a topos of funeral epigrams; see Lattimore (1942) 247–50.

24. Euripides, *Suppliants* 1007, 1040, 1063; Sophocles, *Trachiniae* 720. For further discussion, see Loraux (1985) 53–55. She notes too the "normally feminine" element in Admetus' wish to dwell with Alcestis in Hades and lie with her in the tomb (p. 110, n. 57).

25. Line 196: τοιαῦτ' ἐν οἴκοις ἐστὶν Ἀδμήτου κακά (Such are the woes in the house of Admetus); line 950: τὰ μὲν κατ' οἴκους τοιάδ' (Such are matters in the house).

26. It is perhaps interesting that Admetus gives no thought to the risk of pollution in admitting Heracles, particularly as Apollo mentions the *miasma* of death in the prologue (22f.). The remoter kinship that Admetus alleges for the deceased woman might be regarded as also lessening the risk of pollution, but this would not, of course, affect the real risk for Heracles. On the

question of contracting pollution under such circumstances, see Parker (1983) 39ff.

27. See Kubler-Ross (1970) chap. 3.

28. Admetus' "late learning" has been much discussed; for good comments, see Conacher (1967) 336ff. From a different point of view, his self-abasement in this scene, particularly his feeling that he will now be disgraced, corresponds to the "disturbance of self-regard" in Freud's analysis of the "work of mourning": Freud (1917) 244.

29. The intersection of funeral and wedding is a regular part of what Seaford (1987) calls the "tragic wedding," but it usually applies to the bride-to-be. We may also compare Pindar's juxtaposition of the wedding song when Thetis married Peleus and the funeral and wailing (*goos*) at her son Achilles' death (*Pythian* 3.88–92 and 102–3). The scene of *Alcestis* (915–25) has other verbal links to the previous action. The contrast of marriage song and funeral wail, for example, is conveyed by the adjective *antipalos* in line 922, which suggests Heracles' "wrestling" (*palê*) at the end (1031; cf. Pindar, *Olympian* 8.71, *Nemean* 11.26, *Isthmian* 5.61). Thus this exclusively masculine activity is again brought into contact with the union of male and female in the act that founds a new household.

30. Cf. especially the motif of the coverlet, *demnion*, in lines 183, 186, and 1059.

31. Rosenmeyer (1963) 240f. has a good observation on this change but interprets it too narrowly in terms of guilt; see also Seidensticker (1982) 149.

32. For recent discussion of this endlessly debated subject, see Thury (1988) 198f. For the ironical reading, see, inter alia, Seidensticker (1982) 151. For the more positive view of the "test" of Admetus, see, e.g., Burnett (1971) 45f.; and Lloyd (1985) 129.

33. Cf. lines 1154–56 with 430–33 and 346f.

34. In line 377 Alcestis tells Admetus that he must be "the children's mother instead of me"; and in 646f. he tells Pheres that he considers her his "mother and father" both. Soon after, he calls his father's love of life unmanly (723), but Pheres exits with the same phrase, predicting vengeance from Alcestis' brother, Akastos, or else this latter is "no longer among men" (*en andrasin*, 732). Note too Heracles' introduction of himself by his matronymic in line 505, in contrast to lines 509, 1119f., and 1136f. The reversal of the usual gender divisions, with the man taking on the role of intense, highly emotional grief, is even more striking because of the heroic echoes, on which see above, note 3.

35. On vases depicting funeral scenes, male lament is, as one would expect, less frequent than female and more restrained. See Shapiro (1991) 646, 649, 652–53, who notes a general tendency toward restraint of emotion in the funerary art of the latter half of the fifth century.

36. Weeping for oneself is female behavior in *Iliad* 19.301f., where the captive women around Briseis ostensibly lament for Patroclus but actually weep for themselves. Even Homer's freely weeping Odysseus has to be careful about being seen weeping lest he seem to "float in tears" (δακρυ-πλώειν) as a result of too much wine (*Odyssey* 19.115–22).

37. Pollux 6.202, quoted by Loraux (1986) 45. Cf. Euripides, *Medea* 928. Plutarch, in his treatise on mourning, the *Consolatio ad Apollonium*, not only emphasizes that excessive weeping and grieving is "feminine," "unmanly," "weak," and "ignoble" (e.g., 3.102D, 4.102E, 22.113A), but also in the last passage (22.113A) sets up a hierarchy of weakness in yielding to lamentation: "Women are more fond of mourning [*philopenthesterai*] than men, and barbarians more than Hellenes, and baser men than better; and of the barbarians themselves not the most noble [*gennaiotatoi*], Celts and Galatians and all those who by nature are full of a more manly spirit, but rather the Egyptians, Syrians, and Lydians, and all who resemble them." On the general suspicion of women's tears and the danger of its excess, see Loraux (1990) 33ff., 39ff., 87–99. In Homer, of course, male weeping is quite common; see Monsacré (1984) 138–57, 186–201. There are even some explicit changes of gender, which seem to carry no stigma of feminization: Patroclus can weep like a little girl running after her mother (*Iliad* 16.6–11), and Odysseus can weep as bitterly as a captive woman who has lost her husband (*Odyssey* 8.521–31); but see above, n. 36.

38. Plutarch, *Life of Solon* 21, ad fin., on which see Loraux (1990) 39, with n. 49.

39. In an emotional passage of Pindar's Tenth *Nemean*, Polydeuces weeps "warm tears" over his dying brother, Castor, fatally wounded in battle. But the only spectator is Father Zeus, and the stress on the fraternal and paternal bonds makes this virtually a scene of grief among members of the household (*Nemean* 10.73–90).

40. See Loraux (1990) 21.

41. See Loraux (1990) 41: "L'idéal serait d'enfermer hermétiquement la douleur féminine a l'intérieure de la maison."

42. See Loraux (1986) 48.

43. On the fear of feminization in tragedy, see Loraux (1981) and (1982) = (1989) 49ff., 148ff.; Zeitlin (1985a) 63ff., 76ff.

44. On Heracles' silence here, see C. Segal (1977) 136–38.

45. This effect is characteristic of tragedy in general but is perhaps carried furthest by Euripides. The *Bacchae* is perhaps the clearest example: see C. Segal (1982a) chap. 6, especially 189ff.; Zeitlin (1981) and (1985a) passim.

46. Cf. Menelaus in *Iphigeneia in Aulis* 476–78; also Euripides, frag. 119 Nauck. More commonly in tragedy, however, the male companion tries to lead his friend away from weeping.

47. The "desire" of Admetus here is primarily that for weeping, as the scholiast understood the passage. In addition to Aeschylus, *Suppliants* 79, cited by Dale (1954) in her excellent note ad loc. (following Monk), cf. Gorgias, *Helen* 9: ἔλεος πολύδακρυς καὶ πόθος φιλοπενθής (much-weeping pity and grief-loving longing). On the other hand, the sexual longing is certainly implicit (see Beye [1974] ad loc.), particularly as the eyes are the focal point both for desire and for weeping. Thus Admetus cries out that Heracles' woman should be taken "from his eyes" in line 1064; and a few lines later he exclaims that the tears are flowing "from his eyes" (1067). The two verses have virtually the same line ending (ἐξ ὀμμάτων, ἐκ δ' ὀμμάτων).

48. Sophocles, *Oedipus Tyrannus* 1515; Euripides, *Heracles* 1394, and *Suppliants* 769ff., 838ff.

49. Heracles in the *Trachiniae*, however, is still in a domestic context when he complains about the shame of being reduced to tears.

50. Note too the chorus's full-fledged ode on "Necessity" in lines 962–94.

51. Lines 912ff. and 941ff. also suggest a new understanding of the house, or *oikos*, especially by comparison with lines 882 and 734. Cf. also the slightly different meaning of Admetus' "I myself know too" (1080), where his own emotional need for tears opposes Heracles' advice on the fruitlessness of weeping.

52. For Alcestis' silence see, inter alia, Rosenmeyer (1963) 245; Bassi (1989) 27f.; and Riemer (1989) 100–103, who has a useful review of previous literature. For the ritual reasons, see Betts (1965) passim; and Parker (1983) 37, n. 17, and 329, n. 10.

53. See above, note 43.

54. Cf. *Alcestis* 434f.; also her "noble death" in line 292, with which we may compare Sophocles, *Antigone* 72 and 97. Cf. also Sophocles, *Antigone* 694–99, and *Electra* 973–85, 1082–89.

55. On the implicit parallelism felt between warfare and childbirth, see Loraux (1981) = (1989) 29–53. Women's presence in the theater at the Greater Dionysia remains uncertain. For the negative view, see Pickard-Cambridge (1968) 264f. Their presence in the fourth century seems more likely: see Dover (1972) 16f., who inclines to think that women may have been present at fifth-century performances, at least if accompanied by their husbands.

56. The chorus's pious hope that "good people" may have a better time of it in Hades in lines 744–46 may be a vague allusion to Orphic notions of the afterlife, like those expressed in Pindar's Second *Olympian*, especially as Orpheus is prominent elsewhere in the play. As Dale (1954) observes, however (ad 743), the wish is a modest one and may convey only a conventionally "gentle piety" and a mild hope that virtue somehow finds its reward. We should keep in mind, however, the appeal of the Eleusinian Mysteries, with their promise of a happier life (whatever the details) in the hereafter. More

recent discoveries of "Orphic" or "Orphic-Dionysiac" texts relating to the afterlife suggest that alternative views of defeating "necessity" by mystic initiation may have been more common in the mid-fifth century than we have known; see Burkert (1987) 21ff.; Lloyd-Jones (1985) especially 254ff.; C. Segal (1990).

57. In line 52, Apollo's request from Thanatos implies the normal process of aging and hence the normal downward course of mortal life for Alcestis even after Thanatos releases her from the present day of death (ἐς γῆρας μόλοι, 52). As Gregory (1979) 268f. observes, the return of Alcestis cancels out the extraordinary benefaction of Apollo and implies the restoration of life in this world to the terms of normal mortality. Everyone will now die on schedule.

58. Apollo defines the opening situation of the play as Admetus' not having "found anyone except his wife who wished to die in his place and no longer to look upon the light" (17f.). Contrast Admetus' loss of "joy" in looking at the light in his grief (868) with the reality of Alcestis' "no longer seeing the light" in death (269, 1139, 1146, etc.); cf. also 244f., 722.

5. *Admetus' Divided House: Spatial Dichotomies and Gender Roles*

1. See Alexiou (1974) 5; Kurtz and Boardman (1971) 143f.; Padel (1983) 5–8; Danforth (1982) passim.

2. See Parker (1983) 35ff., with n. 27 on p. 39; Garland (1985) 1–47.

3. Cf. lines 542, 549, 568, 857–60, 1037ff., 1119f., and 1136f.; also the term *to deon* in lines 817 and 1101, in which is implicit the obligations between males in the ties of guest-friendship.

4. For the Greek theater and male fantasy, see Padel (1983) passim, especially 7, 12ff.

5. Vernant (1974b) = (1990) 45ff. points out how mourning in the Homeric corpus is organized by the complementarity of private grief and lament in the family and *kleos* and the warrior's continuing existence in the social memory.

6. For the issue in general, see Shaw (1975) especially 265f.; Easterling (1987) passim, especially 23–25; Henderson (1987) xxxiv f.; Goldhill (1986) 107–15; Padel (1983) 8–12; Walker (1983) 81–91; Gould (1980) 46–50; Lacey (1968) 167f. For the range of variation and the dynamic and dialectical possibilities in such arrangements, see especially Foley (1982) 130–32, 149–62; Humphreys (1983) 4ff., 16f.

7. See Xenophon, *Oeconomicus* 7.16ff.; also Foxhall (1989) 30.

8. The quotations are from Foxhall (1989) 23 and 31, respectively.

9. See Loraux (1985) passim, especially 41ff. For the interconnections of death, marriage, and sacrifice for female figures in Euripides generally, see Foley (1985). For Alcestis, see Burnett (1971) 22–27; Lloyd (1985) 121f.; Seeck (1985) 18–24, with further bibliography on p. 18, n. 5.

10. See Lissarague and Schnapp (1981) 286ff. For the public dimension of the warrior's death, see also "La belle mort et le cadavre outragé" and *"Pánta kalá*: D'Homère à Simonide," in Vernant (1989), pp. 41–79 and 91–101, respectively; also Morris (1989) passim, especially 306–9.

11. Obvious examples are Clytaemnestra's "man-counseling heart" and masculine political power in *Agamemnon*, Deianeira's possessing the poison of the Centaur's blood in the *muchoi* of her house in the *Trachiniae*, Phaedra's desire to hunt in the wood in *Hippolytus*, and the Theban women's flight from the loom to the mountain in *Bacchae*.

12. For discussion and a survey of the scholarship, see Loraux (1986) 23f.; Clairmont (1983) 7ff.; and Shapiro (1991) passim. The arguments of Morris (1989) passim for the continuity of attitudes toward death in the period ca. 800–500 B.C. do not greatly affect the issues of this chapter.

13. See Loraux (1990) 24–27; Bennett and Tyrrell (1990) 453.

14. So, e.g., Euripides' Macaria, Iphigeneia, Polyxena, and Euadna; more ambiguously, Sophocles' Deianeira. See Loraux (1985) passim.

15. See *Hecuba* 1075ff., 1145ff., 1275ff.; and below, chapters 9 and 10.

16. See, e.g., Foley (1981b) 152f.

17. See C. Segal (1982a) chap. 1, and references cited there.

18. Bakhtin (1984) 78ff., 96ff., 198ff.

19. On this effect, see, e.g., Saïd (1979) 33ff.; Rosellini (1979) 11ff.; and Henderson (1987) xxix–xxxvi, and bibliography cited there.

20. See Lefkowitz (1986) 66f.; cf. also Vernant (1974b) = (1990) 42.

21. Garner (1988) 67–69, and (1990) 73ff., and see the discussion above, in chapter 4.

22. The characterization of Admetus continues to divide interpreters. The opposite positions are well staked out by Burnett, in E. Segal (1983); and W. D. Smith, in Wilson (1968) 37–56 (for the positive and negative views, respectively). The negative view has tended to predominate, particularly in view of Admetus' behavior in the scene with Pheres; see Blaiklock (1952) 2ff.; Rosenmeyer (1963) 238f.; Conacher (1981) 8, and (1984) 73f.; Riemer (1989) 155f. Recently, however, there has been a more positive assessment: see Bergson (1985) 19; Lloyd (1985) 127–29; Seeck (1985) 104–8; Dyson (1988) 19ff. For a survey of older views, see Lesky (1925) 77ff.

23. See Zeitlin (1981) 194.

24. Apollo in the prologue, as an Olympian, must avoid the *miasma* of

death in Alcestis' house (223); he thus at least raises the issue of pollution. On the pollution of the house by a death within, see Kurtz and Boardman (1971) 146, 149f.

25. E.g., *Iliad* 6.288ff., 21.510f.; *Odyssey* 8.438–41, 15.104ff.

26. See Vernant (1963) = (1985b) 156, 162ff., 175ff.

27. Cf. lines 141, 242f., 329, 519–21, 525–29, 825, 992–99, 1082, and 1096. See Burnett (1965) 269, and (1971) 37f.

28. See Vernant (1963) = (1985b) 162f., 187ff.

29. The ode also emphasizes masculine activities through various epinician motifs, pointed out by Garner (above, note 21).

30. We may also recall Pheres' appeal to Alcestis' brother in his quarrel with his son, 730–33, another case in which the woman serves only as the focus for transactions between men.

31. See Buxton (1987) 21–23; and Halleran (1988) 126ff. Both scholars, however, view the marriage / death motif differently from one another and also from my approach here. Buxton emphasizes the common symbolism of transition for the woman in the use of the veil in marriage and death; Halleran sees the restoration of the house in the reenacted rite of betrothal. The three views (inter alia) are complementary; and one would expect so evocative and ambiguous a scene (like the play as a whole) to invite varied interpretations.

32. Rabinowitz (1987b) has valuable observations on the importance of the play's ultimate reaffirmation of masculine ties. The scene incidentally shows the movement toward reconciling "competitive" and "cooperative" values; see Adkins (1960) 34–48 and passim.

33. In listing this motive (287), Alcestis conforms to the tendency in Western literature for women to identify loss of love with loss of life. See, for example, Higgonet (1986) 68–83, especially 72: "If Brutus commits suicide for the nation, Portia commits suicide in order not to live without Brutus."

34. For other Iliadic references in the play, see Garner (1990) 65–73.

35. See, e.g., Beye (1974) 6–10 and 78; Patin (1879) 1.204–10.

36. Poole (1987) 143.

37. Dyson (1988) 17ff. points up the parallels between Alcestis' surrender of her role as mother in order to die, in Admetus' behalf, as wife, and Admetus' giving up his grief in order to perform his role as host. Yet the comparison only clarifies how asymmetrical the sacrifices are. See also Lloyd (1985) 129.

38. Cf. also Oedipus' derisory comment on men inside, women outside, in *Oedipus at Colonus* 337–45, doubtless influenced by Herodotus' account of the Egyptians (2.35).

39. See Poole (1987) 146f., who emphasizes the importance of the bed in Alcestis' motivation.

40. See Bradley (1980) 114.

41. For a useful summary and bibliography of the woman's legal rights and expectations in marriage, see Just (1989) 43–50, 62–68, 72f.; Lacey (1968) 109–11, 159–61. The *locus classicus* is Xenophon, *Oeconomicus*, chap. 7. For discussion of this and related texts, see Foucault (1985) 143–84, especially 156ff.

42. Cf. the long debate between Jason and Medea in lines 446–575, especially 496ff. and 533ff.

43. Pericles' remark at the end of his celebrated funeral oration (Thucydides 2.45.2) is perhaps the most famous statement of the exclusion of women from the public realm and the public fame or glory (*kleos, eukleia*) to which the fallen male warriors are here being commended. Cf. also Macaria's brief prologue to her heroic self-sacrifice in Euripides, *Heracleidae* 474–77.

44. For the contradictions, see Kurke (1991) 86ff.

45. Finley (1965) 62ff., 100ff., 129ff.

46. See above, chapter 4.

47. See Humphreys (1983) 42 and 62.

48. See above, chapter 3. Happy endings, it is true, occur in plays that we otherwise consider "tragedies," such as *Eumenides, Philoctetes*, and the Euripidean "melodramas" (*Helen, Ion, Iphigeneia in Tauris*). But even the cancellation of impending disaster by a deus ex machina does not elsewhere go so far as to erase the boundary between life and death.

6. *Language, Signs, and Gender*

1. For the roots of such conceptions of "the race of women" as the Other, see Loraux (1978b), especially 45ff., 52f.; see also Vernant (1974b) 193 (English trans. 1990, 199). The closed conclaves of women in Aristophanes' *Thesmophoriazusae* and *Lysistrata* are comic versions of this potentially threatening female exclusivity and secrecy: see Zeitlin (1981) 175f., 181f. The dialectic of interior and exterior in the play has been much discussed: see C. Segal (1970c) passim, (1986a) 100ff.; also Goff (1990) 2ff.

2. Hippocrates, *Diseases of Women* 62, 8.126 Littré. For discussion, see Pigeaud (1981) 395f., and (1976) 8f.; see also Sissa (1987) 74f. (English trans. 1990, 51f.), and the references cited there.

3. On the erotic implications of vision, and its denial, see Zeitlin (1985b) 90–93, especially 92; also Luschnig (1988a) 5ff., 13f.

4. This excited dialogue between Phaedra and the chorus (565–600) emphasizes voice and hearing (567, 571f., 576, 579–88, 590), with vision reserved for the chorus's impersonal, brief, but climactic "the hidden things have been shown forth" at line 594 (τὰ κρυπτὰ γὰρ πέφηνε). The emphasis on hearing is

all the more striking after the previous ode on the eyes and desire (525–29). Whether or not Phaedra is onstage to overhear the conversation between Hippolytus and the Nurse in lines 601–68 has been much discussed; see W. D. Smith (1960b).

5. Goldhill (1986) 258f.

6. In the following lines, however (424f.), Phaedra includes the shame that may come from the mother *or* the father.

7. The association of the doors with constrained or reluctant speaking is strengthened by Theseus' phrase "the doors of my mouth" shortly after (882f.).

8. See C. Segal (1984) = (1986) 81–84, 92–106; (1982b) = (1987) 288ff.

9. On writing and female sexuality, see C. Segal (1984) = (1986) 93–95; Zeitlin (1985b) 75–77; Rabinowitz (1987a) 134f.; duBois (1982) 98f. On writing in relation to the sophistic movement, see Turato (1976) 173ff.; and Solmsen (1975) 28ff.

10. See Zeitlin (1981) 175ff., 181f., 196. On the Thesmophoria and women's secrets in *Hippolytus*, see Zeitlin (1985b) 85, and 197, with n. 57, noting the possible religious implications of the word *aporrhêta* (unspeakable) to describe the diseases of women in lines 295f. and, more explicitly, the chorus's initial description of Phaedra's starvation as a three-day abstention "from Demeter's grain" to keep her body "pure," as if in preparation for a mystic journey to the underworld (137–40).

11. For a discussion of the problems of staging with a review of recent scholarship, see Ley and Ewans (1985), especially 75–77. They plausibly suggest that during the dialogue between the Nurse and Hippolytus, Phaedra is onstage, perhaps against the skene or hiding behind one of the statues of the goddesses, while Hippolytus moves to the center of the orchestra to deliver his long tirade against women in lines 601ff. In lines 565–600, however, the Nurse and Hippolytus are still inside, whereas Phaedra is outside. Thus she strains her hearing and asks for silence in order to understand the "voice of those within" ("Let me learn the voice of those inside," 567). Her commands "quiet" and "wait" underline the intense listening and expectation.

12. On the unusual nature of the staging, see Taplin (1978) 70f.

13. On this issue in the play, see Fitzgerald (1973) passim; see also Luschnig (1983) 115–23.

14. *Epissutos*, an Aeschylean word, occurs only here in the extant Euripides.

15. Note how language here becomes an active force endowed with the power of movement. We may compare lines 576: οἷος κέλαδος ἐν δόμοις πίτνει, "[Hear] what a shouting falls in the house"; 577: πομπίμα φάτις δωμάτων, "report sent out of the house"; and 588: διὰ πύλας . . . ἔμολε σοι βοά, "The cry went, went through the gate."

16. On speech and silence, see Knox (1952) = (1979) 208ff.; C. Segal (1965) = (1986a) 204; Turato (1976) 173–75; Paduano (1984) 49ff.

17. In Greek tragedy *anômotos* occurs only here and in *Medea* 737 (with weak MS authority); it occurs only one other time in extant fifth-century literature (Herodotus 2.118.12). It becomes more common as a legal term in fourth-century orators.

18. Hippolytus alludes to the possibility of breaking his oath, which, of course, he does not do, in lines 656f., 660, and 1060–63. See Barrett (1964) ad 612.

19. Reiske's *plokon* (lock of hair) in line 514 is widely accepted and is probably correct. It is printed by Diggle in the recent OCT. The manuscripts read *logon* (word), which also occurs in the sixth- or seventh-century Berlin codex (Barrett's K), so that the corruption, if such it is, must be very early. If *logon* were right (admittedly unlikely in the context), it would emphasize the slide of language from rationality and communication to the physical instrumentality of magic. The Nurse's request, then, would also reflect the dangerous slippage of speech into sign.

20. See C. Segal (1984) = (1986a) 100f., and (1987) 289f.

21. Cf. the image of the writing tablets that "fawn" on Theseus in line 863.

22. Viewed psychologically, the bull is also a powerful symbol of what Hippolytus has repressed; see C. Segal (1965) = (1986a) 200ff., (1978–79) = (1986a) 277ff.

23. On *teras* as including the notions of both sign and "marvelous apparition," see Gernet (1968) 131f.

24. Compare the bull's effect on the horses, which prick up their ears "to the sky," and the roar that mounts "to the sky": ἐς οὐρανόν, 1203; οὐρανῷ στηρίζον, 1207f.; cf. also 1215–17.

25. Carson (1986) 91–97; these and the following quotations are from p. 91.

26. See C. Segal (1962) 106f.

27. See C. Segal (1962) 104f.

28. For Derrida this passage is the starting point for writing (*écriture*) as a model for the distances and absences that are inherent (inscribed) in language as it seeks to make present a full reality; Derrida (1972).

29. See Carson (1986) 91ff.

30. For *epôidai* as magical incantations to cure disease, see, e.g., Homer, *Odyssey* 19.457; Pindar, *Pythian* 3.52, and *Nemean* 4.3.

31. For a recent discussion of Phaedra's acceptance of the *pharmakon* and its ambiguities, see Michelini (1987) 289f., with n. 59. For the *pharmakon* as an objectification of the seductive power of language, see Turato (1976) 168–73, who cites (inter alia) Aeschylus, *Eumenides* 885–87; *Suppliants* 447, 1039–47, 1056. For Hippolytus too the words of desire are a tangible substance, like a poison or a polluting stain that he needs to wash away (653–55). Sophocles'

Trachiniae also weaves together notions of magic, poisonous drugs, and erotic persuasion; cf. 660–62, 706–11, 1141ff.; C. Segal (1977) 111f., and (1981b) 94f.

32. The little scene between Phaedra and the Nurse might even be viewed as a displaced version of Gorgias' theories of language itself as a quasi-incantatory magic that charms its hearer by a kind of hypnotic spell. See Walsh (1984) 82, on Gorgias, *Helen* 17, and the "magical power of speech."

33. For Phaedra's yielding to the Nurse's appeal to the irrationality implicit in the spell and philters, see Barrett (1964) on lines 507–24 (pp. 252f.); C. Segal (1965) = (1986a) 180–82.

34. For other aspects of this motif of "letting forth" words, see below, note 38.

35. Both lines 971f. and 1076f. use the legalistic vocabulary of "witness" and "give evidence" (*martus, mênuein*), on which see C. Segal (1992a) 438f.

36. See Diano (1968) 248–51; also Turato (1976) 171, with n. 67; and Sikes (1931) 30f.

37. *Epôidos, goêtês*, 1038; *psychên kratêsein*, 1040. Cf. *Bacchae* 234, Pentheus' scornful accusation of Dionysus as γόης ἐπῳδὸς Λυδίας ἀπὸ χθονός.

38. See especially lines 930f. and 944f. For the motif of inanimate objects acquiring speech, see Knox (1979) 215f.; Turato (1976) 174; Longo (1985) 92f.; Zeitlin (1985b) 90–93.

39. For the two forms of "shame" (*aidôs*), see C. Segal (1970c) passim. For discussion and bibliography, see C. Segal (1987) 218–20; Michelini (1987) 297–304. Interpreters remain divided about whether Phaedra's *dissai* in line 385 refers to "twin pleasures" or "twin forms of *aidôs*" (as I continue to believe). Michelini, for example (pp. 299f.), seems to prefer *aidôs* (though allowing for the ambiguity); and Luschnig (1988a) 42 prefers "pleasures." Kovacs (1980) and Sommerstein (1988) 23–28 apply textual surgery to the problem.

40. Luschnig (1988a) 103 regards the Messenger's speech as the only place where "the speaker's feeling for the man and his tragedy show[s] through." But one cannot forget the larger sexual dichotomies that these sympathies support.

41. See Rabinowitz (1986) 180f., (1987a) 127f., 136.

42. Cf. "slave" in lines 115 and 1249 and "lord" (*anax*) in lines 88 and 1249. The "simplicity" of this judgment, however, is not without its complexity; see below.

43. One may think, of course, of the noble farmer in Euripides' *Electra*. Cf. also the noble slave in *Helen* 728–31 and 1627–41, also ready to die in defense of truth and his mistress. So too the old servant of *Iphigeneia in Aulis* (303ff.) is ready to defend to the death his duty to his master, Agamemnon, even though it means opposing King Menelaus. On this last, see Luschnig (1988b) 118f. In *Hippolytus* the slave's speech, to be sure, belongs to the dramatic

convention of the messenger speech, where the speaker may often be of relatively low status; but this does not detract from the fact that Euripides calls attention to the servile status when he did not have to (1249).

44. See Turato (1976) 180–83; also Gregory (1991) 176–79, who, I think, takes too simplistic a view of a prodemocratic attitude (pp. 54f.). See my review (1993a).

45. Turato (1976) 164ff., also (1974) 150ff., 162f. See also Michelini (1987) 314f., who accepts many of Turato's views.

46. On the figure of the noble slave here, see Vellacott (1975) 214ff.; De Jong (1991) 65–72, especially 66, and also 106. The conventional anachronism of Greek tragedy contributes to the class distinction, since the main figures are kings or queens. Nevertheless, Euripides frequently exploits these differences to call attention to the gap between different classes and their values, most notably, perhaps, in the case of Electra's husband in *Electra*. One need hardly point out how important such matters can be in tragedy (e.g., in Sophocles' *Ajax*). Cf., in general, Citti (1978).

47. See, for example, Rabinowitz (1987a) 136. On Seneca's *Phaedra*, see below, chapter 7, note 71.

48. See Diano (1973) = (1976) 93–109; Turato (1974) 146f., and 152, n. 97.

49. See C. Segal (1965) = (1986a) 221, n. 74; Vernant (1974b) 187–94 (English trans. 1990, 193–201). For the importance of the golden age motif in Hippolytus' velleitarianism, see Turato (1974) passim, especially 149ff.

50. See C. Segal (1965) = (1986a) 209; Zeitlin (1985b) 66–79, especially 78 apropos of lines 1375–77.

51. On these ironies in the ending see below, chapter 7.

52. I keep the manuscripts' order in lines 1455ff.; for the text, see C. Segal (1970b). On the importance of Hippolytus' bastardy, see Fitzgerald (1973) 27f.; Devereux (1985) 79. Some would see here an allusion to Pericles' attempt to legitimize his sons by Aspasia after the death of his two legitimate sons in the plague; see Diano (1973) = (1976) 104; Turato (1976) 180–83. Dimock (1977) 254ff. recognizes the importance of Hippolytus' word *gnêsios* (legitimate) at the end, but he overvalues the notion of "happy" in *chaire*.

7. *Theater, Ritual, and Commemoration*

1. For helpful discussions of the body in Greek theater, especially in relation to the representation of women, see Loraux (1981) and (1982) = (1989) 29–53, 142–170; Zeitlin (1985a) 69–71, (1985b) 66ff. For other aspects of the body in tragedy, see C. Segal (1985) = (1986a) 337ff.

2. See Loraux (1981) = (1989) 48ff.; also Zeitlin (1985b) 77ff.

3. On this passage, see C. Segal (1979) 154.

4. There is perhaps a similar effect in the repeated syllable *pol-* where Hippolytus' citizen status is mentioned; 12f.: Ἱππόλυτος . . . πολιτῶν, 1462: πολλά . . . πολίταις.

5. Barrett and others have raised doubts about the authenticity of lines 1462–66; see Barrett (1964) ad loc.; also G. Lawall and S. Lawall (1986) ad loc. But the manuscript tradition is quite strong, even to the point of resisting attempted interpolations from other plays; see Diggle's apparatus (1984) ad loc.

6. The term *citizen (politês)* is used only three times in the play, each time of Hippolytus and in a significant way (12, 1158, 1462; cf. also 1127).

7. For an apparently unself-conscious example, see Eliade (1981) 4f.

8. Cf. ἰδοῦσα Φαίδρα καρδίαν κατέσχετο / ἔρωτι δεινῷ, *Hippolytus* 27f. (Seeing him Phaedra was held in her heart by a fearful desire); and τὸν δὴ ἔπειτα ἰδοῦσα φιλομμειδὴς Ἀφροδίτη / ἠράσατ’, ἐκπάγλως δὲ κατὰ φρένας ἵμερος εἷλεν, *Homeric Hymn to Aphrodite* 56f. (Then, seeing him, smiling Aphrodite fell in love with him, and desire vehemently seized her mind).

9. The scene, of course, forms part of the strong contrast with the interior of Phaedra's house and the interior space where women suffer, brood, and plot. On the contrasts, see Parry (1966) 325f.

10. On the symbolism of the meadow and the dedication, see C. Segal (1965) = (1986a) 172f., and the references cited there; Turato (1974) 136–51, with ample bibliography; Glenn (1975–76); Pigeaud (1976) 3–7; Zeitlin (1985b) 66f., with further bibliography in n. 34, pp. 194f.; Devereux (1985) 46–48.

11. Note too the contrast between symbolic or "mythical" places (the meadow of Hippolytus or the distant place of the lament for Phaethon) and the "real" place of the action in Athens or Troezen. See Parry (1966) passim, especially 319ff.; also Padel (1974) 232–34; Turato (1974) passim, especially 138, 149–51.

12. For the notion of the play as monument, see Pucci (1977), especially 184ff.

13. Cf. σιγήσατ’—σιγῶ in lines 565–68 with the repetition of "be silent" in 603f., σίγησον—οὐκ ἔστ’ . . . ὅπως σιγήσομαι.

14. For the sexual division of space and the association of the interior realm with women, see Vernant (1963) = (1985b) passim, especially 162ff.; for its scenic representation, see Zeitlin (1985b) 71ff., with nn. 25 and 26.

15. Cf. the Nurse's plea, after line 612, "Child, what will you do? Will you destroy those close to you" (613), and Theseus' cry about destruction when he "shows forth" what the tablets have to say (*oloon kakon,* "woe destructive," 883f.). For other aspects of this passage, see Avery (1968) 25ff.; C. Segal (1970c) 294, (1984) = (1986a) 100f.

16. On the motif of the "tongue out-of-doors" and the inhibiting of female speech, see Rabinowitz (1987a) 131.

17. On the tendency to equate women's speech and women's sexuality, the two female *stomata*, see Sissa (1987) 66ff., 76ff., 190ff. (English trans. 1990, 41ff., 53ff., 166ff.).

18. Cf. Pindar, *Nemean* 5.26–33; cf. also Sophocles, *Trachiniae* 600–623, 660–62.

19. The irony of this reversal is enhanced by the entrance of Hippolytus, after the Nurse's revelation, with his vehement shout to earth and "the unfoldings of the sun" (601).

20. Reading δυσεξέλικτον in line 1237, with Barrett (1964) and Diggle (1984). On this passage, see Zeitlin (1985b) 58. For the implications of the feminine entrapment of the noose that here reaches from Phaedra to Hippolytus, see Loraux (1985) 50, who suggests that the silent speaking by the dead body inside the house is also a symbolic continuation of the seductive, deceptive discourse associated with female guile (*dolos*); see also Loraux (1989) 134f.

21. See C. Segal (1965) = (1986a) 198.

22. For the importance of the mirror in the play, see Avery (1968) 31; and Zeitlin (1985b) 99f., 103.

23. See Avery (1968) 34f.; C. Segal (1972) 177.

24. See C. Segal (1986b) 184–88, 194–201, 218–19.

25. On the reverberations of this oath in the play, see C. Segal (1972) 165–72.

26. See Bacchylides 19.11; Pindar, *Isthmian* 5.28f.; and Barrett (1964) on lines 1423–30; also Alcman, frag. 3.74, μέλημα δάμῳ (a concern to the people).

27. On Hippolytus' feminization, see Loraux (1981) = (1989) 48f.; Zeitlin (1985b) passim, especially 66ff.

28. On the mythic remoteness of the setting here, see Parry (1966) 322.

29. On the social pressures to restrain lamentation, see Alexiou (1974) passim, especially 4, 21f., 28.

30. We may recall the haunting scene of the Mountain Nymphs planting trees around the tomb of Eetion in *Iliad* 6.418–20. With the wordless grief of Phaethon's sisters in Euripides contrast the inscribed monument in Ovid, *Metamorphoses* 2.326f.: "corpora dant tumulo, signant quoque carmine saxum: / 'Hic situs est Phaethon,'" etc. (They place the body in a tomb and also mark the stone with a poem: "Here lies Phaethon . . .").

31. On Artemis' tears, see C. Segal (1965) = (1986a) 214; Taplin (1978) 52; Zeitlin (1985b) 73 and 96.

32. For a discussion of how Hippolytus might be defined as "great," see C. Segal (1970a), which, however, should be modified in terms of the ambiguities of the ending discussed below. For a strongly positive view of the ending, see Newton (1980) 21f., in contrast to which one should read the salutary remarks of Rabinowitz (1986), especially 172 and 182.

33. For the resonances of heroic commemoration in the language of lines 1465f., cf. Pindar, *Olympian* 7.10, and *Pythian* 1.95f.

34. See Zeitlin (1985b) 78.

35. See Knox (1952) = (1979) 217f.; Kovacs (1980) 301f.; Rabinowitz (1987a) 131. On the centrality and complementarity of *eukleia* for both protagonists, see Frischer (1970) 94–96; see also Loraux (1985) 59.

36. Cf. *Bacchae* 971f.; see C. Segal (1982a) 203.

37. On the male / female interchanges in the play, see Zeitlin (1985b) passim, especially 66ff. and 78ff.; see also Frischer (1970).

38. See C. Segal (1978–79) = (1986a) 277–82.

39. There is also an ironic echo of Aphrodite's own description of herself as "not without name" in the play's first line—an attribute she establishes by the grim way Hippolytus becomes "not without name."

40. See Longo (1985) 95. Fitzgerald (1973) 36 suggests that the terms of Hippolytus' fame "ought properly to be taken as an insult." See also Rabinowitz (1987a) 136.

41. On the tomb marker as an essential part of the warrior's *kleos*, see Sinos (1980) 48ff.

42. The manuscripts at line 33 give ὠνόμαζ' ἐνιδρῦσθαι or ὠνόμαζεν ἱδρῦσθαι. Reading ὠνόμαζε(ν) in line 33 would imply that only Phaedra (and the goddess) know the reason for the dedication (i.e., love "for Hippolytus"). The public knows only that it is a temple for Aphrodite. Later, of course (cf. *to loipon*, 33), the full title becomes established, as part of the aetiological myth that the play itself is making "not unnamed" (1429f.). For the text, see Diggle's apparatus (1984). The manuscript reading is now supported, it would seem, by a papyrus fragment. Diggle, however, following Barrett (1964), replaces Murray's manuscript reading with Jortin's conjecture, ὀνομάσουσιν (keeping ἱδρῦσθαι). The fact that Phaedra is unambiguously the subject of the verb ἐγκαθείσατο (founded) just before in line 31 (parallel both in sense and syntax to the verb "named" in 33) also supports the manuscript reading.

43. This irony of the "naming" of the temple in the prologue would apply even if one adopts Jortin's emendation, ὀνομάσουσιν, in line 33, as do Barrett (1964) and Diggle (1984).

44. On other aspects of this passage, see Luschnig (1980) 98.

45. The text is uncertain here, but I cannot regard as likely Fitton's emendation, "of Aphaea," adopted by Diggle (1984) here and also in line 1123. With Barrett (1964), I prefer to stay closer to the reading of manuscripts L and P. Sommerstein (1988) 40f., noting the importance of Athens in lines 34–37, 974f., and 1093–97, provides strong arguments for some form of "Athens" in line 1459.

46. See C. Segal (1970c) 296ff.; also Newton (1980) 21.

47. The model is perhaps the high epic mood of Achilles in his moment of greatest violence and his wrath at Apollo for rescuing Hector (*Iliad* 22.14–20).

48. On this point, see Blomqvist (1982) 411f.

49. Diano (1973) = (1976) 93–109, especially 103–5, views the play as the tragedy of *gennaiotês* for both Hippolytus and Phaedra.

50. E.g., *Medea* 190–203, *Trojan Women* 118–21 and 609f., *Suppliants* 73–82. On the paradoxes of the Homeric "joy in lamentation" in relation to tragedy, see Diano (1968) 244ff., especially 257f.; also Pucci (1980) 25ff.

51. For the ironies involved in this rite, see C. Segal (1978–79) = (1986a) 281f.; Reckford (1972) 414–16. For a more positive view, see Dimock (1977) 254f., who stresses the compensatory nature of the ritual, especially in contrast to the self-curse of lines 1028–31. For the rite as evidence of a continuing harshness in Hippolytus that has to be appeased by fearful future brides, see Devereux (1985) 136f.

52. On this aspect of the marriage ritual, see Vernant (1963) = (1985b) 161.

53. I find grotesque Diano's suggestion of an allegorical identification of Hippolytus with the condemned and then reinstated Pericles: Diano (1973) = (1976) 108. More plausible, though still far from certain, are connections with the death of Pericles' sons in the plague; see Turato (1974) 151ff., and the references cited there.

54. Lines 1300–1312, 1336f., and 1430; cf. 1404. Phaedra's emotional and moral struggles are further kept in the background by the way the goddess even here shifts the agency from the human to the divine plane, from Phaedra to Aphrodite (cf. 1400, 1406).

55. Cf. the arguments for the peaceful, nonpolitical life in the often cited *Ion* 585–647; cf. also Thucydides 1.70.8f. and 2.63.3 on Athenian activism, or *polupragmosunê*. Theseus embodies these latter qualities in Euripides' *Suppliants* and Sophocles' *Oedipus at Colonus*. For the issue in general, see Carter (1986), especially 52–56 and 70–75, on a type of aristocratic youth that Hippolytus embodies; also Gregory (1991) 75.

56. The existence of this secondary chorus has sometimes been doubted: see Barrett (1964) ad 1102–50; and Sommerstein (1988) 35–39; but the alteration of masculine and feminine forms in lines 1102ff. is otherwise hard to explain. See Diggle's critical apparatus, (1984) ad 61 and 1102.

57. These companions might also be implied in the *philoi* of whom Hippolytus speaks in lines 997f. and 1018.

58. For recent discussion, see Easterling (1982) ad loc.; and Kraus (1986) 103, with n. 27.

59. In *Philoctetês*, Neoptolemus' presence at the end is dwarfed by Heracles'; cf. C. Segal (1981b) 348–57.

60. See C. Segal (1981b) 399–404.

61. See C. Segal (1981b) 108.

62. On the shift to the more humane mood at the end, see Knox (1952) = (1979) 228f. For a more negative view, see Rabinowitz (1986) 172.

63. For geographical extent as an expression of the universal power of Aphrodite and Eros, see lines 1–6, 447–58, and 1268–82.

64. Cf. the movement from private, concealed weeping to communal grief in the scene in Menelaus' palace, *Odyssey* 4.113ff., 151ff., 182ff.

65. See Brown (1981) 6, who remarks apropos of the "chasm" opened between mortal and goddess by "the touch of death" in *Hippolytus* 1437f., "We need only compare this with the verse of the Psalms that is frequently applied by Latin writers to the role of the martyrs, 'Oculi Domini super iustos, et aures eius ad preces eorum' [33:16] to measure the distance between the two worlds."

66. Here too there may be an implicit contrast with Phaethon, who is definitively separated from his father and united, only in the mourning ritual, with his sisters.

67. Compare the old Laertes' joy in seeing "son and grandson striving for valor," *Odyssey* 24.514f.

68. Rabinowitz (1987a) 136; see also Rabinowitz (1986) 171ff., 181–83.

69. Loraux (1990) 97 and passim.

70. Sophocles' endings, even more than Euripides', tend to place father figures or other authority figures in healing postures of shared consolation with their families or friends: so Teucer and Ajax, Heracles and Hyllus, Oedipus and his daughters in *Oedipus Tyrannus*, Heracles and Philoctetes, Oedipus and Theseus in *Oedipus at Colonus*, and even Creon and Haemon in *Antigone*.

71. Both Seneca and Racine develop even more fully the forgiveness of the father and the emotional strength of father-son ties, over against the wickedness of Phaedra, even though they raise her level of ethical awareness by having her repent and confess the truth before her suicide.

8. Confusion and Concealment: Vision, Hope, and Tragic Knowledge

1. See, for example, Anaxagoras, 59 B 21a Diels-Kranz; the Hippocratic *Ancient Medicine* 1–2; Thucydides 1.1 and 1.21. For discussion, see Vegetti (1983) 23–40 passim, especially 26ff.; Ugolini (1987) 25ff. On these issues in the *Oedipus* and their relation to the intellectual climate of the time, see Knox (1957) chap. 3, especially 120ff. For the possible dependence of the *Hippolytus* on the *Oedipus*, see Newton (1980) 5–22, especially 11ff.

2. Cf. lines 709ff.; also 9 and 42; Hippolytus in 601ff.

3. On the meaning of the line and the implications of *keuthein*, see Barrett (1964) ad 1105–7, whose translation, however, also plays down the implications of "concealment": "though deep within me I have hopes of under-

standing." The text seems sound, although Barrett makes a tentative emendation, changing the first to the third person; i.e., ξύνεσιν δέ τις ἐλπίδι
κεύθων λείπεται. This is accepted by Willink (1968) 42, but his translation
again weakens the force of *keuthein*: "But anyone who hopes in his heart for
understanding is disappointed when he looks upon the fortunes and deeds of
mankind." Diggle (1984) keeps the manuscripts' reading.

4. The text contains Musgrave's emendation, accepted by Diggle (1984).
The basic sense is not in question.

5. On the meaning of Hippolytus' meadow, see C. Segal (1965) 121ff. =
(1986a) 171ff.; Turato (1974) 136–63 passim; Zeitlin (1985b) 64–66, with further
bibliography in n. 34, pp. 194ff.

6. On Hippolytus' one-sided vision, see Zeitlin (1985b) 93, also p. 109; he
"is unable on his own to initiate the sequence that leads from sight to desire
and from desire to contact with the other."

7. On the motif of the tears here, see Zeitlin (1985b) 98. Contrast the
weeping over Phaethon in lines 738ff. and over Phaedra in 853–55 with
Barrett's note, ad loc., in his *Addendum*, 435. Cf. also lines 1070, 1143ff., and
1178. In the *Odyssey* the hero proves himself mortal by his weeping (16.190ff.,
in contrast to 179ff.). And gods and mortals join in the weeping at the funeral
of Achilles (24.63ff.). In the *Iliad* even Zeus weeps a bloody dew for a beloved
warrior (16.459). Elsewhere in Euripides, to weep at the sorrows of men is a
mark of the common bond of humanity (e.g., *Hecuba*, 29ff.).

8. See above, chapter 6.

9. In his tirade against women in lines 644–55, Hippolytus also suppresses
any visual details and mentions only the polluting effect of what they say and
what he receives through his ears (53ff.). On the relation of ear and eye in
Hippolytus' sexuality, see Zeitlin (1985b) 90ff.

10. For the motif of eyes and eros, see Zeitlin (1985b) 92.

11. On the ironies of Phaedra as "best of women" and the dramatic
significance of Theseus' apostrophe at lines 848–50, see the sensitive remarks
of Sale (1977) 66.

12. *Sôma*: 251, 356, 1353; *demas*: 1222, 132, 1418, 1445. *Sôma* as "dead body" is,
of course, the Homeric usage: see Snell (1953) 5ff. *Sôma* is the "marked" term
for "body," particularly because, as Barrett (1964) observes ad lines 131–34,
p. 187, "*demas* in Euripides is often little more than an elegant substitute for
the reflexive pronoun."

13. On the motif of purity in the play, see C. Segal (1970c) 278–299 (French
trans., with bibliographical addendum = Segal [1987] 183–220).

14. On the anomaly of Aphrodite's punishment, however, which logically
should afflict Hippolytus with unrequited passion, see Zeitlin (1985b) 106ff.
The verb *prospesôn*, "falling against," obviously has a sinister implication
here.

15. Cf. also lines 645–55, where his response to hearing the Nurse's revelation of Phaedra's love takes the form of abhorrence at women's "speech." Like a miasmic pollution it should be confined inside the house and not communicated to others outside (645–48). He will "wash out" his ears, to avoid the infection (653ff.). The wish that the women "not be able to address anyone" (μήτε προσφωνεῖν τινα, 647) is a familiar way of dealing with pollution; cf. Sophocles, *Oedipus Tyrannus* 238, 1437.

16. On the motif of flight as escape from mortality, see C. Segal (1979) 151ff.; also Reckford (1972) 427.

17. In post-Homeric poetry, bodily pain can be a criterion that divides gods and mortals: cf. Aristophanes, *Frogs* 631ff. The Homeric divinities, however, though immortal, are not exempt from physical suffering; see Vermeule (1979) 123–25.

18. For the extent of these reversals, particularly in gender roles, see Zeitlin (1985b) 66–79 and 109ff.

19. For the problems of lines 385ff., see above, chapter 6, note 39.

20. For the text of line 1460, see above, chapter 7, note 45.

21. For the atmosphere of feminine intimacy in the mirror metaphor, see Michelini (1987) 309ff., with n. 144.

22. For the unheroic nature of woman's death, associated with guile or the ugliness of hanging in Greek tragedy, see Loraux (1985) 33ff., 44ff.

23. On the mirror, see Zeitlin (1985b) 95, 99ff.

24. On the problem of the discrepancy and its implications, see Luschnig (1988a) 93f.; and C. Segal (1992b) 88f.

25. Cf. βλέπουσιν ἐς πρόσωπα, 416; also the chorus's "Won't he infer it by looking into your face?" (280); and Hippolytus' "How will you look at him [Theseus], you and your mistress?" (662).

26. On these motifs and their importance for a fifth-century audience, see Avery (1968) 19–35, especially 29ff.; C. Segal (1970c) 288ff.

27. See, for example, Thucydides 1.22; see C. Segal (1983b) passim, especially 30ff.

28. For this mechanism of complementarity in the play, see Frischer (1970) 85–100.

29. Cf. Seneca's elaboration of this scene of forced entry, with a more violent tone, in *Phaedra* 860ff. See C. Segal (1986b) 16off., with n. 20.

30. See C. Segal (1979).

31. Hippolytus' failed passage to adult masculinity is also emphasized by the female form of his death, as his "entangled" body recalls Phaedra's death by hanging (761f. and 1236f.); see Loraux (1981) = (1989) 48ff.; and Zeitlin (1985b) 58f.

32. Sophocles, *Electra* 680–756; cf. *Hippolytus* 1244, and *Electra* 746ff. Cf. also the racing metaphor in *Hippolytus* 87.

33. On the parallels between Hippolytus and Phaethon, see Reckford (1972) passim, especially 414–27. For the myth, see also Wilamowitz-Moellendorff (1883) 396–434; Diggle (1970) 3–32. The parallels between domestic and celestial themes extend further back into the play in the first stasimon's myths of Semele and Iole and in the story of Pasiphae; see C. Segal (1979) passim; and Halleran (1991) 112–15.

34. On *sphallein*, see Knox (1952) 25f. = (1979) 224f., on the significance of its multiple recurrences throughout the play.

35. On Hippolytus' male virginity as a refusal to complete the "course" of life, see Zeitlin (1985b) 64ff.

36. Cf. 86ff., cited above; see Zeitlin (1985b) 64.

9. *Golden Armor and Servile Robes: Heroism and Metamorphosis*

1. This atmosphere of restlessness, suspension, and instability has led to a low valuation of the play and to the suggestion that the material is too diffuse for the dramatic frame. Pohlenz (1954) 1.284, for example, contrasts *Hecuba* with "die grandiose Geschlossenheit der Medea" and goes on, "Man hat das Gefühl, dass durch langen Krieg aufgestaute Erregung zur Ausgestaltung dessen, was den Dichter bewegt, auch über den künstlerischen Rahmen hinaus treibt."

2. Cf. especially *Philoctetes* 331ff., 410–50. This use of Achilles' heroism as an unattainable past glory seen in retrospective vision is already established in the *Odyssey*: cf. 24.58–65.

3. Euripides' play is the first detailed acccount of the metamorphosis of Hecuba, but its connection with Cynossema suggests that there were earlier traditions. See Forbes Irving (1990) 207ff.; also below, chapter 10, note 56.

4. Simonides' lyrical version was outstanding; see Longinus, *On the Sublime* 15.7. In epic there is Achilles' golden armor in *Iliad* 18, Agamemnon's golden scepter, and the various golden possessions of the gods. In his *Electra* Euripides also uses gold to contrast a debased and a heroic world, e.g., 444, 713ff.; see Zeitlin (1970) 653–55, 662.

5. Hecuba's word ἐπῳδόν in line 1272 seems to have the basic meaning of "called after" (so LSJ s.v.); but the word may also carry the association of "song" as well as "magic" and so continue the contrast with heroic song. On the *sêma* and epic monumentalization, see Lynn-George (1988) 252ff.; and Ford (1992) 138ff.

6. On the ironical treatment of Achilles' heroism in the play generally, see K. King (1987) 88ff., especially 91–94.

7. The contrast of gold and blood appears in a different mood in *Iliad*

2.267f., where Odysseus' smiting of Thersites with the "golden scepter" raises a "bloody welt."

8. On the Trojan gold, see lines 10, 27, 713, 775, 994, and also 1002 and 1009, on Hecuba's use of it to entrap Polymestor.

9. Cf. also Hecuba's own lament at lines 619–28 and also her shame at appearing as a slave in 551f. In Ovid's version of the myth she is also explicitly the exemplar of the uncertainty of human fortunes (*Metamorphoses* 13.508–13).

10. On the *ephêmeros* in Greek poetry, see Fränkel (1946) 131–45; also Garzya (1955) ad 55–58. Pindar, *Olympian* 2.30ff., and *Nemean* 6.6f, are noteworthy examples.

11. For the smoking ruins, see lines 476–78, 823, and 1215. For the remnants of the destroyed city, see also lines 11, 16f., 619, 905–13, and 1209–10. For the importance of this nonscenic space to the play, see Hourmouziades (1965) 121f.

12. See Reckford (1985) 113: "Hecuba's own fate illustrates exactly what she denies for Polyxena: namely the power of time and chance to alter the nobility of the soul." On the stability of noble nature in Polyxena and its importance to the play, see, inter alia, Nussbaum (1986) 399f., 405ff.; also Reckford (1985) 115ff.; Michelini (1987) 135ff. We should not, however, allow Polyxena's heroism to obscure the horror and degradation of her death. On the ambiguity of this kind of female tragic heroism, see Loraux (1985) 31ff., 55ff., 81f.

13. The change within Hecuba has been a major focus of interpretation. See, for instance, Pohlenz (1954) 281; Kirkwood (1947) 61ff.; Grube (1941) 82f.; and, with more qualification, Steidle (1966) 133–42, especially 136–40. For a more recent survey of modern views, see Heath (1987) 62ff. Some interpreters suggest a contrast between an "ascending curve" for Polyxena and a "descending curve" for Hecuba; see Méautis (1944) 109, cited with qualified approval by Conacher (1967) 154.

14. Kovacs (1987) 108ff. argues for a more neutral view of Hecuba's final metamorphosis; but this seems to me out of keeping with the grim tone of the ending, on which see, e.g., Grube (1941) 228.

15. Sophocles, *Antigone* 718, and *Ichneutae* 223 (Radt); Euripides, *Andromache* 1003, *Iphigeneia in Tauris* 816, *Oedipus*, frag. 554 Nauck = 97 Austin. The word does not occur in Aeschylus.

16. Cf. *Simonides*, frag. 521 Page. Euripides uses this connotation of the word in his lost *Oedipus* (frag. 554 Nauck = 97 Austin).

17. We may compare the morally ineducable man of Plato, *Protagoras* 322d, who has to be killed "as a disease of the city" if he cannot be socialized.

18. See below, chapter 10.

19. On the reminiscence of the Odyssean Cyclops here, see Schmid (1940)

466. Michelini (1987) 171 also suggests a parodistic allusion to the blinded Oedipus.

20. Cf. Virgil's adaptation of these lines in *Aeneid* 6.362, "nunc me fluctus habet versantque in litore venti" (now the waves hold me, and the winds toss me along the shore) for the shade of Aeneas' hapless pilot, Palinurus, caught between the entrance to the underworld and the River Styx.

21. There is another parallel between these two scenes in the echo between the dark vision of lines 70–72 and 702–5; cf. also 54. For some interesting observations on the two scenes in the light of Greek mantic and oneiric discourse, see Brillante (1988) 429–447, especially 439ff.

22. Line 679 seems to suggest that the body was nude when it was tossed up onshore, as we would also expect from lines 26–30 and 698–701. The phrasing (δέμας περιπτύσσοντες, 735) favors the view that the corpse still had some remnants of clothing clinging to it, and at least one scholiast understood the passage this way. The motif of the peploi here obviously serves the dramatic function of enabling Agamemnon to recognize the body as non-Greek.

23. It is perhaps another stroke of retributive justice that later, in the punishment for this crime, Polymestor will describe himself as "stripped bare" of his arms, his "twofold equipment" of javelins (1156, γυμνόν μ᾽ ἔθηκαν διπτύχου στολίσματος).

24. The motif of burial was begun in lines 508 and 609–18 and then postponed in 726–30 and accomplished, on Agamemnon's order, only at the end in the funeral of these "twofold bodies" (*diptuchous nekrous,* 1287).

25. For discussion, with bibliography, see Griffith (1988) 552–54.

26. On this scene and the typology of supplication, see Gould (1973) 84f.

27. *Bacchae* 618–21, 912–44, 1017–19, 1106–08, 1141–99.

28. In the trial scene of the *Hippolytus,* for example, the false exterior triumphs, at least temporarily, over the truth of the inner man. Hippolytus, falsely accused by Phaedra's letter, wishes for "some skilled Sophist" who could resolve the inversion between appearances and reality that now threatens his life (920f.); Theseus replies with a parallel wish for some clear indication of a man's heart (*diagnôsin phrenôn*), so as to tell the true friend from the false (921–31).

29. On the motif of eyes in the play, see the good discussion by Nussbaum (1986) 410ff.

30. These are the only two places in the play where *aristos* is used of a single individual (134, 580). In the case of Achilles, there is an obvious reference to his Homeric epithet, "best of Achaeans." Interesting too is line 1052, where Hecuba bestows this epithet on the Trojan women who have joined her in killing the sons of Polymestor (σὺν ταῖσδ᾽ ἀρίσταις Τρῳᾶσιν, "with these best Trojan women").

31. The nobility of Polyxena's death, in fact, validates the assumptions about the female acquiescence to male violence which wins the highest praise in this society. See Loraux (1985) passim, especially 79–82; also below, chapter 10.

32. This closing phrase of the play, in this context, recalls Thucydides' famous description of war as a "harsh teacher" (βίαιος διδάσκαλος, 3.82.2).

10. Violence and the Other: Greek, Female, and Barbarian

1. For the problems in the structure of the play and various solutions, see Lesky (1972) 336f.; Abrahamson (1952) 120, n. 1; Kirkwood (1947) 61–63; Conacher (1961) 8ff., 14ff., and (1967) 146, n. 1, and pp. 155ff.; Reckford (1985) 209, n. 1; Kovacs (1987) 80f., 112–14; Michelini (1987) 133–34; Heath (1987) 43ff., 60ff. gives a useful survey of older and more recent views.

2. On Polymestor's "house," see lines 995, 1134, 1212, and 1245; on warfare and horses see lines 1089f.; cf. also lines 9 and 710; see also Herodotus 5.6.2.

3. See Thucydides 7.29.4–5; Herodotus 5.6.2; Aristophanes, *Acharnians* 153ff.; also below, this chapter. For Thracian savagery as a topos in the fifth century, see Long (1986) 143; also Bacon (1961) 150f., citing Euripides, *Erechtheus*, frag. 367 Nauck; and now Hall (1989) 105. For a useful collection of passages on the Thracian character, from the fifth century B.C. on, see Bömer (1976) 131f., ad Ovid, *Metamorphoses* 6.458. The savagery of Tereus here may owe something to Sophocles' *Tereus* (via Accius' version). This play too may have influenced the unflattering picture of Thracians in Aristophanes' *Birds*, where Peisthetaerus sends off to Thrace the violent young man who wants to beat his father (1368–71). See also Rosellini and Saïd (1978) 949–1005, especially 955ff., 985ff.; Hartog (1988), especially 36–50, 109–11, 212–37.

4. See Aélion (1983) 2.183.

5. Odysseus in lines 321–25 has a much harder version of this motif of common suffering: many Greek mothers and wives are in pain too, and the Trojan women have to endure their share. Cf. also line 934, where the women of the Trojan chorus compare themselves to a Dorian girl. Note too that in line 834 Hecuba suggests that the murdered Polydorus is a kind of relation in marriage (*kêdestês*) to Agamemnon; then in 1202f. she reverses this argument and points out that a Thracian, as a barbarian, could never have such a relation with a Greek. Hecuba is clearly manipulating the Greek / barbarian dichotomy to her own advantage, but the very fact that she could use the argument about kinship in line 834 suggests that the Trojans are not as hopelessly alien to Greeks as the Thracians—a bias which the *Iliad*, of course, helped support.

6. On these details of dress, see Bacon (1961) 125f. Euripides is not entirely

consistent in the Greekness of the Trojans' dress. The robe of Polyxena (558–61), for instance, seems distinctly Greek, while the remnants of Polydorus' clothing make him recognizably Trojan (733–35). By contrast, the Thracians never exhibit Greek features in their dress; note the "native" quality of Polymestor's clothes and weapons in lines 1153–56. The Trojans, in any case, can approximate Greekness more closely than the Thracians.

7. The eye-for-an-eye motif is underlined by the repeated emphasis on the "two" children by both Hecuba and Polymestor: cf. lines 45 and 1051. On Hecuba's "retributive and mimetic" revenge, see Nussbaum (1986) 410.

8. The sons of Theseus played an important part in the post-Homeric epics on the fall of Troy (*Little Iliad*, frag. XVIII, and *Iliou Persis*, frag. III, Allen), and so their presence in *Hecuba* is not entirely unexpected. Nevertheless, the detail could have been omitted; their presence, especially in an assembly, is striking to an Athenian audience. Compare the praise of Athens in *Medea* 824ff. wih the role of Athens as the refuge of the murderess Medea at the end of the play (*Medea* 1384f.).

9. Aeschylus, *Agamemnon* 228–47. For a good discussion of the implicit eroticism in the Aeschylean scene, see Lebeck (1971) 80ff. For speculations on the sexual implications of Polyxena's sacrifice, see Burkert (1983) 67, who suggests a possible parallel with a funeral sacrifice in early Russia: "There, before being strangled on the dead man's bier, the victim, a volunteer, had to offer herself to all the participants in the funeral." He goes on to ask whether the name Πολυξένη may not reflect a similar rite, noting the term πολύξεναι νεάνιδες in Pindar, frag. 122.1 Snell-Maehler, of courtesans at Aphrodite's temple at Corinth.

10. Although Talthybius is narrating the event to Hecuba, and although Polyxena herself is presumably trying to stir pity, not awaken lust, nevertheless, it is hard to avoid the sexual implications.

11. Commentators point out how much Virgil's account of the sack of Troy in the second book of the *Aeneid* owes to the descriptions of Euripides here and in the *Trojan Women*; cf. Garzya (1955) ad 905–51.

12. I cannot agree with the lighter view taken of this ode (as of the other odes) by Gellie (1980) 43f. On the importance of women's vulnerability in war in this play and in Euripides generally, see Nussbaum (1986) 413.

13. Cf. *Iliad* 22.469–72, with the analysis of Nagler (1974) 45ff.

14. Alcestis' and Deianeira's addresses to the marriage bed in their respective plays offer some parallel; but the chorus of the *Hecuba*, with the women actually getting ready to lie beside their husbands, takes the intimacy even further.

15. Euripides may have in mind here the powerful simile of *Odyssey* 8.523–29.

16. See Murray (1946) 43: "The only light that shines through the dark

fury of the *Hecuba* is the lovely and gentle courage, almost the joy, with which the virgin martyr [!] Polyxena goes to her death." See also Gellie (1980) 34: "The character and behavior of Polyxena have been designed to meet certain specifications: she must be the kind of girl who can make us feel good when she dies. . . . Part of the good feeling is achieved by allowing some teasing physical detail to add its own kind of warmth." Exactly the opposite view is maintained by Aylen (1964) 138: "We are not allowed to go away from the theatre having had a good cry, and feeling better. We are not to feel better; we are to be horrified."

17. Rivier (1975) 154f. (my translation); the passage is virtually unchanged from the first edition (Lausanne, 1944, p. 173). For similar views, see Garzya (1955) 27, on Polyxena's "dolcissima nobiltà" and "profumo di giovinezza." Recent scholars have been more moderate in their praise of Polyxena's death: see Conacher, *Drama* (1967) 159; Nussbaum (1986) 405f. The lack of moral justification for the sacrifice, even as a reward for Achilles' martial valor, is well set forth by Conacher, pp. 149 and 153f.; Abrahamson (1952) 122ff.; and O'Connor-Visser (1987) 63–67, which includes a review of earlier literature; see also the latter's discussion of earlier scholarship on human sacrifice in Euripides, pp. 5–18. Various other modern views of Polyxena's death are cited and examined by Michelini (1987) 63f., with n. 127.

18. For Vellacott (1975) 209f., "the light of a religious experience" seems "strong enough to transcend the physical barbarity enacted." Michelini (1987) 180 writes of "the erotic charm that plays over [Polyxena's] death scene," for this "anticipates a time when *erôs* will emerge rehabilitated, purified of its physical attachments and refined into a longing of the soul."

19. For the reality of such fears among women in cities at war, see Schaps (1982) passim.

20. See *Homeric Hymn to Ceres* 3, 9, 30. The most familiar example in tragedy is Sophocles' *Antigone* 814–16. See Lattimore (1942) 192ff.; Loraux (1985) 68–75; K. King (1987) 186ff., especially 186–88.

21. Detienne (1988) 159–75, especially 163ff.; see also his "Violentes 'eugénies' en pleines Thesmophories: des femmes couvertes de sang," in Detienne and Vernant (1979) 213f. (English trans. 1989, 146f.). Aeschylus, *Danaids*, frag. 44 Radt, is perhaps the most famous classical text for this association of violence and sexual union.

22. See Rehm (1989) 111f.

23. See, in general, Seaford (1987) 106–30; Foley (1985) 68ff., 84ff., especially 84–88. Euripides, *Iphigeneia in Aulis* 668–80, is an illuminating passage for the association of wedding ritual and the enactment of deathlike loss and separation. For the *Hecuba*, scholars have sometimes hypothesized an early legend of Achilles' love for Polyxena as the motivation for his ghost's demanding her in sacrifice, but strong evidence for an early erotic connection is

lacking: see the scholion ad *Hecuba* 41; further discussion in Conacher (1967) 146–51, and (1961) 3–7; Méridier (1956) 166, who believes in a pre-Euripidean erotic version; and K. King (1987) 185ff., who does not. King (85f.) also cites the story of a hero at Temesa, told in Pausanias (6.6.4–11), who was put to death for rape but then demanded a virgin bride as a sacrificial offering each year; see also Devereux (1985) 136f.

24. See C. Segal (1975) 30–53, especially 33ff.

25. Cf. the related *portis* in Sophocles, *Trachiniae* 530; see, in general, Calame (1977) 1.413ff.; Loraux (1985) 65–68; Seaford (1988) 119.

26. Cf. also the bird imagery of lines 178 and 337f. On the animal imagery generally, see Michelini (1987) 171, with n. 155; also O'Connor-Visser (1987) 65.

27. In the closely parallel myth of Iphigeneia, marriage ritual, the sacrifice of the virgin, and the implicit equivalency of virgin and animal at the altar also come together. On this convergence, see Burkert (1985) 151f. It is a crucial difference, however, that Iphigeneia's sacrifice belongs to the cult of Artemis, whereas Polyxena's is to a heroized warrior. In Polyxena's case, the martial bloodthirstiness receives even greater emphasis. For human victims substituted for animals in myths of wind sacrifice, see Burkert (1981) 115, with n. 1. For the Greek horror of human sacrifice generally, see Henrichs (1981) 195–235: such rites are "something which uncivilized men inflict on one another but which no Greek in his right mind would even contemplate" (p. 234).

28. The verb χραίνειν regularly connotes sexual violation; cf. *Hippolytus* 1266, where it is used to describe the adulterous violation of Theseus' bed.

29. See H. King (1983) 109–27, especially 120.

30. See Michelini (1987) 161ff.

31. Rivier (1975) 154.

32. On the unusual nature of the simile, see Michelini (1987) 150, n. 76, who also has some interesting remarks on the mixture of tones in Polyxena's death scene, pp. 163ff.

33. The most widely used translation, which is otherwise quite sensitive—Arrowsmith (1955) in the University of Chicago Series—flattens both the syntax and the physical details of line 571 into a bland nominative absolute, "The execution finished." The repetition of "breath" is also lost in Arrowsmith's condensation of Euripides' expressive periphrasis, "the channels of her breathing's flow" (*pneumatos diarrhoas*, 567), taking up two-thirds of the verse, into the single word "throat."

34. Neoptolemus was the sacrificer in the *Iliou Persis* of Arctinus (apud Proclus, p. 107 Allen) and of Stesichorus (frag. 205 Page, "Tabula Iliaca"); also Ibycus, frag. 307 Page; Pindar, *Paean* 6.98–120. Cf. the different version in the *Cypria* (frag. XXVI Allen = scholion ad *Hecuba* 41). Euripides suppresses the name of Neoptolemus in his version of Priam's death in *Trojan Women* 16f.,

481ff., on which see Petersmann (1977) 146–58, especially 153–58. Neoptolemus is named as the killer on the celebrated sixth-century vase (ca. 570 B.C.) in the British Museum depicting the sacrifice of Polyxena (London 97.7–27.2). In this brutal scene, incidentally, the girl is fully clothed, and her death is far from voluntary: she is held like a log by three Greek warriors while a fully armed Neoptolemus plunges the sword into her exposed throat. Neoptolemus is said to be the killer of Priam as early as Arctinus' *Iliou Persis* (apud Proclus, p. 107 Allen) and the *Little Iliad* (frag. XVI Allen = Pausanias 10.27.1); and he also appears here as the killer of the infant Astyanax (frag. XIX Allen = Pausanias 10.25.9).

35. Steidle (1966) 136–40 rightly points out that Hecuba, even in the first part of the play, is never entirely a passive sufferer but even there "von einer zwar verzweifelten, aber fast wilden Aktualität beherrscht wird" (136); see also Kovacs (1987) 99. Her activity, however, is almost entirely directed toward her suppliant status and remains ineffectual until she directs it toward revenge in the second part of the play.

36. *Hecuba* 1181f. is perhaps another allusion to this celebrated ode; cf. Aeschylus, *Choephoroe* 585–88.

37. For further discussion, see above, chapter 9.

38. Cf. *Bacchae* 117f., 1236f., where the women of Thebes leave the looms to go raging on the mountain. In *Hecuba* 1151–54 the weaving is only a pretext to enable the Trojan women to get close to their victims; but, as in *Bacchae*, the motif negates the submissiveness of the familiar female role in the house. Here, too, *pollai* (many, 1152) suggests their massed collectivity. In *Hecuba* 363f. and 471f. the loom is also the sign of female enslavement and weakness, to be reversed in the use of the weaving motif later. The garments (peploi) that serve the Trojan women as a pretext to laying hands on their victims are also the means of concealing the daggers that will kill them (1161). Cf. also lines 1013 and 1153f., where the supposedly civilized Trojan women use the pretext of Thracian women's weaving as part of their stratagem to destroy men. Presumably, the pins with which they blind Polymestor (1170) were used to hold up their peploi. Contrast the association of the peploi with Trojan helplessness in lines 486f. (echoing Polyxena's gesture of line 432) and also in lines 246, 432, 558, and 578 (for Polyxena), and 734 (for Polydorus). Weaving is a familiar cultural representation of "tame" femaleness and therefore a focal point of female instability and danger. The association of female weaving with both virtue and guile goes back at least to Homer's Helen and Penelope. See Jenkins (1985) 115f.; see above, chapter 9.

39. For the octopus as a creature of guile, see Detienne and Vernant (1974) 45ff. (English trans. 1991, 37ff.). In this respect too, Hecuba's plotting imitates Odyssean guile, which has semantic affinities with accounts of the octopus: see Detienne and Vernant (1974) 47 (English trans. 1991, 39).

40. In contrast with Ovid's elaboration of the monstrosity (*Metamorphoses* 13.567–71), Euripides keeps the supernatural understated and in the background.

41. For the associations of the bacchantic *sparagmos*, see Porson (1847) ad 1058ff. Polymestor's hysterical reference here to the exposure of his children (ἐκβολάν, 1078) may also recall Hecuba's accusations of the "exposure" of her son's body by Polymestor (699, 781), again with the suggestion of retributive justice. On this scene and the Dionysiac element in the play generally, see Schlesier (1988) 124f., which appeared after the original version of this chapter was published.

42. The only other occurrence of this verb in Greek tragedy is in Euripides' *Hippolytus* 1376, as the injured youth calls for death. For διαμοιράω of dividing up the meat of sacrificial victims, see Homer, *Odyssey* 14.434. Note too the repetition of Hecuba's line 723 by the chorus in their taunting of Polymestor in 1087. Diggle (1984) and Méridier (1956), following Hermann, delete line 1087 (unjustly, in my opinion). The line is retained by Murray (1902) and by Daitz in the Teubner edition (1973).

43. Cf. the story of the women's attack on King Battus of Cyrene in Aelian, frag. 44 (ed. R. Hercher, Leipzig: Teubner, 1866), discussed by Detienne, in Detienne, Vernant, et al. (1979) 184 (English trans. 1989, 129f.). Having discovered him at their festival, the women "rush upon Battus all together (ἀθρόαι) with one accord, to take from him [the means of] being still a male." For the association of eyes and male genitals, see Devereux (1973) 42ff. Hecuba's ploy to lure Polymestor's children into her grasp depends on their role as potential successors and heirs to their father (cf. 1005f., and note the irony of Hecuba's supposed motive of telling the secret of the treasure to the one surviving child of her line in line 1003). Thus, if the blinding suggests castration, Hecuba would be destroying both the father's present heirs and his potential for other children later. In this respect too she is like Medea, who also destroys both the new bride and the father's two male heirs.

44. For the similarities with the revenge plot of the *Medea*, see Strohm (1957) 72f.

45. The parallel with Clytaemnestra is not complete here, for Hecuba's revenge is aimed at the killer of her son, not the killers of her daughter. These latter, in fact, are (in part) her allies and accomplices in her vengeance. The play nevertheless exploits the associations of Iphigeneia and Polyxena to suggest some parallelism, particularly at the very end of the play; see below, this chapter.

46. Note Hecuba's reliance on the motif of *charis*, unsuccessfully, with Odysseus in lines 254, 257, 276, and 320. The importance of *charis* in the play is often noted: see Conacher (1961) 22f., and (1967) 149; also Adkins (1966) 193–219 passim, especially 194 and 201ff.

47. In *Trojan Women* 247–71 Euripides also links Polyxena's fate and Cassandra's: the former's sacrifice immediately follows upon the news that Cassandra will be the concubine of Agamemnon.

48. The degeneration in this movement from nomos to persuasion and eros has often been noted: Kirkwood (1947) 66–68; see Conacher (1967) 162f., and (1981) 20f.; Vellacott (1975) 213; Reckford (1985) 120ff.; and Michelini (1987) 151ff. For further discussion, see below, chapter 11.

49. Both Murray (1902) and Diggle (1984), in the last two editions of the Oxford Classical Texts, follow Matthiae in deleting the lines. Other editors, however, such as Méridier (1956) in the Budé edition and Daitz (1973), allow them to stand. Matthiae's objections to the lines do not seem to me insuperable, and I am inclined to view them as genuine, although my argument does not rest on this fact. It is gratifying to see that Kovacs (1987) 102 and Michelini (1987) 151, n. 81, also believe in the authenticity of the lines.

50. He is "wie ein missglückter Deus ex machina," remarks Schmid ([1940] 472); see also Steidle (1966) 140; Gellie (1980) 38f.; Kovacs (1987) 108, with n. 66.

51. Although Polymestor calls on his Thracian army for help in lines 1089–90, it seems powerless to intervene in his behalf. Is this just a detail that Euripides neglects, or does he mean to indicate thereby the disorganized, ineffectual nature of Thracian society? In Ovid's version, the Thracian people (*gens*) do, in fact, pursue Hecuba, and she is metamorphosed in the midst of her flight from them (*Metamorphoses* 13.565–71).

52. There is perhaps a further pattern of retributive justice in the deception of Polymestor through the repetition of the verb *sêmainein* for the handing on of the supposed secret of the treasure. Polymestor uses it (and the related noun *sêmeion*) four times in his greedy, urgent request for the vital information (983, 999, 1003, 1009). Later, when he returns, blinded, to the stage, he uses the same verb, but now he asks not about the treasure but about the whereabouts of his destroyer, Hecuba (1125), so that he can rip her apart with his bare hands: σήμηνον, εἰπὲ ποῦ 'σθ', ἵν' ἁρπάσας χεροῖν / διασπάσωμαι καὶ καθαιμάξω χρόα. As his revenge, in turn, is the prophecy of her transformation into a *sêma* for sailors (1273), that word may again mark the next twist of the retributive pattern.

53. The affinities of Polymestor with Polyphemus have often been noted: see Schmid (1940) 466; also above, chapter 9. His rage and desperation as he cries out to Helios to heal his bloodied eyes (1066–68) may also evoke the violent rapist-giant Orion, blinded because of his hubristic behavior and sent to seek Helios to cure the wound. Cf. Hesiod, frag. 148a Merkelbach-West = Pseudo-Eratosthenes, *Catasterismi* 32. For the myth, see Fontenrose (1981) 8ff. Note that Polymestor actually mentions Orion (as a constellation) in line

1101. For some interesting suggestions about the connections between Orion and the raging Polymestor, see Schlesier (1988) 132.

54. Polymestor's prophecy also has the structural role of Polyphemus' prayer and curse to Poseidon in *Odyssey* 9.526–36; see below, chapter 11. There is still another ironic collapsing of differences in the first part of the play in the way the wily, ignoble Odysseus champions the cause of his opposite, Achilles. See K. King (1987) 93, who observes how Odysseus' defense of Achilles' prerogatives in *Hecuba* 306–8 echoes Achilles' speech in the embassy of *Iliad* 9.318f.; see also K. King (1985) 47–66, especially 51f. It may be part of the play's ironic reflection on the heroic traditions associated with Achilles that Neoptolemus is always referred to by his patronymic (24, 224, 523, 528).

55. See Michelini (1987) 171: "Avenger and victim join in a lower realm, where the two struggle endlessly on, each seeking to achieve parity." See also Reckford (1985) 122f.

56. See Erbse (1984) 59, who also suggests that the dog may evoke a "bestial embodiment of the revenge-goddess, the Erinys" (n. 16). In a version that seems to go back to sixth-century lyric poetry, the Erinyes transform Hecuba into a dog: see Fragmenta Adespota 965 (Page); also Euripides, frag. 968 Nauck; and *Iliad* 24.212ff.; and, in general, Forbes Irving (1990) 207ff.

57. On this passage, and the "irony of the play [*Trojan Women*] in which the savages are not the Trojans but the Greeks," see Bacon (1961) 13.

58. The Thracians could also appear more sympathetically, as in Euripides' (?) *Rhesus*, e.g., 300ff. If that play is, in fact, among the early works of Euripides, as some think, it may reflect a prewar view of the Thracians. Cf. also Herodotus' "anthropology" of the Thracians (5.3–10), which includes their exact reversal of Greek burial and marriage customs.

59. Cf. *Odyssey* 9.506–21; see Kovacs (1987) 108.

60. This phrase repeats the expression used of Phaedra's suicide in *Hippolytus* 787, another female plot that threatens to destroy patriarchal authority in the house.

61. Meridor (1978) 32ff., seems to me unduly skeptical in questioning the validity of Polymestor's prophecy. Ugly and brutal as he is, he predicts events as ugly as himself. Euripides is careful to give him the authority of a god (1267), even if he is a debased version of the deus ex machina. See also above, note 53.

62. Agamemnon's "May it somehow be well" in line 902 may also be an echo of the choral refrain, "Lament, lament, but may the good win out" in the *Agamemnon* (121, 137, 159).

63. Schlesier (1988) 133 suggests still another parallel, in the Dionysiac realm: the imprisonment of Lycurgus, as in Sophocles, *Antigone* 956–58.

64. See lines 37–41, 109–25, and 534–41. Méridier (1956) 169, n. 1, conve-

niently summarizes the play's contradictory statements about the winds. See also Conacher (1961) 2, with n. 3. For further discussion see below, chapter 13.

65. See C. Segal (1982a) chap. 7, especially 223ff.

66. For the Greek theater's capacity to make the audience see itself in the actions of the protagonist, see, for example, Knox (1957) 77.

11. *Law and Universals*

1. Abrahamson (1952) 12.

2. Euripides' fusion of these diverse elements has often been discussed; see, e.g., Kamerbeek (1960) 3–25.

3. Cf. also the repeated phrase "avoiding blame" in lines 384 and 1249 (ψόγον φυγεῖν, φύγω ψόγον), to be discussed below.

4. On the issue of *charis* in the play, see Conacher (1967) 147 and 161f., and (1981) 20–22; Adkins (1966) 194 and 201ff.

5. Some of the lines in this passage are suspect. Diggle (1984), following Nauck, excises lines 793–97, but this is probably excessive; see Diggle's critical apparatus ad 797.

6. On Polyxena, see Nussbaum (1986) 405f.

7. For detailed discussions and bibliography, see Heinimann (1945) 110ff.; Guthrie (1969) 55ff. For the unwritten laws, see Cerri (1979) chaps. 2 and 4, with further bibliography; Kerferd (1981) chap. 10.

8. See Hippias, 86 C 1, and Antiphon the Sophist 87 44 A and B (both in Diels-Kranz). For discussion and further bibliography, see Guthrie (1969) 160–63.

9. Familiar examples are the slaves in *Hippolytus* 1249ff.; *Helen* 728–31, 1627–41; *Iphigeneia in Aulis* 303ff. See also *Melanippe*, frag. 511 Nauck, and *Phrixus*, frag. 831. See, generally, Guthrie (1969) 157ff.; also above, chapter 6, notes 43 and 46.

10. See Heinimann (1945) 65ff.

11. For recent discussion and bibliography, see Cerri (1979) passim, especially chaps. 1 and 3.

12. Cf. Euripides, *Suppliants* 378; frag. 148.8 Austin; frags. 346.1 and 853 Nauck; also Aeschylus, *Choephoroe* 92ff. Cf. also Euripides, *Hippolytus* 97f., on mortals following "the laws of the gods"; *Ion* 642 ff., and *Bacchae* 890ff. on the identification of *nomos* and *phusis* that applies to all life. Also Euripides, *Heracles* 1316, *Ion* 1045–47, and *Suppliants* 299–303 on a generalized *nomos*. For these and related issues, see Heinimann (1945) 163–69; Cerri (1979) 81ff., with the bibliography cited in n. 16, pp. 92f.; Guthrie (1969) 76ff.; Kerferd (1981) chap. 10.

13. Text in Diels-Kranz, number 89 (vol. 2, pp. 402 and 404, respectively).

For discussion, see Guthrie (1969) 71ff.; Kerferd (1981) 126–28; Untersteiner (1943–44), in Classen (1976) 591–611, especially 597f.

14. See Kerferd (1981) 112.

15. E.g., Antiphon the Sophist 87 B44 A and B in Diels-Kranz; Aristophanes, *Clouds* 1067–82, with the note ad 1075 by Dover (1968) 227; *Birds* 753ff.

16. Cf. *Iphigeneia in Tauris* 465; *Helen* 1241, 1258; also *Bacchae* 483f., cited above.

17. The ambiguity that (as I believe) Hecuba is deliberately exploiting is reflected in the division among interpreters. The two most recent interpreters I have seen, for example, take opposite views. Nussbaum (1986) takes *nomos* to mean "convention" (400–403), although she observes that this meaning "does not licence us to regard them [conventions] lightly. Nor does it seem that we can replace or alter them at will"; see also p. 417. Kovacs (1987), however, recognizes the importance of *nomos* as a broadly valid moral "law" (p. 101), but he unnecessarily limits the meaning of the passage by suggesting that Hecuba is here typical of the Trojans who cling to "old-fashioned notions of the gods' dealings with men," in contrast to the more secular mentality of the Greeks (p. 83). For a useful survey of previous views of the question, see Conacher (1961) 10ff.; and see the references cited above, in notes 9–13.

18. The phrase *graphai nomôn* in line 866 may also suggest that the *nomos* in lines 799ff. refers to *agraphoi nomoi*, the "unwritten laws."

19. See H. Rankin (1983) 131; also Guthrie (1969) 170; Conacher (1961) 22, n. 32; and Kerferd (1981) 170f., who points out that the view of gods as owing their existence to human belief "need not mean however that their existence was merely subjective to individual human beings" (171).

20. After I had written the lecture on which this chapter is based, I was happy to find this view of the passage shared by Kullmann (1986) 47; see also Heinimann (1945) 121.

21. Kirkwood (1947) 66f.

22. See C. Segal (1981b), especially chaps. 1–3.

23. Plato, *Protagoras* 327d; see, in general, Turato (1979) 96–101.

24. Translation by C. Smith (1920) in the Loeb Classical Library Thucydides, vol. 2.

25. See, e.g., line 823 and the ode at 905ff. on the Trojans' suffering at the capture and destruction of their city.

26. Some ancient interpreters referred the vocative of the two-termination adjective, δύστηνε, to Polydorus, who had, in fact, called himself δύστηνος in the prologue (46); but the harshness of the self-address only brings out the desperate self-searching that Hecuba goes through here. For a good discussion, see Bain (1977) 13–16. Conacher (1961) 21 aptly calls this scene "an eerie little passage of self-interrogation by Hecuba."

27. See Bain (1977) 32f.

28. Snell (1928).

29. Note that Agamemnon now grants to Hecuba the *charis* that had previously been associated with Cassandra, although in a different sense: 832 (if genuine) and 855.

30. Diggle (1984), deletes lines 974f. But the manuscripts indicate no problems, and the lines are retained by Daitz (1973). For the importance of the motif of eyes as the mark of honest relations, see Nussbaum (1986) 406 and 410–14. It is interesting to contrast the careful plotting of Hecuba's cat-and-mouse game in manipulating Polymestor into her trap with the direct outburst of anger and the immediate attack of the Ovidian Hecuba at her first encounter with her enemy (*Metamorphoses* 13.558ff.).

31. For *hosios* in this sense of "pure," free of crime, cf. Aeschylus, *Choephoroe* 378; Sophocles, *Oedipus at Colonus* 470.

32. Adkins (1966) 198ff. For a criticism of Adkins from a somewhat different point of view, see K. King (1985) 55, with n. 38.

33. This aspect of Thucydides has often been noted; for an interestingly nuanced discussion, see Crane (1992), especially 13f. and 26.

34. For the development of the concept of natural law in the Stoics, see Striker (1987) 79–94, with the comment by Brad Inwood on pp. 95–101; also Watson (1971) 216–38.

12.   *The Problem of the Gods*

1. Zuntz (1960) 201–41. See Whitman (1974) 32–34; Grube (1941) 41–62. Less ironical positions are taken by Burnett (1971) and Kovacs (1987). Kovacs (1987), especially 105, 110f., and 118, takes a more optimistic view of Euripidean theology and views this absence of the gods more positively. Lefkowitz (1989) argues well for a cautious approach to Euripides' attitudes to the gods and suggests that his apparent critique of traditional views may be due to his realism. Schlesier (1985) 10–16 and 23–37 emphasizes the cruelty of the gods' justice and the incommensurability between gods and men. For a useful survey of post-World War II views of Euripidean theology, see Kullmann (1987) 10f. It is worth noting that Ovid has his gods take pity on Hecuba's suffering: *Metamorphoses* 13.572–75.

2. On this aspect of Euripides' presentation of the gods, see Chapouthier (1954) passim; Kullmann (1987) 11–17.

3. This passage has been much discussed; for recent interpretations and bibliography, see Schlesier (1985) 23–27; and Kullmann (1987) 16f.

4. This passage is much discussed; see Barrett (1964) ad loc.; Willink (1968) 42; and above, chapter 8.

5. On this point, see Nancy (1981) 17–30; especially 29f. On this tragic shift of *eukleia* to the female, see Loraux (1985) 79–82.

6. Chapouthier (1954) 206, cf. also 210.

7. See C. Segal (1982a) 277–88, 292–309.

8. This is Herwerden's widely accepted emendation for ἀναγκαῖον in the manuscripts.

9. See above, chapter 11.

10. See also Agamemnon's feeble endorsement of justice in lines 902ff., discussed in chapter 11.

11. The verb σφαγείς of Priam's death in line 24 also evokes sacrificial killing, and the collocation πίτνει σφαγείς in lines 23f. recurs in Polyxena's death: πεσεῖν . . . σφαγῇ, 569–70.

12. Zuntz (1960) 215.

13. Kullmann (1987) 18–20 suggests that the play acts out the contradiction between amoral, anthropomorphic gods of the Iliadic type and more morally concerned gods of the Odyssean type and thus raises the audience's consciousness of theological questions by dramatizing extreme positions. But the *Hecuba's* gods, like Sophocles', seem more puzzling for their absence than for anthropomorphic intervention as in the *Iliad*.

14. Cf. Aeschylus, *Persians* 688–92, where the gods of the lower world also relent, though their austerity and reluctance are stressed. They are presumably also merciful in Euripides' lost *Protesilaus*.

15. See Heath (1987) 66f.

16. The only textual evidence that divine justice is at work in the recovery of Polydorus' body is perhaps the sequence of thought in lines 790ff., especially 797–801. After accusing Polymestor of impiety and of "not fearing the gods below the earth nor those above" (791), Hecuba cites his having cast his victim's corpse into the sea (ἀφῆκε πόντιον, 797) and only two lines later asserts the gods' strength and the power of law (799f.). But even here the link is far from explicit.

17. The analysis in Heath (1987) 66f. has the merit of raising the question of divine intervention without pressing the case for their providential interference.

18. Kovacs (1987) 110.

19. For Polymestor's role as deus ex machina, see Schmid (1940) 472; and, in a lighter vein, Gellie (1980) 38. Polymestor does not say explicitly that Dionysus is a god here; perhaps (like Pentheus) he does not fully grasp his divine status. Herodotus 7.111 mentions a *manteion* of Dionysus among the Thracians.

20. For some of these bacchantic elements, see Schlesier (1988) 128ff.; see also above, chapter 9.

21. On the Dionysiac background see above, chapter 9.

22. For interesting parallels with the story of Lycurgus, see Schlesier (1988) 131ff., who, however, pushes these further than I find convincing.

23. The chorus's brief remarks on retributive justice in lines 1028–30 and 1085f. have an un-Aeschylean colorlessness. The dubious reference to a "heavy *daimon*" in line 1087, even if genuine, would not add much (cf. 723). Kovacs (1987) 110 suggests that over Agamemnon's closing announcement of setting sail hangs the threat of the god-sent storm in the *Odyssey* that will wreck the fleet and thus avenge the atrocities done here (cf. *Odyssey* 3.151ff., 4.499ff.). But the text offers no indication that such events are relevant here. Euripides' stresses the personal sufferings of Agamemnon back home in Greece (cf. 1277), not at sea.

24. On the cruelty and personal enmities in this closing scene, with its "atmosfera di cupa desolazione," see Di Benedetto (1971) 101.

25. Cf. also Hecuba's blaming of Helen in lines 264–70.

26. Note too the contrast between the Trojan women's separation from "the paternal land" and the prayer (which we know will not succeed) that Helen not arrive "at her paternal house" (γαίας ἐκ πατρίας and πατρῷον ἐς οἶκον, 952).

27. See also lines 25–30, 47–50, 701, and 782.

28. The *Hecuba* illustrates the shortcomings of a Girardian approach to Greek tragedy (Girard 1979). Here the divinely commanded act of sacrifice is a symptom and a symbol of an ingrained violence that can only be perpetuated, not resolved.

13. Conclusion: Euripides' Songs of Sorrow

1. On the Dionysian elements in Hecuba's revenge, see above, chapter 9; also Schlesier (1988) passim; also Schlesier (1993).

2. The process is already implicit in what is probably the earliest literary epiphany of Dionysus, *Homeric Hymn* 7, where the apparently helpless youth, captured by pirates, eventually appears in the form of a lion that seizes the chief, and then transforms the rest of the crew into dolphins. See also C. Segal (1982a) 32ff., 156f., 230ff.

3. See C. Segal (1982a) 195ff.

4. See above, chapters 4, 6, and 7, and the references cited in chapter 7, notes 1 and 2.

5. On the prologues and epilogues, see C. Segal (1992b) 104–10.

6. See, for instance, the conservative Euripides of Gregory (1991), and my review (Segal 1993a).

7. On such reversals in connection with Dionysus and the theater, see

C. Segal (1982a) 219ff. Euripides' play seems to be the first literary text that makes any connection at all between Hecuba's metamorphosis and Dionysus. In Fragmenta Adespota 965 (Page) the Erinyes are the agents of the transformation, a version that does not, of course, necessarily contradict Euripides'; see, in general, Forbes Irving (1990) 207ff.

Bibliography

Abrahamson, Ernst L. (1952). "Euripides' Tragedy of Hecuba." *Transactions of the American Philological Association* 83: 120–29.

Adkins, A. W. H. (1960). *Merit and Responsibility: A Study in Greek Values.* Oxford: Clarendon Press.

———. (1966). "Basic Greek Values in Euripides' *Hecuba* and *Hercules Furens.*" *Classical Quarterly*, new series, 16: 193–219.

Aélion, Rachel. (1983). *Euripide Héritier d'Eschyle.* Paris: Les Belles Lettres.

Alexiou, Margaret. (1974). *The Ritual Lament in Greek Tradition.* Cambridge: Cambridge University Press.

Ariès, Philippe. (1982). *The Hour of Our Death* (1977). Trans. H. Weaver. New York: Vintage Books.

Arrowsmith, William. (1955). *The Complete Greek Tragedies.* Vol. 3, *Euripides.* Chicago: University of Chicago Press.

Avery, Harry. (1968). "My Tongue Has Sworn, But My Mind Is Unsworn." *Transactions of the American Philological Association* 99: 19–35.

Aylen, Leo. (1964). *Greek Tragedy and the Modern World.* London: Methuen.

Bacon, Helen. (1961). *Barbarians in Greek Tragedy.* New Haven: Yale University Press.

Bain, David. (1977). *Actors and Audience.* Oxford: Oxford University Press.

Bakhtin, Mikhail. (1984). *Rabelais and His World* (1965, 1968). Trans. H. Iswolsky. Bloomington: Indiana University Press.

Bibliography   Barnes, Hazel E. (1960). "The Hippolytus of Drama and Myth." In Donald Sutherland and H. E. Barnes, *Hippolytus in Drama and Myth.* Lincoln: University of Nebraska Press, 71–123.

————. (1964–65). "Greek Tragicomedy." In John R. Wilson, ed. (1968), *Twentieth Century Interpretations of Euripides' Alcestis.* Englewood Cliffs, N.J.: Prentice-Hall.

Barnes, Jonathan, Malcolm Scholfield, and Richard Sorabji, eds. (1978). *Articles on Aristotle.* Vol. 4, *Psychology and Ethics.* New York: St. Martin's Press.

Barrett, W. S., ed. (1964). *Euripides, Hippolytos.* Oxford: Oxford University Press.

Barthes, Roland. (1974). *S/Z* (1970). Trans. R. Miller. New York: Hill and Wang.

————. (1986). *The Rustle of Language* (1984). Trans. R. Howard. New York: Hill and Wang.

Bassi, Karen. (1989). "The Actor as Actress in Euripides' *Alcestis.*" *Themes in Drama* 11: 19–30.

Bennett, Larry J., and William B. Tyrrell. (1990). "Sophocles' *Antigone* and Funeral Oratory." *American Journal of Philology* 111: 441–56.

Bergson, Lief. (1985). "Randbemerkungen zur Alkestis des Euripides." *Eranos* 83: 7–22.

Bernays, Jacob. (1880, 1978). *Zwei Abhandlungen über die aristotelische Theorie des Drama* (Berlin). Excerpted and translated as "Aristotle on the Effect of Tragedy," in Barnes, Scholfield, and Sorabji (1978) 154–65.

Betts, G. G. (1965). "The Silence of Alcestis." *Mnemosyne,* 4th series, 18: 181–82.

Beye, Charles Rowan. (1959). "Alcestis and Her Critics." *Greek, Roman and Byzantine Studies* 2: 111–27.

————. (1974). *Alcestis by Euripides. A Translation and Commentary.* Englewood Cliffs, N.J.: Prentice-Hall.

————. (1987). *Ancient Greek Literature and Society.* 2d ed. Ithaca: Cornell University Press.

Blaiklock, E. M. (1952). *The Male Characters of Euripides.* Wellington: New Zealand University Press.

Blomqvist, Jerker. (1982). "Human and Divine Action in Euripides' *Hippolytus.*" *Hermes* 110: 398–414.

Bömer, Franz. (1976). *P. Ovidius Naso, Metamorphosen, Buch VI–VII.* Heidelberg: Winter.

Bradley, Edward M. (1980). "Admetus and the Triumph of Failure in Euripides' *Alcestis.*" *Ramus* 9: 112–27.

Brillante, Carlo. (1988). "Sul prologo dell'*Ecuba* di Euripide." *Rivista di Filologia e Istruzione Classica* 116: 429–47.

Brown, Peter. (1981). *The Lives of the Saints.* Chicago: University of Chicago Press.

Burian, Peter. (1974). "Suppliant and Savior: Oedipus at Colonus." *Phoenix* 28: 408–29.

——, ed. (1985). *Directions in Euripidean Criticism: A Collection of Essays*. Durham, N.C.: Duke University Press.

Burkert, Walter. (1979). *Structure and History in Greek Mythology*. Berkeley and Los Angeles: University of California Press.

——. (1981). "Glaube und Verhalten: Zeichengestalt und Wirkungsmacht von Opferritualen." In *Entretiens sur l'antiquité classique*. Vol. 27, *Le sacrifice dans l'Antiquité*, 91–125. Vandoeuvres-Geneva: Fondation Hardt.

——. (1983). *Homo Necans: The Anthropology of Ancient Greek Sacrificial Ritual and Myth* (1972). Trans. P. Bing. Berkeley and Los Angeles: University of California Press.

——. (1985). *Greek Religion* (1977). Trans. J. Raffan. Cambridge, Mass.: Harvard University Press.

——. (1987). *Ancient Mystery Cults*. Cambridge, Mass.: Harvard University Press.

Burnett, Anne Pippin. (1965). "The Virtues of Admetus." *Classical Philology* 60: 240–55. Reprinted in E. Segal (1983) 254–71, which is cited here.

——. (1971). *Catastrophe Survived: Euripides' Plays of Mixed Reversal*. Oxford: Oxford University Press.

——. (1983). *Three Archaic Poets: Archilochus, Alcaeus, Sappho*. Cambridge, Mass.: Harvard University Press.

Buxton, R. G. A. (1987). "Euripides' *Alkestis*: Five Aspects of an Interpretation." In Lyn Rodley, ed., *Papers Given at a Colloquium on Greek Drama in Honour of R. P. Winnington-Ingram*. Supplementary Paper no. 15, 17–31. London: Society for the Promotion of Hellenic Studies.

Calame, Claude. (1977). *Les choeurs de jeunes filles en Grèce archaïque*. 2 vols. Rome: Ateneo e Bizarri.

Caldwell, Richard. (1973–74). "Tragedy Romanticized: The *Iphigeneia Taurica*." *Classical Journal* 70: 23–40.

Cameron, Averil, and Amélie Kuhrt, eds. (1983). *Images of Women in Antiquity*. Detroit: Wayne State University Press.

Carey, Christopher. (1988). " 'Philanthropy' in Aristotle's Poetics." *Eranos* 86: 131–39.

Carson, Ann. (1986). *Eros the Bittersweet*. Princeton: Princeton University Press.

Carter, L. B. (1986). *The Unquiet Athenian*. Oxford: Clarendon Press.

Cerri, Giovanni. (1979). *Legislazione orale e tragedia greca*. Naples: Liguori Editore.

Chapouthier, Fernand. (1954). *Euripide et l'accueil du divin. Entretiens sur l'antiquité classique*. Vol. 1, *La notion du divin depuis Homère jusqu'à Platon*, 205–37. Vandoeuvres-Geneva: Fondation Hardt.

Bibliography

Citti, Vittorio. (1978). *Tragedia e la lotta di classe in Grecia.* Naples: Liguori Editore.

Clairmont, Christoph W. (1983). *Patrios Nomos.* Oxford: Oxford University Press.

Classen, C. J., ed. (1976). *Sophistik,* vol. 187 of *Wege der Forschung.* Darmstadt: Wissenschaftliche Buchgesellschaft.

Cleary, John J., ed. (1987). *Proceedings of the Boston Area Colloquium in Ancient Philosophy,* vol. 2. Lanham, Md.: University Press of America.

Cole, Susan L. (1985). *The Absent One.* University Park: Pennsylvania State University Press.

Conacher, Desmond J. (1961). "Euripides' *Hecuba.*" *American Journal of Philology* 82: 1–26.

——. (1967). *Euripidean Drama: Myth, Theme and Structure.* Toronto: Toronto University Press.

——. (1981). "Rhetoric and Relevance in Euripidean Drama." *American Journal of Philology* 102: 3–25.

——. (1984). "Structural Aspects of Euripides' *Alcestis.*" In Douglas E. Gerber, ed., *Greek Poetry and Philosophy: Studies in Honour of Leonard Woodbury,* 73–81. Chico, Calif.: Scholars Press.

——. (1987). *Aeschylus' Oresteia: A Literary Commentary.* Toronto: University of Toronto Press.

Cook, Albert. (1971). *Enactment: Greek Tragedy.* Chicago: Swallow Press.

Crane, Gregory. (1992). "Power, Prestige, and the Corcyrean Affair in Thucydides 1." *Classical Antiquity* 11: 1–27.

Daitz, S. G., ed. (1973). *Euripides, Hecuba.* Leipzig: Teubner.

Dale, A. M., ed. (1954). *Euripides' Alcestis.* Oxford: Clarendon Press.

Danforth, Loring. (1982). *The Death Rituals of Rural Greece.* Princeton: Princeton University Press.

De Jong, Irene. (1991). *Narrative in Drama: The Euripidean Messenger-Speech. Mnemosyne,* Supplement 116. Leiden: Brill.

Derrida, Jacques. (1972). "La pharmacie de Platon." In *La dissémination,* 71–196. Paris: Seuil.

Detienne, Marcel. (1988). "Les Danaïdes entre elles ou la violence fondatrice du mariage." *Arethusa* 21: 159–75.

Detienne, Marcel, and Jean-Pierre Vernant. (1974). *Les ruses de l'intelligence: La métis des Grecs.* Paris: Flammarion. English translation: *Cunning Intelligence in Greek Culture and Society.* Trans. J. Lloyd. Chicago: University of Chicago Press, 1991.

Detienne, Marcel, Jean-Pierre Vernant, et al. (1979). *La cuisine du sacrifice en pays grec.* Paris: Flammarion. English translation: *The Cuisine of Sacrifice among the Greeks.* Trans. P. Wissig. Chicago: University of Chicago Press, 1989.

Devereux, George. (1973). "The Self-Blinding of Oidipous in Sophokles: *Oidipous Tyrannos.*" *Journal of Hellenic Studies* 93: 36–49.

——. (1985). *The Character of the Euripidean Hippolytos. An Ethno-psychoanalytical Study.* Chico, Calif.: Scholars Press.

Diano, Carlo A. (1968). "La catarsi tragica." In *Sagezza e poetiche degli antichi*, 215–69. Vicenza: Pozza.

——. (1969) = (1976). "L'Alcesti di Euripide" (1969). In Oddone Longo, ed., *Euripide: Letture critiche*, 70–78. Milan: Mursia.

——. (1973) = (1976). "Le virtù cardinali nell' 'Ippolito' di Euripide" (1973). In Longo (1976) 93–109.

Di Benedetto, Vincenzo. (1971). *Euripide: teatro e società.* Turin: Einaudi.

Diels, Hermann, and Walther Kranz. (1950–52). *Fragmente der Vorsokratiker.* 5th ed., 3 vols. Zurich and Berlin: Weidmann.

Diggle, James, ed. (1970). *Euripides, Phaethon.* Cambridge: Cambridge University Press.

——. (1984). *Euripidis Fabulae*, vol. 1. Oxford Classical Texts. Oxford: Oxford University Press.

Dimock, George. (1977). "Euripides' *Hippolytus*, or Virtue Rewarded." *Yale Classical Studies* 25: 239–58.

Dover, Kenneth J., ed. (1968). *Aristophanes, Clouds.* Oxford: Oxford University Press.

——. (1972). *Aristophanic Comedy.* Berkeley and Los Angeles: University of California Press.

DuBois, Page. (1982). *Centaurs and Amazons.* Ann Arbor: University of Michigan Press.

Dyson, M. (1988). "Alcestis' Children and the Character of Admetus." *Journal of Hellenic Studies* 108: 13–23.

Easterling, Patricia E., ed. (1982). *Sophocles, Trachiniae.* Cambridge: Cambridge University Press.

——. (1987). "Women in Tragic Space." *Bulletin of the Institute of Classical Studies, London* 34: 15–26.

——. (1988). "Tragedy and Ritual 'Cry "Woe, woe," but May the Good Prevail.' " *Metis* 3: 87–109.

——. (1991). "Euripides in the Theatre." *Pallas* 37: 49–59.

Eliade, Mircea. (1981). *Autobiography.* Vol. 1, 1907–37. Trans. M. L. Ricketts. San Francisco: Harper and Row.

Else, G. F. (1965). *The Origin and Early Form of Greek Tragedy.* Cambridge, Mass.: Harvard University Press.

——. (1967). *Aristotle's Poetics: The Argument.* Cambridge, Mass.: Harvard University Press.

Erbse, Hartmut. (1984). *Studien zum Prolog der euripideischen Tragödie.* Berlin: De Gruyter.

Bibliography

Finley, Moses. (1965). *The World of Odysseus*. New York: Viking Press.

Fitzgerald, G. J. (1973). "Misconception, Hypocrisy and the Structure of Euripides' *Hippolytus*." *Ramus* 2: 20–44.

Foley, Helene. (1981a). "The Conception of Women in Athenian Drama." In Foley (1981b) 127–68.

——, ed. (1981b). *Reflexions of Women in Antiquity*. New York: Gordon and Breach.

——. (1982). "The 'Female Intruder' Reconsidered: Women in Aristophanes' *Lysistrata* and *Ecclesiazusae*." *Classical Philology* 77: 1–21.

——. (1985). *Ritual Irony: Poetry and Sacrifice in Euripides*. Ithaca: Cornell University Press.

Fontenrose, Joseph. (1981). *Orion: The Myth of the Hunter and Huntress*. University of California Classical Studies 23. Berkeley and Los Angeles: University of California Press.

Forbes Irving, P. M. G. (1990). *Metamorphosis in Greek Myth*. Oxford: Clarendon Press.

Ford, Andrew. (1992). *Homer: The Poetry of the Past*. Ithaca: Cornell University Press.

Foucault, Michel. (1985). *The Use of Pleasure* (orig. publ. 1984), vol. 2 of *The History of Sexuality*. Trans. R. Hurley. New York: Pantheon Books.

Foxhall, Lin. (1989). "Household, Gender and Property in Classical Athens." *Classical Quarterly*, new series, 39: 22–44.

Franco, Carlo. (1984). "Una statua per Admeto." *Materiali e Discussioni per l'Analisi dei Testi Classici* 13: 131–36.

Fränkel, Hermann. (1946). "Man's 'Ephemeros' Nature According to Pindar and Others." *Transactions of the American Philological Association* 77: 131–45.

Freud, Sigmund. (1917). "Mourning and Melancholia." In *The Standard Edition of the Complete Psychological Works of Sigmund Freud*, vol. 14, 243–58. Trans. James Strachey. London: Hogarth Press, 1957.

Frischer, Bernard. (1970). "*Concordia Discors* and Characterization in Euripides' *Hippolytus*." *Greek, Roman and Byzantine Studies* 11: 85–100.

Garland, Robert. (1985). *The Greek Way of Death*. Ithaca: Cornell University Press.

Garner, Richard K. (1988). "Death and Victory in Euripides' *Alcestis*." *Classical Antiquity* 7: 58–71.

——. (1990). *From Homer to Tragedy: The Art of Allusion in Greek Poetry*. London and New York: Routledge.

Garzya, Antonio. (1955). *Euripide, Ecuba*. Rome: Società editrice Dante Alighieri.

Gellie, G. H. (1980). "Hecuba and Tragedy." *Antichthon* 14: 30–44.

Gentili, Bruno. (1988). *Poetry and Its Public in Ancient Greece and Rome*. Trans. A. T. Cole. Baltimore: Johns Hopkins University Press.

Gernet, Louis. (1968). "La notion mythique de la valeur en Grèce." In *Anthropologie de la Grèce antique*, 93–137. Paris: Maspero.

Girard, René. (1979). *Violence and the Sacred* (1972). Trans. P. Gregory. Baltimore: Johns Hopkins University Press.

Glenn, Justin. (1975–76). "The Phantasies of Phaedra: A Psychoanalytic Reading." *Classical World* 69: 432–45.

Goff, Barbara. (1990). *The Noose of Words*. Cambridge: Cambridge University Press.

Golden, Leon. (1992). *Aristotle on Tragic and Comic Mimesis*. American Philological Association, American Classical Studies 29. Atlanta: Scholars Press.

Golden, Leon, and O. B. Hardison, Jr. (1981). *Aristotle's Poetics: Translation and Commentary for Students of Literature* (1968). Tallahassee: University Presses of Florida.

Goldhill, Simon. (1984). *Language, Sexuality, Narrative in the Oresteia*. Cambridge: Cambridge University Press.

——. (1986). *Reading Greek Tragedy*. Cambridge: Cambridge University Press.

——. (1990). "The Great Dionysia and Civic Ideology." In J. J. Winkler and F. I. Zeitlin, eds., *Nothing to Do with Dionysus*, 97–129. Princeton: Princeton University Press.

Gould, John. (1973). "*Hiketeia*." *Journal of Hellenic Studies* 73: 74–103.

——. (1980). "Law, Custom and Myth: Aspects of the Social Position of Women in Classical Athens." *Journal of Hellenic Studies* 100: 37–59.

Gravel, P., and T. J. Reiss, eds. (1983). *Tragique et la tragédie dans la tradition occidentale*, 25–41. Montreal: Déterminations.

Gregory, Justina. (1979). "Euripides' Alcestis." *Hermes* 107: 259–70.

——. (1991). *Euripides and the Instruction of the Athenians*. Ann Arbor: University of Michigan Press.

Griffith, R. D. (1988). "Disrobing in the *Oresteia*." *Classical Quarterly* 38: 552–54.

Grillone, Antonino. (1974–75). "Vita e realtà quotidiana nell' *Alcesti* di Euripide." *Atti dell' Accademia di Scienze Lettere e Arti di Palermo*, 4th series, 34: 39–61.

Grube, G. M. A. (1941). *The Drama of Euripides*. London: Methuen.

Guthrie, W. K. C. (1969). *A History of Greek Philosophy*, vol. 3. Cambridge: Cambridge University Press.

Hall, Edith. (1989). *Inventing the Barbarian: Greek Self-Definition Through Tragedy*. Oxford: Oxford University Press.

Halleran, Michael R. (1988). "Text and Ceremony at the Close of Euripides' *Alkestis*." *Eranos* 86: 123–29.

——. (1991). "*Gamos* and Destruction in Euripides' Hippolytus." *Transactions of the American Philological Association* 121: 109–21.

Bibliography   Halliwell, Stephen. (1986). *Aristotle's Poetics*. Chapel Hill: University of North
             Carolina Press.

Hartog, François. (1988). *The Mirror of Herodotus* (1980). Trans. J. Lloyd.
             Berkeley and Los Angeles: University of California Press.

Havelock, Eric A. (1982). "The Oral Composition of Greek Drama" (1980). In
             his *The Literate Revolution*, 261–313. Princeton: Princeton University Press.

Heath, Malcolm. (1987). " 'Jure Principem Locum Tenet:' Euripides' *Hecu-
             ba*." *Bulletin of the Institute of Classical Studies, London* 34: 40–68.

Heinimann, Felix. (1945). *Nomos und Physis*. Basel: Reinhardt.

Henderson, Jeffrey, ed. (1987). *Aristophanes, Lysistrata*. Oxford: Oxford Uni-
             versity Press.

Henrichs, Albert. (1981). "Human Sacrifice in Greek Religion." In *Entretiens
             sur l'antiquité classique*. Vol. 27, *Le sacrifice dans l'Antiquité*, 195–242. Van-
             doeuvres-Geneva: Fondation Hardt.

——. (Forthcoming). " 'Why Should I Dance?': Ritual Self-Referentiality in
             the Choral Odes of Greek Tragedy." *Arion*.

Herington, John. (1985). *Poetry into Drama*. Sather Classical Lectures, 49.
             Berkeley and Los Angeles: University of California Press.

Higgonet, Margaret. (1986). "Speaking Silences: Women's Suicide." In Susan
             Rubin Suleiman, *The Female Body in Western Culture*, 68–83. Cambridge,
             Mass.: Harvard University Press.

Hourmouziades, Nicolaos C. (1965). *Production and Imagination in Euripides*.
             Athens: Greek Society for Humanistic Studies. 2d series, vol. 5.

Humphreys, S. C. (1983). *The Family, Women, and Death: Comparative Studies*.
             London: Routledge and Kegan Paul.

Janko, Richard. (1992). "From Catharsis to the Aristotelian Mean." In Rorty
             (1992a) 431–58.

Jebb, Richard C. (1893). *Sophocles: The Plays and Fragments*. Part 1, *The Oedipus
             Tyrannus*. 3d ed. Cambridge: Cambridge University Press.

Jenkins, I. D. (1985). "The Ambiguity of Greek Textiles." *Arethusa* 18: 109–
             32.

Just, Roger. (1989). *Women in Athenian Law and Life*. London and New York:
             Routledge.

Kamerbeek, J. C. (1960). "Mythe et réalité dans l'oeuvre d'Euripide." In
             Entretiens sur l'antiquité classique. Vol. 6, *Euripide*, 3–25. Vandoeuvres–
             Geneva: Fondation Hardt.

Keesey, Donald. (1978–79). "On Some Recent Interpretations of Catharsis."
             Classical World 72: 193–205.

Kennedy, George, ed. (1989). *Cambridge History of Literary Criticism*, vol. 1.
             Cambridge: Cambridge University Press.

Kerferd, G. B. (1981). *The Sophistic Movement*. Cambridge: Cambridge Univer-
             sity Press.

King, Helen. (1983). "Bound to Bleed: Artemis and Greek Women." In Cameron and Kuhrt (1983) 109–27.

King, Katherine Callen. (1985). "The Politics of Imitation: Euripides' *Hekabe* and the Homeric Achilles." *Arethusa* 18: 47–66.

———. (1987). *Achilles.* Berkeley and Los Angeles: University of California Press.

Kirkwood, G. M. (1947). "Hecuba and Nomos." *Transactions of the American Philological Association* 78: 61–68.

Knox, Bernard M. W. (1952). "The *Hippolytus* of Euripides." *Yale Classical Studies* 13: 3–31 = Knox (1979) 205–30.

———. (1957). *Oedipus at Thebes.* New Haven: Yale University Press.

———. (1979). *Word and Action: Essays on the Ancient Theatre.* Baltimore: Johns Hopkins University Press.

Kovacs, David. (1980). "Shame, Pleasure, and Honor in Phaedra's Great Speech." *American Journal of Philology* 101: 287–303.

———. (1987). *The Heroic Muse: Studies in the Hippolytus and Hecuba of Euripides.* Baltimore: Johns Hopkins University Press.

Kraus, Walther. (1986). "Bemerkungen zum Text und Sinn in den 'Trachinierinnin.'" *Wiener Studien* 99: 87–108.

Kubler-Ross, Elisabeth. (1970). *On Death and Dying.* New York: Macmillan.

Kubo, M. (1967). "The Norm of Myth: Euripides' Electra." *Harvard Studies in Classical Philology* 71: 15–31.

Kullmann, Wolfgang. (1986). "Euripides' Verhältnis zur Philosophie." In H. Koskenniemi, S. Jäkel, and V. Pyykkö, eds., *Literatur und Philosophie in der Antike,* vol. 174: 35–49. *Annales Universitatis Turkuensis,* series B. Turku, Finland.

———. (1987). "Deutung und Bedeutung der Götter bei Euripides." *Innsbrucker Beiträge zur Kulturwissenschaft* 5: 7–22.

Kurke, Leslie. (1991). *The Traffic in Praise: Pindar and the Poetics of Social Economy.* Ithaca: Cornell University Press.

———. (1992). "The Politics of *habrosynê* in Archaic Greece." *Classical Antiquity* 11: 91–120.

Kurtz, Donna C., and John Boardman. (1971). *Greek Burial Customs.* Ithaca: Cornell University Press.

Lacey, W. K. (1968). *The Family in Classical Greece.* Ithaca: Cornell University Press.

Lattimore, Richmond. (1942). *Themes in Greek and Latin Epitaphs.* Illinois Studies in Language and Literature, vol. 28, nos. 1–2. Urbana: University of Illinois Press.

Lawall, Gilbert, and Sarah Lawall, eds. (1986). *Euripides, Hippolytus.* Bristol: Bristol Classical Press.

Lear, Jonathan. (1992). "Katharsis." In Rorty (1992a) 315–40.

Bibliography

Lebeck, Ann. (1971). *The Oresteia: A Study in Language and Structure.* Cambridge, Mass.: Harvard University Press.

Lefkowitz, Mary R. (1986). *Women in Greek Myth.* London: Duckworth.

———. (1989). " 'Impiety' and 'Atheism' in Euripides' Dramas." *Classical Quarterly* 39: 70–82.

Lesky, Albin. (1925). *Alkestis, der Mythus und das Drama.* Sitzungsbericht der Akademie der Wissenchaften zu Wien, Phil.-Hist. Klasse, vol. 203, Heft 2. Vienna.

———. (1972). *Die tragische Dichtung der Hellenen.* 3d ed. Göttingen: Vandenhoeck and Ruprecht.

———. (1983). *Greek Tragic Poetry.* Trans. M. Dillon. New Haven: Yale University Press.

Ley, Graham, and Michael Ewans. (1985). "The Orchestra as Acting Area in Greek Tragedy." *Ramus* 14: 75–84.

Lissarague, François, and Alain Schnapp. (1981). "Imageries des Grecs ou Grèce des imagiers." *Le temps de la Réflexion* 2: 275–97.

Lloyd, Michael. (1985). "Euripides' *Alcestis.*" *Greece and Rome* 32: 119–31.

Lloyd-Jones, Hugh. (1985). "Pindar and the Afterlife." In *Entretiens sur l'antiquité classique.* Vol. 31, *Pindare,* 245–83. Vandoeuvres-Geneva: Fondation Hardt.

Lloyd-Jones, Hugh, and Nigel Wilson. (1990). *Sophoclis Fabulae.* Oxford Classical Texts. Oxford: Oxford University Press.

Long, A. A., ed. (1971). *Problems in Stoicism.* London: Athlone Press.

Long, Timothy. (1986). *Barbarians in Greek Comedy.* Carbondale: Southern Illinois University Press.

Longo, Oddone, ed. (1976). *Euripide. Letture critiche.* Milan: Mursia.

———. (1985). "Ippolito e Fedra fra parola e silenzio." In R. Uglione, ed., *Atti delle giornate di studio su Fedra,* 79–96. Turin: Associazione italiana di cultura classica.

Loraux, Nicole. (1978a). "La gloire et la mort d'une femme." *Sorcières* 18: 51–57.

———. (1978b). "Sur la race des femmes et quelques-unes de ses tribus." *Arethusa* 11: 43–87.

———. (1981) = (1989). "Le lit, la guerre." *L'Homme* 21 (1981) 37–67 = Loraux (1989) 29–53.

———. (1982). "Mourir devant Troie, Tomber pour Athènes." In J.-P. Vernant and G. Gnoli, *La mort, les morts dans les sociétés anciennes,* 27–43. Cambridge and Paris: Cambridge University Press.

———. (1982) = (1989). "Héraklès: le surmâle et le féminin." *Revue Française de Psychanalyse* 26 (1982) 679–99 = Loraux (1989) 142–70.

———. (1985). *Façons tragiques de tuer une femme.* Paris: Hachette.

——. (1986). *The Invention of Athens*. Trans. A. Sheridan. Cambridge, Mass.: Harvard University Press.

——. (1989). *Les expériences de Tirésias: Le féminin et l'homme grec.* Paris: Gallimard.

——. (1990). *Les mères en deuil*. Paris: Seuil.

Loraux, Nicole, and Laurence Kahn-Lyotard. (1981). "Mort. Les mythes grecs." In Yves Bonnefoy, ed., *Dictionnaire des Mythologies*, 117–24. Paris: Flammarion.

Luschnig, C. A. E. (1980). "Men and Gods in Euripides' Hippolytus." *Ramus* 9: 89–100.

——. (1983). "The Value of Ignorance in the *Hippolytus*." *American Journal of Philology* 104: 115–23.

——. (1988a). *Time Holds the Mirror: A Study of Knowledge in Euripides' "Hippolytus."* Mnemosyne Supplement, vol. 102. Leiden: Brill.

——. (1988b). *Tragic Aporia: A Study of Euripides'* Iphigeneia at Aulis. Ramus Monographs 3. Berwick, Victoria, Australia: Aureal Publications.

Lynn-George, Michael. (1988). *Epos: Word, Narrative and the Iliad*. Houndmills, Basingstoke: Macmillan.

Manetti, Giovanni. (1987). *Le teorie del segno nell' antichità classica*. Milan: Bompiani.

Méautis, G. (1944). *Mythes inconnus de la Grèce antique*. Paris: A. Michel.

Meier, Christian. (1990). *The Greek Discovery of Politics* (1980). Trans. D. McLintock. Cambridge, Mass.: Harvard University Press.

Méridier, Louis. (1956). *Euripide*, vol. 2. 2d ed. Paris: Les Belles Lettres.

Meridor, Ra'anana. (1978). "Hecuba's Revenge." *American Journal of Philology* 99: 28–35.

Michelini, Ann Norris. (1987). *Euripides and the Tragic Tradition*. Madison: University of Wisconsin Press.

Moles, John. (1984). "*Philanthropia* in the *Poetics*." *Phoenix* 38: 325–35.

Monsacré, Hélène. (1984). *Les larmes d'Achille*. Paris: Albin Michel.

Morris, Ian. (1989). "Attitudes Toward Death in Archaic Greece." *Classical Antiquity* 8: 296–320.

Murray, Gilbert. (1902). *Euripidis Fabulae*. Oxford: Oxford University Press.

——. (1946). *Euripides and His Age* (1913). 2nd ed. New York: Oxford University Press.

Nagler, Michael N. (1974). *Spontaneity and Tradition: A Study in the Oral Art of Homer*. Berkeley and Los Angeles: University of California Press.

Nagy, Gregory. (1973). "Phaethon, Sappho's Phaon, and the White Rock of Leukas." *Harvard Studies in Classical Philology* 77: 137–77.

——. (1989). "Early Greek Views of Poets and Poetry." In Kennedy (1989) 1–77.

———. (1990). *Pindar's Homer: The Lyric Possession of an Epic Past.* Baltimore: Johns Hopkins University Press.

Nancy, Claire. (1981). "Φάρμακον Σωτηρίας: Le mécanisme du sacrifice humain chez Euripide." In *Théâtre et spectacles de l'antiquité*, 17–30. Actes du colloque de Strasbourg, 7–11 novembre, Université des Sciences Humaines de Strasbourg.

Neumann, E. (1954). *The Origins and History of Consciousness.* Trans. R. F. C. Hull. Princeton: Princeton University Press.

Newton, Rick M. (1980). "*Hippolytus* and the Dating of *Oedipus Tyrannus*." *Greek, Roman and Byzantine Studies* 21: 5–22.

Nielsen, Rosemary M. (1976). "*Alcestis*: A Paradox in Dying." *Ramus* 5: 92–102.

Nussbaum, Martha C. (1986). *The Fragility of Goodness.* Cambridge: Cambridge University Press.

O'Connor-Visser, E. A. M. E. (1987). *Aspects of Human Sacrifice in the Tragedies of Euripides.* Amsterdam: B. R. Grüner.

Padel, Ruth. (1974). "Imagery of the Elsewhere: Two Choral Odes of Euripides." *Classical Quarterly* 24: 227–41.

———. (1983). "Women: Model for Possession by Greek Daemons." In Cameron and Kuhrt (1983) 3–19.

Paduano, Guido. (1984). "Ippolito: la rivelazione dell' eros." *Materiali e Discussioni per l'Analisi dei Testi Classici* 13: 45–66.

Parker, Robert. (1983). *Miasma: Pollution and Purification in Early Greek Religion.* Oxford: Clarendon Press.

Parry, Hugh. (1966). "The Second Stasimon of Euripides' *Hippolytus* (732–775)." *Transactions of the American Philological Association* 97: 317–26.

———. (1978). *The Lyric Poems of Greek Tragedy.* Toronto and Sarasota: Samuel Stevens.

Patin, M. (1879). *Etudes sur les tragiques grecs: Euripide.* 5th ed. 2 vols. Paris: Hachette.

Perdicoyianni, Hélène. (1992). *Commentaire sur les Troyennes d'Euripide.* Athens: Basilopoulos.

Petersmann, Gerhard. (1977). "Die Rolle der Polyxena in den Troerinnen des Euripides." *Rheinisches Museum für Philologie* 120: 146–58.

Pickard-Cambridge, Arthur. (1968). *The Dramatic Festivals of Athens.* 2d ed. Revised by J. Gould and D. M. Lewis. Oxford: Oxford University Press.

Pigeaud, Jackie. (1976). "Euripide et la connaissance de soi: Quelques reflexions sur *Hippolyte* 83 à 82 et 373 à 430." *Les Etudes Classiques* 44: 3–24.

———. (1981). *La maladie de l'âme.* Paris: Les Belles Lettres.

Pohlenz, Max. (1954). *Die griechische Tragödie.* 2 vols. Göttingen: Vandenhoeck and Ruprecht.

Poole, Adrian. (1987). *Tragedy: Shakespeare and the Greek Example*. Oxford: Blackwell's.

Porson, Ricardus, ed. (1847). *Euripidis Hecuba*. London.

Prier, R. A. (1978). "Sêma and the Symbolic Nature of Pre-Socratic Thought." *Quaderni Urbinati di Cultura Classica* 29: 91–101.

Pucci, Pietro. (1977). "Euripides: The Monument and the Sacrifice." *Arethusa* 10: 165–95.

———. (1980). *The Violence of Pity in Euripides' Medea*. Ithaca: Cornell University Press.

Rabinowitz, Nancy Sorkin. (1986). "Aphrodite and the Audience: Engendering the Reader." *Arethusa* 19: 171–85.

———. (1987a). "Female Speech and Female Sexuality: Euripides' *Hippolytos* as Model." *Helios* 13: 127–40.

———. (1987b). "Male Friends and Female Guests." Paper presented at Classical Association of Atlantic States conference, Princeton, N.J.

Ramnoux, Clémence. (1986). *La nuit et les enfants de la nuit*. 2d ed. Paris: Flammarion.

Rankin, A. V. (1974). "Euripides' Hippolytos: A Psychopathological Hero." *Arethusa* 7: 71–94.

Rankin, H. D. (1983). *Sophists, Socratics and Cynics*. Totowa, N.J.: Barnes and Noble Books.

Reckford, Kenneth J. (1972). "Phaethon, Hippolytus and Aphrodite." *Transactions of the American Philological Association* 103: 405–32.

———. (1985). "Concepts of Demoralization in the *Hecuba*." In Burian (1985) 112–28.

Rehm, Rush. (1989). "*Medea* and the λόγος of the Heroic." *Eranos* 87: 97–115.

Reinhardt, Karl. (1979). *Sophocles*. Trans. H. Harvey and D. Harvey. Oxford: Oxford University Press.

Riemer, Peter. (1989). *Die Alkestis des Euripides*. Beiträge zur klassische Philologie, vol. 195. Frankfurt am Main: Athenäum Verlag.

Rivier, André. (1975). *Essai sur le tragique d'Euripide*. 2d ed. Paris: Boccard.

Robert, Carl. (1921). *Die griechische Heldensage*. In L. Preller and Carl Robert, *Griechische Mythologie*. 4th ed., vol. 2, pt. 2. Berlin: Weidmann.

Roberts, Deborah H. (1988). "Sophoclean Endings: Another Story." *Arethusa* 21: 177–96.

Rohdich, Hermann. (1968). *Die Euripideische Tragödie*. Heidelberg: Winter.

Rorty, Amélie Oksenberg, ed. (1992a). *Essays on Aristotle's Poetics*. Princeton: Princeton University Press.

———. (1992b). "The Psychology of Aristotelian Tragedy." In Rorty (1992a) 1–22.

Rösler, Wolfgang. (1984). "Die frühe griechische Lyrik und ihre Interpretation." *Poetica* 16: 179–205.

Bibliography

Rosellini, Michèle. (1979). "*Lysistrata*: Une mise en scène de la féminité." *Cahiers de Fontenay* 17: 11–32.

Rosellini, Michèle, and Suzanne Saïd. (1978). "Usage des femmes et autres 'nomoi' chez les 'sauvages' d'Hérodote: Essai de lecture structurale." *Annali della Scuola Normale Superiore di Pisa*, Classe di Lettere e Filosofia, 3d series, 8: 949–1005.

Rosenmeyer, Thomas G. (1963). "Alcestis: Character and Death." In *The Masks of Tragedy*, 201–48. Austin: University of Texas Press.

Saïd, Suzanne. (1979). "*L'assemblée des Femmes*: Les femmes, l'économie et la politique." *Cahiers de Fontenay* 17: 33–69.

Sale, William. (1977). *Existentialism and Euripides: Sickness, Tragedy and Divinity in the Medea, the Hippolytus and the Bacchae*. Ramus Monographs. Berwick, Victoria, Australia: Aureal Publications.

Schadewaldt, Wolfgang. (1966). *Von Homers Welt und Werk*. 4th ed. Stuttgart: Koehler.

Schaps, David. (1982). "The Women of Greece in Wartime." *Classical Philology* 75: 193–213.

Schlesier, Renate. (1985). "Der Stachel der Götter: Zum Problem des Wahnsinns in der Euripideischen Tragödie." *Poetica* 17: 1–45.

——. (1988). "Die Bakchen des Hades: Dionysische Aspekte von Euripides' *Hekabe*." *Metis* 3: 111–35.

——. (1993). "Mixtures of Masks: Maenads as Tragic Models." In Thomas H. Carpenter and Christopher A. Faraone, eds., *Masks of Dionysus*. Ithaca: Cornell University Press.

Schmid, Wilhelm. (1940). In W. Schmid and Otto Stählin, eds., *Geschichte der griechischen Literatur*, vol. 1, pt. 3. Munich: Beck.

Seaford, Richard. (1986). "Wedding Ritual and Textual Criticism in Sophocles' Women of Trachis." *Hermes* 114: 50–59.

——. (1987). "The Tragic Wedding." *Journal of Hellenic Studies* 107: 106–30.

——. (1988). "The Eleventh Ode of Bacchylides." *Journal of Hellenic Studies* 108: 118–36.

——. (1989). "Homeric and Tragic Sacrifice." *Transactions of the American Philological Association* 119: 87–95.

——. (1990). "The Imprisonment of Women in Greek Tragedy." *Journal of Hellenic Studies* 110: 76–90.

Searle, John R. (1969). *Speech Acts*. Cambridge: Cambridge University Press.

Seeck, Gustav Adolf. (1985). *Unaristotelische Untersuchungen zu Euripides: ein motivanalytischer Kommentar zur "Alkestis."* Heidelberg: Winter.

Segal, Charles. (1962). "Gorgias and the Psychology of the Logos." *Harvard Studies in Classical Philology* 66: 99–155.

——. (1965). "The Tragedy of the *Hippolytus*: The Waters of Ocean and the

Untouched Meadow." *Harvard Studies in Classical Philology* 70: 117–69 =
Segal (1986a) 165–221.

———. (1970a). "Hippolytus 'The Great.' " *L'Antiquité Classique* 39: 519–21.

———. (1970b). "The Order of Lines in *Hippolytus* 1452–6." *Greek, Roman and Byzantine Studies* 11: 101–7.

———. (1970c). "Shame and Purity in Euripides' Hippolytus." *Hermes* 98: 278–299. In French, with bibliographical addendum, in Segal (1987) 183–220.

———. (1971). "The Two Worlds of Euripides' Helen." *Transactions of the American Philological Association* 102: 553–614 = Segal (1986a) 222–67.

———. (1972) "Curse and Oath in Euripides' Hippolytus." *Ramus* 1: 156–80.

———. (1975). "Mariage et sacrifice dans les *Trachiniennes* de Sophocle." *L'Antiquité Classique* 44: 30–53.

———. (1977). "Sophocles' *Trachiniae*: Myth, Poetry, and Heroic Values." *Yale Classical Studies* 25: 99–158.

———. (1978–79). "Pentheus and Hippolytus on the Couch and on the Grid: Psychoanalytic and Structuralist Readings of Greek Tragedy." *Classical World* 72: 129–148 = Segal (1986a) 268–93.

———. (1979). "Solar Imagery and Tragic Heroism in Euripides' Hippolytus." In G. Bowersock, W. Burkert, and M. Putnam, eds., *Arktouros: Hellenic Studies Presented to B. M. W. Knox*, 151–61. Berlin and New York: De Gruyter.

———. (1980–81). "Visual Symbolism in Sophocles." *Classical World* 74: 124–42 = Segal (1986a) 113–36.

———. (1981a). "Griechische Tragödie und Gesellschaft." In *Propyläen Geschichte der Literatur*, vol. 1: 198–217. (Berlin, 1981). English version, "Greek Tragedy and Society," in Segal (1986a) 21–47.

———. (1981b). *Tragedy and Civilization: An Interpretation of Sophocles.* Martin Classical Lectures, vol. 26. Cambridge, Mass.: Harvard University Press.

———. (1982a). *Dionysiac Poetics and Euripides' Bacchae.* Princeton: Princeton University Press.

———. (1982b). "Tragédie, Oralité, Ecriture." *Poétique* 50: 131–54 = Segal (1987) 263–98.

———. (1983a). "Greek Myth as a Semiotic and Structural System and the Problem of Tragedy." *Arethusa* 16: 173–98 = Segal (1986a) 48–74.

———. (1983b). "*Logos* and *Mythos*: Language, Reality and Appearance in Greek Tragedy and Plato." In P. Gravel and T. J. Reiss, eds., *Tragique et la tragédie dans la tradition occidentale*, 25–41. Montreal: Déterminations.

———. (1984). "Greek Tragedy: Truth, Writing, and the Representation of the Self." In Harold J. Evjen, ed., *Mnemai: Classical Studies in Memory of Karl K. Hulley*, 41–67. Chico, Calif.: Scholars Press = Segal (1986a) 75–109.

———. (1985). "Tragedy, Corporeality, and the Texture of Language." *Classical World* 79: 7–23 = Segal (1986a) 337–58.

———. (1986a). *Interpreting Greek Tragedy: Myth, Poetry, Text.* Ithaca: Cornell University Press.

———. (1986b). *Language and Desire in Seneca's Phaedra.* Princeton: Princeton University Press.

———. (1986c). *Pindar's Mythmaking: The Fourth Pythian Ode.* Princeton: Princeton University Press.

———. (1987). *La musique du Sphinx. Poésie et structure dans la tragédie grecque.* Trans. C. Malamoud and M.-P. Gruenais. Paris: La Découverte.

———. (1989). *Orpheus: The Myth of the Poet.* Baltimore: Johns Hopkins University Press.

———. (1990). "Dionysus in the Golden Tablets from Pelinna." *Greek, Roman and Byzantine Studies* 31: 411–19.

———. (1992a). "Signs, Magic, and Letters in Euripides' *Hippolytus.*" In Ralph Hexter and Daniel Selden, eds., *Innovations of Antiquity,* 420–55. New York and London: Routledge. Reprinted, in part, as chapter 6 of this volume, with revisions.

———. (1992b). "Tragic Beginnings: Narration, Voice, and Authority in the Prologues of Greek Drama." *Yale Classical Studies* 29: 85–112.

———. (1992c). "Time, Oracles, and Marriage in the *Trachiniae.*" *Lexis* 9–10: 63–92.

———. (1993a). Review of Justina Gregory (1991). In *American Journal of Philology* 114: 163–66.

———. (1993b). *Sophocles' Oedipus Tyrannus: Tragic Heroism and the Limits of Knowledge.* New York: Twayne-Macmillan.

Segal, Erich, ed. (1968). *Euripides, A Collection of Critical Essays.* Englewood Cliffs, N.J.: Prentice-Hall.

———. (1983). *Oxford Readings in Greek Tragedy.* Oxford: Oxford University Press.

Seidensticker, Bernd. (1982). *Palintonos Harmonia: Studien zu komischen Elemente in der griechischen Tragödie. Hypomnemata,* vol. 72. Göttingen: Vandenhoeck and Ruprecht.

Shapiro, Alan. (1991). "The Iconography of Mourning in Athenian Art." *American Journal of Archaeology* 95: 629–56.

Shaw, Michael. (1975). "The Female Intruder: Women in Fifth-Century Drama." *Classical Philology* 70: 255–66.

Sikes, E. E. (1931). *The Greek View of Poetry.* London: Methuen.

Sinos, Dale. (1980). *Achilles, Patroklos and the Meaning of Philos.* Innsbrucker Beiträge zur Sprachwissenschaft, vol. 29. Innsbruck.

Sissa, Giulia. (1990). *Greek Virginity* (1987). Trans. A. Goldhammer. Cambridge, Mass.: Harvard University Press.

Slater, Philip E. (1968). *The Glory of Hera.* Boston: Beacon Press.

Smith, C. M. (1920, 1965). *Thucydides.* Loeb Classical Library. Cambridge, Mass.: Harvard University Press.

Smith, Wesley D. (1960a). "The Ironic Structure in *Alcestis.*" *Phoenix* 14: 127–45. Reprinted in Wilson (1968) 37–56, which is cited here.

——. (1960b). "Staging in the Central Scene of the *Hippolytus.*" *Transactions of the American Philological Association* 91: 162–73.

Smoot, J. J. (1976a). "Hippolytus as Narcissus: An Amplification." *Arethusa* 9: 37–51.

——. (1976b). "Literary Criticism on a Vase-Painting: A Clearer Picture of Euripides' Hippolytus." *Comparative Literature Studies* 13: 292–303.

Snell, Bruno. (1928). *Aischylos und das Handeln im Drama. Philologus*, Supplement 20, Heft 1. Leipzig: Dieterich.

——. (1953). *The Discovery of the Mind.* Trans. T. G. Rosenmeyer. Cambridge, Mass.: Harvard University Press.

Solmsen, Friedrich. (1975). *Intellectual Experiments of the Greek Enlightenment.* Princeton: Princeton University Press.

Sommerstein, Alan. (1988). "Notes on Euripides' *Hippolytos.*" *Bulletin of the Institute of Classical Studies, London* 23: 23–41.

Stanford, William Bedell. (1983). *Greek Tragedy and the Emotions.* London: Routledge and Kegan Paul.

Steidle, Wolf. (1966). "Zur Hekabe des Euripides." *Wiener Studien* 79: 133–42.

Stinton, T. C. W. (1975). "*Hamartia* in Aristotle and Greek Tragedy." *Classical Quarterly* 25: 221–54.

Striker, Gisela. (1987). "Origins of the Concept of Natural Law." In John J. Cleary, ed., *Proceedings of the Boston Area Colloquium in Ancient Philosophy,* vol. 2, 79–94. Lanham, Md.: University Press of America.

Strohm, Hans. (1957). *Euripides. Interpretationen zur dramatischen Form. Zetemata* 15. Munich: Beck.

Suleiman, Susan Rubin. (1986). *The Female Body in Western Culture.* Cambridge, Mass.: Harvard University Press.

Taplin, Oliver. (1978). *Greek Tragedy in Action.* Berkeley and Los Angeles: University of California Press.

——. (1986). "Fifth-Century Tragedy and Comedy: A Synkrisis." *Journal of Hellenic Studies* 106: 163–74.

Thury, Eva M. (1988). "Euripides' *Alcestis* and the Athenian Generation Gap." *Arethusa* 21: 197–214.

Turato, Fabio. (1974). "L'Ippolito di Euripide tra realtà e fuga." *Bolletino dell' Istituto di Filologia Greca* (Università di Padova) 1: 136–63.

——. (1976). "Seduzioni della parola e dramma dei segni nell' Ippolito di Euripide." *Bolletino dell' Istituto di Filologia Greca* (Università di Padova) 3: 159–83.

———. (1979). *La crisi della città e l'ideologia del selvaggio nell' Atene del V secolo a. C.* Rome: Ateneo e Bizarri.

Ugolini, Gherardo. (1987). "L'Edipo tragico sofocleo e il problema del conoscere." *Philologus* 131: 19–31.

Untersteiner, Mario. (1943–44). "Un nuovo frammento dell' 'Anonymus Iamblichi.'" In *Scritti Minori* (Brescia, 1971), 422–39. Reprinted in Classen (1976) 591–611, which is cited here.

Vegetti, M. (1983). "Forme del sapere nell' *'Edipo re.'*" In *Tra Edipo e Euclide*, 23–40. Milan: Il Saggiatore.

Vellacott, Philip. (1975). *Ironic Drama.* Cambridge: Cambridge University Press.

Vermeule, Emily. (1979). *Aspects of Death in Early Art and Poetry.* Berkeley and Los Angeles: University of California Press.

Vernant, Jean-Pierre. (1963) = (1985b). "Hestia-Hermes. Sur l'expression de l'espace et du mouvement chez les Grecs" (1963). In *Mythe et pensée chez les Grecs*, 155–201.

———. (1971) = (1985b). "Figuration de l'invisible et catégorie psychologique du double: le colossos" (1971). In *Mythe et pensée chez les Grecs*, 325–38.

———. (1974a) = (1990). "Le mythe prométhéen chez Hésiode." In *Mythe et société en Grèce ancienne* (1974), 177–94. English translation in *Myth and Society in Ancient Greece*, 183–201.

———. (1974b) = (1990). *Mythe et société en Grèce ancienne.* Paris: Maspero. English translation: *Myth and Society in Ancient Greece.* Trans. J. Lloyd. New York: Zone Books, 1990.

———. (1974c). "Paroles et signes muets." In J.-P. Vernant et al., *Divination et rationalité*, 9–25. Paris: Seuil.

———. (1985a). *La mort dans les yeux: Figures de l'Autre en Grèce ancienne.* Paris: Hachette.

———. (1985b). *Mythe et pensée chez les Grecs.* Nouvelle édition. Paris: La Découverte.

———. (1989). *L'individu, la mort, l'amour.* Paris: Gallimard.

Vernant, Jean-Pierre, and Pierre Vidal-Naquet. (1990). *Myth and Tragedy in Ancient Greece* (1972, 1986). Trans. J. Lloyd. New York: Zone Books.

Von Fritz, Kurt. (1962). "Euripides' Alkestis und ihre modernen Nachahmer und Kritiker." In *Antike und Moderne Tragödie*, 256–321. Berlin: De Gruyter.

Walker, Susan. (1983). "Women and Housing in Classical Greece: The Archaeological Evidence." In Cameron and Kuhrt (1983) 81–91.

Walsh, George B. (1984). *The Varieties of Enchantment: Early Greek Views of the Nature and Function of Poetry.* Chapel Hill: University of North Carolina Press.

Wankel, Hermann. (1983). "Alle Menschen müssen sterben: Variationen eines Topos der griechischen Literatur." *Hermes* 111: 129–54.

Watson, G. (1971). "Natural Law and Stoicism." In A. A. Long (1971) 216–38.

Whitman, Cedric H. (1974). *Euripides and the Full Circle of Myth.* Cambridge, Mass.: Harvard University Press.

Wilamowitz-Moellendorff, Ulrich von. (1883). "Phaethon." *Hermes* 18: 396–434.

Willink, C. W. (1968). "Some Problems of Text and Interpretation in the *Hippolytus.*" *Classical Quarterly*, new series, 18: 11–43.

Wilson, John R., ed. (1968). *Twentieth Century Interpretations of Euripides' Alcestis.* Englewood Cliffs, N.J.: Prentice-Hall.

Zeitlin, Froma I. (1970). "The Argive Festival of Hera and Euripides' Electra." *Transactions of the American Philological Association* 101: 645–69.

——. (1980). "The Closet of Masks: Role-playing and Myth-making in the *Orestes* of Euripides." *Ramus* 9: 62–73.

——. (1981). "Travesties of Gender and Genre in Aristophanes' *Thesmophoriazusae.*" In Foley (1981b) 165–217.

——. (1985a). "Playing the Other: Theater, Theatricality, and the Feminine in Greek Drama." *Representations* 11: 63–94.

——. (1985b). "The Power of Aphrodite: Eros and the Boundaries of the Self in the *Hippolytus.*" In Burian (1985) 52–111, 189–208.

Zuntz, G. (1960). "On Euripides' *Helena*: Theology and Irony." *Entretiens sur l'antiquité classique.* Vol. 6, *Euripide*, 201–41. Vandoeuvres-Geneva: Fondation Hardt.

Absence, 31; in *Alcestis*, 44, 49–50; and funerary ritual, 30

Acharnians, by Aristophanes, 165

Achilles, 27, 55, 65, 75, 88, 127, 132, 157–58, 169, 175, 182, 217, 222, 226; in *Odyssey*, 24–25; in *Trojan Women*, 30

Achilles Tatius, 49

Acropolis, 9, 114

Adkins, Arthur, 209–10

Admetus, character of, 251 n.22. *See also Alcestis*

Adrastus, 66

Aegeus: in *Medea*, 182

Aegisthus, 10

Aeneid, by Virgil, 173, 225

Aeschylus, 19, 66, 117, 145, 228, 232

Aetiology, 15, 232

Afterlife, 12, 71–72. *See also* Death

Agalma, 177

Agamemnon, 11, 65–66, 231

Agamemnon, by Aeschylus, 9, 17, 22, 67, 76, 77, 145, 172, 182, 187

Agave, 134

Agora, 114

Agraphoi Nomoi, 196

Aidôs, 105, 166, 183, 192, 256 n.39. *See also* Shame

Airs, Waters, Places, by Hippocrates, 198

Aischron, 194, 208. *See also* Shame

Ajax, 128

Ajax, by Sophocles, 17, 22–24, 30, 32, 53, 66, 110, 130, 133, 228

Alcestis, 4, 227

Alcestis, by Euripides, 9, 145, 175, 229, 233; Admetus, character of in, 39, 55–56, 59–62, 67–72, 80–86; Admetus' recognition of truth in, 39, 61–62, 70; Apollo in, 42–44, 83; art, theme of in, 37–50; Asclepius in, 38–45; children in, 51; comedy in, 85–86; commemoration in, 44–50, 77; death in, 50, 51–62, 67–72, 86, 229–30; folktale elements in, 54; funeral rites in, 53–55, 59–60, 84–85; gender roles, reversal of in, 63, 82–86;

Index

Alcestis (cont.)
Heracles in, 40–41, 49, 67–72; heroism of Alcestis in, 69–70, 77–78, 82; heroization of Alcestis in, 46–47, 52, 77; hospitality in, 41, 46, 54, 62, 73, 80–86; house in, 78–86; marriage in, 61, 79–86; marriage and funeral in, 47–49, 53, 61–62, 80, 86; mourning in, 53–56, 83, 85; necessity in, 39, 41, 49, 72, 85; Orpheus in, 38–45; Pheres in, 53, 79, 83; pollution in, 42, 73, 77, 79; satyr-play and, 40, 54; self-reflexivity in, 48–50; silence of Alcestis in, 49, 82, 86; space in, 11–12, 41–46, 78–86; statue in, 37–39, 44–50; substitution in, 37, 39, 45–50, 54; tears in, 62–63, 67–69
Alcinous, 21
Alexander, by Euripides, 132
Amphitryon, 65
Anakalypteria, 80
Anankê. See Necessity
Anaxagoras, 136
Andromache, 130, 186; in *Trojan Women*, 30
Andromache, by Euripides, 11, 27, 54, 65, 134, 157, 171, 177
Andromeda, 86
Antigone, 19, 60, 71, 74, 77, 228
Antigone, by Sophocles, 19–20, 39, 65, 67, 72, 76–77, 110, 128, 130, 134, 175, 197
Antiphon, the Sophist, 196, 198
Aphrodite, 113, 134, 198, 216, 228, 228, 230. *See also* Kypris
Apollo, 83, 229
Apology, by Plato, 33
Appearance: versus reality, in *Hippolytus*, 4, 101, 108–109, 114, 119, 136–37, 146–50, 267 n.28; in *Hecuba*, 168. *See also* Concealment; Truth; Vision
Apragmosynê, 128
Aretê, 145
Ariès, Philippe, 59

Aristophanes, 16, 38, 56, 93, 116, 127, 165
Aristotle, 25, 110, 213. *See also Poetics*
Art, 44; in *Alcestis*, 37–50. *See also* Statue
Artemis, 3, 24, 216, 222, 228, 230
Asclepius, 40, 43, 45
Assemblies: of citizens, in Athens, 5
Astyanax: in *Trojan Women*, 29–33
Athena, 16, 185, 216, 222
Athens, 9, 232
Athletics, 80, 109, 128, 134, 146, 151, 152
Atomists, 136
Audience, 234, 236; presence of women in, 41–42, 71, 94, 133, 173, 249 n.55; response of in tragedy, 26–29; in theater, 94. *See also* Spectacle; Theater
Austin, J. L., 14

Bacchae, by Euripides, 6–7, 10, 65, 76–77, 134–35, 165, 167–68, 174, 179–80, 189, 196, 216, 228, 231
Bacchants, 76, 158, 167–68, 179–82, 181–82, 221–22. *See also* Dionysus; *Sparagmos*
Bacchylides, 63, 127
Bakhtin, Mikhail, 76
Balaustion's Adventure, by Browning, 38
Balzac, Honoré de, 49
Barbarian, 193–95, 196, 198, 202, 209, 211–12, 231, 235; in *Hecuba*, 170–90
Barthes, Roland, 6, 49–50
Battus, King, 273 n.43
Beasts, in *Hippolytus*, 98–104
Bestialization: in *Hecuba*, 162, 180, 185; in *Hippolytus*, 98–104
Birds, by Aristophanes, 127
Birth, 8, 71
Body, 94, 139, 142–44, 146, 148, 152, 153, 163–65, 168, 178, 181, 182, 232
Bouleutic oratory, 211
Boundaries, 76
Browning, Robert, 38
Bull: in *Hippolytus*, 99, 118, 144

Burial, 23–24, 75; in *Alcestis*, 52, 82; in *Hecuba*, 164, 219. *See also* Funeral; Lament; Mourning

Cadmus, 65, 134
Callicles, 198
Callinus, 75
Cannibalism, 162, 181. *See also* Bestialization; Cyclops
Carnivalesque, 76
Carson, Anne, 100
Cassandra, 17, 22, 164, 173, 179, 182–83, 187–89, 193, 209, 217–18, 221, 223, 230
Catharsis, 25–29, 131
Cephalus, 151
Cerberus, 58
Chapouthier, Fernand, 216
Charis, 81, 183, 192, 195, 206, 209
Charon, 58, 245 n.17
Chef d'oeuvre inconnu, Le, by Balzac, 49
Children of Heracles. See *Heracleidai*
Choephoroe, by Aeschylus, 179
Choral lyric, 33
Choral narrative, 127
Choral poetry: and tragedy, 14–17
Choral song, 233
Chorus, 234; in *Hippolytus*, 129
Circe, 232
Citizenship, 146; in *Hippolytus*, 128–35
Class, 107
Closure, 47; in Euripides, 7; and ritual lament, 22–33; in *Trojan Women*, 29–33. *See also* Metatheatricality
Clothing, 164, 171; in *Hecuba*, 158–69
Clouds, by Aristophanes, 56
Clytaemnestra, 9–11, 74, 76, 117, 179, 182, 187, 202, 212, 223, 228, 232; in Aeschylus, 145
Comedy, 76, 85–86, 127
Commemoration, 4, 6, 13–14, 32, 39, 52; in *Alcestis*, 44–50, 77; in *Hippolytus*, 24–25, 112–15, 123–29, 131–35, 233; in *Trojan Women*, 31–

32. *See also* Funeral; Lament; Memory; Monument
Communication, 91. *See also* Language
Community. *See* Individual
Concealment: in *Hecuba*, 167; in *Hippolytus*, 92–96
Cook, Albert, 38, 46
Corcyrean Revolution, 186, 202
Creon: in *Antigone*, 60, 130, 134; in *Medea*, 9, 182; in *Oedipus Tyrannus*, 29, 65
Creusa: in *Ion*, 210
Critias, 197, 200–201
Crito, by Plato, 33
Cyclops, 43, 162–63, 168, 185, 187, 188, 202, 274 n.53, 275 n.54
Cyclops, by Euripides, 197
Cynossema, 159, 232

Danae, 86
Danaids, 167, 175, 179, 186
Dante, 113
Day, fated, 56–57
Death, 42, 86; and the afterlife, 71–72; in *Alcestis*, 37, 50, 73; and marriage, in *Alcestis*, 252 n.31; in tragedy, 4. *See also* Funeral; Hades; Lament; Mourning
Deianeira, 9, 60, 74, 145, 228, 232
Deliberative oratory, 211
Delos, 222
Demas, 143. *See also* Body; *Sôma*
Democritus, 197
Demodocus, 132
Dêmosion sêma, 75
Desire, 153; in *Hippolytus*, 89–109
Detienne, Marcel, 175
Deus ex machina, 184, 214, 221–22, 236
Diano, Carlo, 108
Dicastic oratory, 211
Dikaion, 194, 197, 199. *See also* Justice
Dikê, 199, 201, 209, 220. *See also* Justice
Diomedes, 84
Dionysia, 5

Index

Dionysus, 16, 168, 189, 196–97, 216, 221–22, 228, 231, 235, 239 n.3, 279 n.19, 280 n.2. *See also Bacchae*; Bacchants; *Sparagmos*
Disease, 90, 110–11, 115, 136–37, 147–148, 230, 232. *See also Nosos*
Diseases of Women, by Hippocrates, 90
Doctors, 89–92, 94, 96
Dolos, 106, 163, 179, 185. *See also Mêtis*

Ecclesiazusae, by Aristophanes, 76
Echthros, 198–99, 206–11
Ekklesia, 128. *See also* Assemblies
Ekphora, 82. *See also* Burial; Funeral
Electra, 18, 71, 128, 130
Electra, by Euripides, 10, 54, 65, 214; by Sophocles, 10, 32, 134, 151
Eleusinian Mysteries, 249 n.56
Eleusinion, 114
Elpis. See Hope
Emotion: in Sophocles, 19
Empedocles, 100
Encomium, 15
Ephêmeros, 161
Epic Cycle, 157
Epic, 4–5, 16, 22, 24–25, 30–33, 72, 115, 127; death in, 53. *See also* Homer; *Iliad*; *Odyssey*
Epigram, 47
Epilogue, 232
Epinician ode, 15, 21, 42, 77. *See also* Pindar
Epitaphios. *See* Funeral speech
Epitaphios, by Lysias, 20. *See also* Funeral speech
Erechtheus, by Euripides, 236
Erinyes, 22
Eros, 103, 106, 123, 142, 150, 210
Escape ode, in *Hippolytus*, 25
Eteocles, 65
Eukleia, 71, 122, 129, 147. *See also* Fame; *Kleos*
Eumenides, by Aeschylus, 3, 22, 228
Eurydice, 45
Evadne, 60

Evidence. *See Hippolytus*
Exchange of women: in *Alcestis*, 42, 78, 81–86; in *Hecuba*, 176. *See also* Marriage; Women
Eyes. *See* Vision

Fame, 25–26, 30, 32, 84, 122–23; in *Hippolytus*, 126–29. *See also* Commemoration; *Eukleia*; *Kleos*; Memory; Monument
Fathers and sons, 104, 107, 120, 127, 130, 133–34
Female, construction of, in tragedy, 8–12, 74, 98, 231. *See also* Gender; Gender roles; Women
Feminization, 66, 82, 121, 126; in tragedy, 63. *See also* Gender roles; Women
Festivals, 5
Finley, Moses, 84
Folktale, 54
Freud, Sigmund, 55
Frogs, by Aristophanes, 16–17, 46, 116
Funeral, 24, 31, 47–48, 59, 73, 75, 84–85, 230. *See also* Burial; Commemoration; Death; *Epitaphios*; Lament; Mourning; Ritual lament; Threnos
Funeral speech, 5; by Pericles, 20, 91

Garner, Richard, 53
Gender: division of, in tragedy, 8–12, 105–106, 108–109. *See also* Female; Feminization; Gender roles; House; Marriage; Sexuality; Space; Women
Gender roles: in Euripides, 227–28; reversal of, in *Alcestis*, 63, 67, 73–86; reversal of, in *Hecuba*, 167–69, 180–81, 184–85; reversal of, in *Hippolytus*, 109, 122–24, 144–49. *See also* Female; Feminization; Gender roles; House; Marriage; Sexuality; Space; Women
Gennaiotês, 144, 147
Gesture, 17
Ghost: in *Hecuba*, 157–58

Glaucus, 84

Gods: in Euripides, 214–15, 229–30;
in *Hecuba*, 188–89, 211, 215–26

Gold: in *Hecuba*, 160–69, 185, 223

Golden Age, 108, 179

Goldhill, Simon, 91

Goos, 48. *See also* Lament; Mourning

Gorgias, the Sophist, 26, 100–102

Gorgias, by Plato, 198

Graphê, 142. *See also* Writing

Graphikê, 101. *See also* Writing

Guest-friendship, 5, 79, 193, 227. *See
also* Hospitality; *Xenia*

Gyges, 145

Hades, 12, 164, 167, 180, 181, 222–23,
225, 246 n.18; bride of, 177; in *Hippolytus*, 151. *See also* Death

Haemon, 60, 134

Hamilla logôn, 194, 208

Hamlet, by Shakespeare, 7

Hearing, 90–91, 93, 101, 142–44, 149–
50, 153

Hearth. See *Hestia*; House

Hecataeus, 196

Hector: in *Iliad*, 24, 53, 55, 159; in
Trojan Women, 29–31

Hecuba, by Euripides, 9, 11, 17, 29–33,
54, 65, 76, 82, 130, 134, 230;
Achilles in, 169; Achilles' tomb
in, 159, 177, 226; bacchants in, 158,
167, 179–82, 221–22; barbarian,
contrasted with Greek in, 170–
90, 192, 194–95, 203, 209; bestialization in, 162, 180–82, 185; body,
theme of in, 163–65, 168, 181;
burial in, 164–65; cannibalism in,
162, 181; Cassandra in, 179, 182–
83, 187, 188–89, 193, 209, 217, 223,
230; *charis* in, 183, 192, 195, 206;
clothing in, 158–69, 171; Clytaemnestra in, 179, 182, 187, 202, 212,
223; Cyclops in, 162–63, 168, 185,
187, 188; Danaids in, 167, 179, 185,
186; deus ex machina in, 184,
221–22, 236; *dolos*, by women, in
163, 179, 185; eroticism in, 172–73,

175, 177, 235; friendship in, 198–
99, 206–11, gender roles, reversals of in, 167–69, 180–81, 184–85;
gods in, 188–89, 211, 215–26; gold
in, 160–69, 223; guest-friendship,
relations of, 193; Hades, bride of,
as theme, 177; Helen in, 160, 217,
223–25; heroism in, 157, 162; justice in, 199–201, 220, 223, 235; *krêdemnon* in, 173; law in, 176, 184,
191–213, 229; marriage and funeral in, 175–76, 230; marriage
and sacrifice in, 171, 175–77, 179,
186, 230; marriage and war in,
171, 230; metamorphosis in, 159–
63, 167–69, 180, 185–86, 191, 225,
233, 235; *mêtis* of women in, 163,
179, 185; mutability of fortune in,
158, 160–62, 207; necessity, theme
of in, 169, 185, 235; Neoptolemus
in, 160, 178, 202; Odysseus in, 163;
Odyssey, use of in, 162–63, 188;
Oresteia, plot of, reflected in, 11,
187, 212, 223; Paris in, 218, 223–25;
prophecy in, 163, 186, 191, 223,
235–36; relativism in, 200–202,
210; sacrifice, human, in, 165–66,
172–73, 177, 181, 184, 202, 212, 217,
218, 223; space in, 11–12, 157, 184,
225, 231–32; *sparagmos* in, 181–82,
222; supplication in, 166–67, 176,
183, 192; Thracians, character of
in, 171, 186; universals in, 191–213;
violence in, 11, 165–66, 167, 170–
90; war, and sacrificial ritual in,
192; winds in, 188–89, 205, 212,
220–21, 222

Hecuba, 228; in *Trojan Women*, 17

Hedda Gabler, by Ibsen, 7

Helen, 18, 22, 83, 130, 145, 216, 217,
223–25, 227, 232; in *Hecuba*, 160;
in *Iliad*, 32

Helen, by Euripides, 10, 18, 22, 38, 49,
66, 157, 165, 173, 175, 198, 214, 216;
by Gorgias, 19, 102–103

Hera, 214

Heracleidai, by Euripides, 74, 236

Heracles, 63, 66–67, 128, 130, 228

Heracles, by Euripides, 15, 21, 65, 69, 110, 126, 130, 133, 135, 215, 233

Heraclitus, 197

Herington, John, 22

Hermione, 11

Herodotus, 145, 172–73, 195–96, 198

Heroism, 158, 162, 169; of Alcestis, 70, 77; in *Hecuba*, 157; in *Hippolytus*, 122, 126–29

Heroization: of Alcestis, 46–47, 52, 77

Hesiod, 20–21, 89, 105, 141, 232. See also *Theogony*

Hestia, 57. *See also* House; Marriage; Space

Hestia, 78–79

Hippias, 196

Hippocrates, 90, 136, 196

Hippolyta, 117

Hippolytus, 228

Hippolytus, by Euripides, 9–11, 14, 31, 57, 65, 82, 198, 214–16, 230–31; Aphrodite in, 103, 113–14, 134, 228; athletics in, 128, 132, 151–52; beasts, as theme in, 98–104; body, as theme in, 91, 93, 98, 110–12, 139–44, 146, 152–53; bull in, 98, 103, 118; chorus in, 129, 234; citizenship in, 120–22, 128–35; class, as theme in, 105–109; commemoration in, 112–15, 123–29, 131–35, 233; communication in, 89, 91, 93, 97–99; disease in, 89–109, 115; doctors in, 89–92, 94, 96; ending of, 24–25; eros in, 103, 106; evidence, as theme in, 97, 103–104; feminization in, 126; gender division in, 105–106, 108–109; gender roles, reversals of in, 122–24; hearing, as theme in, 90–91, 93, 101, 142–44, 149–50, 153; heroism in, 122, 125–29; lament in, 112, 121, 128–35; language in, 89–109, 114; language and women in, 117–20; magic in, 97–98, 102–104, 115; marriage rites at end of, 24– 25, 109, 120–29, 233; meadow of Hippolytus in, 113, 140; mirror, as theme in, 119, 146; mourning in, 126–29, 131–35; Phaethon in, 25, 121, 127, 133, 151–52; *phrên, phrenes* in, 95–96, 115–16, 119, 137–39; 147–48; pollution, 96; purity, 92, 109, 125–26, 139, 142–45; revealing, mode of in, 92–96; self-reflexivity on theater in, 110–20; shame, as theme in, 91, 115, 122, 139, 145, 149; signs in, 97–109; silence, as theme in, 96, 115, 117, 123, 233; *sôphrosynê* in, 140, 145; space in, 9, 11–12, 89–99, 93; space and gender in, 4, 113–20, 151–53, 230; spectacle in, 113–15, 148; tears, as theme in, 121, 131– 35, 139–41; truth, as theme in, 93, 136, 145, 148; vision, as theme in, 89–109, 152–53; writing in, 92– 109, 117–18, 121, 142, 149–50, 230

Homer, 4, 17, 20–21, 33, 63, 72, 78, 123, 145–146, 158, 185, 232. See also *Iliad*; *Odyssey*

Homeric Hymns, 21

Homeric Hymn to Aphrodite, 113

Homilia, in *Hippolytus*, 90, 113, 141– 42, 153. *See also* Communication; Language

Honor, 7, 91, 144. See also *Eukleia*; Fame; *Kleos*

Hope, 138

Horace, 171

Hospitality, 41, 46, 54, 62, 73, 79–80, 83–84, 232. *See also* Guest-friendship; *Xenia*

House, 4, 11, 54, 60, 76, 145, 189, 224, 232; in *Alcestis*, 78–86. *See also* Marriage; Space

Hunting, 9

Hyllus, 64

Iliad, 6, 30, 32, 53–55, 75, 81, 83, 127, 132, 146, 158–59, 173, 222. *See also* Epic; Homer

Illocutionary, 14

Impiety, 193, 202, 220. *See also* Gods
Individual, 129–35, 207
Intertextuality, 7. *See also* Self-reflexivity
Io, 147
Ion, 130
Ion, by Euripides, 49, 65, 82, 174, 210, 214
Iphigeneia, 10, 18, 74, 130, 175, 187, 212
Iphigeneia in Aulis, by Euripides, 65–66, 76, 130, 159, 172–73, 175, 214
Iphigeneia in Tauris, by Euripides, 10, 18, 49, 65, 130, 157, 171, 196, 198, 214
Itys, 18

Jason, 135
Jocasta, 148, 217
Justice, 199–201, 220, 223, 229, 235; in *Hecuba*, 219. See also *Dikaion*; *Dikê*

Kalon, 194
Karteria, 68, 125–26. *See also* Heroism
King Lear, by Shakespeare, 7
Kirkwood, Gordon, 201
Kleos, 84, 122, 126. *See also* Commemoration, *Eukleia*; Fame
Kolossos, 38; in *Alcestis*, 45–50
Kômos, 61
Kore, 175
Krêdemnon, 173. *See also* Marriage; Veil
Kubler-Ross, Elisabeth, 55, 60
Kurios, 10–11
Kypris, 220. *See also* Aphrodite

Lament, 7, 20, 23–33, 48, 52, 62–67, 230, 233; and closure, in *Trojan Women*, 29–33; in *Hippolytus*, 112, 121, 126–35; in Sophocles, 19; and tragedy, 16–20. *See also* Funeral; Mourning; Threnos
Language: and gender, 117–20; in *Hippolytus*, 89–109, 114; in trag-

edy, 4, 17. *See also* Communication; Gender; Gender roles; Women; Writing
Law, 176, 184, 229; in *Hecuba*, 191–213. *See also* Justice; *Nomos*
Law courts, 5, 9, 103, 127, 147, 211, 235
Lemnian women, 167, 179, 186
Libation Bearers. See *Choephoroe*
Literacy, 6
Livy, 171
Logos, 191
Longus, 49
Loom, 76, 167, 272 n. 38. *See also* Clothing; Weaving
Loraux, Nicole, 64, 74, 111, 133, 232
Lycurgus, 222, 280 n.22
Lysias, 11, 20
Lysistrata, by Aristophanes, 76–77

Macaria, 74
Maenads. *See* Bacchants
Magic, 97–98, 104, 106, 115
Marriage, 8, 48, 61, 76, 79–80, 83, 112, 134, 230; and death, in *Alcestis*, 252 n.31; and funeral, 175–76; and funeral, in *Alcestis*, 53; in *Hippolytus*, 109, 120–29; and sacrifice, 171, 175–77, 271 n.27; and war, 171. *See also* Birth; Exchange; Gender roles; House; Space; Women
Masistes, 145
Mater dolorosa, 30, 158, 165. *See also* Funeral; Lament; Mourning; Threnos
Meadow, in *Hippolytus*, 113, 140, 144
Medea, 71, 74, 130, 170, 182
Medea, by Euripides, 9, 15, 20, 54, 82–84, 102, 135, 167, 174–75, 182, 197, 214, 231–32
Medusa, 16
Meleager, 63
Melian debate, 33, 189, 211
Memorabilia, by Xenophon, 101, 197
Memory, and cult, 23–24. *See also* Commemoration
Menelaus, 10, 65–66

Index

Mérimée, Prosper, 49

Metamorphosis, 185–86, 191, 225, 233, 235; in *Hecuba*, 158–63, 167–69. *See also* Mutability

Metaphor, 17–19, 25

Metatheatricality, 7. *See also* Self-reflexivity

Mêtis, 163, 185. See also *Dolos*

Miasma. *See* Pollution

Mirror, 119, 146–147

Moirai, 41

Monument, 6, 30–31, 47, 52, 114, 124, 232–33; of hero, 23

Motherhood, 8, 71. *See also* Birth; House; Marriage; Space; Women

Mourning, 5, 24, 48, 53–56, 76–77, 83, 85. *See also* Burial; Funeral; Lament; Threnos

Muses, in tragedy, 16–22, 31, 121

Music: in *Alcestis*, 44–45; negated, in tragedy, 18–20

Mutability: of fortune, 160–62, 207; in *Hecuba*, 158. *See also* Metamorphosis

Mysteries, 113

Myth, 5, 33, 50, 52, 54, 58, 158, 185, 191, 215

Mytilenean debate, 33, 189, 211

Nature. See *Phusis*

Necessity, 41, 43, 49, 72, 85, 185, 234–35; in *Alcestis*, 39, 41; in *Hecuba*, 169

Neoptolemus, 130, 178, 202; in *Andromache*, 27; in *Hecuba*, 157–60; in *Philoctetes*, 64; in *Trojan Women*, 30

Nessus, 9

Nietzsche, Friedrich, 16, 191

Nightingale, 17–18

Niobe, by Aeschylus, 17

Nomos, 196, 218. *See also* Law; *Phusis*

Nosos, 57. *See also* Body; Disease

Ocean, 12

Ode on Man, in *Antigone*, 72

Odysseus, 127, 132; in *Ajax*, 23; in *Hecuba*, 163; in *Trojan Women*, 31. See also *Odyssey*

Odyssey, 21, 25, 54, 65, 75, 84, 162–63, 185, 188. *See also* Homer

Oedipus, 19, 65, 75, 128

Oedipus at Colonus, by Sophocles, 14, 19, 57, 65, 128, 130, 134

Oedipus Tyrannus, by Sophocles, 14–15, 27, 54, 65–66, 69, 75, 134, 136, 188, 197, 217

Oikos. See House

Olympus, 12

Oral culture, 13–16, 121

Oral poetry, 33. *See also* Epic; Homer

Oresteia, by Aeschylus, 22, 32, 76, 223; by Stesichorus, 20. *See also* Agamemnon; *Choephoroe*; Clytaemnestra; *Eumenides*; Iphigeneia

Orestes, 10–11, 65–66, 130, 196

Orestes, by Euripides, 54, 65–66, 157, 197, 214

Orion, 274 n.53

Orpheus: in *Alcestis*, 38, 40, 43–45

Orphics, 249 n.56

Ovid, 171

Oxymoron, 16

Paean, 15

Pain, 264 n.17. *See also* Body; Disease

Pandora, 232

Panhellenic contests, 128

Panhellenic myths, 131–32

Paradox, 16, 32; in Euripides, 37; in tragedy, 20, 178

Paris, 10, 83, 218, 223–25

Parrhêsia, 128–29, 146. *See also* Assemblies; Law courts

Parthenos, 177

Peace, by Aristophanes, 127

Peithô, 204, 210, 220

Peleus, 65; in *Andromache*, 27

Pelion, 79

Peloponnesian War, 158, 186

Pentheus, 165, 168, 197

Peplos. See Clothing

Pericles, 20, 64, 69, 91, 131. *See also* Funeral speech
Perlocutionary, 14
Persephone, 18, 175
Persians, by Aeschylus, 20, 66, 82, 165
Petrarch, 113
Phaedo, by Plato, 33
Phaedra, 4, 11, 60, 71, 74, 228, 230
Phaedra, by Seneca, 120
Phaedrus, by Plato, 102
Phaethon, 25, 121, 127, 133, 151–52, 265 n.33
Pharmakon, 44, 102
Pherecrates, 202
Pheres, 53, 79, 83, 245 n.12
Philanthrôpon, 26
Philoctetes, 75, 128, 130
Philoctetes, by Sophocles, 64, 110, 130, 157
Philos, in *Hecuba*, 198–99, 206–11
Phoenissae, by Euripides, 65, 130, 148
Phrên, Phrenes: in *Hippolytus*, 95–96, 115–16, 119, 137–39, 147–49
Phusis, 108, 196, 198. *See also* Law; *Nomos*
Pindar, 16, 33, 117, 127, 196
Pity, 14, 26, 28
Plague, in Athens, 108
Plato, 33, 43, 69, 211, 213; on tragedy, 26
Plutarch, 63–64, 69
Poetics, by Aristotle, 25–29
Politics, by Aristotle, 26
Pollution, 42, 73, 77, 79, 96, 252 n.24, 264 n.15. *See also* Purification; Purity
Polybus, 54, 75
Polydorus, 230
Polymestor, 65
Polyneices, 19, 65, 148
Polyphemus. *See* Cyclops
Polyxena, 4, 65, 74; in *Trojan Women*, 30
Polyxena, by Sophocles, 157
Poros, 41, 49
Poseidon, 216

Priam, 127, 132, 178, 202, 226; in *Trojan Women*, 31
Privacy, 207
Procne, 18
Prologue, 232
Prometheus, 65
Prometheus, by Aeschylus, 147
Prophecy, 163, 188–89, 191, 224, 235–36; in *Hecuba*, 186
Protagoras, 200, 202, 212
Protesilaus, 45
Protesilaus, by Euripides, 22, 38
Psuchagogein, 103
Purification, 23. *See also* Pollution
Purity, 109, 114, 125–26, 139, 142–45. *See also* Pollution
Pygmalion, 49
Pythian 12, by Pindar, 16

Racine, Jean, 119
Relativism, 200–202, 210. *See also* Universals
Republic, by Plato, 64, 198, 211
Rescue, 52
Rescue myths, 86
Rhapsode, 22
Ritual, 5, 14–15, 17, 32, 128, 192, 233; and closure, in tragedy, 22–25. *See also* Burial; Commemoration; Funeral; Lament; Marriage; Threnos
Ritual lament, 25–33. *See also* Lament; Threnos
Rivier, André, 174, 177

Sacrifice, 165–66, 171–72, 180–82, 192, 202, 212, 215, 217–18, 223, 235; of Polyxena, 174–79, 184
Sarrasine, by Balzac, 49–50
Satyr play, 3, 40, 54, 62
Searle, John, 14
Secret, 113
Self-reflexivity, 15, 24, 32, 238 n.9; in *Alcestis*, 48–50; in Euripides, 4, 7; of theater, in *Hippolytus*, 110–20, 122, 126–35. *See also* Metatheatricality

Index

Sêma, 123, 159

Sêmeion, 101, 274 n.52

Semele, 151

Seneca, 113, 119–20

Seven Against Thebes, by Aeschylus, 20, 82, 173

Sexuality, 4, 10–11, 117, 145, 147, 173, 184. *See also* Aphrodite; Marriage; Women

Shame, 90–91, 105, 122, 139, 145, 148–49, 194, 256 n.39. See also *Aidôs*; *Aischron*

Shield of Hector, in the *Trojan Women*, 29–31

Sickness. *See* Body; Disease; *Nosos*

Signs. See *Sêma*; *Sêmeion*

Silence, 17, 22; in *Alcestis*, 49, 82; in *Hippolytus*, 91, 94, 96–97, 104, 123, 233. *See also* Language; Writing

Slavery: in *Hecuba*, 204–205

Snell, Bruno, 206

Socrates, 33, 43, 63, 69, 101, 197

Solon, 63

Sôma, 143–44. *See also* Body; *Demas*

Song: negated in tragedy, 16–20

Sophia, 44–45

Sophists, 33, 93, 147, 196

Sophocles, 4, 128, 228, 232; contrasted with Euripides, 130–31, 134

Sôphrosynê, 71, 140, 145

Space, 4, 40–42, 121, 184, 230; and gender, 9–12, 132–35, 151–53; and gender, in *Alcestis*, 73–86; and gender, in *Hippolytus*, 89–99, 113–20; in *Hecuba*, 157, 225; and tragedy, 9; and women, 231–32. *See also* Gender; Gender roles; House; Marriage; Women

Sparagmos, 180–82, 222. *See also* Bacchants; Dionysus

Sparta, 225

Spectacle, 28, 85, 148, 177–78, 235–36; in *Hippolytus*, 114. *See also* Audience; Statue; Theater; Vision

Statue: in *Alcestis*, 37–38, 49–50, 59–

60, 83; in *Hecuba*, 177–78, 235–36. *See also* Art; Spectacle

Stesichorus, 20

Stoics, 213

Substitution: in *Alcestis*, 37–39, 45, 47–49, 54

Sunthanein, 60. *See also* Death; Marriage

Suppliants: by Euripides, 18, 20, 60, 66, 69, 76, 130, 197; by Aeschylus, 19

Supplication: in *Hecuba*, 166, 176, 183, 192

Symposium, 15, 17, 21, 85

Symposium, by Plato, 43

Tablets, of Phaedra. *See* Writing

Talthybius, 65, 175, 215, 235

"Tame Death," 57–62

Tears, 14, 26, 121, 126, 131, 139; of Admetus, 67–72; at end of *Hippolytus*, 132–35; in *Oedipus Tyrannus*, 29; in tragedy, 62–67. *See also* Lament; Mourning; Threnos

Tecmessa, 23, 66

Telephus, by Euripides, 165

Teras, 99

Terpsis, 16, 126

Teucer, 23

Thanatos, 58, 229

Theater, 133, 234. *See also* Audience; Self-reflexivity; Spectacle

Theoclymenus, 10, 66

Theodicy, in *Hecuba*, 219

Theognis, 33

Theogony, by Hesiod, 21, 141

Theonoe, 66, 214

Therapy, and tragedy, 55

Theseus, 9, 11, 60, 66, 228

Thesmophoria, 93

Thesmophoriazusae, by Aristophanes, 77, 93, 165

Thetis, 25, 27

Thoas, 10, 196

Thracians: character of, 171, 186

Thrasymachus, 198

Threnos, 15, 30, 42, 73. *See also*

Burial; Commemoration; Funeral; Lament; Ritual lament
Thucydides, 33, 76, 91, 131, 136, 158, 186, 189, 202, 211
Timê: See Honor
Tomb of Achilles, in *Hecuba*, 159, 177
Trachiniae, by Sophocles, 9, 32, 57, 60, 64, 66–67, 110, 128–30, 134, 175, 228
Trojans: character of, 171
Trojan War, 157. *See also* Homer; *Iliad*
Trojan Women, by Euripides, 4, 6, 17, 21, 29–33, 54, 130, 134, 157, 171, 186, 214, 216, 218–19
Troy, 169; in *Hecuba*, 161; in *Trojan Women*, 31
Truth, 108, 136, 145, 148–49
Turato, Fabio, 107
Tyrtaeus, 75

Universals, 5; in *Hecuba*, 191–213

Vase Étrusque, La, by Mérimée, 49
Veil, in *Alcestis*, 53. See also *Krêdemnon*
Vengeance, 5
Violence, 11, 165, 166–67, 174; in *Hecuba*, 170–90
Virgil, 225
Virginity: in *Hecuba*, 174, 182
Vision, 89–109, 114, 148–50; 152–53. *See also* Appearance; Concealment; Spectacle; Truth

War, 8, 171–73, 182, 192, 230
Weaving: and women, 180, 272 n.38. *See also* Clothing
Wedding, 86. *See also* Marriage
Winds: in *Hecuba*, 188–89, 205–206, 212, 220–22
Winter's Tale, by Shakespeare, 50

Women: and barbarians, 170–71; and body, 111, 140, 142–44; as challenge to masculine order, 227–28; communication with, 91–92, 97–99, 109; construction of, in tragedy, 8–12, 74, 98, 231; and death, 51–54, 57–59, 71, 75, 77, 86; and doctors, 89–92, 94, 96; Euripides' sympathy for, 230; evils of, 105; and exchange, 81, 83–84; and heroism, 74–75, 77, 82–83, 168–69; and hearth, 78; and lament, 30–32, 63–64, 133; and language, 98–99, 104, 115, 117; and marriage, 8, 80, 83, 175–77; "race" of, 89–90; sacrifice of, 172–79; sexuality of, 10–11, 117, 145, 147, 173, 184; and silence, 48–49, 82, 86, 124; and space, 9–12, 41, 73–86; 116, 118, 121, 147, 151–52, 184, 232; as spectacle, 172–73, 177–78, 235–36; strength and weakness of, 167, 179–81, 184; in theater, 41–42, 71, 173, 249 n.55; vengeance of, 167, 187–88; and war, 8, 170–71, 173, 182; and weaving, 272 n.38; and writing, 92–96, 97–98, 103, 105. *See also* Female; Feminization; Gender; Gender roles; House; Marriage; Sexuality
Writing: in *Hippolytus*, 92–109, 117–18, 121, 142, 149–51, 153, 230

Xenia, 54, 77, 85. *See also* Guest-friendship; Hospitality
Xenophon, 100, 197
Xerxes, 66, 165

Zeitlin, Froma, 232
Zeus, 214–15, 217
Zuntz, Gunther, 218

ABOUT

THE AUTHOR

Charles Segal is Professor of Greek
and Latin at Harvard University. He is
the author of numerous books, including
*Lucretius on Death and Anxiety, Orpheus:
The Myth of the Poet*, and *Interpreting
Greek Tragedy: Myth, Poetry,
Text.*

Library of Congress Cataloging-in-Publication Data

Segal, Charles, 1936—
Euripides and the poetics of sorrow : art, gender, and
commemoration in Alcestis, Hippolytus, and Hecuba /
Charles Segal.
p. cm. Includes bibliographical references and index.
ISBN 0-8223-1360-x (cloth)
1. Euripides —Criticism and interpretation. 2. Greek drama
(Tragedy)—History and criticism. 3. Hippolytus (Greek
mythology) in literature. 4. Hecuba (Legendary character) in
literature. 5. Alcestis (Greek mythology) in literature. 6.
Trojan War in literature. 7. Sex role in literature. 8. Grief in
literature. I. Title. (PA3978.S5   1993) 882'.01—dc20
93-15565   CIP